Decentralization
and Self-Government
in Russia,
1830-1870

Decentralization and Self-Government in Russia, 1830-1870

S. FREDERICK STARR

PRINCETON UNIVERSITY PRESS

PRINCETON, NEW JERSEY

This book has been composed in Caledonia
with Melior Semi-bold display

Printed in the United States of America
by Princeton University Press

To *my wife,*
my family,
and my teachers

Contents

CONTENTS

Preface

This book deals with that great set piece of pre-Revolutionary Russian history, the turbulent period of renewal and innovation that followed the crushing Crimean defeat of 1855. It was by no means unusual for change to occur in Russia through dizzying leaps of statecraft rather than a plodding process of evolution. Yet, never since the time of Peter the Great had so many changes been introduced as in this brief span of scarcely more than a decade. Some twenty-four million male serfs owned by the gentry, the crown, and the state were legally emancipated from their long bondage; a judicial system and a legal profession were created virtually *ex nihilo*; the draconian terms of military service were reduced and the army overhauled from top to bottom; the censorship was reformed; the universities received new statutes; a state bank was established; and scores of matters as petty as the cut of a state copy clerk's uniform were altered in accordance with the spirit of the day. Surely these years amply merit their repute as the "Era of Great Reforms."

My focus will be on one of these reforms: the effort to reconstitute the decrepit system of provincial government under which most Russians lived. This restricted range of enquiry seems justified since few areas of governmental activity reveal so clearly the fundamental character of a state as does the manner in which it seeks to organize public functions and civic life in the local communities. Indeed, the attitudes and institutions that define local government constitute a unique index to the mind and structure of a state as a whole.

This particular episode in the history of the Russian state has generally been subsumed under the broader issues of the emancipation debate and the evolution of the land-owning gentry class. This frame of reference has led scholars to valuable insights on the social makeup of the provincial and district councils, or *zemstvos*, the creation of which was such a major legacy of the reform era. At the same time, it has contributed to a general underestimation of the breadth and intensity of the impulse for local reform *per se*, a concern shared by gentry abolitionists, by planters who vigorously opposed emancipation, by westward-looking publicists, and by many stolid bureaucrats within the St. Petersburg ministries and in the provinces. In order to correct this picture I have devoted a major section of this book (Chapter I) to a review of provincial government during the period from 1825 to 1855.

In the course of those years the problem of administering Russia became so acute that it impinged upon the lives of Russians from many levels of society occupying diverse positions of responsibility. The second chapter follows the process by which this issue entered the arena of public debate and how concern over it was manifest in various ideological currents not related exclusively or even directly with the serf question.

The diverse strains of reformist thought and action that coalesced around the issue of provincial rule divide themselves neatly into two sweeping categories: "decentralization," a term which I shall employ in reference to governmental programs that granted provincial bureaucrats more powers and initiative without turning functions over to local public control; and "self-government," which required that local elective bodies so far as possible be empowered to manage public affairs in the provinces and districts. These categories, devised and accepted by the reformers themselves, correspond to two of the three paths by which the Russian autocracy could conceivably have reorganized political power during the reform era; it could give its own local agents more power and initiative; it could invite the local public and particularly the gentry to take a broader role in provincial affairs; or it could attempt to improve the system by exerting more authority directly from Petersburg through bureaucratic or elected agents.[1] Chapter III of this book deals with attempts to follow the first alternative by legislating a program of administrative decentralization, while Chapter IV does the same for public self-government; in Chapter V the third option is considered as the central government renewed its interest in controlling local affairs directly from the capital.

To avoid confusion over my employing for analytic purposes terms made current during the period under study, it may be helpful to keep in mind the more precise synonyms "deconcentration" for decentralization and "devolution" for self-government. I have endeavored to use these modern expressions in those cases where the views of contemporaries themselves are not at issue.[2] The reason for retaining the original terms in all other cases is that their use by the reformers themselves links state development in Russia after 1855 with western European development slightly earlier in the nineteenth century, and at the same time relates talk of local organizations in Russia during the reform era

---

[1] The second and third of these alternatives follow closely the analysis of Alfred J. Rieber, *The Politics of Autocracy: Letters of Alexander II to Prince A. I. Bariatinskii, 1857-1864*, Paris and The Hague, 1966, p. 55.

[2] I am indebted for these terms to Henry Maddick, *Democracy, Decentralization and Development*, London, 1963, pp. 23ff.

with many similar discussions in developing nations today. The former relationship was first perceived several decades ago by Robert C. Binckley in his provocative *Realism and Nationalism*,[3] while the latter has been noted in general terms by several modern political scientists. Due to lack of detailed information on the Russian side it has been impossible until now to explore these parallels further. It is hoped that this book will stimulate investigation of these important issues but, as Gogol said of his novel, *Dead Souls*, it pretends to be nothing more than a front porch to such greater works. My more limited purpose is to examine the process by which a serious malfunction developed in the tsarist autocracy, how it came to be recognized and dealt with, and how the legislative solutions were in turn reintegrated into the realities of a fast-changing nation that was still bound firmly by old habits.

Section VI of the Bibliography which lists some of the major books and articles that I have cited suggests the extent to which my book is indebted to the work of others. Beyond that formal compendium I should like to express my deep gratitude to several individuals from whose counsel and generous assistance I have particularly benefited. Among them I should like especially to thank my Princeton teachers and colleagues, Professors Cyril E. Black and James H. Billington, who, in their different ways, have repeatedly demonstrated that the study of history may still aspire to a position of preeminence among the humane arts. Dr. Nikolai Andreyev and Dr. Peter Squire of Cambridge University patiently encouraged the early stages of this project, and Professors Richard Wortman of the University of Chicago, Charles Ruud of the University of Western Ontario, and Gregory Guroff of Grinnell College offered valuable criticism on later drafts. Mr. Robert V. Abbott kindly allowed me to peruse his research on the Russian adminis-

[3] Robert C. Binckley, *Realism and Nationalism, 1852-1871*, New York, 1935, p. 180.

trative police and Dr. Zdenek David provided invaluable bibliographic advice. Three distinguished senior Soviet scholars to whom I am grateful for sharing an expertise that can only arouse awe in the aspiring historian of Russia are Professors Naum G. Sladkevich and Sergei S. Okun of Leningrad State University and Professor Peter A. Zaionchkovskii of Moscow; due to their interest and concern I was permitted access to invaluable archival materials in the Soviet Union. Finally, I should like to express my gratitude to the administrators of the Inter-University Committee on Travel Grants, the Foreign Area Fellowship Program, the Fulbright-Hayes Program, and Princeton University's Council on International and Regional Studies for their sustaining support.

S. Frederick Starr
Princeton, 1971

Decentralization and Self-Government in Russia, 1830-1870

I | The Undergoverned
Provinces, 1830-1855

*There is nothing more strange
than the entirety of the internal
administration of any province
of Russia.*[1]

Sergei Uvarov, 1827

In the last century the province of Kherson on the Black Sea
coast was a prosperous region noted for its mild climate and
its horses. Its capital, the town of Kherson, was a sleepy
community dominated by the cathedral, the tomb of Catherine II's favorite, Potemkin, and the province's administration buildings. The latter, ample stone structures, housed
the headquarters of all the region's public agencies, the
treasury, and the board of taxes. For two generations before 1861 these same buildings had been the scene of a sys-
tematic embezzlement of public funds by civil servants.
During 1860, for example, 760 rubles vanished from the accounts of the poor relief agency. In the same year another
agency succeeded in spending 150,000 rubles for a bridge

---

[1] Sergei Uvarov, "De l'administration de la plupart des gouvernement de la Russie centrale," *Materialy sobrannye dlia vysochaishei
uchrezhdennoi komissii o preobrazovanii gubernskikh i uezdnykh
uchrezhdenii*, 3 vols., St. Petersburg, 1870, I, Pt. iii, p. 70. Hereafter
cited as *MSVUK*. (All translations throughout the book are mine
unless other sources are cited.)

3

in the Odessa district without so much as the foundations to show for it.[2]

No public institution in the province was immune from corruption. Like all provinces, Kherson had a small hospital under the control of the Ministry of Internal Affairs in St. Petersburg, 625 miles to the north. The hospital was a modest institution and rarely housed more than four or five patients at a time. As was the custom, the doctor treated horses and cows during the frequent periods of idleness his official duties allowed him. In 1860 officials in the Kherson office of the Ministry of Internal Affairs quietly paid local merchants 825 rubles, or the annual salary of three clerks, for soap with which to wash the hospital's linen; secure in the knowledge that the expenditure had gone unnoticed, they allocated 104 more rubles for the same purpose in January 1861, and ten to twenty rubles more in each of the following months.[3]

If we are to believe contemporary accounts, the situation in Kherson was exceptional only in that the evil-doers were finally brought to justice. Otherwise, similar stories could be told of most provinces in the empire.[4] So widespread was this corruption that Nikolai Gogol could exploit it as a fact of common knowledge in his grotesque but disturbingly realistic stories and plays. "Of course I take bribes," declared the district judge in *The Inspector General* (1836) "but there are bribes and bribes." The mayor in the same play accepted this distinction and philosophized that "There is no man who has no sins in his past. This is the way things were arranged by God himself."[5] Such lines were cal-

[2] P. Zelenyi, "Khersonskoe dvorianstvo i Khersonskaia guberniia v 1862-om godu," *Severnyi Vestnik*, viii (August 1889), 59.

[3] *Ibid.*, pp. 57-58.

[4] See M. O. Gershenzon, ed., *Epokha Nikolaia I*, Moscow, 1910, Chap. iii. Also *Materialy ob ustroistve upravleniia zemskimi povinnostiami*, B. E. Trutchenko, ed., St. Petersburg, 1861, p. 25; and V. A. Shompulev, "Provintsialnye tipy 40-kh godov," *Russkaia Starina*, cxv, August 1898, pp. 331-35.

[5] N. G. Gogol, *Sobranie khudozhestvennykh proisvedenii v piatikh tomakh*, 5 vols., Moscow, 1961, iv, 13.

culated to amuse or appall, but certainly not to shock the audience with unexpected revelations. Poorly managed institutions and the consequent bribery and peculation had left their mark on the public.

The fact of large-scale mismanagement and corruption in the provinces is too well documented to be doubted. Its importance for the succeeding period, however, has been questioned. The most recent Soviet specialist on the subject acknowledges the existence of chaos in the provinces but minimizes its impact on the state and society as a whole.[6] In his view, the reforms in provincial government introduced in the sixties are to be explained primarily in terms of the emancipation of the serfs in 1861. This hypothesis inclines him to consider only briefly the concrete problems of regional administration in Russia before passing on to the more dramatic political conflicts in Petersburg at the time of the abolition of serfdom.

Such a perspective distorts the motives of many of the reformers and drastically oversimplifies the dynamics of change in mid-nineteenth century Russia. Unfortunately, it is reinforced by much of the historical writing on the decades before 1861. The primary thrust of research on the reign of Nicholas I has been on the state apparatus in Petersburg and its leading functionaries. The closest attention that the provinces have been afforded has resulted from the populist interests of a variety of writers rather than from a balanced view on the role of the provinces in the state and society of Russia. Accordingly, the only institutions studied are those of the rural peasantry, and the term "society" is understood in its ethnographic rather than its political sense. For opposite reasons, both the "statist" and the "populist" views see the Russian provinces primarily as the stage on which the Russian *Volk* waged its age-old battle against serfdom.

In fact, historical writings on the period have considera-

[6] V. V. Garmiza, *Podgotovka zemskoi reformy 1864 goda*, Moscow, 1957, p. 20.

bly underestimated the importance of the provinces to Russian life. The themes of contemporary literature present a different picture. Gogol's *Dead Souls* (1842), Aksakov's *A Family Chronicle* (1856), and all but one of the novels of Turgenev are set squarely in the provinces at the estates of the middle and lower gentry. Although critics were increasingly impressed by the young Dostoevski's use of urban themes, scores of readers relished the mood of corruption and motley confusion presented by the brilliant vice-governor of Riazan and Tver, Mikhail Saltykov, in his popular *Provincial Sketches*.[7]

The preponderance of provincial themes in the literature suggests that the hegemony of the two capitals in Russian life was far from complete, and the population statistics of the middle years of the century indicate that in this respect literature accurately reflects reality. Though extremely crude and approximate, the census data of the years preceding 1861 indicate the extent to which Russia retained its nonurban character. In the 1840s, majestic Petersburg, Catherine II's "Northern Palmyra," was less than half the size of Paris.[8] As late as the 1850s this center of Russian political life did not have numbered streets, and buildings were identified merely by the names of their owner. Despite Peter I's hopes, so much of the city was built of wood that when Otto von Bismarck arrived in Petersburg in 1859 he was confronted with a ban on cigar smoking in the streets.[9] In 1849 Moscow still had only 349,000 inhabitants[10] and open country began within view of the Kremlin walls.

[7] On Saltykov's administrative career see N. V. Iakovlev, *M. E. Saltykov-Shchedrin v Tveri, 1860-1862*, Kalinin, 1961, and Baron N. V. Driesen, "M. E. Saltykov v Riazane," *Istoricheskii Vestnik*, xxi (February 1900), 598-622.

[8] A. G. Rashin, *Naselenie Rossii za 100 let (1811-1913); statisticheskii ocherk*, Moscow, 1956, p. 90.

[9] *Vest*, No. 13 (1863), 4-5. In this article entitled "Bureaucracy and Sidewalks," the absence of sidewalks, water, and public lighting in Odessa is also criticized.

[10] Rashin, *Naselenie* . . . , pp. 90, 114.

6

At the end of the Crimean War the combined populations of Petersburg and Moscow did not make up even two per- cent of the seventy million people of European Russia.[11] Both cities were expanding steadily, but their greatest growth did not come until the 1870s. Two years after the emancipation of the serfs a journalist could still ask seri- ously, "Are there cities in Russia?"[12]

In a country in which four of every five people were peasants, the raw statistics on population distribution must be further refined to be of significance to political and ad- ministrative history. After all, except that they represented a permanent threat of spontaneous revolt, the serfs were without political weight in the state. Even if they had been invited to take an interest in the life of the society of which they were a part, which they decisively had not been, their low literacy rate would have barred them from participa- tion in all but the most rudimentary practical matters.[13] Nor was political participation the prerogative of all nonserfs. Due to impediments imposed by the government and the poverty of most members of the so-called urban classes, the political significance of this group was minimal.[14] Similarly, the Orthodox clergy was excluded from taking a political role in local society. And the few statesmen who advocated wider civic involvement for the clergy had to apologize for their general ignorance and backwardness.[15]

Thus, the Russian political community was confined to that amorphous group of landlords, small farmers, military

[11] *Ibid.*, pp. 28-29.   [12] *Vest*, No. 13 (1863), 5.
[13] Rashin, *Naselenie.* . . , p. 291, reports that the average rate of literacy in 21 provinces in the 1880s was 10.8 percent.
[14] When the government of the city of Petersburg was reorganized in 1845 the merchant and trading classes played no part and took no interest in the proceedings, which were conducted in the Ministry of Internal Affairs under N. Miliutin. William Bruce Lincoln, "Nikolai Alexandrovich Miliutin and the Problems of State Reform in Niko- laevan Russia," Ph.D. diss., University of Chicago, 1966, pp. 93ff.
[15] TsGIA-SSSR, f. 1143 (1863), op. vi., d. 82, 817-23, *Memoriia No. 8*, July 29, 1863. (See Bibliography, Archival Sources)

officers, and upper civil servants known grandiosely as the gentry. In the late 1850s members of this service class numbered 886,000, or about one and one-half percent of the population.[16] In spite of their small numbers, the Russian gentry held a near monopoly of political skill and power in the tsar's empire. Yet this statement cannot be applied to the gentry as a whole. Thousands of members of this class were, from the standpoint of culture and education, virtually indistinguishable from the peasantry, even to the point of wearing peasant beards.[17]

Where did members of this exclusive political class live? A constant accusation of western visitors was that they circulated idly about the court in Petersburg, to the neglect of their estates.[18] Undoubtedly, scores of noble courtiers were much in evidence at the Winter Palace and at the royal estate of Tsarskoe Selo. But the overwhelming majority of the gentry lived not in the two capitals but in the provinces. In 1831 the gentry domiciled in Petersburg numbered 42,900; in the years 1834 to 1840 the gentry population of Moscow stood at 15,700.[19] During the years 1830 to 1835 the total population of Russia stood at about 48 million, and the number of gentry at approximately 720,000.[20] Accordingly,

[16] Jerome Blum, *Lord and Peasant in Russia, from the Ninth to the Nineteenth Century*, Princeton, 1961, pp. 375ff.

[17] In spite of such notable nongentry intelligentsia as N. Polevoi, N. Pogodin, A. Grigoriev, and V. Belinskii, this group was insignificant in number throughout the reign of Nicholas I.

[18] Baron August von Haxthausen, *Studien über die innern Zustände, das Volksleben, und insbesondere die ländlichen Einrichtungen Russlands*, 3 vols., Hannover and Berlin, 1847-52, III, Chap. 2, contains a lengthy critique of the Russian gentry's way of life.

[19] Rashin, *Naselenie . . .* , pp. 124, 126. The nobility of Petersburg was 9.5 percent of the total urban population and in Moscow only 4.5 percent. These statistics contradict the widespread contemporary impression of Moscow as a city of the aristocracy. See Ivan Golovine, *Russia under the Autocrat, Nicholas the First*, 2 vols., London, 1846, I, 111.

[20] The total population recorded in the 1838 census was 48,825,400 (Rashin, *Naselenie . . .* , p. 29). The percentage of gentry in the population is taken as 1.5.

only about 8 percent, or one out of twelve gentry in the middle of Nicholas' reign, were living under the direct supervision of the central authorities. Even if the figure of 92 percent of the class living in the provinces is adjusted by the subtraction of the large number of those who were only technically gentry but were actually undistinguishable from peasants, we still have a preponderance of the politically relevant members of Russian society living under the wing of provincial rather than central institutions.

Under such circumstances, the day-to-day functioning of the organs of provincial government assumed an importance that it would not have had in a more highly urbanized and geographically concentrated society. The provincial resident's most frequent contact with governmental authority would have been through the local agencies of the ministries rather than with the central authorities themselves. For him, the Russian state was embodied most immediately in its provincial administrative apparatus.[21] Policies could be announced with pious resolution at the parade grounds in Petersburg, but they became concrete facts in the lives of most Russian subjects only when applied at the provincial level.

The ability of provincial administrations to execute policy thus became the prime determinate of the success of domestic rule in Russia. During the reign of Nicholas I many changes affected the performance of local administrations. The cumulative impact of these changes was to be so pernicious as to call forth a broad-based reform movement after 1855.

THE GROWTH OF BUREAUCRACY

No characteristic of the administrative apparatus of Nicholas I stamped its mark more firmly on the minds of

---

[21] "The *chinovnik* is the incarnation of the government." D. K. Schedo-Ferroti (pseud. for Baron Firks), *Études sur l'avenir de la Russie*, 2 vols., Berlin, 1857, I, 8-9.

contemporaries than the seemingly boundless growth of the civil service. The weird image of Gogol's hunched scribe Akakii Akakevich, rising posthumously in the Petersburg sky to haunt the administrator under whom he worked, was transformed into a symbol of the era. Dmitrii Tolstoi, later Minister of Education, observed the shadow cast over government by the bulging chancelleries and declared bureaucrats to be "no less strong and much more dangerous than the Poles."[22] The French *bon vivant*, the Marquis de Custine, visiting Petersburg in 1839, considered the "machines inconvenienced with souls" to have become the very essence of the Russia of Nicholas I.[23]

The overriding importance which contemporaries assigned to the mushrooming of bureaucracy readily became a historian's shibboleth, admitting of no challenge and requiring no proof. I. Kataev, in a book devoted to the pre-reform bureaucracy, did not deem it necessary to investigate the actual number of civil servants during the reign of Nicholas.[24] This has recently been done in a masterly fashion by Professor Pintner, but his study focuses primarily on the composition of the central bureaucracy.[25]

Part of the cause of this lacuna in research was pointed out by the eminent scholar, Vasilii Kliuchevskii. Although thoroughly familiar with the available sources, he had to acknowledge that "Unfortunately, we do not have precise statistical evidence with which to measure the growth of the bureaucracy."[26] During much of Nicholas' reign detailed

[22] D. N. Tolstoi, "Zapiski grafa Dmitriia Nikolaevicha Tolstogo," *Russkii Arkhiv*, xxiii, No. 2, 1885, p. 40.

[23] Astolphe Louis Léonor, Marquis de Custine, *A Journey for Our Time*, Phyllis Penn Kohler, ed. and trans., New York, 1951, p. 55.

[24] I. M. Kataev, *Do-reformennaia biurokratiia po zapiskam, memuaram i literature*, St. Petersburg, 1914.

[25] Walter M. Pintner "The Social Characteristics of the Early Nineteenth-Century Russian Bureaucracy," *Slavic Review*, 29, No. 3 (September 1970), 429-43; Hans-Joachim Torke, *Das russische Beamtentum in der ersten Halfte des 19. Jahrhunderts, Forschungen zur osteuropaischen Geschichte*, Berlin, 1967, Vol. 13, 133-37.

[26] V. O. Kliuchevskii, *Sochineniia*, 9 vols., Moscow, 1956-59, v, 271.

civil service lists were kept, but only a partial set of these is preserved in Soviet archives.[27] Pintner has shown the excellent use to which these can be put, but serious problems are nonetheless present. First, they are incomplete even for single agencies, and the principle of selection is erratic to the extreme. Second, the numerous petty clerks at the lowest two ranks are not included. Third, these records are so incomplete for the early part of Nicholas' reign that it is difficult to make valid growth calculations. And finally, there must be serious question of the accuracy of all records kept by officials whose thoroughness and even honesty was generally doubted by contemporaries.

A second class of data is available in the official *Adres-Kalendar*, published annually by the Academy of Sciences, and in other more reliable lists issued by individual ministries.[28] The Ministry of Internal Affairs' *List of Chinovniks* for 1829 indicates that the overall staffing of top provincial offices was nearly uniform in all of the fifty provinces of European Russia, regardless of their area or population. In 1829 the principal local officials were the civil governors who kept staffs of only two or three assistants.[29] Equally modest were the advisory staffs to the Provincial Directorates (*gubernskie pravleniia*) which varied between five and six members.[30] Thus, the top provincial officers for the

27 TsGIA-SSSR, f. 1349.

28 The *Adres-Kalendar* issued by the government beginning in 1844 provides the names of only the principal officeholders in the provinces and excludes their staffs. Another potential source, the *Spisok glavnykh nachalnikov, chlenov sekretarei, i stolonachalnikov gubernskikh i uezdnikh prisutstvennykh mest*, St. Petersburg, 1851 and 1858, lists only centrally appointed officeholders and is not available for the 1820s and 1830s.

29 *Spisok chinovnikam ministerstva vnutrennykh del i ego vedomstv*, St. Petersburg, 1829.

30 The civil governor of Vladimir had three assistants including a secretary, a titular councillor, and a collegiate assessor. Voronezh's governor had three aides (p. 180), Kostroma's, had two (p. 380), and Viatka's, had two (p. 207). *Ibid.*, Vladimir, 6; Voronezh, 6; Kostroma, 5; Viatka, 5.

11

Ministry of Internal Affairs in the late 1820s never numbered more than nine.

A startling growth occurred in the following decades. The government of Kostroma province, which had managed in 1829 with an advisory staff of 7, in 1848 required 54 officials to do essentially the same work;[31] the governor's chancellors and the Directorate in Viatka grew from 8 in 1829 to 38 by 1863, while those of Voronezh expanded from 9 to 54 between 1829 and 1862.[32] As a control, it should be noted that the rate of population growth in the same provinces for the period from 1830 to about 1860 was in the area of 10 to 50 percent.[33] Top provincial offices for this one ministry, then, increased in number fourfold and even eightfold in an approximately thirty-year period, during which time the population did not expand by more than half. In some provinces the growth was registered within a few hectic years. In Vladimir, for example, the governor's staff of aides was enlarged from 14 to 21 in the two years between 1849 and 1851, and the general force of ranked civil servants in the Provincial Directorate from 85 to 114.[34] It should be noted, moreover, that these figures do not include the army of clerks and scribes who had to copy, mail, and file the reports drawn up by the officials.

A similar growth took place in staffs at the district level. In 1829 few districts in the country required more than six officials to handle the affairs of the Ministry of Internal Affairs. Adding an equal number of representatives from the ministries of Finances and Justice—whose staffs, however, were often smaller—a total of approximately eighteen offi-

31 *Spisok o chinovnikakh Kostromskoi gubernii*, Kostroma, 1848 (pages not numbered).

32 *Spisok lits, sostoiashchikh na sluzhbe v Viatskoi gubernii na 1864*, Viatka, 1864 (?), (pages not numbered); *Spisok dolzhnostnykh lits Voronezhskoi gubernii na 1851 god*, Vladimir, 1851 (pages not numbered).

33 Rashin, *Naselenie . . .* , pp. 28, 29.

34 *Spisok chinam, sostoiashchim na sluzhbe po Vladimirskoi gubernii na 1848 god*, Vladimir, 1849; *Spisok chinam, sostoiashchim na sluzhbe po Vladimirskoi gubernii na 1851 god*, Vladimir, 1851.

cers is reached. By 1853 three sample districts of the steppe province of Orel had 41 to 42 people working in the same offices. A typical Chernigov district in 1857 had 44 ranked civil servants of all ministries, and another in Kursk required 43. A single district in Vladimir province employed a 48-man staff to conduct its affairs in 1851.[35] The unusually low figures of 20 and 26 officials in two Viatka districts were not repeated outside of the far north and the southeastern border where the steppe merges with desert.[36] Thus, the local representatives of the three principal ministries in the approximately five hundred districts of the country more than doubled in number within the two decades after 1829.[37] Taking the entire period of Nicholas' reign it appears that there was a two to eightfold growth of the total staff of provincial and district governments with the greatest expansion occurring in the provincial offices.

To accommodate this mushrooming, a corresponding expansion took place within the government's central organs in Petersburg. Again, the irregularity of the statistics for the early part of the period renders difficult any precise appreciation of the magnitude of change. But to take as an example a single division of the Ministry of Internal Affairs, the Economic Department, the number of its staff members

---

[35] *Spisok chinam grazhdanskogo upravleniia Orlovskoi gubernii na 1853 g.*, Orel, no date: Kromy district, 40 (pp. 69-73); Malo-arkhangelsk, 42 (pp. 73-77); Sevsk, 41 (pp. 61-69). These figures include the district towns as well; the district town administration was also included in the 1829 figures. Excluding the district town administration, the district figures are Kromy, 29; Malo-arkhangelsk, 28; Sevsk, 24 (1853). Unfortunately, the 1829 data are not broken down further. *Spisok dolzhnestnikh lits Chernigovskoi gubernii na 1857*, Chernigov, n.d. Gorodnitskii district, 41 (plus 5 teachers, pp. 39-44). *Spisok chinam, sostoiashchim na sluzhbe po Kurskoi gubernii, 1859*, Kurski, n.d. (pages not numbered), Belgorod district, 43; *Spisok chinam . . . Vladimirskoi . . . 1851*: Murom district, 48 (pp. 52-57); Suzdal district, 42 (pp. 34-38).

[36] Urzhum district, 20; Malmyshsk district, 26. *Spisok lits, sostoiashchikh na sluzhbe v Viatskoi gubernii, 1859*, Viatka, 1859, pp. 204-13.

[37] The incomplete *Adres Kalendar* lists reflect a similar magnitude of change; cf. Torke *Das russische Beamtentum. . .* , p. 135.

with titles listed in the Table of Ranks expanded from 63 to 115 in the decade 1839-1848.[38] Each of these officials would have required in turn more secretaries and helpers. A similar explosion took place within the Ministry of Finances.[39] The new Ministry of State Domains grew rapidly after its foundation in 1837-1838, and the Chief Communications Administration, a quasi-ministry, enlarged its staff repeatedly as functions were transferred to it from other ministries between 1832 and 1847.

It is not enough, however, to point out this startling proliferation of bureaucracy without taking notice of its causes and consequences. Clearly, the impression created by a large staff would be different if it labored to broaden the public services of a province than if it was serving ends largely unrelated to the needs of the region. Official data on government expenditures indicate that the provincial public received few direct benefits from the expanded bureaucracy.

During Nicholas I's reign the cost of governing the Russian state rose precipitously. In the sixteen years between the monetary reform of 1839 and the end of his reign the budget grew by 172,233,000 rubles, or 51 percent, and in the period 1825 to 1839 the rise had been no less startling.[40] Most of this growth was covered by foreign loans, but borrowing alone did not suffice. To meet the deficit, taxes levied in the provinces soared in the half-century after 1814.[41]

[38] *Obshchii sostav ministerstva vnutrennykh del,* St. Petersburg, 1839, pp. 26, 31, 1848, pp. 37-50; *Spisok chinam ministerstva vnutrennykh del,* St. Petersburg, 1857, pp. 93-112, 1862, pp. 119-38. These lists do not include the army of copy clerks required to process the documents prepared by the expanding corps of officials.

[39] *Ministerstvo finansov, 1802-1902,* 2 vols., St. Petersburg, 1902, i, 628-29, shows that the Ministry of Finances required 14,696 rubles more to maintain it in 1854 than in 1840.

[40] Torke estimates a fourfold increase for all central agencies from 1805 to 1851, *Das russische Beamtentum . . . ,* p. 135.

[41] S. Ia. Tseitlin, "Zemskaia reforma," *Istoriia Rossii v XIX veke,*

How were these public funds spent? Due to the dispersal of data among the archives of ten different governmental agencies it is difficult to arrive at even an approximation of the amount of tax money spent in any one province. The fact that the growth in expenditures at the local level was modest at best must be deduced instead from the available data on the total governmental budget, broken down by ministries and principal agencies. These indicate that the annual expenditures of several important branches of the government either remained static or registered only a slight absolute increase in the period from 1839 to 1854. Among these were the Orthodox Church, the postal service, and the ministries of Justice and Education, all of which together show an absolute growth of less than a million rubles. These agencies all performed functions closely related to the life of the provincial population. Most important, the Ministry of Internal Affairs, whose role in local life exceeded that of all other central organs of the government, did not substantially enlarge its expenditures over the same years, in spite of a 9 percent growth in the population!

In stark contrast is the military budget. The militarization of Russian life during the reign of Nicholas "The Stick" is well known. Though Russia was not engaged in any full-scale wars between the departure of Napoleon from the European scene until the outbreak of the Crimean War, it remained a nation in arms. To ensure the tranquility of the continent, Alexander I had adopted the formula that Russia's army should be equal in numbers to the combined strength of the Prussian and Austrian armies. When after 1815 Prussia, too, continued to adhere to the principle of a mass army, Russia's self-assigned task became all the more onerous. Added to this burden was a series of small-scale campaigns against Turkey (1828-30), Poland (1830), and

9 vols., St. Petersburg, 1906, III, 186-87n puts the figure at 1.6 times. Garmiza, *Podgotovka* . . . , p. 34, n.6, argues that taxes increased by a factor of six.

15

Hungary (1849) and continual western diplomatic pressure on several fronts that served to justify a costly military policy in the minds of the tsar and his advisers.[42]

In 1840 the military consumed half of the state's annual budget. Fourteen years later the expenditures of the army and navy had doubled. The Ministry of Finances, which was charged with the processing of all state taxes after their collection, increased its operating budget at the same time from 30,034,000 to 44,727,000 rubles. Further, the annual interest charges on foreign loans increased by 32,507,000 rubles between 1840 and 1854. Together, the direct military bill, the expenses of the finance ministry, and the interest on foreign loans account for all but nine million of the 172,223,000 ruble growth in the annual budget.[43]

Besides expenditures which appeared in the budget of the central government, there were other military expenses which were paid through locally levied taxes and services. Chief among these was the quartering of troops at the expense of the provinces. The original military function of Peter I's provincial divisions is still evident in the nineteenth-century quartering system. When a military unit was in permanent garrison in a particular province it was the duty of the locality to provide it with basic accommodations and rations. These and other so-called natural duties were paid in labor or goods. By their very nature it was—and is —impossible to determine their exact cost to any given province. But whatever the actual value may have been of

[42] John Shelton Curtiss, *The Russian Army under Nicholas I, 1825-1855*, Durham, N.C., 1965, pp. 100ff.
In contrast to Russia. the economizing English Parliament forced through a severe reduction of British armed strength; between 1815 and 1821 the British army was slashed from its strength of 685,000 to 100,000. Richard A. Preston and others, *Men in Arms: A History of Warfare and Its Interrelationships with Western Society*, New York, 1956, p. 201.

[43] *Ministerstvo finansov* . . . , I, 628-29. The proportion of the budget going to military expenses had reached 50 percent first during the war years at the beginning of the 19th century.

the goods and services provided under the quartering duty, we can be sure that it was great and that the burden did not fall equally on every province. When the provincial reform idea gathered momentum after the Crimean War this archaic system became a major focus of criticism.[44]

To be sure, the provincial populace of Russia did receive certain new services in return for the general tax increases. When the new Ministry of State Domains was established, provision was made for a national system of fire insurance which, however, was inadequately implemented; the gentry benefited from the founding of a special estate bank in 1833; a modest number of new gymnasiums were founded in provincial and district capitals; a new Council on Manufactures in the Ministry of Finances promoted internal trade while a Commercial Council with five local branches was created to foster foreign trade. But for most improvements bearing directly on their own lives the provincial populace was expected to look to its various corporate institutions, to special taxes levied by the provincial estates, and to *zemskii* or local public taxes.[45]

Two aspects of the nonstate tax system should be noted. First, responsibility for collecting these taxes, as for all others, lay with the executive police and even their disbursal was entrusted not to those upon whom they were levied but to the police or other local representatives of the central organs. The road and building commissions established in 1833 and 1849 were typical: though both contained *de jure* representatives of the body of provincial taxpayers, their work, according to the report of the gov-

[44] D. P. Gavrilov, ed., *Materialy i svedeniia o sushchestvuiushchem poriadke i sposobakh otpravleniia naturalnykh zemskikh povinnostei v tsentralnykh guberniiakh imperii* (Ministry of Finances), St. Petersburg, 1860, pp. 16-20.

[45] The precise definition of the word "zemstvo" and of "zemskii" taxes was the subject of heated debate during the 1850s. In the 1840s its meaning was closer to "public" than to the German "land" with its geographical overtones.

17

ernment's own investigating commission, was actually controlled by police and civil servants and by the ministries to which the latter were responsible.[46]

A second aspect of the nonstate tax system is that the portion of the local gentry legally empowered to participate in its administration was reduced by governmental decree in 1831. In that year participation in the provincial and district gentry assemblies from whose members elective offices in the tax agencies were filled was restricted to those landlords who owned 100 or more male serfs or 8,000 acres (3,000 *desiatiny*) of land.[47] The stated purpose of this decree was to elevate the authority of the gentry. Its obvious effect, however, was to deprive large numbers of that class of a role in public affairs at the very time when the provincial civil service was undergoing an unprecedented expansion. Most provincial gentry responded to this provocative measure with their habitual indifference. After all, the corporate organization of the gentry had been established by Catherine the Great more to satisfy the administration's need for personnel than to stimulate political activity by the gentry. But a powerful minority felt otherwise. They enjoyed the right to petition the throne, but this was a frustrating and fruitless process.[48] So keen was the feeling of ineffectiveness that when the marshals of the provincial gentry gathered in Petersburg in 1833 for the dedication of the Alexander monument, they expressed their discontent not to the Tsar but to the Minister of Internal Affairs.[49]

Such demonstrations serve to summarize the situation that was developing. Its elements, as we have seen, were the

[46] *Materialy po zemskomu obshchestvennomu ustroistvu (Polozhenie o zemskikh uchrezhdeniiakh* (Ministry of Internal Affairs), 2 vols., St. Petersburg, 1885-86, I, 38-47.

[47] Blum, *Lord and Peasant* . . . , p. 353.

[48] A. I. Skrebitskii, ed., *Krestianskoe delo v tsarstvovanii Imperatora Aleksandra II-ogo. Materialy dlia istorii osvobozhdeniia krestian,* 4 vols., Bonn, 1862-68, I, 776.

[49] A. Romanovich-Slavatinskii, *Dvorianstvo v Rossii ot nachala xviii veka do otmeny krepostnogo prava,* 2nd edn., Kiev, 1912, p. 447.

18

numerical growth of the local civil service, the steady increase in taxes and imposts which yielded no direct return in services to the provincial taxpayer, and the restriction of the right to participate in local civil affairs to only the wealthiest minority of the gentry class. All of these factors forced upon the provincial gentry in general a heightened awareness of the Russian state and of its claims on the provinces.

If the growth of the bureaucracy amplified the state's impact on the public, it had equally significant consequences for the government itself. The burgeoning administrative apparatus created vexing problems of both personnel and procedure. During the reign of Nicholas I these problems were felt in the central chancelleries in Petersburg, but were especially acute in the provinces. So serious were they, in fact, that doubts arose within the government itself whether the administration could effectively fulfill its local functions and make good its claims on the provinces.

Although the civil service underwent a great expansion, the rapid increase in numbers does not in itself account for its chaotic condition. In Prussia, by comparison, the provincial administration was substantially enlarged in the same period but without most of the problems that plagued Russia. Among these problems none was more serious than the backwardness and incompetence of the green-uniformed army of clerks and scribes and "executive" police. Year by year this personnel problem grew more pressing. Eventually the search for a solution led to the consideration of alternative forms of local administration.

A conspicuous aspect of Russian society in the early nineteenth century was the absence of a literate middle class from which qualified recruits for administrative posts could be drawn. Unlike the nations of western Europe with their ample class of *Fachleute*, Russian society had no secure middle group from which the government could recruit office workers and the like. This inadequacy was poignantly described by the civil governor of Kaluga province in his

19

annual report for 1848. With rare and disarming frankness, he told his superiors that his administration was in trouble, in spite of his own "constant and unflagging efforts." For years, he wrote, he had attempted to form a staff but had failed, "due to the difficulty of finding educated people to serve in the district institutions." So bad was the situation that many of his clerks, aides, and police were farmers who worked their fields on weekends and eventually retired to their small holdings.[50] In Vladimir the situation was equally bad, with most of the nonelective police posts being filled by draftees impressed into civil service from the local garrison.[51] And yet Kaluga and Vladimir were far better provided with educated personnel than were many more sparsely settled areas in the north, east, and south. Even in Kaluga, however, official documents were riddled with misspellings and made illegible by sloppy handwriting.

Carelessness was the least of the undesirable effects of this situation. Though civil servants generally devoted their entire careers to their administrative duties, by functional standards they did not constitute a professional corps.[52] The large-scale recruitment of nearly uneducated rural folk into the ranks of officialdom drastically retarded the development of a sense of professionalism within the civil service. Clerks in public offices rarely comprehended the general purpose of the institution which they served and hence could not share in the awareness of common objectives that alone can bind a diffuse administrative apparatus together. Baron Haxthausen was conscious of this problem and characterized the Russian civil servant of 1843 as "ungifted" and "insecure."[53]

An essential element in the modern bureaucracy is that it possess a virtual monopoly of certain administrative

[50] TsGIA-SSSR, f. 1281, op. 4, d. 43.
[51] TsGIA-SSSR, f. 1281, op. 6, No. 44, p. 25.
[52] Pintner argues the case for professionalization on the basis of the career patterns of civil servants rather than on functional grounds, "The Social Characteristics . . . ," pp. 441-42.
[53] TsGIA-SSSR, f. 1180, d. 81, p. 383.

skills.[54] But members of Nicholas' provincial and central bureaucracy were so poorly trained in their work that measures had to be taken by the state itself to educate them to their duties. The Ministry of Justice founded a legal academy in 1835 to train its future judges and lawyers. For its future administrators the Ministry of Finances formed the Technological Institute (1825) and the School of Mining Technology (1834). Conspicuously lax in this regard was the Ministry of Internal Affairs, which was increasingly responsible for all provincial administration. Even if this ministry had acted promptly in the 1830s, a generation would have to elapse before provincial capitals felt the benefits of more competent officials.

The mere improvement of educational facilities would not alone have made the provincial service attractive to an ambitious young man. A life of poverty awaited him. When new provincial organs of government were instituted in 1775, salary levels were already low. Then, by offering pay only in *assignats* at a time when their purchasing power was plummeting, the situation was further worsened. By 1816 salaries were so depressed that representatives of the ministries of Internal Affairs, Justice, and Police convened to study the problem. In 1820 the governors general took up the issue at the request of Alexander I. Though they approved a substantial increase in salary levels, the treasury rejected the proposals because of the state deficit. Equally well-intentioned calls for change were raised in 1824, 1826, 1834, and 1835, but each time budgetary considerations prohibited increases on the scale proposed.[55]

By the 1840s the Minister of Internal Affairs, Count Perovskii, had to admit that salaries of members of the Pro-

[54] See Reinhard Bendix, "Bureaucracy and the Problem of Power," *Reader in Bureaucracy*, Robert K. Merton, ed., New York, 1952, pp. 114-35, 118ff.

[55] E. Anuchin, *Istoricheskii obzor razvitiia administrativnykh-politseiskikh uchrezhdenii v Rossii s uchrezhdeniia o guberniiakh 1775 g. do poslednego vremeni* (Ministry of Internal Affairs), St. Petersburg, 1872, p. 41.

vincial Directorates were "so poor that they do not suffice for the most essential needs of man."[56] More than a few local administrators sought temporary—and illegal—relief by dipping into pension and philanthropic funds to pay their executive police.[57] But when the Crimean War brought a general price rise that turned the already deflated salaries into a pittance even this "green-collar crime" was unavailing.[58] In rural Russia economic life was largely uncomplicated by the daily need for currency, but such desperate conditions nonetheless severely hampered the development of a modern class of civil servants and invited graft, bribery, and embezzlement.

Budgetary considerations alone do not explain the miserably low pay levels. Count Krankrin, Minister of Finances, hinted at a more important factor when he observed to Nicholas that, considering the low place of the civil servant in society, there was no basis for the accusation that his salary was inadequate.[59] Clerks, in other words, did not deserve more than they received. And since no substantial middle class existed in Russia, the government saw no reason to pay men as if they belonged to such a group. Consequently, for years after Peter I the tendency was to raise top administrators to the gentry and to consider the remaining clerks as on the same level as military conscripts or state peasants.

With the expansion of the civil service, however, the existence of a new group, neither peasant nor gentry, had finally to be acknowledged. The gentry-bureaucrat-novelist, Mikhail Saltykov, contemptuously referred to its members as "a special breed of proletariat," while others described them with stronger invective.[60] The first step toward the

---

[56] TsGIA-SSSR, f. 1149 (1843-44), d. 94, p. 12.

[57] TsGIA-SSSR, f. 1389, op. 3, 11, p. 60.

[58] On the influence of the Crimean War see TsGIA-SSSR, f. 869, op. 1, d. 393, p. 3.

[59] *Ministerstvo finansov* . . . , I, 207.

[60] Cited by K. K. Arseniev, ed., "Materialy dlia biografii," *Polnoe sobranie sochinenii M. E. Saltykova*, 12 vols., St. Petersburg, 1905-06,

legal recognition of this group was taken in 1832 with the establishment of a special rank of "honorary citizenship," with privileges roughly comparable to those of the merchant guild.[61] To distinguish "honorary citizens" from the gentry, the government raised the service level for entry into the hereditary gentry to the fifth grade on the fourteen-level Table of Ranks and then, in 1856, to the fourth.

These measures drew a hard line horizontally through the state administration. They underscored the division that had long existed between higher and lower civil servants and redefined it in social terms. As a consequence, they reduced the possibility that subordinate officers would identify their own interests with the aims of the bureaucracy as a whole. At the same time, the new ruling affected adversely the incentives within the system. New "honorary citizens" enjoyed freedom from bodily punishment, were exempted from military service, and were spared the degradation of the "soul tax." Having achieved this measure of security and faced with the risk involved in taking the large step to the next rank, most civil servants were inclined to remain content with their lot. The few who resolved to compete for the superior ranks were shrewd enough to realize that the battle could not be waged successfully in the obscurity of a district or provincial office; from members of this rising group came ever-mounting pressure for positions in the capital and for the "exposure" to the notice of higher officials which such posts alone could provide.[62]

Recent research into the nature of bureaucratic organizations has clarified their potential role as a stabilizing element in society. By enrolling their worst critics into their own ranks bureaucracies neutralize possible threats to their habitual patterns of operation. True assimilation implies

---

I, lxviii, lxvix. See also V. P. Bezobrazov, "O soslovnykh interesakh," *Russkii Vestnik*, III, No. 3 (1858), 89.

[61] A. A. Kizevetter, "Vnutrennaia politika v tsarstvovanii Nikolaia Pavlovicha," *Istoriia Rossii v XIX veke*, I, 211-12.

[62] *Ibid.*, p. 210.

23

that a degree of power has been transferred to a new element. This can be avoided through "cooptation," that is, by involving discontented social groups in the bureaucracy's work without surrendering any real authority to them. By this means potential critics become the virtual prisoners of an administration.[63]

Russia's expanded provincial civil service was unsuccessful either in assimilating or in coopting its critics during the reign of Nicholas I. True, the fact that elected officials such as the marshals of the provincial nobility wore civil service uniforms and wrote on ministerial stationery does imply a degree of "bureaucratization of society's representatives," as Alexander Kizevetter claimed.[64] Those few gentry who for one reason or another accepted office generally held on to it for years, their fellow lords gratefully reelecting them whenever their three or six year terms of service expired.[65] Needless to say, this situation did much to undermine the prestige of the gentry assemblies and the willingness of intelligent landlords to take an active part in them. Most gentry sought by all means to avoid election. Frequently, those who could not escape election simply failed to fulfill their duties.[66] This evasion of responsibility can be blamed in part on the social stigma attached to work in provincial agencies. Why should a hereditary gentry seek election to a post where he would work alongside a professional administrator of humble origin? This theme sounded clearly in a play entitled *The Chinovnik*, which delighted St. Petersburg audiences in 1856. It depicts the fate of a dedicated administrator, Nadimov, who appears at a local estate whose proprietress is an unmarried gentry woman. As a

[63] On the concepts of cooptation see Philip Selznick, "Co-optation: A Mechanism for Organizational Stability," Merton, ed., *Reader* . . . , pp. 135-40. See also Robert Michels "Assimilation of the Discontented into the State Bureaucracy," *ibid.*, pp. 140-41.

[64] Kizevetter, "Vnutrennaia politika . . . ," p. 210.

[65] Romanovich-Slavatinskii, *Dvorianstvo v Rossii* . . . , Chap. v, Sec. 3, Pt. v.

[66] *Ibid.*, pp. 507-14.

provincial civil servant he is treated in a patronizing fashion and is not invited to dine at the same table with the proprietress and her gentry guests. Only at the end of the play are the barriers thrown down and virtue rewarded, when Nadimov wins the hand of the lady of the house.[67]

Merely to give official posts to critics, however, did not ensure that they would be assimilated. Once within the civil service many were frustrated by the glacial slowness with which promotions came and by the heavy torpor which reigned in the chancelleries. Otto von Bismarck perceived the results of this at a meeting of the gentry of Petersburg province in 1861-1862: "These debates and votes on . . . principles which so little agree with the existing structure of the empire leave an impression all the more strange because one can see by the uniforms in which the members appear that the majority of them occupy high positions in the military and civil service."[68]

As early as the 1840s this problem of assimilation had become chronic. In that decade a generation of young men began to point out the faults of the administration of which they were a part. Such criticism drew attention to them, and occasionally, if the critics happened to be well connected in learned circles, actually served to promote their careers. So bitterly did the brilliant young Nikolai Miliutin criticize the civil service that the bureaucracy became a kind of negative springboard for his own advancement within it.[69] It is no accident that it was Miliutin who later envisaged the proposed *zemstvo* provincial organs as a means of neutralizing the strivings of the government's critics in the hinterland. In 1862, Miliutin proposed to his fellow officials that the new organs whose establishment they were considering could serve as "safety valves" for the

---

[67] Count Vladimir Sollogub, "Chinovnik," *Russkii Vestnik*, I, No. 3 (1856). See also Pintner, "The Social Characteristics . . . ," pp. 431-32.

[68] B. E. Nolde, *Peterburgskaia missiia Bismarka, 1859-1862*, Prague, 1925, p. 256.

[69] Lincoln, "Nikolai Alexandrovich Miliutin . . . ," p. 111.

hostility of provincial critics. The *zemstvos*, in other words, should fulfill the cooptative function that the bureaucracy itself had abdicated.[70]

THE IDEAL OF CENTRALIZATION

The critics whom Miliutin had in mind were demanding changes. Some demanded changes in the emancipation statutes issued the year before. All demanded changes in the day-to-day functioning of the provincial bureaucracy. Probably no single aspect of prereform Russia irritated the public at large quite so much as the ordinary workings of local administrations.

A poignant briefing paper issued in 1843 by the Minister of Internal Affairs, Count Lev Perovskii, brought the question of procedure in local agencies to the attention of the tsar. Modern research could scarcely evoke the situation more clearly:

The mechanical work of writing has long since exceeded the physical capabilities of the staff of the Provincial Directorates. The accepted procedures for deciding issues and the forms of processing papers are extremely burdensome, due to their great complexity and slowness. The essence of matters is choked out by formalism . . . [the Provincial Directorates have become], in the public mind, places for civil servants who are not wanted in any other department.[71]

Perovskii bolstered his argument with statistics. For the period 1839 to 1843 the number of papers written and processed per annum in each of nineteen sample provincial gov-

[70] V. V. Garmiza, "Iz istorii razrabotki zakona o vvedenii zemstva v Rossii," *Vestnik Moskovskogo Universiteta*, No. 1 (1958), 131-45.
[71] L. Perovskii, "O neobkhodimosti nekotorykh uluchshenii po gubernskim pravleniiam," 1843, TsGIA-SSSR, f. 1149 (1843-44), d. 94, p. 12. A shortened version of this document was published in *MSVUK*, I, otd. 2 (see also Torke *Das russische Beamtentum . . .*, pp. 211-13).

ernments averaged 60,304. The normal work year in a chancellery was officially set at 272 days, but Perovskii notes that this did not include Saints' days, in which the Orthodox calendar is particularly rich. Nevertheless, using the figure of 272 workdays, Perovskii computed that each day the office staff of every Provincial Directorate had to compose, write, and mail 222 letters in order to keep abreast of its basic work load. In a central province the chancellery could be expected to have ten clerks, so that each one of them had to write an average of twenty-two letters per day.

This figure does not convey completely the full chaos of the situation, for it considers only outgoing mail. Each day the provincial offices received two to three times the number of letters that they sent. Every letter had to be read, entered in a general register, then in the reader's private register, then in a topical reference list and, after that, in an alphabetical index. Whenever an issue was settled, it had to be noted in the report register and a protocol filed in duplicate. Finally, all outgoing mail had to be entered in the general register and copies of all letters sent and received filed in the provincial archive and noted in the archival catalogue.[72]

The Russian equivalent for the term "red tape" was coined in the years when these conditions prevailed.[73] The hydra of red tape enmeshed every aspect of provincial life to such an extent that no local official, however exalted his rank, could avoid it. When Prince Alexander Suvorov, Governor-General of the Baltic provinces, discovered a smoking flue in his residence in Riga he informed the local Building Commission whose responsibility it was to approve the repair. Though the Commission was in the same building that contained the defective flue, official permis-

[72] *Ibid.*, p. 13.

[73] In the seventeenth century "volokita" was occasionally used to refer to bureaucracy, though its primary meaning was "affliction" or "wandering." (*Zhitie protopopa Avvakuma*, Moscow, 1960, p. 456.) It does not appear at all in *Slovar iazika Pushkina.*

sion to carry out the repair was not approved until ten reports had been issued and sixteen days spent in formalities. Once repaired, Surovov's flue was not forgotten. For another two weeks the Building Commission busied itself with terminal reports, which numbered fourteen when the case was finally laid to rest.[74]

Attempts to improve the situation had been made from the time of the foundation of the provincial institutions. In 1806 the Military Governor of Moscow province and in 1826 the Civil Governor of Petersburg sought unsuccessfully to cut back the tangle of formalities. An interministerial committee appointed to explore the problem in 1830 labored for five years and concluded that the solution was to rank all provincial documents in five classes of importance, in other words, to add more formalities. Perovskii's own proposal was no more imaginative: in his report of 1843 he suggested that the staff be enlarged by the addition of a vice-governor, an extra secretary for each section, and "several chancellery clerks and scribes." He perceived the need to simplify procedures but left the fundamental structure of provincial management unchanged.[75] When Mikhail Saltykov quit his own post in the provincial service almost two decades later he named formalism as the chief cause of frustration among would-be reformers.[76]

The specter of the impending inundation of paperwork was so awesome that it distracted attention from the underlying cause of the problem. In retrospect, however, it seems clear that bureaucratic formalism in the provinces was an unacknowledged substitute for the correct hierarchical organization of authority which the Russian administration lacked. It was an attempt to reduce to apparent order the fragmentation of authority caused by the proliferation of

[74] Schedo-Ferroti, *Études* . . . , II, 42n-43n.
[75] Anuchin, *Istoricheskii obzor* . . . , pp. 47-48, 55-63; TsGIA-SSSR, f. 1149 (1843-44), d. 94, pp. 32ff; *MSVUK*, I, otd. 2.2.
[76] K. K. Arseniev, "Materialy dlia biografii . . . ," pp. lxxviff.

poorly staffed and uncoordinated bureaus in regional and district capitals. Because the central ministries could not trust their local personnel they checked them at every turn. In the end, the central authorities sought to eliminate rule by caprice by hiding it behind an opaque wall of petty procedures. Indeed, the entire system was built on the false hope that the relation of the provinces to the capital could be reduced to a matter of form and not of power.

This confusion over the nature of power pervades Russian administrative thought of the first half of the nineteenth century. In the first place, the fundamental laws of the empire (Article 80) scarcely acknowledged the existence of a civil administration. The declaration that "the power of administration in all its aspects belongs to the Emperor" implies that decision making and administration were really one and the same thing. The establishment of the ministries in 1811 did not alter this formula, for they were conceived as the sovereign's will. By definition, autonomous administrative power could not exist. Committed to this notion, the autocracy saw little need for setting up elaborate systems for dealing with bureaucratic formalism, red tape, and misuse of administrative power.

In the second place, the new ministries shared the autocracy's passive and one-sided conception of power. According to the law, they were to be "institutions of means of which the Supreme Authority acts upon all parts of the administration."[77] Power here is the right to issue orders; once the ministries issued their orders they simply assumed that compliance would follow. When orders were speedily implemented the system worked. When they were not the true nature of administrative power became evident; in practice, power was the ability to elicit obedience from subordinates.

[77] *Polnoe sobranie zakonov Rossiiskoi Imperii, sobranie vtoroe,* 55 vols. in 12, St. Petersburg, 1830-84, xxiv, 686, Sec. 206. (Hereafter cited as *PSZ.*) See Marc Raeff, *Michael Speransky: Statesman of Imperial Russia,* The Hague, 1957, p. 112.

As in administrations everywhere, the key to administrative power as a whole was locked up in the ability to inspect and control the lower bureaucracy.[78]

This problem of administrative inspection or control (*nadzor*) had not been treated as a major issue when the provinces were refounded in 1775 or when the ministries were introduced in the years from 1802 to 1811. This initial neglect, together with the great expansion of the bureaucracy in the nineteenth century, forced the issue upon the government during the reign of Nicholas I. In other states such problems fell into the domain of administrative law and were dealt with through the legal system as a whole. But Russia lacked a developed *Rechtsstaat* concept. The backward judiciary provided no solid foundation upon which an efficient system of administrative law could be erected.[79] As a consequence, Russia was forced to deal with the essentially juridical problem of control as a purely administrative issue. Administrative inspection became the *sine qua non* for administrative power as a whole. Describing its importance, a contemporary concluded that without it "there can be no guarantee of correctness and justice, there can exist no society whatsoever."[80]

Legislative decisions were executed at the grass-roots level by the executive police or by other paid civil servants. The most suitable officials for supervising this implementation process were the provincial governors. In the eighteenth century governors were considered the stewards

[78] Cf. Herbert A. Simon, Administrative Behavior, New York, 1957, pp. 11-12; Arnold S. Tannenbaum, *Control in Organizations*, New York, 1968, Chap. 1.

[79] Baron S. A. Korf, *Administrativnaia iustitsiia v Rossii*, 2 vols., St. Petersburg, 1910, presents a more optimistic view of the possibilities of developing administrative justice on the basis of existing Russian legal institutions. See I, 283.

[80] P. Polezhaev, "O gubernskom nadzore," *Zhurnal Ministerstva Iustitsii*, No. 5, 1859, p. 4. More recently Michel Crozier has identified controllers as the unique element of Soviet bureaucracy as opposed to the French system, *The Bureaucratic Phenomenon*, Chicago, 1967, p. 230.

(*khoziainy*) of their provinces, with authority to review all local affairs as agents of the Senate. Even after they were made responsible to the new Ministry of Internal Affairs their duties were enormous. But duties do not necessarily entail power, and recent scholars who have claimed that the authority of the governors was excessive fail to distinguish these two elements.[81]

The inability of governors to exercise power by eliciting obedience from subordinates was due partly to the countless petty responsibilities resting upon them. Just signing routine correspondence required several hours a day. And since no public employees could travel within the province without a pass, governors had to approve some 20,000 of these annually.[82] Such trivia were alone sufficient to restrict the time available to governors for exercising leadership.

An even more important factor in weakening the role of the governorship arose from the very structure of provincial government. Throughout the eighteenth century collegiate rule had prevailed in Russian administration. The *kollegii* introduced by Peter I were based on the functional division of duties. Peter's personality dictated that no strong leader could be allowed to rise within the administration, that function being performed by the tsar, who endeavored to supervise all work in the colleges from above. Lower officials simply coordinated the work of their own staffs. This practice was reversed with the introduction of the ministries in the years from 1802 to 1811. With this measure a single responsible figure was designated in each branch of the government.

For all its merits, the ministerial system was not extended to the provincial governments. Throughout the reign of Nicholas I the governors continued to coordinate the activities of the eighteen agencies under them, without wielding

[81] Raeff, . . . *Speransky*, p. 283.
[82] TsGIA-SSSR, f. 1314, op. 1, d. 55, pp. 1-4. Passes were written for every trip taken by the land captains, the *zasedateli* and the *stanovye pristavy*.

powers adequate to exert control. Though retained to ensure supervision and inspection, this system in fact destroyed the governorship as a check on the local administration and police. Count Zakrevksii made this point in the
Committee of December 6, 1826, in a memorandum entitled
"On the Excessive Number of Duties Entrusted to the Civil
Governor."[83] A later commission concluded that "The affairs
and interests of the provinces are so diverse and numerous
that the governor, with his huge number of responsibilities,
cannot do all that is demanded of him no matter how much
he might want to."[84] A further consequence of the collegiate
system was the impossibility of the governor criticizing the
activities of committees and commissions of which he was
chairman. He could not be expected to turn in adverse reports on himself, and in practice governors rarely exposed
fundamental abuses in agencies subordinate to them except
after their initial inspection of the provincial offices following their appointment.[85]

Under these circumstances, only two means of restoring
the governor's role as chief inspector and controller were
possible. First, the existing collegiate system could be simplified and trimmed to a point that would free the governor
to coordinate effectively the diverse committees under him.
This course was strongly advocated in 1843 by a group of
governors who thought it possible to revitalize the collegiate system.[86] What they failed to realize, however, was
that the committees nominally under their collegiate control
were agents of central ministries, to which they owed their
first allegiance. Moreover, the governors ignored the fact
that they themselves were agents of only one ministry, In-

[83] *MSVUK*, I, otd. 2. Extracts in Anuchin, *Istoricheskii obzor* . . . ,
p. 83.
[84] TsGIA-SSSR, f. 1287 (1860), op. 21.9, pp. 7-8.
[85] V. N. Kliushin, Kherson's new governor in 1862, submitted an
analysis of his province's administration rare for its detail. It brought
immediate action from the Minister of Internal Affairs. Zelenyi,
"Khersonskoe dvorianstvo . . . ," pp. 48ff.
[86] *MSVUK*, I, otd. 4, pp. 58-60; Anuchin, pp. 56-70.

ternal Affairs, and could not coordinate the work of other ministries without a direct link with them. And in a government with no prime minister or single top administrative officer beneath the tsar there was a natural tendency toward competition among the ministries which virtually ruled out forming such a link.

A second alternative was to extend the ministerial system down to the provincial level and make the governors powerful but dependent agents of the central ministries. This view was strongly advocated in the Committee of December 6, 1826, by Count Kankrin and in 1843 by Count Perovskii, as well as by the majority of provincial governors who responded to the latter's questionnaire on the subject.[87] One senator, an outspoken advocate of the ministries, saw the governors principally as agents of the central ministries with wide powers of surveillance over, but not participation in, the local committees and police; in his report he spoke at length of the need "not theoretical but practical, for centralization in the higher government."[88]

This approach was embodied in the final law of January 2, 1845.[89] Governors were granted considerable responsibility for seeing that ministerial decisions were executed and that local affairs in general were conducted properly. The assignment of this responsibility, however, was not intended to increase the governor's autonomous authority, a fact that Count Perovskii underscored in his memorandum on the law.[90] Governors acquired no new powers of initiative nor any new means with which to fight corruption within their administrations.

An earlier law of 1837 had had essentially the same centralizing end. This law transferred all governmental supervision and surveillance from the governors-general to the

[87] *MSVUK*, I, otd. 1.3; Anuchin, pp. 57-63. *MSVUK*, I, otd. 2.2, contains several of the governors' responses.
[88] *MSVUK*, I, otd. 2.2, pp. 49-55; Anuchin, pp. 62-63.
[89] Korf, *Administrativnaia iustitsiia* . . . , I, 332-33.
[90] *MSVUK*, I, otd. 2.2.

ministries and the governors proper. The governors-general had been established in 1775 specifically to serve as an intermediate agency for inspecting the provincial administrations. Under Alexander I strong forces in St. Petersburg had promoted this office as a means of relieving the central ministries of the burden of inspection but without abandoning this crucial function to the provinces themselves.[91] By 1837 advocates of still greater ministerial control in the provinces took a new tack and demoted the governors-general everywhere but in the border regions of the empire.[92]

The law of 1837 deputized governors to conduct inspections of their provinces and required them to report every finding to Petersburg. Another law of the same year introduced new and infinitely time-consuming procedures for the Provincial Directorates, through which the governors acted.[93] To the surprise of no one, paperwork in the chancelleries immediately doubled, effectively nullifying whatever increase in the governors' prerogatives had been achieved in theory. The same tendency was further stimulated by legislation on procedures in 1845. Promulgation of this law was postponed while it was being tested in selected provinces, and when it was finally promulgated in 1852 the Crimean War already loomed and provincial governors were too busy with immediate concerns to consider its ill effects. As soon as the war was over, however, they acknowledged its harmful influence and immediately sought a new basis for the organization of control in provincial governments.

[91] A. D. Gradovskii, *Istoricheskii ocherk uchrezhdeniia general-gubernatorstv v Rossii*, St. Petersburg, 1869; reprinted in *Sobranie sochinenii*, 9 vols., St. Petersburg, 1899-1908; Gradovskii argues that in theory the law of 1837 vastly increased the power of the governors. If this had been true the movement among the governors for provincial autonomy after 1855 would be unintelligible.

[92] Korf, *Administrativnaia iustitsiia* . . . , I, 292ff. For the law itself see, *PSZ*, I, No. 10303.

[93] *PSZ*, XII, No. 10304, Korf, I, 321ff., and Anuchin, p. 54.

Legislation on inspection and supervision in the 1830s and 1840s failed. Whether conducted by governors responsible to Petersburg or representatives sent from the separate ministries or from the Senate, *nadzor* or administrative control remained abominable. Nothing attests more eloquently to the ineffectiveness of all supervision over the administration than the manner in which reports on local conditions were written and processed. Thanks to the 1837 reform, the annual reports from governors were the chief means of checking on local affairs. With few exceptions these were hopelessly superficial. Rather than describe and analyze substantive problems facing his administration the average governor simply listed the number of letters answered and processed during the year. Petty gossip was frequently recounted in lurid detail while the fact that a district had no police force at all might be mentioned only *en passant*.[94] Few governors submitted reports which were consistent in form, and the ministerial archives contain distressingly few letters indicating that the central authorities raised issues ignored by the governors.

The Senate's investigations or revisions were no better. Though occasionally it did bring to light cases of blatant corruption, the revisions were neither frequent or thorough enough to serve as a true check on local government. It was possible, for example, for a district government in Kiev province to survive twenty years without building an office building to house itself.[95] One can suppose that the Senate agent was told a story not unlike that suggested by the district police chief in Gogol's *The Inspector General*: "If they ask why the orphanage church, for which money was allo-

[94] TsGIA-SSSR, f. 1281, op. 6, No. 25. Report of governor of Vladimir province for 1860. Other governors' reports consulted are: TsGIA-SSSR, f. 1281, op. 6, No. 44; f. 1389, op. 1, d. 85; f. 1281, op. 6, No. 64; f. 1281, op. 6, No. 37; f. 1281, op. 7, d. 111; f. 1281, op. 6, d. 19; f. 1281, op. 4, d. 43. On the absence of police in a district see f. 1281, op. 6, No. 29, p. 25.

[95] TsGIA-SSSR, f. 869, op. 1, d. 393, p. 29.

cated five years ago, has not been built, don't forget to say that the work was begun but that it burnt down . . . but then someone will probably forget and stupidly let out that it was never begun."[96]

The value of both governors' reports and Senate revisions was further diminished by the extraordinary slowness with which they were read and digested by the central ministries. The fate of the annual report for 1848 on Kaluga province, written by the civil governor in January 1849, is characteristic. As soon as it was received in Petersburg—two months after being dispatched—it was forwarded via the Ministry of Internal Affairs' Department of General Affairs and the Medical Division to the Committee of Ministers. After a preliminary reading by the Committee on April 26, 1849, the report was sent around to all departments of the Ministry of Internal Affairs, each of which copied it on its own letterhead and added its own comments and suggestions in the wide margins. By October 20, 1849, the last of these comments was received and the entire package sent to the Council of the Ministry of Internal Affairs which discussed it on November 20. A month and a half later the governor of Kaluga finally received the preliminary answers to his requests and at the end of December 1849, he was at length able to continue the exchange with his superiors that he had opened ten months before.[97]

Under such conditions it was idle to believe that the interest of the central ministries could be served successfully by the civil governors. Nor did the half-hearted attempts of 1837 and 1845 to solidify the governor's role bring any improvement. Governors in the field felt as estranged as ever from the central administration and the local public still suffered from unchecked misrule.[98] On the rare occasion when a governor actually discharged incompetents

[96] N. G. Gogol, *Sobranie* . . . , IV, 26.
[97] TsGIA-SSSR, f. 1281, op. 4, p. 43, pp. 1-164.
[98] "Biurokraticheskaia voina 1839-ogo g.," *Russkaia Starina*, XXXII, 1881, 890-91.

from his staff he could justly brag to his superiors of his resourcefulness.[99] Inspection and control over the provincial administrations of Russia were all but paralyzed.

FUNDS FOR LOCAL AFFAIRS

The first function of provincial administration in Russia was to supervise the apportionment and collection of taxes from the populace and to direct them toward their designated purposes. When Peter I reformed provincial rule he was chiefly preoccupied with the problem of tax collection; when Catherine restructured the provinces again in 1775 the tax issue remained the central policy factor. Because of its tie with the military budget, taxation was of paramount importance to the government itself, but it was scarcely of less critical concern to every taxpayer in Russian provincial society. When a movement to reform provincial government developed after the Crimean War, all the many points of criticism yielded place to the question of taxes. More than anything else, the relation of province to central administration is determined by the system of taxation.[100]

The manner in which taxes were levied and collected in the Russian provinces combined strict rationality with astonishing elements of caprice. The rationality was evident in the general procedure to be followed in levying a tax.[101] The first steps were taken simultaneously in the ministries in Petersburg and in the fifty provincial capitals. While the ministries worked to set the budget for each ensuing three-year fiscal period, the governors met locally with members of the General Offices on Taxes. This agency was composed

[99] TsGIA-SSSR, f. 1281, op. 4, d. 43, p. 6.

[100] Fred W. Riggs, "Bureaucrats and Political Development: A Paradoxical View," Merton, ed., *Reader* . . . , pp. 120-67. Riggs defines the degree of local autonomy in terms of the amount of local-based taxation (pp. 132-34).

[101] Data on tax procedure is from A. A. Golovachev, "O zemskikh povinnostiakh" (MS with annotations), TsGIA-SSSR, f. 572, op. 1, d. 7, pp. 1-33; also *Materialy po zemskomu . . . ustroistvu*, I, 72ff.

of representatives of the four ministries involved with provincial life (Finances, Internal Affairs, State Domains, and Crown Lands), the marshal of the provincial gentry and the mayor of the provincial capital. Its purpose was to gather data from the districts and to draw up estimates on the tax base in their province. Also, in conjunction with representatives of the local commissions on buildings, roads, etc., they determined the provinces' financial needs. Objections to any of their estimates could be raised at hearings before the governor and the local Committee on Duties; the decisions of these bodies could be appealed either to the Ministry of Finances or the Ministry of Internal Affairs.

Once settled, the estimates were forwarded to the various ministries which added their comments and passed them to the Ministry of Finances (Department of the State Treasury) which in turn presented them for approval to the Council of Ministers. From there the material was again turned over to the Ministry of Finances and Council of Ministers (Committee on Duties) where detailed tax schedules were prepared in accordance with the government's needs and the provinces' tax base. The Department of Economy of the State Council then examined these schedules and passed them on to the State Council itself for its approval. Should any agency, including the State Council, suggest fundamental changes the tax schedule reverted to the Ministry of Finances and was then returned through the same elaborate channels back to the State Council. Finally, the schedules were sent to the tsar for his signature. The Senate then distributed them to the provincial governors who turned the assessment lists over to the district treasuries whose job it was to oversee the actual collection of the tax by the executive police.

This system of nine levels of review assured every branch of the central government a chance to alter the final tax levies. But, as one specialist pointed out to the Ministry of Finances, most agencies were too overburdened with other affairs to bother with an effective review of the levies. And

38

should any central ministry change the assessments, no provisions existed for checking the alterations with the locally based Committees on Duties or even with the governors. Usually the tax lists glided along routine channels from office to office.[102] For all practical purposes taxes were levied and schedules prepared by the Ministry of Finances alone. Hence, the astonishing degree to which the entire process was governed by capriciousness.

The only point at which this ponderous system might have made contact with provincial reality was at the first step of the process, in the Committees on Duties and the General Offices. Even here contact was rarely achieved. In the first place, the operations of these tax committees were chaotic. In Orenburg province the members were wholly unfamiliar with their duties and rarely began their deliberations in the provincial capital until a month after the reports were due.[103] In the second place, they had no data with which to work. By law, statistics were to be gathered by the General Office of the Committees on Duties, but, according to a Ministry of Finances investigator, "neither the provincial nor district authorities . . . do anything demanded in the way of such data."[104] When the gentry of Tula province finally spoke out about this condition they noted that the local data for revising the estimates were always at least three years old.[105] In the third place, should the committees err in their assessments it was impossible for local residents to learn of the fact until it was too late for them to act, due to the slowness of communication. The attempt by the Ministry of Finances to remedy this condition by having the assessments published in provincial newspapers achieved nothing, for they were printed only *after* the tsar had approved them.[106]

---

[102] Golovachev, "O zemskikh povinnostiakh," p. 23.
[103] Trutchenko, *Materialy* . . . , pp. 9-10.
[104] Gavrilov, *Materialy i svedeniia* . . . , pp. 87-88.
[105] TsGIA-SSSR, f. 572, op. 1, d. 7, p. 58.
[106] *Ministerstvo finansov* . . . , I, 278.

The lack of adequate data seriously hampered the work of tax accounting on the local level. In some provinces the archives were nonexistent, and in others they were rotting under leaky roofs.[107] The result was that the provincial bureaucracy had no memory or useful record of its own fiscal transactions. In the 1850s the Tula gentry tried to exercise their limited powers by determining the amount of revenue gathered on a local toll pike. They found that: "Significant sums are gathered from this but how great are they? We don't know. Where are they used? This is unknown. It is said that they go for maintenance of the road, but what repairs are made? We have no data, and for checking the tax accounts such data are essential."[108] Under such circumstances the attempt by the State Council in 1834 to introduce detailed rules for the keeping of tax accounts in the provinces was naive at best. Until accounts were kept it was futile to bring them under a standard system.[109]

The actual collection of taxes of all sorts fell to the executive police, that motley and ill-trained band of incompetents who were the only representatives of the autocracy with whom most rural folk had any direct contact. When agents from Petersburg inspected the agencies of Vladimir province in 1859 they found the police bureaucrats working under hideously cramped conditions in a couple of dank first-floor rooms with papers piled everywhere in complete disarray.[110] These papers presumably included data for the reports to the local representatives of the Ministry of Finances that were the sole means of checking on the thoroughness and equity of the actual collections. In this case the police had kept no records at all for over a decade, with the result that the details of many tax matters under current discussion had long since been forgotten. Leaving the police offices, the government inspector noted dryly in his

---

[107] TsGIA-SSSR, f. 1389, op. 3, d. 11, pp. 24, 38.
[108] TsGIA-SSSR, f. 572, op. 1, d. 7, pp. 52-53.
[109] Law of April 39, 1834. *Ministerstvo finansov* . . . , I, 279.
[110] TsGIA-SSSR, f. 1389, op. 3, d. 11, pp. 25ff.

report that "The police fail almost totally to fulfill their legal obligations regarding procedures for financial duties, taxes, and assessments."[111]

One of the beneficial results of the ninefold central review of provincial tax schedules should have been the equalization of state levies throughout the empire. But to the end of Nicholas' reign all forms of duties varied erratically from province to province. An irate landlord wrote to the editors of the *Odessa News* (*Odesskii Vestnik*) that he had paid a total of 127,769 rubles in taxes for a road to be built between Moscow and Kharkov, but had he lived in the next province the assessment for this national highway would have been substantially less.[112]

Tax burdens were especially inequitable in the case of "natural" duties paid with labor or provisions. A government study of the 1850s revealed that in two adjoining districts of the same province the money value of natural duties differed by a factor of six. Such differentials, apparently, were especially common in districts where the provincial capitals were situated.[113]

The government was slow to recognize the existence of these inequalities. Count Kankrin, who believed that the structure of local government needed no fundamental alterations and proposed none during his term as Minister of Finances, first began to act on this problem in 1834.[114] His plan was to create a reserve fund in his ministry that could be applied to the tax budget of any province which was unduly burdened as a consequence of natural catastrophe or other temporary conditions. This modest proposal did not meet the real issue, but the State Council rejected it and in its place founded a Committee on Equalizing Duties. The

---

[111] *Ibid.*, p. 47.

[112] "Derevenskie pisma," *Odesskii Vestnik*, No. 12 (1862).

[113] Gavrilov, *Materialy i svedeniia* . . . , p. 102: "Correct or even approximately accurate evidence on the amount and annual cost of natural duties is never gathered and, under the present state of things, cannot be." See also *Materialy po zemskomu . . . ustroistvu*, I, 37ff.

[114] *Ministerstvo finansov* . . . , I, 219.

few records of this committee that do survive in Soviet archives are insufficient to form a clear idea of its activities. But the silence of other sources of the period suggests that it dragged out its six-year existence (1852-1858) in complete lethargy.[115] Though minor adjustments in the system of natural duties were introduced by the Statute of 1851, the gross inequalities between tax levels in different provinces and districts remained into the reform era.

Unequal taxation aroused strong feelings whenever people from neighboring provinces or districts gathered. When taxpayers of one area came together, however, they were more concerned with the confusing mixture of taxes levied within their own locality. The formal tax categories included national or "state" taxes of the kind that have been discussed, "private" duties levied by the estates on their members, and "local public" assessments. The legal definitions of each of these categories were hopelessly imprecise, and in the actual levying and collecting of taxes the formal lines distinguishing one from another were all but obliterated.[116] In fact, the entire system of taxation seemed calculated to baffle and anger the public.

At the heart of the problem was the absence of any rigorously delineated provincial tax for local needs. The concept of local public affairs (*zemskie dela*) and local taxes had been a feature of Russian life since Muscovite times, but was not formulated in law until the eighteenth century. In that century alone the sphere of local taxation was redrawn four times but without once distinguishing it sharply from natural levies or substantially diminishing the role of the central treasury in local affairs. This legacy of ill-defined but highly centralized fiscal activity was passed intact to nineteenth-century Russia.[117]

New statutes in 1805 codified tax policy and tentatively

[115] TsGIA-SSSR, f. 1313.

[116] *Doklad pervogo otdeleniia komissii dlia peresmotra sistemy podatei i sborov*, TsGIA-SSSR, f. 908, op. 1, d. 161, pp. 29, 34.

[117] *Ibid.*, pp. 34-46.

set down lines for distinguishing between national and local levies. This measure lacked any theoretical rigor and was intended only as a preliminary to a more thoroughgoing law. But the more precise code failed to appear and the 1805 guides remained in effect until 1851. Only when local levies rose sharply from eight to twelve million rubles in the three years after 1845 did the State Council attempt to define the line between national and local taxes.[118] Far from clarifying the situation, however, the Council further confused it by creating yet a fourth category of tax, the so-called state-local or national-provincial levy, introduced in 1851.

By mid-century the entire provincial tax system had degenerated to the point of ineffectiveness. Boxed in by the inadequacy of its own funds and by the lack of organs for obtaining more funds through normal channels, the central government simply dipped directly into local treasuries.[119] This precipitous move threw governmental and estate-based financial institutions in the provinces into chaos. They could no longer be sure what funds were properly theirs to dispose of and what belonged to the central government. This in turn drastically affected their credit at the very time that many local public and private agencies increasingly needed money.[120]

To rectify the situation, two alternatives were open: either to establish a tax system based unequivocably on state levies, under which provincial treasuries would be wholly subordinated to the central financial agencies, or to move in the other direction and establish the province as a solid entity with defined powers of taxation. No sooner was the 1851 Statute promulgated than the Crimean War sus-

[118] B. B. Veselovskii, *Istoriia zemstva za sorok let*, 3 vols., St. Petersburg, 1911, I, 2ff.

[119] I. Kh. Ozerov, *Osnovy finansovoi nauki*, 2 vols., Moscow, 1905, II, 142.

[120] TsGIA-SSSR, f. 1282, op. 2, d. 1180, p. 52. Report of P. A. Valuev, February 1, 1863.

pended consideration of both possibilities. Once the campaign was over these issues were taken up once more by the best minds in Russian government and society.

THE PARADOX OF UNDERINSTITUTIONALIZATION

Russians of the 1840s needed no special expertise to discern that their provinces were misgoverned. The corruption; the burgeoning hierarchy; the incompetence of personnel; the inefficient procedures and absence of inspection and control; the inequities of the tax system—all were well known to those affected by them. No sooner were these individual problems perceived than thoughtful observers began to classify and arrange them. Sorting through the symptoms, they sought the generalizations which best described the patient's disease. The two characterizations that best satisfied contemporary Russians were first, that the internal administration of the empire was highly bureaucratized, and second, that this bureaucratic administration was centralized to an extraordinary degree.

These general statements, posited in the 1840s, were subsequently accepted by nearly all critics of local government, who bequeathed them to the reformers of the 1850s. Historians then borrowed this point of view and incorporated it as the basis of their own analysis of the paralyzed administration. In this form the perspective of the 1840s has come down to our own day.

But are these characterizations valid? Granted their historical importance, it must be asked whether they are compatible with what is now known about the nature of bureaucracy and centralization. The answer in both cases is that the assertions of the 1840s obscure almost as much as they explain.

It is evident that the government's intention was to develop a strong bureaucratic regime in the countryside.

44

Legislation adopted during the reign of Nicholas I was geared to the creation of a system under which, in Max Weber's words, "authority to give and execute commands [would be] ordered in a stable and consistent manner."[121] This goal was not achieved under Nicholas I. The failure of the autocracy to forge a functionally professional civil service was the chief impediment to its realization. Because of this failure fruitless debates over procedures constantly embroiled the entire structure and vitiated its effectiveness in ruling. Whether Russian society could have produced an efficient bureaucracy before the social changes brought by industrialization is highly questionable. At any rate it had not happened by 1855. As the astute Mikhail Saltykov observed as he tendered his own resignation from the provincial service, "Bureaucracy as a disciplined corporate body which serves defined political ends does not exist in Russia."[122]

Similarly, centralization was the expressed goal of much of the legislation of the period, but it was achieved in only the most formal sense. True concentration of decision-making is inconceivable without swift communications, a staggering demand in a country with no good roads and either snow or mud for nine months of the year. As long as a rush letter from Orenburg province to the capital required forty-four days in transit, substantive authority could not be focused in St. Petersburg.[123] Good communication is essential to a concentrated bureaucratic regime because it makes possible the feedback and correction performed otherwise by a local voting electorate. The slipshod system of inspec-

---

[121] H. H. Gerth, C. Wright Mills, eds. *From Max Weber: Essays in Sociology*, New York, 1948, pp. 96-98.

[122] *Sovremennaia Letopis* (supplement to *Russkii Vestnik*), No. 30 (1861), 8.

[123] TsGIA-SSSR, f. 1281, op. 2, d. 1180, p. 106. Fourteen months were required to receive a reply to a government circular from Tambov province. Bureaucratic delays in Tambov accounted for only half of this time. TsGIA-SSSR, f. 1282, op. 2, d. 1110.

45

tion and control and the poorly kept archives attest to the absence of feedback and hence of effective centralization in the Russian system.

Recognizing these shortcomings and also the weak financial condition of the central ministries, Nicholas I extended the control of St. Petersburg only to certain selected public functions in the provinces. The local estates, especially the corporate organizations of the gentry, controlled the rest. All welfare activities and some provisioning and grain storage were left to the local corporate bodies. Most provincial judicial and police functions as well were fulfilled without recourse to central institutions.[124] Judging by the harshness with which the execution by the gentry of its non-centralized functions was criticized, often by gentry themselves, it is clear that bureaucratic concentration alone cannot bear the blame for provincial misrule. Nonetheless, because the government held centralization as its stated objective, that policy was vulnerable even when difficulties stemmed from its failure rather than its implementation.

Bureaucratization and centralization reigned as formal models for provincial rule rather than as accomplished facts. The reality, obscured by contemporary characterizations, was a *pastiche* of poorly assimilated procedures that were anything but rationalized. Even the police, whose nefarious activities were the talk of Europe, maintained such a minimal presence in many provincial centers that the head of the national force questioned whether Russia in fact had a police system.[125] Its claims notwithstanding, the Russian government faced what Michel Crozier has aptly

---

[124] On the police see the excellent study by Robert J. Abbott, "Police Reform in Russia, 1858-1878," Ph.D. diss., Princeton University, 1970.

[125] S. Zhdanov, October 5, 1857, TsGIA-SSSR, f. 869, op. 1, d. 520, p. 28; also TsGIA-SSSR, f. 1389, op. 3, d. 11, pp. 27ff, 47. In fairness it must be acknowledged that the police discussed in literary *salons* were almost always those under the Third Section and not the executive police considered here.

termed "the paradox of the weakness of the ostensibly omnipotent central power."[126] Petersburg simply could not provide active leadership in the provinces on a day-to-day basis.

Had effective bureaucratization and centralization actually existed in the Russian provinces, we could expect that the administrators would have been criticized for performing tasks that local inhabitants could have done with equal or greater ease. In spite of the capricious distribution of functions among administrative and elective agencies, this was not the common complaint. Instead, inhabitants of the provinces complained that nothing was being done for them at all. Russia's provinces were, in fact, undergoverned. Vital civic functions were not being fulfilled. In all of Vladimir province there were only two communities with adequate fire companies in 1850. In spite of the fact that Vladimir's historical importance was due to its position on the Volga river system, the government had only built one wharf in the province.[127] Libraries were almost nonexistent, even for the gentry.[128] Insurance programs of all sorts were inadequate or nonexistent. Public grain stores against famine were insufficient. Veterinary services were sporadic and ineffective. Schools were abominable. More serious, the number of doctors per thousand of population in Russia was less than half of that of any country in western Europe, notwithstanding the fact that, unlike France or England, the local practice of medicine in Russia was controlled by the Ministry of Internal Affairs.[129]

If contemporaries had not been blinded by the formal claims of the autocracy, they might have perceived better the actual weakness of the governmental presence in the

[126] Crozier, *The Bureaucratic Phenomenon*, p. 225.
[127] TsGIA-SSSR, f. 1281, op. 6, No. 29, p. 27.
[128] TsGIA-SSSR, f. 1281, op. 6, No. 64, pp. 37ff. In the province of Kaluga in 1863 (pop. 964,800) there were 3,105 books.
[129] TsGIA-SSSR, f. 1284, op. 66, No. 11, pp. 190-91. Also Garmiza, *Podgotovka . . .* , pp. 30-31.

provinces. For instance, the total population of Chernigov province in 1857 was 1,374,700. For this population the total number of civil servants of all ranks from all branches of provincial and district government, including school teachers and doctors, was only 1,807. The only group excluded from this figure were the heads of the local peasant communes, but their number would not have been greater than the total of state servants. Hence, in this typical province of average size there were about 1.3+ functionaries per thousand inhabitants.[130] Other indexes yield similar results. The censor A. V. Nikitenko refers in his diary to 80,000 civil servants in 1861.[131] Taking the population as sixty million for that year[132] the ratio of 1.3 per thousand is again reached. The Berlin scholar, Torke, derived the same ratio from figures published by Köppen, and elsewhere he calculated the mid-century total as 1.1 civil servants per thousand.[133] Clearly, the ratio of 1.1 to 1.3+ civil servants per thousand is reasonably sound.

By comparison, there were 4.1 public employees per thousand of the British population in 1851,[134] and approximately 4.8 per thousand in France in 1845.[135] For more recent developing countries the Filipino figure of 4.2 civil servants per thousand population is normal, while higher ratios, such as 11 per thousand in Malaya (1962), or 12 per thousand in Japan (1930) are not unusual.[136] By any meas-

[130] *Spisok dolzhnostnykh lits Chernigovskoi gubernii na 1857 god*, Chernigov, n.d.

[131] A. V. Nikitenko, *Dnevnik A. V. Nikitenko*, 3 vols., Moscow and Leningrad, 1955, III, 243.

[132] Rashin, *Naselenie* . . . , pp. 28-29.

[133] Torke, *Das russische Beamtentum* . . . , pp. 133-36.

[134] Based on data from Moses Abramovitz, Vera F. Eliasberg, *The Growth of Public Employment in Great Britain*, Princeton, 1956, p. 16.

[135] Félix Ponteil, *Les Institutions de la France de 1814 à 1870*, Paris, 1966, p. 167. Ponteil cites the figure 250,000 for 1845, which includes 40,000 clerics and 40,000 university functionaries. The remainder, 170,000, divided by the population (1846) 35,404,500, produces the above figures.

[136] Data from O. D. Corpuz, *The Bureaucracy in the Philippines*, Manila, 1957, p. 222; Robert O. Tilman, *Bureaucratic Transition in*

ure, then, the bureaucracy in the time of Nicholas I was woefully small and inadequate, and could not provide a strong governmental presence beyond the limits of a few population centers. The fact that this administration divided its attention unequally among gentry, peasants, and townsfolk does not alter the case, for all three groups were spread geographically across the countryside.

Such figures suggest the possibility that what the government was doing badly in the provinces was not as important as what it was not doing at all. Merely to perform successfully the functions it had already claimed for itself would have required an extraordinary effort on the part of the state administration. And to expand into the many areas which called for new public or administrative initiative would have been impossible without fundamental changes.

By mid-century, every group with an interest in provincial life had grounds for dissatisfaction: taxpayers found that their payments brought no benefit either to themselves or their province; gentry watched with alarm as their corporate influence suffered a relative decline; intellectuals were disturbed by the state's lack of interest in the indigenous life of the localities; governors felt excluded from their rightful place as head of the civil life of their provinces; and ministers of the tsar were frustrated by the seeming impossibility of performing the most simple tasks in the provinces. Each of these groups had a motive for supporting reform. Each sought to acquire for itself or for those whose interest it defended the power it lacked under Nicholas I.

Diverse as their aims were, all of these groups had one objective in common: to strengthen the provincial units of Russia to the extent necessary to enable them to carry out the local and national programs that were either being ignored or nullified through mismanagement under Nicholas I. The task of the Great Reforms was not merely to substi-

---

Malaya, Durham, N.C., 1964, p. 85; the ratio for Japan was provided by Professor H. D. Smith, II, Princeton University.

tute public power for what had previously been the private authority of the gentry estate nor to reassert the claims of the gentry against the state apparatus; rather, it was to create new centers of authority in Russia's undergoverned provinces.

II | The Ideology
of Reform

*Thoughts on self-government are
in fashion here after the western
mode.*

Konstantin Lebedev[1]

However grave a situation might appear to have been in
hindsight, it does not become the object of legislation until
those who hold power have recognized and defined the
problem. Even then, what Marxists term the "objective demands" of the circumstances rarely coincide with those factors to which legislators respond. It is instead the particular
manner in which a social or political crisis is conceived by
contemporaries that is all important, for it is that conception which to a large measure determines the way in which
legislative countermeasures are molded.

In an autocracy, the autocrat and his advisers formally
claim a monopoly on the process which translates an irk-
some situation into a call for action. In the Russian autocracy in the nineteenth century this monopoly was rarely, if
ever, complete and, at every hand nongovernmental influ-
ences, particularly intellectual ones, were felt. Especially
when the problem under consideration was of a domestic
nature, the educated populace felt itself to be somehow in-

---

[1] K. N. Lebedev, "Iz zapisok senatora K. N. Lebedeva," *Russkii
Arkhiv*, XLIX, No. 1, 1911, p. 551.

volved. Through discussion and debate it could create a form of public opinion. The tsar and his officials claimed complete control over legislative initiative and barely acknowledged the links which tied them to public opinion, but such links existed nonetheless, as what Tocqueville called "a kind of intellectual atmosphere in which both governed and governors move and from which they draw the principles of their conduct, often without realizing it."[2]

The crisis in Russia's provinces did not spring into being in the 1850s, yet it was only in that decade that public discussion wove the many strands of the problem into a single cord strong enough to raise the banner of reform. To be sure, the provincial chaos had been discussed sporadically since the eighteenth century, but few of these analyses had challenged the basic structure of local institutions. The quiescence of governmental and public opinion on the matter of institutional change during the reign of Nicholas I (1825-1855) was especially surprising, considering the seriousness of the problem. But the pre-Crimean generation had created an ornate ideology which proudly rejected institutional arrangements, no matter how clever, as possible sources of national welfare.[3] Such matters as the state administration and provincial agencies were too important to be wholly ignored, but their significance was ascribed not to any functional roles they filled but to their ability to embody the higher realities of "Autocracy, Orthodoxy, and Nationality." Not even these were understood in their everyday sense of a system of government, specific theological doctrines, or a body of shared cultural traits. Instead,

---

[2] Alexis de Tocqueville, *Oeuvres complétes*, 9 vols., Paris, 1864-66, IX, 123.

[3] See Nicholas V. Riasanovsky, *Nicholas I and Official Nationality in Russia, 1825-1855*, Berkeley and Los Angeles, 1959, Chaps. 3, 4. Also, Nikolai Barsukov, *Zhizn i trudy M. P. Pogodina*, 22 vols., St. Petersburg, 1888-1906, for the best published collection of materials on the official ideology and its relation to other contemporary intellectual movements, see especially Vol. XVII and Vol. XVIII.

they were raised to the exalted level of psychological truths ingrained in the minds of Russians.

If Russia's concrete institutional arrangements were considered of secondary importance, those of other countries were simply unworthy of serious attention. Encouraged by the fears of certain French and German sages that the West was dying, official Russia under Nicholas I looked contemptuously at the institutions which embodied the principles of western European nations. Had Peter I not brought to Russia all that she had previously lacked and thereby completed the process of borrowing? As a St. Petersburg daily disarmingly put it, "In Russia there exists everything necessary for national welfare."[4]

Even the opponents of this official dogma did not reject it entirely. Slavophiles, admirers of French utopians, and scholars of the Roman legal tradition all agreed that the abstract values underlying civil life were more important than any practical administrative or political arrangements derived from them. To the Slavophiles these values were religious and communal, and were best embodied in the life of ancient Moscovy;[5] for the utopian "westernizers" the relevant values were either "scientific" after the fashion of Saint-Simon or Comte or "communitarian" in the spirit of Fourier; and to the older juridical experts the legal mentality of western Europe was far more crucial to its development than were its councils and parliaments. All of these groups and the proponents of "Official Nationality" as well would have firmly opposed any suggestion that the existing institutions of the West could serve as textbooks for Russia. To be sure, each group had its favorite institutional scheme, but these were seen only in terms of the ethical first princi-

[4] *Severnaia Pochta*, No. 159 (1852).

[5] For the Slavophiles, see A. Gratieux, *A. S. Khomiakov, 1804-1860*, 2 vols., Paris, 1939, ii, 184-94; Andrzej Walicki, *W Kregu Konserwatywnej Utopii*, Warsaw, 1964, pp. 207-31; and Nicholas V. Riasanovsky, *Russia and the West in the Teaching of the Slavophiles*, Cambridge, Mass., 1952.

ples on which they were founded: loyalty to the autocracy, the faith of the community of Orthodox believers, the West's mixture of cooperation and positive knowledge, or its legalistic mentality. Nikolai Pogodin, chief apologist for "Official Nationality" in the academic world, wrote that "There is no institution or law which cannot be abused and this is actually happening everywhere. Consequently, institutions and laws are of less importance than the people on whom their function depends."[6] Slightly modified, this comment could have come from any of Pogodin's adversaries in the 1840s or from the government itself.

The unintended consequence of this widespread cast of mind was that it placed all mundane matters of public administration beyond the pale of serious analysis. Those few public or private figures who concerned themselves with administrative reform, such as the Minister of State Domains, Count Kiselev, or a handful of the younger men who frequented the Petersburg salon of Mikhail Petrashevskii, were not sufficiently conversant with the alternative models presented by western Europe to shape a reform ideology of their own.[7] The strong feelings of discontent with the administrative hierarchy revealed in the literature of the 1840s took literary form precisely because they were otherwise unchanneled.

The entire problem of provincial government was put in a stark new light by the utter collapse of Russian arms in the Crimea between 1853 and 1855. So devastating was the final defeat that, before the capitulation could be signed in Paris, the higher Russian bureaucracy had to be combed to find a man whose reputation in conservative circles was suf-

[6] Barsukov, *Zhizn . . . Pogodina*, v, 22.

[7] On Kiselev's support for foreign research on Russia, see P. O. Morozov, ed., *Istoricheskie materialy iz arkhivov ministerstva gosudarstvennykh imushchestv*, St. Petersburg, 1891, pp. 190ff.; on the administrative concerns of the Petrashevskii circle, see Frances M. Bartholomew, "The Petrashevskii Circle," Ph.D. diss., Princeton University, 1969.

ficiently secure to survive the humiliation of signing it.[8] The absence of heroic murals in public buildings erected after the war indicates the degree to which the government's self-respect had suffered. Few monuments were raised even to the defense of Sevastopol; the popularity of young Count Tolstoi's account of that siege was due in large measure to the fact that he had made the best of a national disaster.

The war affected the Russian people as profoundly as it did the government. To the crowds of peasants that flocked to Moscow after the fall of Sevastopol and gathered on street corners moaning and crossing themselves, it seemed as if Russia were under divine judgment.[9] Educated people were no less disturbed. "Russia is on the verge of collapse," wrote an alarmed Moscow scholar,[10] and a young journalist surveying the public's mood found that "Everyone agrees that an internal crisis is inevitable but how and when it will come nobody can decide. At the present time there is not a satisfied man in Russia."[11]

The cause of this anguish was the fact that the war sensitized Russians to their own national weaknesses. As the frightened scholar put it, "All the faults of the social organism that had been hidden in peacetime had come to the surface."[12] Serfdom, the basis of local economic life, was exposed to attacks of unprecedented virulence, even though censorship confined all discussion of the subject to the semilegal realm of manuscript literature. Without the press telling them, scores of people knew that impassable roads and the lack of railroad lines leading south from supply depots

[8] E. V. Tarle, *Krymskaia Voina*, 2 vols., Moscow and Leningrad, 1950, п, 558.

[9] O. M. Bodianskii, "Vyderzhki iz dnevnika," *Sbornik obshchestva liubitelei russkoi slovesnosti*, Moscow, 1891, p. 130.

[10] B. N. Chicherin, *Zapiski proshlogo (vospominaniia i pisma)*, S. V. Bakrushin, M. A. Tsiavlovskii, eds., Moscow, 1929, p. 249.

[11] I. S. Aksakov, *Dnevnik*, St. Petersburg, 1910, p. 8.

[12] Chicherin, *Zapiski proshlogo*, pp. 249ff.

had thwarted the war effort. In the war zone itself, rampant inflation had wiped out the fruits of earlier economic reforms.[13] At war's end the government was faced with a staggering deficit of half a billion rubles, while a glut of hastily printed paper currency complicated the settlement of private debts and mortgages. The judiciary, meanwhile, proved itself to be woefully inadequate to the task of regularizing such matters.[14]

For a brief period, reform-minded intellectuals in the two capitals relished the prospect of a government crisis and eagerly awaited it. "We were convinced," a contemporary later confessed, "that only calamity and a disastrous war could bring about a salutary overturn and stop further putrefaction."[15] In view of the effect of military and diplomatic triumphs on Russia's internal policy earlier in the nineteenth century, such a pessimistic view may not have been entirely groundless. Had not Alexander I's victories on the battlefield and in Vienna led to a decade of the most retrograde policies at home? And did not Nicholas' "defeat" of the revolutions of 1848 at home and in Budapest only harden his determination to preserve Russia from all change? Whatever its basis, though, this apocalyptic mood was confined to a very limited group of young intellectuals and quickly evaporated when the humiliation of defeat became a reality.[16]

The military disaster, followed by the coronation of the thirty-seven-year-old Alexander II in the summer of 1856,

[13] Walter M. Pintner, "Inflation During the Crimean War," *The American Slavic and East European Review*, xviii (February 1959), 85ff.

[14] For the role of the judiciary in mortgage settlements, see the study on judicial reform by Richard Wortman, University of Chicago, now in preparation.

[15] Professor S. M. Soloviev, cited in *Russkaia istoricheskaia literatura v klassovom osveshchenii*, M. I. Pokrovskii, ed., 2 vols., Moscow, 1927, I, 267.

[16] This was acknowledged by the historian K. N. Bestuzhev-Riumin, *Vospominaniia K. N. Bestuzhev-Riumina (do 1860g.)*, St. Petersburg, 1900, p. 42.

served to cool the more rancorous antigovernmental feelings. In a conciliatory mood, the jurist Konstantin Kavelin urged the author of a bitter tract to assume "a softer and more respectful tone in regard to the government."[17] "The time for radicalism has passed in Russia," declared an anonymous essayist of 1856, "just as it has passed in western Europe."[18] The extravagant and illegal criticism of the war years dropped off sharply, but at the same time public self-examination by Russians rose to new heights. Iurii Samarin was one of scores of skilled polemicists who called on his fellow Russians to "turn to ourselves, study the fundamental causes of the weakness and devise a cure."[19] Never before had such a grandiose perspective been opened to pamphleteers, essayists, and drawing-room oracles.

The energetic exchange of views that ensued generated the closest thing to a modern public opinion that Russia had ever seen. Public journals appeared by the dozens to express every shade of opinion tolerable to the somewhat more lenient censors. During the entire preceding reign the average number of newspapers and journals founded per annum was a paltry 8.3, whereas in the period 1856 to 1863 an average of 33.4 new periodicals came from the presses annually.[20] Even the government participated in this movement, and by the end of the 1850s the house organs of the various ministries were well on the way to becoming public forums from which the ministers could make known their views on the problems of the day. Should the new tsar and

[17] Chicherin, *Zapiski proshlogo*, p. 159.

[18] Chicherin, *Zapiski proshlogo*, p. 162. N. P. Ogarev wrote the following statement on the purpose of the émigré *Polar Star (Poliarnaia Zvezda)* and *Bell* in 1857: "No, we are not called upon to be a wrathful opposition to the new government, but to provide a firm and clear critique of its deeds, a critique from which the government itself can nobly and openly see its errors." *Izbrannye sotsialno-politicheskie proizvedeniia*, 2 vols., Leningrad, 1957, I, 117.

[19] Iurii F. Samarin, *Sochineniia Iu. F. Samarina*, 10 vols., Moscow, 1877-1911, II, 18.

[20] N. V. Lisovskii, *Bibliografiia russkoi periodicheskoi pechati, 1703-1900 gg.*, Petrograd, 1915, pp. 67-183.

his advisers be more accessible to the pressure of public opinion than the military regime of Nicholas had been, broad sections of educated society wanted to be in a position to edify them.[21]

The ideas that impelled these public-spirited thinkers were simple in form and sweeping in implications. Clearly, the official ideology had erred in picturing the western powers as in a state of imminent collapse. Equally clear was the fact that Russia's vaunted uniqueness had failed to save her from ruin. For the first time since the Napoleonic invasion of 1812, Russians were forced to view their nation as relatively backward and relatively weak vis-à-vis the West. Worse still, the circumstances that had impelled Russians to this realization destroyed their earlier confidence that their nation possessed in her own institutional traditions all that was needed for national welfare. Like their counterparts in developing nations today, Russians tended naturally to look abroad for ideas and suggestions and to reject their own discredited principles.[22] "There is no thought from yesterday," wrote the Petersburg censor A. V. Nikitenko, "that would not seem old today."[23]

WESTERN MODELS FOR LOCAL ADMINISTRATION

Simply to admit the possibility that institutions in general and those of the victorious allies in particular were able to impart health and power to a social organism was not enough. It only raised the central issue. Since Russia had been beaten by a coalition, which of the nations that com-

---

[21] V. N. Rosental, "Narastanie krizisa verkhov v seredine 50kh godov XIX-ogo veka," *Revoliutsionnaiia situatsiia v Rossii, 1859-1861 gg.*, M. V. Nechkina, ed., 4 vols., Moscow, 1960-65, I, 46.

[22] See Fred Riggs, *Administration in Developing Countries: The Theory of Prismatic Society*, Boston, 1964, p. 338.

[23] A. V. Nikitenko, *Dnevnik A. V. Nikitenko*, 3 vols., Moscow and Leningrad, 1955, I, 46.

prised it most warranted study? England, France, and Austria presented such contrasting political, social, and administrative structures that, until they were accurately classified, no lessons could be drawn from them. For guidance the public looked to the burgeoning number of magazine articles and journal essays on western nations. In 1855 the total number of articles on European countries appearing in Russian publications was only 97, but in 1856 the number jumped to 269 and then to 300 in the following year.[24] At first the majority of articles was devoted to France, whose tricolor had flown over the captured fortress of Sevastopol. In 1856 analyses of France exceeded the combined total for Germany and Austria and was almost double the number of titles on England. The gap between France and England quickly closed by 1860 to 1861, years of the most intense political activity, and England replaced France as the first object of study. Prussia and the United States, which had not figured in the anti-Russian coalition, played but a modest role in the journalistic campaigns of the years 1855 to 1859. Gradually they came to prominence as the movement toward unity in Germany and toward disunity in North America gathered momentum and finally exploded in war.

As the pace of Russian writing on the West intensified in 1856 and 1857 a more or less consistent alignment of Russia's internal issues with foreign countries began to emerge. Emancipation immediately called to mind the very recent experience of Austria, which had freed its serfs in 1849, and the more distant experience of Prussia. Of the two countries, the example of Prussia was far the more interesting to Russian publicists, partly because Prussia had not waged war against Russia, partly because its emancipation had been carried out with a minimal loss to the landholding

[24] These approximations are made from P. P. and B. P. Lambin, *Russkii bibliograficheskii ukazatel za 1855, g.*, St. Petersburg, 1855, and *Ruskaia istoricheskaia bibliografiia*, St. Petersburg, 1856-62.

Junkers, and also because "Beaten and humiliated [by France], she [Prussia] set about internal reform at the very time that French garrisons occupied her fortresses."[25]

The vital question of credit and banking brought forth considerable interest in the new credit societies in Germany and France.[26] Advocates of change in the Russian universities generally turned to Germany, where the innovative Nikolai Pirogov seized on the reform slogan "Freedom of Research, Teaching, and Study."[27] Other pedagogical reformers campaigned for the concept of a university completely open to the public, modeled after the Collège de France.[28] As specialists debated legal reform, they constantly turned to the example of Roman law justice in France and to the British system; and, during the hard-fought struggle over the censorship laws, journals frequently carried laudatory essays on the press laws of France, Belgium, and England. Finally, the looming problem of the role of industry in modern society often drew attention to the United States.[29]

After 1856, every western nation seemed to have something to offer as replacement for Russia's outworn ideas and institutions, but, above all, the challenge of France and England had to be faced. Their stature was more than that

[25] Samarin, *Sochineniia* . . . , II, 19ff.; see also, Baron August von Haxthausen's comparative essays "Ob otmenenii i vykupe pomeshchichikh gospodskikh prav v Prussii," *Russkii Vestnik*, XII (1857), 426-43, and "Ob otmenenii i vykupe pomeshchichikh gospodskikh prav v Avstrii," *Russkii Vestnik*, XII (1857), 571-82. The Grand Duchess Elena Pavlovna brought the Prussian example to bear at several points in the emancipation debate, even supporting a project to introduce Baron Stein's reforms into Russia. The German text is preserved at TsGAOR, f. 647, op. 1, ed. khr. 39; also *Materialy dlia biografii kn. V. A. Cherkasskogo*, O. Trubetskaia, ed., 2 vols., Moscow, 1901-04, II, 66.

[26] *Trudy komissii vysochaishei uchrezhdennoi dlia ustroistva zemskikh bankov*, 4 vols., St. Petersburg, 1861, I, i-xxxv.

[27] N. I. Pirogov, *Universitetskii vopros*, St. Petersburg, 1863, p. 12.

[28] G. Dzhanshiev, *Epokha velikikh reform*, 7th edn., Moscow, 1898, p. 282.

[29] A. Zimmerman, "Puteshestvie po Amerike," *Russkii Vestnik*, XXVIII (1859).

of victors. Arsenii, Bishop of Kiev, lauded them as "the ideals of contemporary civilization."[30] An anonymous journalist writing in 1863 argued that the problems vexing Russia had been solved long ago in France and England and that, by following their example, "people could not demand anything better in the way of new institutions."[31]

Educated Russia was swept by a flood tide of interest in England and France unparalleled since the early years of Alexander I's reign. The opening of borders to foreign travel encouraged this development. Grand Duke Konstantin visited Napoleon III in 1859 and, in spite of the Emperor's previous attitude toward Russia, concluded that he was "a fine fellow"; on the same trip Konstantin visited England, all the while reading Macaulay's *History of England* in spare moments.[32] Nikolai Ogarev arrived in London in 1857 to help found the influential journal *The Bell* (*Kolokol*); in the second issue the emigré editor admitted Russia had much to learn from France and England but warned that Germany had only "metaphysics and bureaucracy" to offer.[33] Other Russians flocked to Paris. Nikolai Chernyshevskii complained bitterly that many contributors to his journal, *The Contemporary* (*Sovremennik*), were moving abroad and that, as a result, public opinion was becoming "Europeanized."[34] The same thing was occurring in Petersburg itself where two-thirds of the reference material gathered for the commissions preparing the emancipation proclamation was from abroad.[35] The public's thirst for ad-

[30] Barsukov, *Zhizn . . . Pogodina*, xix, 58.

[31] *Severnaia Pchela*, No. 205 (1863), 905.

[32] TsGAOR, f. 722 (Marble Palace archive), op. 1, ed. khr. 91, 11.62, pp. 73-74. (Diary of Grand Duke Konstantin Nikolaevich)

[33] *Kolokol* (February 1, 1858), 64. Article unsigned but written by Ogarev as shown in (February 15, 1858), 68.

[34] N. G. Chernyshevskii, *Polnoe sobranie sochinenii*, 16 vols., Moscow, 1939-53, xiv, 343. Nekrasov, Turgenev, Fet, Herzen, Ogarev, Botkin, Druzhinin, Kraevskii, and Dolgorukov were among those either abroad or just leaving.

[35] Ia. A. Soloviev, "Zapiski senatora Iakova Aleksandrovicha Solovieva; krestianskoe delo v tsarstvovanii Aleksandra II," *Russkaia Starina*, xxvii-xlvii, 1880-85, February 1880, p. 353.

vice from their victors was no less keen, and a completely fraudulent memorandum on reform purported to be from the pen of Guizot was earnestly read and passed from hand to hand.[36]

In many respects, England and France in the 1850s were not unlike one another. In population they ranked as the second and third largest states in western Europe after Austria. Both had embarked early on the path of industrialization and, by the mid-nineteenth century, were the first and second greatest industrial powers in Europe. Both were moving rapidly in the direction of free trade and, in 1860, were able to join hands in the so-called Cobden-Chevalier Treaty which marked the debut of that issue in international politics. The two countries cooperated after 1858 to wage war against China. Both had adorned their capitals with world expositions in the early 1850s to symbolize their preeminence in the modern world. Both were the most rapidly urbanizing and already the most highly urbanized societies in the world. Most of all, they alone of the major European powers were not in the late 1850s undergoing fundamental upheavals over the unification of the country. Important as were the other points of comparison, it was the ability of France and England to serve as patterns for the internal organization of a modern state that most excited Russians.

Precisely on this issue everything which England and France shared diminished to insignificance. In the eyes of Russian observers, the two powers epitomizing modernity stood absolutely opposed to one another, embodying contrary institutions and principles. At the core of this juxtaposition were their opposite approaches to the problem of provincial government. One of the earliest specialists on this subject and a participant in the ideological movement

[36] N. G. Sladkevich, *Ocherki istorii obshchestvennoi mysli v Rossii v konste 50-kh—godov nachale 60-kh godov XIX-ogo veka*, Leningrad, 1962, pp. 93-95.

of the fifties, Alexander Vasilchikov, only expressed the conviction of most educated Russians when he declared that:

> Just as in arithmetic one operation can be checked by another, adding by subtracting, and division by multiplication, so in considering what is the best system of internal government, the French system can serve as a check for the English. Throughout the entire organism of internal social life and for each separate administrative department there have been introduced in England principles which are the complete opposite of those which prevail in France.[37]

So obvious was this to Vasilchikov and his peers that they required no substantiation of the basic proposition beyond a straightforward enumeration of the differences. This accomplished, Russians moved on to what were for them more important questions: what fundamental principles did each system embody, and which of these principles would become the model for the internal organization of modern states, including Russia?

The very immediacy of these questions prescribed the form of the acceptable response. Having been disenchanted with their long-held faith in the model for administrative organization championed by Nicholas I, Russians found themselves at sea. The stark questions they posed demanded answers of the utmost directness. Learned caution and scholarly equivocation were of little value to them. The ideological, rather than abstractly philosophical, nature of their quest required that the terminology used to characterize the local administration of England and France be highly evocative even at the expense of precision.

On one point there was general agreement: that the conduct of public affairs was thoroughly bureaucratized in the French *départements* but not in English counties. Whatever

[37] A. I. Vasilchikov, *O samoupravlenii*, 3rd edn., 2 vols., St. Petersburg, 1869-70, I, ix.

63

the justice of this assertion, Russian writers of all opinions accepted it so wholeheartedly as to suggest that bureaucracy was for them more a system of government than a simple tool of state administration. Some denounced bureaucracy as evil, the vehicle for a morality in which "men are unable to distinguish formal from moral responsibility."[38] Others viewed it with more mixed feelings, but no one denied the accuracy of the characterization. Consequently, everyone was prepared to accept the English term "self-government" as the polar opposite of bureaucratic rule. This thoroughly evocative expression had been bandied about for a generation by continental political thinkers, who assigned it a new definition whenever circumstances required.[39] Now it made a belated appearance in Russian thought and language. Since no Russian term existed for the notion of public involvement in the execution of local affairs, the English expression "self-government" was translated literally into *samo-upravlenie*. This newly coined word made its first appearance in the literature of publicists but not yet in dictionaries—in 1856.[40]

A second generalization on administrative practice that was almost universally subscribed to in Russia was that the French bureaucracy was highly centralized while that of England was not. Again, the empirical accuracy of the statement or its intrinsic merit for analysis was of less moment to Russian thought than its ability to encapsulate a welter of commonly held beliefs within the one term "centralization." The precise meaning of the expression re-

[38] *Sovremennaia Letopis* (supplement to *Russkii Vestnik*), No. 30 (1861), 7-8.

[39] For an account of the genealogy of this principle in Germany, see Heinrich Heffter's masterful *Die Deutsche Selbstverwaltung im 19. Jahrhundert*, Stuttgart, 1950, especially pp. 258, 359ff.

[40] In V. I. Dal's *Tolkovyi slovar zhivogo Velikorusskogo iazyka*, 1st edn., Moscow, 1856, v, 123, *samoupravstvo* (capriciousness) is the only form given. The Tver abolitionist, Aleksei Unkovskii, writing in 1857, still used the adjective *samoupravnyi* only in this old sense. He did not refer to *samoupravlenie* until 1859. TsGIA-SSSR, f. 1291, op. 33, d. 2, pp. 359-61.

mained inchoate, but it was generally assumed that "centralization" related somehow to the phenomenon of "bureaucracy"; many publicists, in fact, used these terms interchangeably. Accordingly, if bureaucracy found its opposite in self-government, the analogous alternative to centralization was decentralization. Once more a precise Russian equivalent was lacking, so the French term *décentralisation* was adopted and became *detsentralizatsiia*.[41]

Bureaucracy and self-government, centralization and decentralization—these unfamiliar western European expressions quickly established themselves in the political language of Russia and became common usage in reformist discussion after the Crimean War. Granted that their precise application to the French and English systems of government, let alone the Russian, was at first poorly understood, the mere fact that such narrowly administrative terms were widely accepted indicates the fundamental reorientation in Russian political thought that occurred when the old verities were cast in doubt. Only a few years after the Crimean War a powerful Russian statesman could decry the old bureaucratic centralization and declare that Russia's future, like that of the leading nations of western Europe, lay with the "new principles of decentralization and self-government."[42]

Yet the widespread adoption of a new administrative jargon, no matter how important a step, signified little until the alien vocabulary was domesticated and refined. This process took place in Russia during the first four years after the Paris settlement. During the period when actual legislative work was only beginning, scholars and publicists

[41] Count Kankrin's comments on Speranskii's reform project of 1829 indicate the state of terminology at that time. He used the word "centralisation" in its original French form, but instead of describing the Speranskii plan for the provinces as "decentralized" he used the Russian adjective for "insular" and the Latin "divergenum." Apparently he was unacquainted with the more fitting term, "decentralization." *MSVUK*, Chap. I, otd. 1.3. pp. 58-60.
[42] TsGIA-SSSR, f. 1291, op. 5, III, d. 65, p. 39. (Baron Korf)

65

undertook a kind of ideological crash program to clarify in their own minds the meaning of "decentralization" and "self-government" for contemporary state development. To this end they followed the same path to England and France that they had taken to find the new principles in the first place.

At this point the position of the would-be reformers in Russia must be put in perspective. Those who had so readily taken up the notions of decentralization and self-government included many, but by no means all, representatives of official and unofficial educated society. Of necessity they were acutely aware of their opponents, those who adhered to the old Nicholaevan ideal of governance. Even if those apologists for the old regime constituted a minority, they enjoyed the immeasurable advantage of having their ideas already enshrined in institutional form. This fact imparted a sense of pioneering urgency to the innovators' campaign. Even when they agreed among themselves, the reformers had to choose their arguments carefully for maximum polemic impact. They would gladly forego primary research on France and England if authoritative and sharply worded commentaries by western experts would be more effective against the opposition. As it happened, such commentaries were in ample supply.

Turning to the writings of western publicists, Russians discovered that their own search for viable local institutions coincided with a remarkable flowering of interest in precisely the same problem in France and elsewhere. This concern flowed initially from opposition to the French Revolution and the Napoleonic restructuring of the traditional provinces into administrative departments. Over the next half century both liberal and royalist opponents of the Napoleonic idea had worked to develop and spread an anticentralist model for state and administrative development.[43] This perspective constituted a *leitmotiv* of French

[43] See F. Béchard, *Essai sur la centralisation administrative*, 2 vols.,

political thought and even spilled over to Germany, where it emerged in titles such as Robert von Mohl's *Über Bürokratie* (1846) and in numerous articles in the reform press.[44] Similar currents attracted the attention of writers in England, where they reached fruition somewhat later than on the continent. The introduction to Toulman Smith's widely read study of local government differs little from scores of works published in western Europe in the 1840s: "There are two elements to which every form of government can be reduced. These are local *self-government* on the one hand, and *centralization* on the other. According as the former or the latter of these exists more or less predominant, will the state of any nation be more or less free, happy, progressive, truly prosperous and safe."[45]

This widespread attitude toward public administration reached its zenith on the continent amidst the revolutionary tumult of 1848. For a heady moment opposition to centralized and bureaucratic organization became official ideology and the blueprint for future development. But before the French liberal ideologists succeeded in translating their doctrines into practice they were swept aside, first by social radicals from the left and then by the Bonapartist restoration from the right which hailed a return to the most criticized practices of Napoleonic administration. Acting in the name of the electorate of all eighty-four French departments, Louis Napoleon restricted local autonomy in 1852. First he rescinded the right, instituted in 1848, of provincial councils to hold public sittings and then he replaced the

Paris, 1836-1837. P. Hauser, *De la décentralisation*, Paris, 1832, etc. This literature is briefly reviewed in Félix Ponteil, *Les Institutions de la France de 1814 à 1870*, Paris, 1966, pp. 29-37, 163-67.

[44] Heffter, *Die Deutsche Selbstverwaltung . . .* , Chaps. 4-5.

[45] J. Toulman Smith, *Local Self-Government and Centralization: The Characteristics of Each; and Its Practical Tendencies as Affecting Social, Moral and Political Welfare and Progress*, London, 1851. For a Russian view on Smith, see A. D. Gradovskii, *Sobranie sochinenii*, II, 26. For Toulman Smith's impact in Germany, see Heffter, *Die Deutsche Selbstverwaltung . . .* , pp. 383-85.

locally elected heads of these councils with crown appointees. Although he went on to turn over various ministerial functions to the departmental *préfets*, Napoleon had already touched off his enemies' fire. And however weak their capabilities at practical politics, the ex-leaders of the provisional government of 1848 were adept polemicists.[46]

Typical of Napoleon's opponents was Camille Hyacinthe Odilon-Barrot, whose cabinet held power briefly during December 1848. The 1852 law, Odilon-Barrot fumed, instituted a stifling centralization, "l'apoplexie au centre et la paralysie dans les extrémités."[47] Though a member of the dynastic opposition, the former prime minister had long mingled in constitutionalist circles, and in fact, had been among the first leaders of the banquet campaign preceding the outbreak of revolution. After several years spent in criticizing the Napoleonic principles of state and Paris-centered administration from the lecture platform, Odilon-Barrot finally collected his thoughts into a fiery book, *De la centralisation et de ses effets*, in which he fulminated against the blatant disequilibrium of power between Paris and the provinces and called for decentralization and self-government.

Elias Regnault, *chef du cabinet* of the Ministry of the Interior under Odilon-Barrot and editor of the *Bulletin de la République*, was equally incensed at Napoleon's "strange abuse of the word decentralization." In historical works on the revolution of 1848 and in a tireless public campaign in the 1850s, Regnault condemned the 1852 law and pleaded for the province "to reclaim its place in the life of society

[46] Ponteil, *Les Institutions* . . . , pp. 371ff. The most thorough analysis of French local administration from the perspective of centralization is by the Georgian, Z. Avalov, *Detsentralizatsiia i samoupravlenie vo Frantsii*, St. Petersburg, 1905, pp. 201-53.

[47] Camille Odilon-Barrot, *De la centralisation et de ses effets*, Paris, 1861, pp. 154ff. The statement cited here was quoted by Barrot from a speech of Lamennais' in 1848. For Russian praise of Barrot (Katkov), see *Sovemennaia Letopis* (supplement to *Russkii Vestnik*), No. 14 (1861), 19-20; for a Russian critique of Barrot, see Gradovskii, II, 41-43 ("Gosudarstvo i provintsiia").

and in the political and intellectual domains, and its position as the source of the light vivifying France."[48]

When Russians began their search for western insights on decentralization and self-government, writers like Odilon-Barrot and Regnault immediately struck their attention. Their vigorous, argumentative style, their broadside attacks on Louis Napoleon, and their polished and practical defense of decentralization endeared them at once to educated readers in Petersburg and Moscow. Odilon-Barrot's book was frequently cited and Regnault became better known in Russia than in France. Probably their least restrained disciple was the flamboyant émigré Prince Peter Dolgorukov, who met them both in Paris, apparently at the French Society of Political Economy to which all three belonged.[49] Dolgorukov occupied a peculiar position in Russian society, for he was descended from the medieval founder of Moscow and was also an outspoken critic of the prereform government. His distinguished name caused his schemes and projects to reach more ears than those of less well-connected people. In the immediate postwar years he was mentioned as a candidate for Minister of Internal Affairs and, although the nomination was not actually considered by the tsar, Dolgorukov was deeply disappointed when he was not offered the post. A master at the use of acid *ad hominem* attacks in the press, Dolgorukov had found himself in periodic trouble with the government and private citizens since his youth. With no official position, scores of enemies, and an adverse domestic situation, he finally departed his Tula estate and secretly fled his homeland.[50]

[48] Elias Regnault, *La Province, ce qu'elle est, ce qu'elle doit être,* Paris, 1861, p. 38. For a scathing Russian critique of Regnault, see Gradovskii, *Sobranie sochinenii,* II, 43-53.

[49] *Pravdivyi-La Véridique,* No. 1, Leipzig (May 17, 1862), 4.

[50] For this and other details relating to Dolgorukov's life, see M. Lemke, "Kniaz Petr Vladimirovich Dolgorukov v Rossii/emigrant," *Byloe,* February 1907, pp. 188-235; March 1907, pp. 153-91. Judging from Dolgorukov's letter to Pogodin of March 13, 1858, while

Even before his emigration Dolgorukov had expressed his views on provincial government in private memoranda. He had attacked the officials sent from Petersburg, "who are for the most part untalented and no more acquainted with the internal life of Russia than with the Isle of Ceylon," and had demanded broader participation in provincial government by local residents of all classes.[51] In Paris, Dolgorukov contacted Regnault and Odilon-Barrot and further developed his views. He found several Russian and French language papers to promote his campaign and in them frequently alluded to the work of his new French friends. Finally he wrote a book, *On Changing the Form of Rule in Russia*, in which he advocated the plan proposed by Regnault for the creation of new, nearly autonomous provinces or territories.[52]

Dolgorukov's greedy borrowing from Regnault's plans for local government is instructive, for its demonstrates the process by which an ideology was transplanted from the France of 1848 to the Russia of Alexander II. Other Russians followed suit, apparently oblivious to the fact that the brand of reformism which so attracted them had just been rejected by France herself. Ironically, the pursuit of fresh inspiration in the West ended with Russians importing a batch of ideological castoffs! In their new environment, however, the western notions of decentralization and self-government lost their musty aura of the 1830s and 1840s

---

Dolgorukov was abroad on an earlier trip, he did not anticipate his permanent departure from Russia. GBL, f. 231 (M. P. Pogodin archive), II, carton 11, ed. khr. 17, p. 12.

[51] "O vnutrennom sostoianii Rossii" (November 1857), Sec. 4, O tsentralizatsii, TsGAOR, f. 647 (Grand Duchess Elena Pavlona archive), op. 1, ed. khr. 50, pp. 23-25. Another copy is in TsGAOR, f. 722 (Marble Palace archive). Other copies of this memorandum were presented to Bludov and to the Minister of Foreign Affairs, Gorchakov, with whom Dolgorukov met while in Petersburg in November 1857. GBL, f. 231 (Pogodin archive), II, carton 2, ed. khr. 17, pp. 10-11.

[52] P. V. Dolgorukov, *O peremene obraza pravleniia v Rossii*, Leipzig, 1862, pp. 31-36, 72-73. The slightly modified French edition of the same work is *Des Réformes en Russie*, Paris, 1862.

and could be paraded as the latest Paris fashions. In this way the administrative thought of the moderates of 1848 was revitalized and given a second chance in the vast tsarist empire. To a great extent, the history of the reform of local government in Russia after 1855 is bound up with the process of discussing, applying, and ultimately rejecting this older heritage of reformism.

THE RUSSIANS' TOCQUEVILLE

In the first half of the nineteenth century whenever European thinkers concerned themselves with the role of state administration in social life, they turned to a common source of inspiration, the brilliant French Anglophile, Alexis de Tocqueville. Amidst the wave of theorizing which swept the continent as the French Revolution subsided, Tocqueville's clear analysis of political systems provided a fixed landmark on which men could take their bearings.[53] His meticulous studies of the United States and England and lesser known monographs on Ireland and Algeria were invaluable even to those who disagreed with his conclusions, for in them he analyzed the effects of "centralization" and "self-government" in a variety of polities and presented the first theory on the social basis for each form of administration. Through his writings and, more concretely, by his participation in the Odilon-Barrot government of 1848 as Foreign Minister, he was inseparably linked with the other

[53] J. S. Mill wrote in his autobiography that it was Tocqueville who "led him to attach the utmost importance to the performance of as much of the collective business of society as can safely be so performed by the people themselves." J. S. Mill, *An Autobiography of John Stuart Mill*, New York, 1924, pp. 134-38. See also Iris Wissel Mueller, *John Stuart Mill and French Thought*, Urbana, 1956, pp. 160-62. For this and all aspects of the mutual flirtation of Tocqueville and England, see Seymour Drescher's competent *Tocqueville and England*, Cambridge, 1964. Other thinkers in this school include Léon Fauchet, *Études sur l'Angleterre*, 2 vols., Paris, 1845, I, 118-155; and Charles Comte de Montalembert, *De l'avenir politique de l'Angleterre*, Paris, 1855.

71

reformist politicians whose turn of mind so attracted Russians after the death of Nicholas I.

Tocqueville established his reputation with his study on *Democracy in America*, in which he argued that participatory local government could serve as a bulwark against the tyranny of a national majority and of the central government.[54] Members of the Russian provincial civil service were reading *Democracy in America* a generation before it was translated by Ukrainian federalists in 1861.[55] But, since this work dealt with the influence of a democratic social structure on deconcentrated and elective administrative organs, it had no direct bearing on Russian conditions and was largely ignored.

This was not the case with *The Old Regime and the French Revolution*. No sooner did this great work appear in 1856 than it drove all other foreign comparisons for the Russian predicament from the field. Its evocation of France on the eve of revolution gave a tense mood of immediacy to the problem of reforming Russia. Whether or not there actually existed a "revolutionary situation," as Soviet scholars have argued, Tocqueville's book helped Russians of all persuasions to accept the full urgency of the national condition as well as to see their problems in a European perspective.

The ordinarily optimistic jurist, Konstantin Kavelin, was startled by the implications of *The Old Regime and the French Revolution*: "The formula of Russian history is terrifyingly reminiscent of the formula of French history; reading Tocqueville's book makes one tremble, so much does the pre-revolutionary France call to mind the condition and prevailing ideas of Russia at the present."[56]

[54] See Drescher, *Tocqueville* . . . , p. 79.

[55] Alexis de Tocqueville, *De la démocratie en Amérique*, 2 vols., Paris, 1835. Russian translation, *Demokratiia v Amerike*, 4 vols., Kiev, 1861; N. G. Chernyshevskii's review is in *Polnoe sobranie sochinenii*, VI, 313-36. Alexander Herzen received his copy as a gift from a provincial administrator, *Polnoe sobranie sochinenii*, VII, 296.

[56] *Pisma K. D. Kavelina i I. S. Turgeneva k A. I. Gertsenu*, Geneva,

Tocqueville's impact on the wealthy planter wing of public opinion was equally sharp. S. I. Maltsev, a proprietor of 200,000 serfs and a major industrialist, read *The Old Regime and the French Revolution* and drew up his extremely defensive conclusions in a widely distributed manuscript essay.[57] Another provincial magnate recalled how all the representatives of the provincial gentry called to Petersburg in 1859 saw their local interests in terms of Tocqueville's study and how one of them, the wealthy Count Vladimir Orlov-Davydov, pulled him aside at a soiree and delivered a dogmatic lecture on the subject.[58] Nor were governmental figures immune to Tocqueville's message. In 1858 a copy of *The Old Regime and the French Revolution* was given to the Grand Duke Konstantin.[59] Upon reading it he found that the book contained "awful lessons" of great significance for Russia. "Our position is terrible," he told the Minister of Finances, "God grant that our eyes are opened."[60] In the meanwhile, the Minister of Internal Affairs, Peter Valuev, was finding that "whole pages [of *The Old Regime and the French Revolution*] were, as it were, written for us" and hoped that Russia's eyes would be opened by a native-born Tocqueville. "When will Russians write like this?" he asked rhetorically. "When will we have our own Tocquevilles?"[61]

Tocqueville's book helped replace the bothersome image

1892, p. 56, cited by Sladkevich, *Ocherki* . . . , pp. 97-98. The brief study by Sladkevich, to whom I acknowledge my indebtedness, is the only attempt to assess the overall effect of Tocqueville on his Russian readers. This pioneering account, however, suffers from the author's conviction that Tocqueville was simply a reactionary appealing to foes of reform and to Slavophiles.

[57] Sladkevich, *Ocherki* . . . , p. 95, n30, and pp. 95-96.

[58] Barsukov, *Zhizn . . . Pogodina*, xvii, 130-31. For Tolstoi's response to *The Old Regime and the French Revolution*, see his *Polnoe sobranie sochinenii*, 90 vols. Moscow, 1928-58, xlvii, 123ff.

[59] TsGAOR, f. 722 (Marble Palace archive), op. 1, ed. khr. 91, p. 61.

[60] B. N. Chicherin, *Zapiski proshlogo*, p. 154.

[61] Valuev, *Dnevnik*, i, 76, 285.

of a victorious France with that of a nation suffering from chronic institutional diseases. At the same time, its appearance provided a cover under which Russian development could be discussed obliquely but legally. Because of this, the many Russian reviews of *The Old Regime and the French Revolution* provide a convenient index to the range of thought on administrative reform. For it was precisely in this exchange that the main lines of opinion on decentralization and self-government were first presented to Russian readers.

The first published notice of *The Old Regime and the French Revolution* in Russia was a lengthy review by Prince Vladimir Cherkasskii, published by the *Russian Colloquy* (*Russkaia Beseda*) in the spring of 1857, only months after the first Paris edition appeared. Cherkasskii was a wealthy, Moscow-educated landlord with deep ties to his native Tula province and personal links with the Slavophiles.[62] As genial as he was intelligent, Cherkasskii was lionized by the polite society of Petersburg and enjoyed direct access to the tsar during the entire period of reforms. At the same time he was reviewing Tocqueville, he prepared a memorandum on the emancipation of the serfs which was one of only three examined in detail by the government in 1857.[63] This success guaranteed him a brilliant career as an officially designated "expert" in the Editing Commissions that prepared the 1861 manifesto.

Cherkasskii established his point of view at the outset by citing the conclusions reached by Tocqueville in the "renowned chapter" of *Democracy in America* devoted to the political effects of administrative decentralization. "Centralization," Tocqueville had written, "is capable only of hindering development, and not of helping and furthering it . . . it can only preserve society in a certain status quo."[64]

[62] "Kritika," *Russkaia Beseda*, II (1857), 25-88.
[63] See Trubetskaia, *Materialy . . . Cherkasskogo*, II, 36-45, for his memorandum to Alexander II.
[64] *Russkaia Beseda*, II (1857), 62.

Cherkasskii strongly supported Tocqueville's contention that concentrated and bureaucratic forms of organization were not inevitable concomitants of the modern state but diseases which must be cured. The review of *The Old Regime and the French Revolution* was organized around this idea and therefore focused on the middle section of Tocqueville's analysis, where the Norman thinker presented his critique of "centralization." The first and third sections treating the policies of the French government on the eve of revolution were scarcely mentioned by Cherkasskii.

At first glance, Cherkasskii wrote, eighteenth-century France appeared to have been covered with local institutions, but in fact these were too few and too weak to execute the complex web of provincial functions.[65] Stated differently, Cherkasskii agreed that prerevolutionary France suffered from the same undergovernment and underinstitutionalization, both in structural and in functional terms, that beset present-day Russia. Control over civil life had been transferred to the central ministries and to the *conseil du roi*: "The most distant communes from Paris, even the rural ones, were all subject to the same formalities."[66] Those issues not decided in the capital were delegated to the *Intendants*. With unconcealed relish the Tula reformer recounted Tocqueville's tales of inefficiency, confusion, and corruption in provincial administrations under the *Intendants*. "And over all this chaos," he declaimed, "there reigned deep disrespect for the law." Here Cherkasskii equated "disrespect for the law" with disrespect for the monarch, whose decisions could be qualified or nullified locally due to the absence of a rigorous system of inspection and controls.

How could administrative control be established? Cherkasskii bluntly stated that control could be introduced only by going outside of the administrative hierarchy itself, by turning this function over to the local public.

[65] *Ibid.*, pp. 73-74. [66] *Ibid.*, p. 76.

The notion of self-administration propounded by Cherkasskii assumed the prior existence of a modern state with its hierarchical, bureaucratic administration which was to be whittled back to its proper proportions. He interpreted Tocqueville to be advocating what political scientists today term "devolution," or "the legal conferring of powers to discharge specific or residual functions upon formally constituted local authorities."[67] Nowhere in his review does Cherkasskii indicate sympathy toward a policy of administrative deconcentration since such a policy would leave the state—now represented by local bureaucrats rather than the ministries—in control of the same sphere of activities as before. This would not have satisfied the Tula reformer.

At the same time that Cherkasskii acknowledged the existence of a complex administrative system, he followed Tocqueville in idealizing a form of provincial independence that antedated the modern state. He took his ideal for a self-governing province from the famous appendix to *The Old Regime and the French Revolution* on the province of Languedoc. In Tocqueville's eyes, Languedoc, administered largely by *les gens des trois états*, was not a feudal anachronism holding out against modern state authority but an integral part of the French state with institutions perfectly adapted to modern needs:

> The more I studied the rules and regulations issued by the estates of Languedoc with the King's permission (but seldom on his initiative) as regards such departments of the public administration as were left under their control, the more did I admire their wisdom, equity, and, indeed, benevolence; and the more superior did I find the methods of this local government to those prevailing in districts administered by the King exclusively.[68]

[67] Maddick, *Democracy . . .* , pp. 23ff.
[68] Alexis de Tocqueville, *The Old Regime and the French Revolution*, Stuart Gilbert, trans., New York, 1955, p. 217.

The note of anachronism is less prominent in the passages devoted to the social composition and tax powers of Languedoc's self-rule. Neither for Tocqueville nor, even less, for Cherkasskii, did the system of self-rule prevailing in Languedoc represent an assertion of the prerogatives of the nobility against the throne. Provincial affairs there were conducted by the *three* estates rather than the nobility alone and Cherkasskii took pains to divorce Tocqueville's and his own conception of Languedoc from the oligarchic program of certain Russian noblemen-planters.[69] The value which both Tocqueville and Cherkasskii found in Languedoc's self-government was that it involved all "men of substance" in local affairs. By analogy, Russia's emancipated peasants, as communal property owners, should enjoy representation in the future local government. Only in this manner could an adequate institutional counterweight to the bureaucracy be erected and only in this manner could wide social support be gained for local programs carried out through locally levied and controlled taxes.[70] Indeed, Cherkasskii explained, other provinces in France had not shared in Languedoc's "flowering of local institutions" because they had allowed the power of taxation for local needs to fall into the hands of the state without any participation by the local populace. Like Tocqueville, Cherkasskii saw the power to tax as the *sine qua non* for local self-government.

The review concluded with remarks on the contemporary implications of "the question of centralization and of the evil which it brings."[71] In the tone of the French pamphleteers, Cherkasskii asked if Napoleon III could be expected to establish the needed provincial organs. Approvingly, he cites the campaign of the council-general of Herault to cre-

[69] For this aspect of Cherkasskii's thought, see Richard Wortman, "Koshelev, Samarin, and Cherkassky and the Fate of Liberal Slavophilism," *Slavic Review*, xxi, No. 2 (June 1962), 261-79.

[70] Tocqueville, *The Old Regime* . . . , pp. 214-15.

[71] *Russkaia Beseda*, ii (1857), 86.

ate a completely new form of administrative unit by combining several small Napoleonic departments. Such provinces would be so nearly self-sufficient economically as to reestablish in France the regional life that had been crippled when the country was divided "into eighty-six capriciously drawn subdivisions." Could Napoleon III introduce these? Cherkasskii doubted it for Napoleon sat precariously on an unearned throne.

> Such an achievement of elevated and unselfish policy can be brought about only by a sovereign who was born on the throne, surrounded from the cradle with the affection of his people and loving them no less sincerely and warmly than they him. The possibility of accomplishing such a feat is reserved by the miserly hand of History for only those few who are especially beloved by Her.[72]

And so, beginning with an analysis of eighteenth-century France, Cherkasskii arrived at the conclusion that the Russian tsar alone was fated to fulfill Tocqueville's ideal by abolishing the old bureaucratic provinces and replacing them with new units in which regional life would flourish under the protection, but not the administrative wardship, of a modern central government.

Anyone advocating regional self-rule and opposing all manifestations of central administrative control flirts with federalism. At a time when quasi-federal schemes were under consideration in most nations of western Europe, Cherkasskii pressed a private campaign for such a division of Russia.[73] His plan was to use the emancipation discussions as a lever for grouping provinces into federal territories. After all, he reasoned, the regional peculiarities within Russia "are not characteristic of a single province but of the particular region to which a province belongs. In this

[72] *Russkaia Beseda*, II (1857), 87.
[73] This theme is discussed at length in Robert C. Binckley's provocative *Realism and Nationalism, 1852-1871*, New York, 1935, pp. 180ff.

respect the provinces group themselves into several regions or zones."[74] In each of these territories Cherkasskii proposed to establish a "commission" with members drawn from the local populace and administration. These commissions would not only work out details of emancipation and serve as superior agencies for its enactment, but would also provide a basis for the future administration of the federation. Powerful forces in the Ministry of Internal Affairs supported this idea as late as the autumn of 1858 but it was finally abandoned in the face of an antireform onslaught that threatened to paralyze all administrative reform.[75]

Cherkasskii's staunch opposition to bureaucracy and his federative idea of self-administration were better received by Russian publicists than by the government. His friend from university days, Iurii Samarin, was delighted by the review and concluded from it that Tocqueville and his school were nothing less than "western Slavophiles."[76] The grandees assembled at the Moscow English Club also read the review with enthusiasm and Cherkasskii's old Slavophile mentor, the ailing Alexander Khomiakov, added his weak praise to the chorus.[77] Even Nikolai Chernyshevskii, acerbic editor of the *Contemporary* and a future martyr to the radical cause, found the "remarkable essay" so provocative that he reprinted its concluding proposal to federalize Russia in the most widely circulated journal of the day.[78]

Tocqueville's second Russian reviewer, Mikhail Katkov, brought to his subject the most fervent Anglophilia in mid-nineteenth century Russia. From his lofty pulpit as editor of the *Russian Messenger* he tirelessly drew his readers' attention to the achievements of Victorian civilization:

[74] TsGIA-SSSR, f. 1291, 1858, op. 1, d. 11, pp. 17-18. "Poriadok rassmotreniia proektov gubernskikh krestianskikh polozhenii."

[75] *Ibid.*, p. 12. A. I. Levshin supported Cherkasskii's plan in a note to Alexander II, October 1858: "This memorandum, in my opinion, warrants special attention . . ."; Minister of Internal Affairs Lankoi supported it as well. TsGIA-SSSR, f. 1180, op. xv, d. 109, pp. 211-19.

[76] Samarin, *Sochineniia* . . . , I, 401.

[77] *Materialy* . . . *Cherkasskogo*, I, 80n.

[78] Chernyshevskii, *Polnoe sobranie sochinenii*, IV, 789-98.

If we speak of England often on the pages of this journal, if we often turn the attention of our readers to her and represent her as the classic land of the most contemporary civilization, then, let it be remembered that we are not alone in thinking this.[79]

Never has this country aroused such strong and constant interest as in our own time . . . the English system unfolds before the eyes as an inexhaustibly diverse and complex world which demands the same techniques of study as does Nature . . . the English system is like Life and Nature in its development and creation.[80]

For Katkov, contemporary England was the new Rome, embodying all the positive forces of modern life.[81]

Not surprisingly, the man who held these views had long been associated with the so-called westernizing faction in Russian social thought, which held that Russian development must follow the model of advanced nations in western Europe. The reading of Tocqueville's *The Old Regime and the French Revolution* forced Katkov to define his westernism more closely, specifically to take a careful look at the role of administration in the more developed nations. On this issue Katkov agreed wholeheartedly with Cherkasskii and the "western Slavophile," Tocqueville, that civil life was being set upon by a sinister phalanx of bureaucrats. He agreed, too, that the advance of this army could be checked only by establishing "self-government."

In his review of *The Old Regime and the French Revolution* and in other writings, Katkov developed a view of self-government which, while fundamentally similar to Cherkasskii's included several quite distinctive features. "The notion of centralization is odious to Tocqueville," he claimed, "because he considers it alien to the concept of

[79] *Sovremennaia Letopis*, No. 51 (1861).
[80] Cited by S. Nevedenskii, *Katkov i ego vremia*, St. Petersburg, 1888, p. 114.
[81] Nevedenskii, *Katkov . . .* , p. 114.

freedom."[82] Unlike Cherkasskii and Tocqueville, Katkov did not relate this freedom to the existence or nonexistence of territorial units within the nation. Moscow-born and educated and acquainted with provincial life only through occasional forays into the countryside, Katkov generalized about self-government from a purely national perspective.

This disinclination to take the territorial issue seriously was reinforced by Katkov's reading of the German philosophers. Through Hegel and the minor Stuttgart luminary, Wilhelm Riehl, Katkov was assured that history worked through the unit of society as a whole, the national *Volk*. This society could function as an organic unit at the national level alone. Thus Katkov's distaste for the excesses of administrative concentration was tempered by his overriding concern for the political unity of the state. He rejected territorial unions within the nation as threats to that unity and, following the German theorists, centered his hopes for self-government on more modest corporate entities of cities, townships, and societal estates. The point at which Katkov agreed completely with Cherkasskii was in his insistence that the administration should not interfere with the affairs of these corporate bodies. "The principle of non-intervention," he wrote, "is the highest governmental wisdom, a principle upon which rests all progress of both government and society."[83]

To this point, Katkov's consideration of self-government parallels closely that of west European liberals in general and John Stuart Mill in particular. A general fear of revolution pervaded his thought, though, and when he followed out its implications he emerged in a different light. From Tocqueville he claimed to have derived the belief that the best assurance against revolution were institutions free from administrative interference and endowed with ample authority of their own. As a Russian he knew that only the gentry exercised real power locally, and as an Anglophile

[82] Barsukov, *Zhizn . . . Pogodina*, xvi, 127.
[83] Cited by Dzhanshiev, *Epokha . . .* , p. 299.

he accepted this condition as fitting and proper. Katkov's general plan for local reform nominally included all-class representation as specified by Tocqueville, but, following what he understood to be the British model, he granted the predominant voice in local affairs to justices of the peace elected by the gentry alone. Whereas Cherkasskii interpreted Tocqueville in favor of a local union of property-owning classes, Katkov now used the same source to justify the virtual disenfranchisement of the peasantry and the protection of the noble estate as a bulwark against bureaucracy; in contrast to Cherkasskii and Tocqueville, he simply refused to consider the peasant communities as having a place in provincial and district self-rule.[84]

Compared with Cherkasskii's federative view of self-government, Katkov's nonterritorial and socially narrow conception seems much closer to the Russian *status quo* of the period. Yet his strong defense of corporate rights against the state and his specific inclusion of locally controlled public agencies within the category of corporate bodies clashed with Russian law and raised a question of great significance for the future: would the reformed local organs continue to be governmental bodies or would they have instead the status of semiprivate corporations wholly independent of the central administration and its local representatives? Katkov believed that the latter should be the case. Hence the knotty problem of administrative control over local public agencies would simply vanish: there would be none. "Government" would henceforth exist only to serve the national society while fully autonomous corporations would look after all local needs.

The full import of this notion did not immediately become apparent since it occupied a secondary position in

[84] *Moskovskie Vedomosti*, No. 34 (1863), 82; Joseph Backor, "M. N. Katkov, Introduction to His Life and His Russian National Policy Program," Ph.D. diss., Indiana University, 1966, p. 291; for other aspects of Katkov's social conservatism, see Martin Katz, *Michael N. Katkov*, The Hague, 1966, pp. 50ff.

Katkov's review and because it was further veiled by Katkov's facile and persuasive analogies between Russia and England. This literary sleight-of-hand, practiced earlier by Tocqueville himself, made the most fundamental changes of governmental practice appear merely as the logical steps necessary to bring a developing nation in line with England, the "protectress of civilization."[85] Katkov's review appealed naturally to those gentry who supported basic changes in local government but believed that their own class should retain political dominance of the countryside. His indifference to autonomy based on territorial divisions made his program appear far less bold than Cherkasskii's federalism. Yet his secondary assertions were in this case more important than his main propositions. He flatly denied that the state administration could successfully organize local life and insisted instead that this task be performed by corporative bodies outside the bureaucratic apparatus; these assertions promoted and yet already reflected the dualistic thinking about "administration" and "zemstvo," "state" and "society," that was later to grow so important and justify antagonism on both sides.

Katkov's editorials left the major problems of what to do with the existing provincial administrative organs unsolved. Yet precision and thoroughness are never essential ingredients of popular ideology. If they were, Boris Chicherin's writing would surely have been greeted with enthusiasm, for in his unrelenting attacks on both Tocqueville and England and his dogged opposition to policies of devolution he surpassed his opponents in these qualities. But the public met his opinions with coldness and disdain. In promoting what he termed "centralization," Chicherin insulted the vague but widely held attitudes toward reform which Cherkasskii and Katkov flattered.

The reasons that motivated Chicherin to make a radical defense of the state bureaucracy during the post-Crimean

[85] Barsukov, *Zhizn . . . Pogodina*, xv, 10.

years have yet to be adequately explained. His doctrinaire training is always cited—students at Moscow University called him "Hegel"—and inconclusive arguments based on his social origins have been advanced.[86] In lieu of a more substantial explanation, it can be noted that Chicherin, though born in Tambov province, felt no deep ties to provincial life and that as a scholar in Moscow he had never been exposed at firsthand to the central ministerial apparatus in Petersburg whose interests he so vigorously championed.[87]

Chicherin first wrote his lengthy critique of Tocqueville for the press, and when it was rejected he grouped it with other short studies in a volume appropriately entitled *Essays on England and France*. In the introduction to this collection Chicherin wrote: "Comparative study of the two leading nations of Europe doubtless is highly instructive. We meet there all the questions which occupy thinking men today: medieval elements and the new order, aristocracy and democracy, freedom and equality, state administration and private undertakings, industry and proletariat, centralization and local autonomy."[88]

The rival claims of administrative leadership and local public autonomy dominated the essays that followed. Through Hegel and especially the historian Sergei Soloviev, Chicherin had absorbed a deep theoretical interest in the role of the state in civil society. In the first of the four studies, a review of Montalambert's sanguine work *On the Political Future of England*, he argued that the state alone is competent to guide the destiny of a modern nation, and

[86] The bravest attempt to do so is that of P. Soloviev, "Filosofiia istorii Gegelia na sluzhbe russkogo liberalizma," *Russkaia istoricheskaia literatura v klassovom osveshchenii*, M. I. Pokrovskii, ed., 2 vols., Moscow, 1927, I, 121-204.

[87] Darrell Patrick Hammer, "Two Russian Liberals: The Political Thought of B. N. Chicherin and K. D. Kavelin," Ph.D. diss., Columbia University, 1962, p. 48.

[88] B. Chicherin, *Ocherki Anglii i Frantsii*, Moscow, 1858, p. ix.

that "True liberalism does not consist in denying the state principle."[89]

Though he was not above Hegelian bombast, Chicherin preferred to set forth this important thesis indirectly, by cutting the particular European moorings of his opponents. By this means he hoped to upend the entire lexicon of provincial reform. First he attacked the symbolic homeland of decentralization and self-government, England. In his essays he sliced away at the romantic mist surrounding that island. His accusing finger sought out the misery of the laboring poor, the monopolies, and sinecures, "—in a word, a whole series of phenomena growing from the inadequate development of the central organs of government."[90] English statesmen must stop talking of rights and think about welfare; then they would realize that the public weal could only be promoted through administrative "centralization" and efficient bureaucratization.

In recent English civil service reforms Chicherin detected evidence that this change was actually occurring; the innovations of 1853 to 1855 instituted examinations and review boards as a step toward forging a truly efficient bureaucracy. It is revealing of the state of Russian opinion at the time that, except for Chicherin's lavish praise, this monumental legislation and the celebrated Trevelyan-Northcote Commission which drafted it were otherwise unnoticed by the Russian press. Chicherin's England, even if it actually existed, was rejected in favor of Tocqueville's beautiful isle.

Having humbled England to the level of a nation suffering from deep social ills and gradually remedying them through centralized administrative means, Chicherin moved on to France, the archenemy of the Russian provincialists. Mockingly he alluded to French liberal thinkers who in 1852 threw off their calling as scholars to become

[89] *Ibid.*, pp. xi-xii, review of *De l'avenir politique de l'Angleterre.*
[90] *Ibid.*, p. xiii.

85

carping publicists. With special scorn he turned on Tocqueville, knowing full well that unless he could wipe out the effects of Cherkasskii's adulatory review the ideas of this defeated Frenchman would hold the field in Russia.[91] Chicherin's review of *The Old Regime and the French Revolution* was an explicit attempt to refute Cherkasskii's view on France and an implicit attack on his proposals for Russia. Throughout its seventy pages the author left little doubt that he intended his reader to read "Russia" whenever "France" was mentioned: "It seems that the spirit of political opposition, denying the very existence of the new administrative system, had gone too far in its criticism. It has heaped the blame for all set-backs in France on centralization and the supremacy of Paris."[92] What did France owe to its central organs of government? Only through the efforts of the state, Chicherin wrote, was civil society created out of chaos. The abstract force of the state was manifest in an administrative class which comprised "the most zealous servants of the king";[93] moving to and fro from the capital, they worked in the name of general ends, of *raison d'état*. This they understood intuitively because they were citizens of the whole state, men for whom "the spirit of local independence did not exist." Their crowning achievement was not to destroy local life but to create a nationally integrated society.

But what about Languedoc, which Tocqueville and in turn Cherkasskii had cited as evidence of the viability of a regionalized nation state? To Chicherin, Languedoc appeared not as "a provincial state after which all France could be modeled" but a feudal holdover, a denial of national principle, a call for a *status in statu*, and a defense of the local public's *rights* against the state's concept of delegated administrative *functions*.[94] Indeed, Chicherin concluded, the form of self-government that Tocqueville sought in his panegyric of Languedoc was neither possible

[91] *Ibid.*, p. 154.   [92] *Ibid.*, p. 269.
[93] *Ibid.*, p. 173.   [94] *Ibid.*, p. 226.

nor desirable, for it "destroys public and governmental unity. It leads to federalism to which not one Frenchman would accede."[95]

Taken as a whole, the reappraisal of England, France, and of Tocqueville's *The Old Regime and the French Revolution* undertaken by Boris Chicherin was a major achievement. He brusquely rejected the romantic and static notion of England prevalent in Russia and demonstrated that England had need for a stronger administration and more concentrated forms of control. Likewise, he showed that France had developed more in spite of, than because of, the autonomy of regional and provincial public bodies. For Chicherin, as for Katkov, the achievement of national unity was the most noble drama of social and political history. But Chicherin, unlike Katkov, saw the civil administration as the leading actor: "Bureaucracy is the over-all tie in this body of the French people whence comes its ability to function as a society; centralization leads this structure to unity by creating a focal point from which and to which flow the movements of government."[96] Given this perspective, both Cherkasskii's and Katkov's brands of self-government could only appear as steps backward.

Much as Chicherin opposed the devolution of civic functions on the provincial public, he was at least cognizant of the need for reform. Almost alone among publicists in the 1850s, he realized that the fault with the Nicholaevan administration of the provinces was that it had been too crudely constituted to function in a centralized manner. Rather than invite the provincial public to substitute another imperfect system for the existing chaos, he proposed to reform and improve the civil service. Chicherin recognized that, given slow communications, local administrators could not avoid taking independent action. To this he did not object, and, in fact, favored the delegation of certain authority to the locally based representatives of central ministries. Although he elsewhere stressed the importance of

[95] *Ibid.*, p. 270.   [96] *Ibid.*, p. 7.

87

"centralization" both in the sense of administrative rather than public control and in the sense of concentration of administrative authority in the capital, Chicherin here defended deconcentration as an answer to those advocating devolution. Never prominent in his writings, this current was scarcely noticed by outraged contemporaries, who saw only his call to quell localist sentiments.[97]

Chicherin presented a masterful brief but lost the case. He not only lost it but was roundly abused by everyone in the court. Reformist Russian followers of Tocqueville recoiled at being told that Bonapartist France was "the central point of western European history" whose pattern of development they should and must follow.[98] Katkov flatly refused to publish Chicherin's review of Tocqueville in his *Russian Messenger*, an action which marked a decisive rupture in the ranks of the old "westernizing" party.[99] Needless to say, all salons sympathetic to Cherkasskii's reformist Slavophilism closed their doors to the young professor. And Chernyshevskii used the strongest language yet to appear in his popular *Contemporary* to condemn the *Essays on England and France*. "We want to be stern with Mr. Chicherin," he began: "You, my friend, are a good soul, but a fool."[100] No major faction of opinion rushed to Chicherin's defense and in disgust he left Russia to travel in England and France. At the same time, Katkov soared to the forefront of Russian journalism and Cherkasskii's views on reform won him the position of chief editor of the emancipation statutes.[101]

Much of the furor over Chicherin was more smoke than substance, but it did demonstrate that a rough consensus

[97] *Ibid.*, p. 18.　　　　　　　[98] *Ibid.*, p. 274.

[99] Barsukov, *Zhizn . . . Pogodina*, xvi, 125-35. V. N. Rozental, "Obshchestvenno-polititicheskaia programma russkogo liberalizma v seredine 50-kh godov XIX v," *Istoricheskie zapiski AN SSSR*, Moscow, 1961, No. 70, p. 221; Katz, *Katkov*, pp. 54-56.

[100] Chernyshevskii, *Polnoe sobranie sochinenii*, "Chicherin kak publitsist," vi, 651-52.

[101] Chicherin, *Zapiski proshlogo*, p. 254.

on local reform had emerged through the debates over France, England, and the writings of Tocqueville. By and large, publicists followed Katkov and Cherkasskii in concluding from the British and French experience that bureaucracy was an evil to be cured by turning administrative functions over to elected representatives of local society. They conceived of self-government as a policy set in conscious opposition to the central ministries and their agents. Accordingly, they did not support administrative decentralization, or deconcentration, with the same enthusiasm since it left ministerial power intact. This position was reinforced by news from France—again filtered through the writings of liberal critics—that Louis Napoleon was using administrative decentralization as a means of pre-empting advocates of public participation in local affairs.

It was a short step from drawing such conclusions about western Europe to applying them directly to Russia.[102] But the ease with which countless Russians took this step is deceptive. Their imported ideology, for all its practical appeal, was just that, an import. It flatly contradicted the administrative verities that had guided Russian policy for generations and the deeper historical traditions on which those precepts were based. Some of Russia's most profound political thinkers, including Nikolai Karamzin, had long felt that the administrative unification and expansion of the state constituted the very fulfillment of the nation's destiny. Likewise, the incisive German scholar, Baron von Haxthausen, had only recently argued on sociological grounds that "centralization and generalized forms of government in the higher departments of administration correspond perfectly with the character of the Slavonic race, and are peculiarly adapted to Russia."[103]

[102] *Russkii Invalid,* No. 182 (1863), 780. Thus, the Minister of War, D. A. Miliutin, argued in his ministry's newspaper that "Our country, not at all similar to France in its physical character, laws, customs, and the historical fate of the population, has come to the same point as France in respect to its administrative structure."

[103] Baron August von Haxthausen, *Transcaucasia, Sketches of the*

Such distinguished spokesmen for the idea of concentrated bureaucratic leadership could not simply be ignored, let alone scoffed at in the person of their youngest disciple, Boris Chicherin. Advocates of self-government and decentralization had eventually to face their arguments or acknowledge their own theories to be superficial and derivative. They had to interpret their reform ideas in the specific context of Russian experience or fall prey to the accusation that their habit of reasoning by analogy was irrelevant to Russia. In this effort they were fortunate to receive the utmost support from Russian historians themselves.

THE SEARCH FOR A PROVINCIALIST PAST

The decade after 1855 witnessed a flood of historical writing in Russia. In a few short years most of the great scholars who shaped the fiercely contested debates of the late nineteenth century made their professional debuts. In the years after the fall of Sevastopol these men were still young and, though serious researchers, were unwilling to abandon the great issues of the day to the influence of mere politicians. This determination caused them, perhaps unconsciously, to integrate their own chief concerns closely with the ideological problems of reform, which in turn imparted to their writings a compelling sense of immediacy.

The public responded to this scholarly *engagement* with the keenest enthusiasm. In university lecture halls, frock-coated civil servants and journalists rubbed elbows with radical students to hear popular scholars expound on Russian antiquity.[104] Historians dazzled the public for which they wrote and the public, in turn, was gratified to discover historians who could project its own concerns onto the topography of the past.

Nations and Races between the Black Sea and the Caspian, London, 1854, p. 69.

[104] Nikitenko, *Dnevnik* . . . , II, 113, 175.

Of all the many and significant reforms under public debate, none presented a more fundamental historical challenge than the question of local government. At the same time, on no other issue were the reformers in such need of historical justification as this. Advocates of administrative decentralization and provincial self-government faced a monumental task: to prove that their ostensibly alien programs were rooted in Russian tradition, and to map out the way in which these policies had influenced Russian development in the past.

The easiest period on which to base this argument was the years between the American Revolution and 1825 when Nicholas I came to the throne. These years had witnessed the birth and first development of western European and American thinking on self-government and on federative relations among provinces.[105] The rich ferment of ideas on the structure of modern states which the American Constitution inspired had quickly spread to every corner of Europe, especially to those opposing the Napoleonic reforms of local government. Further afield, in the Americas leaders dreamt of establishing a federated United States of Central America and in South America a decentralized administrative apparatus was being planned for Brazil.

It is quite natural that veterans returning to Russia should have carried back with them the sympathy for regional autonomy and hostility to provincial bureaucratism that was so widespread in the Europe they had conquered. No sooner was Napoleon safely on Elba than numerous schemes for the reorganization of Russia's provinces blossomed in Moscow, Petersburg, and even in far-off Siberia. In 1817 a leading senator sent Alexander I a proposal to establish elective governors-general; the next year the tsar received an anonymous proposal for establishing a "provincial state," and in the year following, Jeremy Bentham in-

---

[105] See Avalov, *Detsentralizatsiia* . . . , Pts. 1 and 2; also Hedwig Hintze, *Staatseinheit und Föderalismus in alten Frankreich und in der Revolution*, Berlin and Leipzig, 1928, Chap. XIIff.

formed him that the Russian autocracy was ill-informed on provincial affairs.[106] Between 1820 and 1825 the government was bombarded with proposals for localized administration, many of which received the rather confusing title of "constitutions." Typical of these was the "constitution" of N. N. Novosiltsev (1820)—nearly half of the 191 articles dealt with local rule.[107]

Before 1825, politically respectable Russians could advance such proposals with impunity because they directly countered what was believed to be the centralizing influence of the French Revolution. For this reason Alexander I was not unsympathetic to them and even encouraged a top administrator to conduct a limited experiment in provincial reorganization in the province of Voronezh.[108] Only when the ideas of deconcentration and local public autonomy appeared in Russia in a revolutionary guise with the Decembrist conspiracy was this attitude broken.[109] Henceforth, mention of such policies would evoke dark fears of Italian Carbonari and cabalistic German student unions. Though the committee appointed to investigate the Decembrist uprising gave thoughtful consideration to certain decentralizing proposals, this strain of reform had fallen into disrepute by 1827.

During most of Nicholas I's reign the provincial reform program was kept alive by the lone figure of Nikolai Turgenev in Paris, since its partisans in Russia were, for the

[106] A. V. Predtechenskii, *Ocherki obshchestvenno-politicheskoi istorii Rossii v pervoi chetverti XIX veka*, Leningrad and Moscow, 1957, pp. 373, 380ff.

[107] Georges Vernadsky, *La charte constitutionelle de l'empire russe en l'an 1820*, Paris, 1933.

[108] Predtechenskii, *Ocherki . . .*, pp. 398ff.

[109] On Decembrist attitudes toward local rule, see N. Druzhinin, *Dekabrist Nikita Muraviev*, Moscow, 1933, pp. 180, 189; G. G. Krichevskii, "Konstitutsionyi proekt N. Muravieva i amerikanskie konstitutsii," *Izvestiia AN SSSR; seriia istorii i filosofii*, Moscow, 1945, No. 6, pp. 397-406; Georges Luciani, *La Société des Slavs Unis (1823-1825)*, Bordeaux, 1963, pp. 64ff.

most part, in exile.[110] The situation changed drastically with the general amnesty of 1856, the return of many exiled Decembrists, and the easing of censorship. These changes finally enabled the suspended debates of the 1820s to be revived publicly. Forgotten propaganda for self-government by leading statesmen of the 1820s was republished, ostensibly as historical texts.[111] Old reform projects were brought out from cabinets. Biographies and memoirs on political figures of the era of Alexander I appeared in print, giving rise to more debate.[112]

The revival of interest in this earlier reformism was of undeniable value in the post-Crimean era, for it provided the generation educated in the 1840s with a link to the discussions on local government broken off in 1825. And since members of that generation were now prominent in Russian public life,[113] the reform movement as a whole was thereby strengthened. But the opposition was untouched and unperturbed. The trouble was that nothing had been proven by recalling that something akin to decentralization or self-government had been advocated in the time of Alexander I; even the warmest admirers of this earlier movement admitted that it had been an import. Given this fact, they still had to prove that their program had indigenous Russian roots. Meanwhile, opponents of fundamental change in provincial rule grew daily more convinced that the whole of Russian history justified their position. Their claim to Russian authenticity gained immensely in prestige when the most prominent historian of the day, Professor Sergei

[110] See Nikolai Turgenev, *La Russie et les Russes*, 3 vols., Paris, 1847, III, 208ff.

[111] M. M. Speranskii, "Zamechaniia o gubernskikh uchrezhdeniiakh," *Arkiv istoricheskikh i prakticheskikh svedenii otnosiashchikhsia do Rossii*, St. Petersburg, 1859, No. 4, pp. 92ff.

[112] See N. G. Sladkevich, "Problema reformy i revoliutsii v Russkoi publitsistike nachala 60-kh godov (Polemika vokrug knigi M. A. Korfa, *Zhizn Grafa Speranskogo*)," *Revoliutsionnaia situatsiia* . . . , I, 509-21.

[113] Torke, *Das Russische Beamtentum* . . . , pp. 86-87.

Soloviev of Moscow, reinterpreted the entire Russian past in terms of the development of the centralized state.[114] The "state" or "juridical" school of Russian historiography which Soloviev established reached its fullest development in the 1860s and 1870s when it fused with the emerging Russian *Rechtsstaat* movement. In the 1850s its proponents sided vigorously with all the advanced reform programs including the abolition of serfdom and their favorite cause, the reorganization of the courts. Only on the question of provincial government did their historical perspective set them at odds with the popular currents of the day.

Sergei Soloviev had begun his scholarly career in the 1840s by positing a view of Russian history that stressed the inner logic of Russian development rather than ethical battles between actual events and what should have been. With voluminous and original documentation he defended his conviction that the chief force for political and social development in Russia was the state and its administration.[115] All the apparent contradictions of the Russian past became intelligible, Soloviev claimed, if viewed from the perspective of the progressive evolution of a unified government. Indeed, all cultural phenomena and even Russian society itself had been called into being by the state.[116]

Before 1856, historians of the "state" school struggled to defend this general thesis against those who accused them of partiality toward the Nicholaevan autocracy. After 1856, the statists were freed from this accusation and rapidly became a powerful force in Russian academic circles. At this

---

[114] On this movement, see P. Melnikov, "Iuridicheskaia shkola v Russkoi istoriografii," M. M. Pokrovskii, ed., *Russkaia istoricheskaia literatura . . .* , Vol. I; and Klaus Detlev Grothusen, *Die historische Rechtschule Russlands*, in *Osteuropastudien der Hochschulen des Landes Hessen*, Series I, Giessen, 1962.

[115] S. M. Soloviev, *Istoricheskie otnosheniia mezhdu Russkimi kniaziami Riurikogo doma*, Moscow, 1847, pp. 697-700.

[116] S. M. Soloviev, "Istoricheskie pisma," *Russkii Vestnik*, No. 4 (1858).

critical moment a younger colleague of Soloviev's took over as public champion of the statist school, the same man whose disconcerting insights on France and England were to be so widely criticized, Boris Chicherin. With his usual contentiousness, Chicherin applied the statist interpretation to local history. Specifically, he hoped to prove that the Russian provinces and their institutions were not autonomous societal forces but themselves the creation of the central government. In this effort he became, as he later confessed, "a defender of the hated centralization."[117]

Chicherin based his claim on a study of provincial administration in the seventeenth century.[118] Even before Peter the Great forged the modern Russian provincial system, he argued, the haphazard Muscovite administration was quickly evolving into a rationalized system of local organs directly responsible to the central power. This system, Chicherin claimed, had to be created from above, for geographic and sociological conditions had dictated that Russia would have no local unities which might spawn provincial institutions from below.[119] Pre-Muscovite Russia was itself based on hierarchical relations and consequently bequeathed nothing to posterity on which autonomous local institutions could have been constructed. Toiling in a vacuum, Ivan the Terrible and his successors had forged all the institutions of provincial Russia.

Three points of Chicherin's highly legalistic argument emerge with special clarity. First, before a unified state developed in Russia there had existed only a disarray of conflicting rules applied irregularly and inconsistently. In this world neither administrative decentralization nor local self-government played any significant part and to the extent

[117] B. N. Chicherin, *Zapiski proshlogo*, p. 216.
[118] B. N. Chicherin, *Oblastnye uchrezhdeniia Rossii v XVII-m veke*, Moscow, 1856.
[119] *Ibid.*, p. 589. (Also, *Opyt po istorii russkogo prava*, Moscow, 1858, p. 380.)

that they existed at all they impeded the unremitting march of progress. Second, the victory of the centralized state and the rule of law was assured by the competence of the local administrators or *voevody*, who were responsible solely and directly to the tsar in Moscow.[120] So warmly did Chicherin praise these functionaries that he all but obliterated the critical distinction between political unification and administrative concentration that he at least recognized in speaking of western development; in Russia, he claimed, political unification was achieved only through administrative centralization. Third, Chicherin and the state school allowed the possibility of only one pattern of political development: that based on the unified and internally homogeneous state. For reasons of logic they flatly denied that "history" could create any other form of organization than what it had actually produced. With their teacher, Hegel, they averred that "whatever is, is right."[121]

All three of these points posed a direct challenge to the provincial reformers. By "proving" that the reformist program had no Russian genealogy, historians of the state school offered ideological support to anyone dedicated to maintaining the *status quo*. Against this background, the campaign of the reformist historians to find Russian precedents for their ideas assumed special urgency. To do nothing was to lose.

Historians who responded to this challenge were of a different sort from the statists.[122] Soloviev, Chicherin, and their colleagues were all Moscow-educated and Muscovite to the core in outlook; the provincialists were, with few ex-

[120] *Ibid.*, pp. 337-38.
[121] It is important to separate Chicherin's beliefs of the late 1850s from his later commitment to the *zemstvo* movement. This is not done by P. Melnikov, "Iuridicheskaia shkola . . ." or N. L. Rubinstein, *Russkaia istoriografia*, Moscow, 1941, pp. 301-10.
[122] For general studies on this school see M. A. Rubach, "Federalisticheskie teorii v istorii Rossii," M. M. Pokrovskii, ed., *Russkaia istoricheskaia literatura . . .* , ii, 3-120; Anatole G. Mazour, *Modern Russian Historiography*, Princeton, 1958, pp. 146-69.

ceptions, born in the countryside and imbued with a deep antiurban perspective that persisted long after they moved to the capitals to teach. The statists had all enjoyed a cosmopolitan education, Soloviev having spent two years in Berlin and Paris attending the lectures of Ranke, Ritter, Guizot, and Michelet; the provincialists characteristically began their education at provincial Russian universities and looked abroad only after their point of view was set. Finally, historians of the state school, while led by the priest's son, Soloviev, were, for the most part, gentry, while the provincialists, led by Nikolai Kostomarov, a son of the lower gentry, were generally of non-noble birth. This social difference imparted to the provincialists sympathies more broadly democratic than those of the statists.[123]

All these biographical factors might have come to nothing had the provincialists not made early contact with the new fields of ethnography, statistics, and local history. While the statist historians derived intellectual stimulus from philosophy and historical jurisprudence (two areas in which Moscow University excelled), the provincialists applied the findings of these burgeoning disciplines to the study of Russian history.

The origins of these new fields date to the reign of Nicholas I. As early as 1841 the Department of Laws on Tax and State Finance at St. Petersburg University had offered a prize for the best essay on "the degree to which the success of financial institutions depends on the influence of local and temporary conditions in the state which change the rules of pure theory."[124] In 1842 a nearly moribund sta-

[123] Soviet scholars have followed Rubinstein (p. 377) in assigning this factor paramount importance. Their argument on the statists is that in upholding the interest of the government they tacitly acknowledged the dependence of their own gentry class on governmental favor. The trouble with this hypothesis is that it should apply equally to the gentry Slavophiles, whose ideology was so opposed to that of the statists. For the provincialists this line of reasoning is somewhat more fruitful for it at least accounts for the general cast of their thought.

[124] V. V. Grigoriev, *Imperatorskii Sankt-Peterburgskii Universitet*

97

tistical commission founded seven years earlier by the Ministry of Internal Affairs was reorganized. This agency gathered material for a five-volume study of the regions of Russia, the manuscript of which was accidentally destroyed by fire.[125] After 1837 the General Staff began gathering local statistics, too, although their classified status closed them to civilian use until after the death of Nicholas I. In the provinces themselves, the official newspapers (*gubernskie vedomosti*) founded in 1838 became active in publishing local surveys, many of which were conducted by amateur investigators.[126]

These were but a foretaste of the explosion of statistical and ethnographic research on the provinces that occurred in the 1850s under the aegis of the Ministry of Internal Affairs, the Imperial Geographic Society (founded in 1845), and numerous secondary institutions. Nikolai Miliutin, who later presided over the commission on local reforms, completely overhauled the statistical organs of the Ministry of Internal Affairs in 1852. Thanks to his efforts, part-time correspondents were replaced by a permanent staff of eighteen and the province was accepted as the prime unit of study. In a pioneering effort the entire force descended on Nizhnii Novgorod and Iaroslavl provinces to gather data. These innovations were paralleled by the energetic correspondents of the Imperial Geographical Society, who coordinated independent studies throughout the empire.[127] Within four years after the fall of Sevastopol the volume of local studies issued during Nicholas I's reign had been surpassed, and detailed analyses of Vologda, Nizhnii Novgorod, Perm, Kharkov, Iaroslavl, Novgorod, Kiev, Tver, Tula, and Pskov

v techenii pervogo piatidesiatiletiia ego sushchestvovaniia, St. Petersburg, 1870, p. xl.

[125] I. Miklashevskii, "Statistika," Brockhaus and Efron, *Entsiklopedicheskii slovar*, xxxi-a, 497-98.

[126] A. N. Pypin, *Istoriia russkoi etnografii*, 4 vols., St. Petersburg, 1890-91, i, 305-06.

[127] *Dvadsatipiatiletie Imperatorskogo Russkogo Geograficheskogo Obshchestva*, St. Petersburg, 1872, p. 94.

provinces and Olonets district were in press.[128] The province had arrived as an object of serious study.

Such compilations of tables and dry description demanded that their reader consider the province, district, or region as a distinct economic and social entity with its own characteristic history and resources rather than merely as an administrative unit. Reading them, the sensitive reader could scarcely fail to wonder whether the Russian unity vaunted by historians of the state school actually existed. At the very least, one was required to appreciate the difficulties that any uniform bureaucratic system would face in attempting to serve adequately the varying needs of each region. From this honest recognition of fact, the conclusion followed easily that the existing concentrated system of administration was totally unsuited to its assigned task.

The emergence of this localist attitude in the 1850s is doubly ironic. On the one hand, such competent observers as Baron Haxthausen had marvelled at the integration of Russia's economic regions as early as the 1840s.[129] Now, a decade and a half later, when the local economies should have been even more closely tied together, the focus of attention had shifted to the region. On the other hand, the attitude became widespread on the very eve of the sweeping economic changes in Russia which were to move the country rapidly in the direction of geographical integration.

[128] N. Vkonadu, "Ocherki mestnostei i nravov Vologodskoi gubernii," *Vologodskie Gubernskie Vedomosti*, No. 5 (1856); N. Khramtsovskii, *Kratkii ocherk istorii i opisanie Nizhnego Novgoroda*, Nizhnii Novgorod, 1857; typical of these were Ivan Afremov, *Istoricheskii obzor Tulskoi gubernii*, Moscow, 1850-57; S. I. Kovanko, "Istoriia Kharkovskoi gubernii," *Kharkovskie Gubernskie Vedomosti*, Nos. 3-9 (1856); M. Duev, "Istoricheskii obzor obshchestnosti drevnei kostromskoi oblasti," *Kostromskie Gubernskie Vedomosti*, Nos. 34, 36, 40 (1857); D. I. Lomachesvskii, "Istoricheskii obzor Olonetskoi gubernii," *Olonetskie Gubernskie Vedomosti*, Nos. 3, 6, 8 (1858); I. F. Shtukenberg (Johann Ch. Stuckenberg), *Statisticheskie trudy*, 2 vols., St. Petersburg, 1857-60.

[129] August von Haxthausen, *Studien über die innere Zustände, das Volksleben, und insbesondere die ländlichen Einrichtungen Russlands*, 3 vols., Hannover and Berlin, 1847-52, i, xiv.

Whatever its historical justification, provincialism became widespread in the disciplines of statistics, ethnography, and economics and spread rapidly to the study of history. In 1850 a Petersburg savant could still claim that "So far as we know, the regional unit has not yet been submitted to special research."[130] This situation changed totally after 1855 with the rapid-fire publication of a round of provincial histories, many by previously unknown researchers. Even the history of Russian law was affected by the new localizing influence, as evidenced in the change in title of a major course at Petersburg University from "Russian Civil Law" to "Local Law."[131] As the movement toward local studies gathered momentum it also gained in stature when the works of distinguished provincialist historians came to public attention. By 1858 the provincialists could claim several eminent scholars for their school.

The first complete reinterpretation of early Russian history from a provincial perspective was the creation of a Ukrainian by adoption, Nikolai Kostomarov (1817-1885). His provincialism grew naturally from a passionate interest in ethnography which evidently appealed to him for highly personal reasons.[132] He was born on his family's modest estate near the western border of Voronezh province. The decisive event in Kostomarov's childhood occurred when his father, a member of the Russian gentry who was more interested in the Petersburg *beau monde* than in the welfare of his serfs, was murdered by Ukrainian peasants.[133] Given this background, young Kostomarov's idealization of everything provincial, his study of the Ukrainian language (which he was still learning when twenty-eight years

---

[130] A. Tiurin, *Obshchestvennaia zhizn i zemskie otnosheniia v drevnei Rusi*, St. Petersburg, 1850, p. 2.

[131] Grigoriev, *Imperatorskii* . . . , p. 159.

[132] N. I. Kostomarov, *Ukrainskii separatizm. Neizvestnye zapreshchennye stranitsy*, Iu. G. Oksman, ed., Odessa, 1921, p. 4.

[133] N. I. Kostomarov, "Avtobiografiia Nikolaia Ivanovicha Kostomarova," *Russkaia Mysl*, 1885, Bk, 5, p. 195.

54040

old),[134] and his subsequent denunciation of every governmental attempt to exert authority from the capital appear
as much the working out of a psychological drama as the
fruit of scholarly analysis. As he grew, his provincialism was
fed by Gogol's Ukrainian tales and third-rate French novels
such as Jules Sandeau's *Le Docteur Herbeau* (Paris, 1841),
from which he concluded that "The province is the measure
of public development. . . . Of what use is the capital to
us?"[135] As if answering his own question, Kostomarov
founded in Kiev the Society of Sts. Cyril and Methodius
(1846), whose members boldly advocated that the Russian
Empire be abolished and a federation established in its
place encompassing all the regions of Russia and the other
Slavic nationalities as well.[136]

The closing of this group by the police in 1848 and Kostomarov's six-year exile in Saratov left him bent on exposing
the roots of the provincial problem by completing a historical study of pre-Mongol Russia that he had conceived
years earlier.[137] During the six centuries since the fall of
Kiev, he claimed, Russia had been on the wrong course, the
course of administrative centralization and bureaucratization. "The fall of independence and freedom" that Kostomarov bemoaned was occasioned first by the Mongol inva-
sions but was subsequently pushed to its conclusion by
Moscow's heinous "strangulation" of the Russian city-
states.[138] Like Soloviev and Chicherin, Kostomarov conceived of Russian history in linear terms but, unlike them,
he pictured the line as leading only downward.

[134] *Ibid.*, pp. 209-10.
[135] N. I. Kostomarov, "Pisma N. I. Kostomarova k K. M. Sementov-
skomy," *Russkii Bibliofil—Le Bibliophile Russe*, Petrograd, 1916, III,
18.
[136] See P. A. Zaionchkovskii, *Kirillo-Mefodievskoe Obshchestvo*,
Moscow, 1959, pp. 85ff.; N. I. Kostomarov, "K bratiam ukraintsam,"
Byloe, February 1906, pp. 67-68.
[137] N. I. Kostomarov, "Pisma . . . ," p. 20.
[138] N. I. Kostomarov, *Istoricheskie monografii Nikolaia Ivanovicha
Kostomarova*, 3rd edn., 16 vols., St. Petersburg, 1886, VII, 153.

101

The earliest Russian people, Kostomarov believed, had been organized not into clans fighting among themselves, as the statists claimed, but into Slavic tribes (*plemia*). The tribe which grouped itself around Kiev was but one of these, along with the Novgorodians, Vladimirians, Pskovians, etc. These tribes were sufficiently differentiated among themselves as to constitute distinct nationalities (*narodnosti*),[139] yet their common origins, language, culture, and, later, their Christian faith provided firm bonds among them. On this basis, pre-Mongol Russia existed as a single entity, but one founded on "unity in diversity."[140] Far from being the archaic confusion of mutually hostile princes fighting for precedence that the statist historians pictured, Russia in the appanage period was the very ideal of civil society, achieving order without bureaucratic compulsion.

To this pre-Mongol system of territorial states Kostomarov applied the term "federation." Its components were not "provinces" but "lands," bound together by geographical contiguity and the need for defense against external foes. The ancient Russian federalism precluded the need for regional or provincial separatism and even the idea of Ukrainian independence was rendered unnecessary and undesirable.[141] "Although the principle of unity among the lands was strong enough to prevent them from breaking away from one another to set up life independently, it was nonetheless not so powerful as to drown out every local peculiarity and to merge all the parts."[142]

Could the ancient federation of self-governing lands be revived in the nineteenth century? Though for half a millennium the federative spirit had been maintained only by

[139] In his "Dve russkie narodnosti," *Osnova* (March 1861), 33, Kostomarov argues the case for differentiating the Ukraine from Great Russia as a whole but elsewhere he applies the term *narodnost* to the separate cities of Great Russia. Kostomarov, "Mysli o federativnom nachale v drevnei Rusi," *Osnova* (January 1861), 131, 142.

[140] Kostomarov, "Mysli . . . ," p. 145.

[141] *Ibid.*, p. 158.

[142] Kostomarov, *Ukrainskii separatizm . . .* , p. 16.

the popular masses, Kostomarov believed such a revival possible. This had been his intent in founding the Society of Sts. Cyril and Methodius and in asking the public "Would it not be better, instead of repeating the tired, modish phrase 'Onward' to cry out instead 'Reverse'?" Yet he stopped short of advocating his radical march into the past and even denied in print that his provincial ideas had contemporary applications.[143] Instead, Kostomarov applied the practical experience he had gained in exile as editor of the newspaper in Saratov[144] and translated his historical theories so as to mesh with those of moderate provincial re- formers throughout Russia; he retained this stance until after the emancipation of the serfs was promulgated.

Kostomarov's disciples were far less reticent in pointing out the relevance of his ideas for present-day Russia. In Kiev, a graduate student argued that in ages of reform the social sciences come to the fore, and that now history taught that the provinces must be restructured and made as auton- omous as they had been in the distant past.[145] Meanwhile in Moscow a future leader of the historical profession, Kon- stantin Bestuzhev-Riumin, hailed the effort "to bring from behind the apparent homogeneity these distinct ethno- graphic and geographic unities" as "a task worthy of the historian."[146] Criticizing Chicherin and praising Kosto- marov, he demanded the immediate establishment of ad- ministrative decentralization and provincial self-govern- ment within a Russian federation.[147]

---

[143] *Den*, No. 29 (1863), 349-61; M. A. Rubach insists nonetheless that Kostomarov's federal ideas were revolutionary: "Federalisticheskie teorii . . . ," p. 24.

[144] Kostomarov, "Avtobiografiia . . . ," pp. 27ff.; V. I. Semevskii, "N. I. Kostomarov, 1817-1885," *Russkaia Starina*, xvii, 1886, p. 195.

[145] A. V. Romanovich-Slavatinskii, in *Kievskii Telegraf*, No. 26 (1859), 110-11; see also *Moskovskie Vedomosti*, Nos. 239, 276 (1859).

[146] K. Bestuzhev-Riumin, "Kritika," *Otechestvennye Zapiski*, cxxxiv (1861), 55.

[147] K. Bestuzhev-Riumin (unsigned), "O neobkhodimosti novogo metoda v naukakh gosudarstvennykh," *Moskovskoe Obozrenie*, No. 2

The argument presented by the provincialist historians squared neatly with the reformist ideology of the day and was quickly absorbed into respectable public debate. The provincial theory of early Russian history was not entirely stable, however, and at several points could be turned to support more radical programs. Kostomarov and his followers, for instance, neglected to specify how the tsar might fit into their federal system and could rightly be accused of seeking to limit the autocracy. Similarly, Kostomarov's belief that the peasant masses alone retained the ancient spirit of locality could easily be read to support a strongly populist program.

The man who provided these radical interpretations and thereby went far to destroy the respectability of the provincial school after 1862 had himself risen from the peasantry through an Orthodox seminary to become a popular, if erratic, teacher at Kazan University. Unlike Kostomarov, Afanasii Shchapov detested provincial life but hated the central government even more.[148] Under the influence of Cherkasskii's essay on Tocqueville and the urgings of a disciple of Kostomarov's at Kazan, Shchapov channelled these aversions into a belief in self-government and a form of federalism which he termed "regionalism" (*oblastnost*).[149] Shortly after becoming the first professor openly to preach these principles, however, he was arrested and exiled to Siberia for delivering an oration at the funeral of people killed when government troops repressed an uprising of peasants protesting the emancipation, which had just been promulgated. This experience quickly radicalized Shchapov

---

(1859), 22-23; "Istoricheske i politicheskoe doktrinerstvo v ego prakticheskom polozhenii," *Otechestvennye Zapiski*, cxxxix (1861), 3-6; Bestuzhev-Riumin abandoned these views by 1865 and treated them condescendingly in his memoirs: *Vospominaniia* . . . p. 57.

[148] A. P. Shchapov, *A. P. Shchapov v Irkutske* (*neizdannye materialy*), V. K. Kuzmin, ed., Irkutsk, 1938, pp. i-iv.

[149] G. A. Luchinskii, ed., *Sochineniia A. P. Shchapova*, 3 vols., St. Petersburg, 1906-08, iii, xxii; on Kostomarov's disciple, S. V. Eshevskii, see his *Sochineniia*, 3 vols., Moscow, 1870, especially i, 125-251.

who, as a populist martyr, came eventually to exercise influence over Siberian separatists.[150]

In view of his humble origin and personal identification with the Old Believers whom he studied, Shchapov's democratic beliefs are not at all surprising. What is striking, though, is the extent to which his historical work before 1861 fits squarely within the broad movement for provincial reform. His *déclaration de foi* could have been penned by most of the moderate reformers who later denounced him:

> I declare from the very start that I bring with me to the chair of Russian history at this university not the idea of the State, not that of centralization, but that of *nationality*, and of *regionalism*. Here is a new principle not yet firmly established in our scholarship: the principle— please allow the expression—of regionalism. Until now the prevailing idea has been that of centralization; all the strands of provincial history have been swallowed in the general theory of the development of the state. But the history of Russia is, more than anything, the history of . . . the various regions before and after centralization.[151]

He believed separatism to be impossible and undesirable[152] and much as he opposed the alien "boyar class" he was quite willing to allow the gentry a place in provincial rule if that would reduce the role of the central administration.[153] The extent to which Shchapov before his exile was typical of provincial reformers of the era can be seen most clearly in an unsolicited letter which he managed to hand to Alexander II. In it he cited historical precedents to sup-

---

[150] Mikhail Lemke, *Nikolai Mikhailovich Iadrinstsev,* St. Petersburg, 1904, p. 41.

[151] Luchinskii, ed., *Sochineniia* . . . , p. xxxi.

[152] Josef Wachendorf, *Regionalismus, Raskol und Volk als Hauptprobleme der Russischen Geschichte bei A. P. Shchapov,* Cologne, 1964, pp. 67ff.

[153] Shchapov, "Zametka o samoupravlenii," *Ocherki,* 1862, Nos. 2-3, in *Sochineniia* . . . , I, 789.

port the cause of provincial banks, locally controlled schools, and the establishment of provincial councils in rural centers to supervise local taxation and public works. In Shchapov's proposal the principle of national taxation emerged intact and provision was made even for the review of local governments by the Ministry of Internal Affairs![154] For all his later radical populism, Shchapov before 1861 helped rewrite Russian history to serve the ends of the provincial reformers.

IDEOLOGY AND ACTION

Thanks to the efforts of Nikolai Kostomarov, Afanasii Shchapov, Konstantin Bestuzhev-Riumin and the numerous minor historians and ethnographers whose works filled the scholarly and popular journals of the day, a truly "provincial" outlook on the Russian past emerged after 1855. Though they never referred to themselves as such, these historians were fully as much a school as the statists. Its hallmarks were a warm admiration for what was believed to have been Russia's pre-Mongol federation, hatred of Moscovy for destroying it, and a boundless optimism that political unity could be preserved without submitting the natural diversity of the land and people to an administrative straitjacket. These beliefs suffused all of their individual writings in the years from 1856 to 1862 and made them appear as parts of a single endeavor.

Subsequent scholarship has generally rejected the main assertion of the provincialist school that a federation of provinces or regions once thrived in ancient Russia.[155] Moreover, the romantic and, at times, pathetic sense of longing

---

[154] A. P. Shchapov, "Pisma k Aleksandru II," *Krasnyi Arkhiv*, 1926, VI, 160-64.

[155] L. V. Cherepnin, *Obrazovanie Russkogo tsentralizirannogo gosudarstva v XIV-XV vekakh*, Moscow, 1960, Chaps. I, IV; a scholar who maintains the federal view is George Vernadsky, *A History of Russia*, 5 vols., New Haven, 1943-69, II, *Kieven Russia*, Chap. VIII, pp. 1-3.

for a lost golden age that motivated Kostomarov and his school is easy to discern in retrospect.[156] Yet, the provincialists should not be judged by their influence on later scholars but rather by their impact on the times in which they lived. In terms of numbers of adherents, quantity of works published, and total sway in their society—especially on its younger members—the provincialists quickly eclipsed the rival state school and for a few years before 1862-1863 could claim to represent the dominant attitude toward the national past.

The provincialist perspective appealed to educated Russians because it harmonized with the broader ideology of reform of which it was a part. Unlike the statist view, it took cognizance of the faults of provincial government that had become acute during the previous reign and pointed the way toward their solution. Its function was not to convert Russians to new beliefs but instead to assure them that their own observations on provincial life and government were correct and that they could advocate reform without disloyalty to the national past. Even those who, like the Grand Duke Konstantin, rejected the more extreme statements of Kostomarov and considered Shchapov a dangerous radical, could find in the scores of local studies a refreshing emphasis with which they could innocently sympathize.

Whatever its historical accuracy, the reinterpretation of early Russian history was an ideological event no less important than the reinterpretation of western European development that the Russians undertook during the same years. Both movements of thought realigned the landmarks on which contemporaries took their political bearings and both developments, while pertaining nominally to geographically or temporally remote issues, had as their subject Russia in the 1850s. By nurturing a frame of mind attuned to administrative problems and by translating this

[156] See, for example, Kostomarov's speech in honor of the 100th anniversary of the establishment of the Russian state in 1862, GPB, Kostomarov archive.

general mood into goals for provincial reform they stimulated the growth of a cast of mind which, like all ideologies, was potentially the first step on the road to power.[157]

In what direction would this ideology lead Russia? It must be stressed that in the mid-nineteenth century the broad directions of state development were far less clear than they are to us today—that the localist state seemed a living possibility. But for all their apparent contemporaneity, were the principles of local self-government and administrative decentralization really what Russia's ailing provincial system required? Advocates of the provincialist ideology assumed quite logically that the underdevelopment of the Russian provinces was a consequence of the prevailing system of local administration. But their reasoning, however logical, may have been inverted. The underdevelopment of the provinces can with equal logic be viewed as a cause rather than an effect of the inadequate local administration. If this were so, to turn the administration over to elected or appointed local authorities would deny to the provinces the regular contact with the economically and socially more advanced capitals that alone could induce development. It would deny them national tax funds at a time when the demand and need for new local functions was growing faster than the provincial tax base. It would deny them the help of top civil servants who, but for central regulations, would never have consented to serve even briefly in Riazan or Smolensk. According to this line of thought, the proposed reforms were likely to aggravate the very tendencies that they were designed to alleviate.

This paradoxical interpretation corresponds closely to the experience of many developing nations today with administrative deconcentration and public self-rule.[158] It bears emphasis, however, that nobody in the post-Crimean dec-

---

[157] Barrington Moore, *Political Power and Social Theory*, Cambridge, 1958, pp. 9-27.

[158] Maddick, *Democracy* . . . , p. 134; Riggs, *Administration* . . . , pp. 338-44.

ade considered this as a possibility. The statists, whose beliefs placed them within reach of it, did not grasp it on account of their persistently abstract and antiempirical frame of mind, while the provincialists, confined as they were by their mistaken belief that the Russian administration had been successfully concentrated, were deaf to any suggestion that self-government and decentralization were not the sought-for panaceas.

Yet, ironically, the provincialists, who surpassed everyone in their hostility to the existing provincial apparatus, ended by not taking it seriously. They were content to denounce it as a historical mistake and thus to minimize grossly its importance to Russia and the extent to which it was woven into the fabric of national life. By failing to consider the historical and practical roots of the state's attempt to rule Russia from the center through administrative means, they became like the farmer who, disappointed in his stunted corn, sought to improve his yields by pulling out the crop and beginning anew with rice, rather than by fertilizing the corn. They blithely assumed that the mere substitution of new administrative structures for the old would renovate the entire system from top to bottom. This belief cast them in the most ironic light possible: in their unflagging faith in the efficacy of structural change they fell prey to the formal and mechanistic way of thinking that characterized the system which they so despised!

III | The Politics
of Decentralization

If the strength of an ideology is measured in terms of the numbers of its adherents, the ideology of provincial reform in Russia was very powerful indeed. Within two years after the end of the Crimean War scores of educated Russians came to believe, explicitly or tacitly, that administrative decentralization and self-government were entirely within the natural order of things and the sole means by which the provinces could be saved from bureaucratic suffocation. If, however, the strength of an ideology is measured in terms of its ability to mold reality to accord with its precepts, then Russian provincialism cannot be so easily judged. At once questions arise as to the process by which reform might come to the existing provincial institutions and the role that ideas and models might play in that process. Fortunately, it is possible in the case of administrative decentralization to follow with some precision the metamorphosis of ideological goals into working policies.

Local administrative reform might never have become an issue of prime urgency had it been left to the normal processes of government. Lacking an efficient system of inspection and control, the central ministries were prevented from perceiving the full depth of the problem. Professionally insecure local bureaucrats shared responsibility for the resultant inaction by covering up shortcomings within their administrations. Together the central and local functionaries reduced to a trickle the flow of critical appraisals and feedback that is the hallmark of the healthy administrative organization.

Bureaucracies suffering from these defects commonly reform themselves only as a response to crisis.[1] A strong shock may at once drastically increase the flow of data to and from the center, force central and local leaders to suspend their habitual distaste for unsettling "showdown" situations and compel them to search for alternatives to existing models of organization. The Crimean War had precisely this effect on the Russian civil service. Yet even before this, in 1852, important preliminary steps toward reform were taken in response to lesser crises. Among these the most significant was the creation of a "Committee on Reducing Correspondence." Notwithstanding its eminently bureaucratic name, this body served as a reform commission which, by the fall of Sevastopol, was already well organized and ready to consider any ideas on provincial reform. It was here that the possibility of deconcentrating the administration was first raised.

THE COMMITTEE ON REDUCING CORRESPONDENCE

The 1837 law on governorship had been designed to offset the inertia born of bureaucratic formalism.[2] To the surprise of its sponsors, the law had precisely the opposite effect due to grotesquely complex procedures introduced into the Provincial Directorates during the same year. Larger staffs were required, but the high cost of the military ad-

[1] See Crozier, *The Bureaucratic Phenomenon*, pp. 226ff.
[2] See pages 33-34.

venture in Hungary in 1849 left the state's treasury unable to support them. By 1851 the cost of maintaining a clerical force adequate to meet the complex demands imposed in 1837 was so great that Sergei Lanskoi, acting Minister of Internal Affairs, was compelled to reopen the entire administrative issue. He presented the Senate with a series of proposals designed to reduce the size of his ministry's staff without impeding the flow of work.[3] Meanwhile, the Senate had been studying the same problem on its own initiative and had independently reached the conclusion that procedural reform was overdue. It therefore issued an urgent order in 1852 for the ministries to explore all means of unraveling procedural tangles and limiting correspondence so that a reduced staff would be effective as well as economical.[4] Within months, an initial set of guidelines or "Rules for Reducing Correspondence" had been drawn up, and a Committee on Reducing Correspondence established to elaborate them further.

The chairman of the new committee was a military man known for his executive vigor, Adjutant General Dmitrii Bibikov, who was later to serve briefly as interim Minister of Internal Affairs. His first act upon taking command of the Committee on Reducing Correspondence was to admit the failure of normal control procedures and to issue an appeal to all provincial governors for suggestions and proposals relating to the problem of red tape.[5] By the time replies began to arrive from the provinces late in 1852 the committee had been organized with representatives drawn from all those ministries and departments with branches at the provincial level. Though Bibikov served as chairman, the guiding light

---

[3] *Ministerstvo vnutrennykh del, istoricheskii ocherk*, 3 vols., St. Petersburg, 1902, I, 55.

[4] TsGIA-SSSR, f. 1314 (archive of the Committee on Reducing Correspondence), op. 1, ed. khr. 27, p. 1. The new rules on correspondence included six sections and touched on everything from the Senate to the lowest provincial scribe. E. Anuchin, *Istoricheskii obzor* . . . , pp. 73-74.

[5] *Ibid.*, p. 12. Memorandum of S. S. Lanskoi, December 16, 1857.

of the committee from its first tentative talks to its dramatic work of the late fifties was the aging but dedicated Sergei Lanskoi.[6] Also, the committee welcomed outside support from the efficient Grand Duke Konstantin Nikolaevich and Count Peter Kleinmichel.[7]

During 1853 the State Council reviewed proposals on administrative practices submitted by the committee and by year's end had adopted a number of them as law.[8] In the early phase of its work the committee proceeded on the assumption that greater efficiency alone would render the provinces better governed, enable the ministries to reduce their staffs, and thus bring about the desperately needed fiscal savings. Compared with the earlier efforts of Count Perovskii, the committee was eminently successful in achieving at least the second and third of these objectives. As a result, the Department of General Affairs of the Minis-

[6] The precise membership of the Committee on Reducing Correspondence is not known. The entire list of names appearing on documents in the committee's archive is as follows: Grand Duke Konstantin Nikolaevich, Count P. Kleinmichel, D. Bibikov, A. Taneev, D. Gavrilovich, S. Laskoi, and Baron M. A. Korf.

[7] The Grand Duke, however, was soon appointed first admiral of the fleet, so his interest in administrative reform was channeled into military affairs during the years that the committee worked most intensively. Kleinmichel's interest in the application of the telegraph to military administration made it impossible for him to participate in the committee's work on a day-to-day basis. TsGIA-SSSR, f. 1314, op. 1, ed. khr. 27, pp. 1-3. On Kleinmichel and the telegraph see *Ministerstvo vnutrennykh del . . .* , I, 140ff. Even after Konstantin entered the Naval Ministry he was not lost to the cause of administrative decentralization. M. A. Korf, writing in 1866 on the reform era (*Vzgliad na vnutrennye preobrazovaniia poslednogo desiatiletiia*) states that the Grand Duke's reforms of the navy in 1855 to 1858 served as a stimulus to reform in other agencies. "From this time on," wrote Korf, "the [navy] itself began everywhere to recognize the slowness and unsatisfactoriness of procedure . . . as a consequence, work was begun everywhere to institute all possible decentralization, with the idea of giving in each instance more independence and freedom." TsGAOR, f. 728, No. 2863, op. 1, 1866, p. 22.

[8] On November 26, 1853, Bibikov reported on the committee to the tsar; on December 12, 1853, the report was turned over to Bludov. TsGIA-SSSR, f. 1314, op. 1, ed. khr. 27, pp. 1ff.

try of Internal Affairs was eliminated entirely and a further sixty-seven offices abolished elsewhere in the central ministry.[9] But the advent of war in March 1854 quickly obliterated this gain, so the committee was granted only a year in which to bask in the glory of having reduced central administrative staffs to below their 1837 levels.

At the same time that it was attempting to reduce duplication of effort in Petersburg, the committee was alert to the jumbled relations among the provincial and district agencies and between province and capital. Urged on by memoranda from governors in the field it submitted several proposals to the State Council before and during the Crimean War. Typical of these was a plan to return control of surveying to district authorities and a ruling which enabled local building and road commissions to deal with their clients directly rather than through the central ministerial offices.[10] The fact that such changes were being undertaken before the Sevastopol crisis suggests that more feedback and hence greater prospects for self-reform existed in the administration than has been pictured above. Yet, on the one hand, few reports critical of the administration were submitted from the provinces—no more than ten; on the other hand, the committee which received them remained isolated, and far more of its proposals were tabled than were accepted.[11] In this respect the obvious compari-

---

[9] *Ministerstvo vnutrennykh del* . . . , I, 55, lists the reduction in the central organs of the MVD as: 40 ministerial aides, 18 scribes, 9 others (total, 67). In comparison to 1839, the reduction reported is as follows (staff after reduction): Executive Police, 49; Spiritual Affairs, 20; Department of Economics, 80; Medical Section, 39; Military Medical, 40; others, 42 (total, 270). (*Ibid.*, pp. 55-56.) It is claimed in the official history of the MVD that in 1839 it required 287 people to perform these same tasks.

[10] TsGIA-SSSR, f. 1314, op. 1, khr. 27, pp. 22-23.

[11] TsGIA-SSSR, f. 1314, op. 1, ed. khr. 27, pp. 16-23. Also, f. 1314, op. 1, d. 55. Report of Governor A. D. Ignatiev of Saratov to the committee, November 30, 1854, and f. 1314, op. 1, d. 48; proposals of the Governor of Riazan, P. P. Novosiltsev, concerning accounting in the provinces. This last issue lay dormant until 1857 when it was finally resolved by order of the tsar (p. 11).

son between the Russian Committee on Reducing Correspondence and the contemporary British Northcote-Trevelyan Commission breaks down, for the latter had the full support of leading statesmen in its pursuit of civil service reform.

The Crimean disaster electrified the sponsors and members of the Committee on Reducing Correspondence. In his annual report for 1856 the Minister of Internal Affairs acknowledged that the cost of government had again risen, due to the wartime deluge of paperwork; the problem had reached "enormous proportions," he declared, and a solution would have to be discovered immediately if the entire provincial apparatus were to be saved from collapse.[12] At this juncture the tsar promoted the committee's unofficial helmsman, Sergei Lanskoi, to the post of Minister of Internal Affairs. Once in his new office Lanskoi was beset by a host of critical problems but, in recognition of the importance of the provincial administration, he took personal charge of the Committee on Reducing Correspondence.[13]

The financial situation in 1856 was considerably more grim than in 1851. The sudden inflation that took place in Russia at the end of the war enabled the propertied classes to recoup the losses they had suffered during the fighting, but for the government it brought no relief at all.[14] Revenues from customs duties had fallen during the war and the yield of direct taxes did not rise significantly. Over the whole period from 1851 to 1857 the state's income remained virtually static at 220 to 230 million rubles per annum. During the same years the debt rose precipitously, reaching 2,310 million in 1860. To make matters worse, nearly 15 million rubles of hard currency were being drained abroad annually for luxuries and only 3 millions of gold and silver

[12] TsGIA-SSSR, f. 1314, op. 1, ed. khr. 27, pp. 12-13.
[13] For a view of Lanskoi see A. I. Levshin, "Dostopamiatnye minuty v moei zhizni. Zapiska Alekseia Iraklevicha Levshina," *Russkii Arkhiv*, xxiii, No. 3, 1885, p. 528.
[14] Walter M. Pintner, "Inflation during the Crimean War," *American Slavic and East European Review*, xviii (February 1959), 87.

were being mined in Siberia each year.[15] Foreign investors were understandably dismayed by these conditions and Russian financial leaders were forced to undertake stringent economy measures. Restrictions on foreign travel were considered, as was the introduction of state lotteries, luxury taxes, and restrictions on the import of English machinery.[16] The militarily oriented autocracy even consented to cut back the navy's shore establishments and to reduce administrative staffs in both the army and navy in the hope of effecting savings.

In the Ministry of Internal Affairs the campaign against paperwork had this same end. Several means of reducing expenditures were explored: cutbacks in public works construction, the sale of state properties, and even the transferal of certain expenses from public to nonstate tax funds. In this atmosphere of stringent parsimony the old nostrum that all problems in the provincial administration could be cured with periodic injections of additional personnel was irrelevant—it was simply impossible to pay more staff. Nor did the mere reduction of paperwork hold the promise that it had five years earlier—the situation was too grave to be remedied so simply.[17]

Recognition of this state of affairs was widespread by 1856. The many proposals submitted to the committee that year were marked by the sense of liberation that comes from having rejected outworn shibboleths. Although no new conception of the relationship of provincial administrations to the capital had yet established itself, there was a general awareness in official circles that the local side of the local-central equation had to be emphasized.

[15] K. N. Lebedev, "Iz zapisok senatora K. N. Lebedeva," *Russkii Arkhiv*, XLIX, No. 1, 1911, pp. 9-91.

[16] Lebedev, "Iz zapisok . . . ," pp. 92ff.

[17] TsGIA-SSSR, f. 1389, op. 3, d. 11 (1859-62 revision of Vladimir province by Senator Karger), p. 60. In 1860 in Vladimir province there was no money to pay the police. This problem was only partially rectified by the pay raise of 1860-61 discussed in TsGIA-SSSR, f. 1286 (1860), op. 21, d. 1090.

For example, a memorandum by State Councillor Nikolai Bakhtin called on the state to prepare reforms based upon the new local statistical studies and on historical research into provincial life.[18] Other proposals went beyond Bakhtin's by advocating specific and fundamental changes. That presented by the Petersburg censor and senator, Vladimir Tsie, during the coronation festivities in 1856 is of particular interest in this respect, for it epitomized and, in fact, helped mold the policy followed by the committee during the last and most important phase of its existence. Tsie took his title from the full name of the committee: "Measures Necessary for Limiting Correspondence and Simplifying Procedure in State Institutions."[19] In it he posited two possible courses of reform: either "to diminish useless formalism and superfluous letter-writing" or "to increase the degree of power and the sphere of action of local and subordinate powers, that is, to limit centralization."

> The first [policy] can relieve civil servants and save them from burdensome and fruitless labor . . . the second [i.e., decentralization] eliminates all of the superfluous barriers and red tape which are inevitable whenever there exists a multiplicity of governmental institutions and a huge scale of distances as in Russia; finally, it gives local powers the freedom of movement without which one cannot expect the requisite ardor for public affairs from them or, in all fairness, hold them legally responsible for its absence. But to achieve the former, i.e., to cut down on correspondence, it is necessary immediately to undertake the latter, i.e., to increase the degree of local power, for otherwise no reduction of correspondence will be achieved in reality and, as experience shows [the allusion is to the 1837 law on procedure in the Provincial Directorates] there might even be an increase. Obviously, as

[18] TsGAOR, f. 722 (Marble Palace archive), op. 1, ed. khr. 605, pp. 2-10. On Bakhtin see TsGIA-SSSR, f. 1161, op. 7, d. 62.
[19] GPB, f. 833 (V. A. Tsie archive), ed. khr. 292.

117

long as the essential cause exists its consequences will inevitably remain.

It is impossible to determine whether Tsie's analysis was prompted primarily by his reading of French writers and study of foreign systems or by direct observation of Russia's bureaucracy. But he himself acknowledged that he was "inspired by the example of many other states"[20] and that the experience of England and France were prominent in his mind. Indeed, his analysis of local administration reads like contemporary French publicists:

> The chief and almost sole cause of the constant growth of correspondence in Russia is the huge and all-swallowing centralization, and the cause of centralization can be called the absence of trust. Consequently, in order to cut down on correspondence it is necessary to diminish superfluous centralization; one must devote all energy to establishing relations between the central and local powers on a cornerstone of *trust*.
>
> For trust to rest on a firm basis . . . it is necessary:
>
> 1) to raise the prestige of the local authorities;
> 2) to define with precision the extent of their power;
> 3) to secure their existence materially;
> 4) to be decisive in the choice of responsible people . . .

Having set forth these general principles, Tsie then attempted to define a standard by which the sphere of provincial administrative authority could be distinguished from the entirety of state functions: "it is essential to define not those cases where the local authorities should act on their own power, for such instances are innumerable and the listing of them would lead to restrictions, difficulties, and endless misunderstandings; *instead, we must specify precisely only those areas where, for the good of society, it is beneficial to limit the local powers by the central.*" [Italics

[20] GPB, f. 833 (V. A. Tsie archive), ed. kh. 292, p. 4.

118

added] With this definition Tsie broke through the wall that had obstructed reform during the reign of Nicholas I by introducing a nonbureaucratic standard for measuring the effectiveness of civil administration. Rather than ask whether the ministries were in regular and harmonious communication with their local agents, he asked what the substance of these communications were. Recognizing that the provinces were underdeveloped and undergoverned, he made "the good of society" the measure of the administration and was willing to change the administration to achieve this objective. In other words, efficiency was not an end in itself and structural changes should be welcomed if they would benefit the localities ruled. Tsie's brand of bureaucratic deconcentration was particularly bold in that he rejected the notion that local functions were those duties *not* performed by the central authorities; rather, he conceived of the central apparatus as performing only those tasks beyond the capacities of local administrators. In effect, he set the relationship of local to central government on its head.

Tsie's analysis would be familiar to anyone acquainted with the constitutional history of federalized governments, but in Russia his solution was a considerable innovation, the more so because he spoke from a responsible post within the Petersburg bureaucracy itself. The Committee on Reducing Correspondence was swayed by Tsie's reasoning and in 1856 and 1857 it adopted several of his proposals. Provincial governors were empowered to make sales of certain immovable state properties without central authorization; governors could henceforth approve punishments imposed by the judiciary without referring back to the capital; another measure simplified financial relations between governors and the Ministry of Finances; monthly gubernatorial reports on the movement of convicts en route to Siberia were abolished; and governors were empowered to decide on civil service pensions without central authorization.[21]

[21] TsGIA-SSSR, f. 1314, op. 1, ed. khr. 27, pp. 16-23.

Though individually inconsequential, these measures together reflect an unprecedented willingness on the part of the committee to enhance the influence of top provincial administrators at the expense of the central bureaucracy.

Whatever doubt remained about the intention of the government to undertake a policy of administrative deconcentration was removed by Alexander II. At the time of his coronation the tsar had astounded the gentry of Moscow province with hints that the liberation of the serfs was unavoidable. Sergei Lanskoi, who favored a gradual form of emancipation, had objected to what he considered the tsar's imprudent haste in addressing the Moscow lords. Although Lanskoi's aide, Alexander Levshin, strongly censured him for this opinion, the Minister was not guilty of dragging his feet. On the contrary, Lanskoi knew from his own investigations that the majority of gentry opposed emancipation and that a precipitous approach to that issue would spoil the long-range program of improving local administration through structural and procedural reform.[22]

In pursuit of this end, Lanskoi prevailed on Alexander on October 21, 1856, to proclaim that the governorships would be strengthened by providing them with "greater means of getting at local needs." Echoing the decentralizing theme of the Tsie memorandum, Alexander II declared that this could be accomplished ". . . by strengthening their influence on affairs and on individuals, broadening their power to utilize financial resources for matters relating to the general welfare, and by instituting other similar measures while not disturbing the general order of provincial government, and in particular by seeking to cut down the formalities and impediments which hinder the provincial governors in their action."[23]

With this seal of royal support on his own policy, Lanskoi

[22] On Levshin's criticism see Levshin, "Dostopamiatnye minuty . . . ," p. 477. On Lanskoi's investigation of the attitudes of the gentry gathered for the coronation, see Levshin, *ibid.* pp. 483-84.

[23] *MSVUK*, I, otd. 3, p. 4.

immediately issued a confidential circular to selected governors. In it he repeated verbatim the text of the tsar's announcement and added:

> . . . I request Your Excellency, after carefully examining the essence of the proposals which I have communicated to you,[24] to compose separate memoranda on every local agency of each ministry outlining those procedures which require modifications. You, Sir, are constantly following such matters and can define better than anyone else what hinders you in benefiting the province entrusted to you and what is needed to achieve the goals which you set.
>
> It is desirable that you begin work on this without delay and that you express your opinions to me with complete frankness.

Finally, so that it might be quite clear that the Committee on Reducing Correspondence had taken a new turn, Lanskoi concluded: "In the present circumstances you should not be limited to the proposals which you have heretofore submitted concerning the reduction of correspondence, for now the widest possible sphere of enquiry has been opened to you."[25] The provincial governors responded immediately, forwarding their proposals to the Ministry of Internal Affairs where they were studied by Lanskoi and the Committee on Reducing Correspondence. Thus the seventy-one-year-old architect of the local reform movement gave it a decisive new thrust.

With the consideration of replies to Lanskoi, the debate over administrative decentralization entered a new phase. During the years 1857 to 1858 the primary focus of attention shifted back from the Ministry of Internal Affairs to the newly formed Committee of Ministers in Petersburg. There the two-pronged effort of Lanskoi and his ministry's agents,

[24] These proposals were not extant in 1870 when the *MSVUK* was collected and they cannot be found today in either TsGIA-SSSR, TsGAOR, or PD. *MSVUK*, I, otd. 3, p. 2n.

[25] *MSVUK*, I, otd. 3, p. 2.

the governors, to restructure the provincial apparatus encountered rigid opposition from the other ministers. These politically astute functionaries sensed quite correctly that the proposed deconcentration placed their own local agencies in imminent danger of falling under the direct tutelage of the Ministry of Internal Affairs.

If the intention of Vladimir Tsie and Sergei Lanskoi had been to translate local reform from the realm of ideology to concrete action they had succeeded by 1857. But in succeeding, they unintentionally sparked a struggle in the top levels of the autocracy which partook more of power politics than of pragmatic disagreement over policy.

Before turning to this interministerial showdown, however, one element in the spectrum of forces requires further clarification: the governors. Officials in the Petersburg offices of the Ministry of Internal Affairs might well have considered the problems besetting these top provincial administrators to have been solved. Had not the minister himself invited the governors to express their views on their work? Had he not championed their cause before the other ministries and even the tsar? Yet things were not quite so ideal. In fact, the governors had long since taken affairs into their own hands and had independently established themselves as a new pressure group in the autocracy. For the first time in its history the Ministry of Internal Affairs had to face a serious challenge from its own local officials. In taking up the cause of decentralization Lanskoi acted as much to co-opt this incipient revolt in his own ranks as to lead the Russian government to a new administrative policy.

PROVINCIAL GOVERNORS TURN TO REFORM

By its nature the Russian governorship of the mid-nineteenth century was a conservative institution dedicated to maintaining the even flow of public business amidst the flux of provincial life. The men who filled gubernatorial posts were selected for their ability to achieve this end. Though on the whole an able group, they were certainly not distinguished for their ingeniousness at initiating reform proposals or boldness at striking defiant political poses. Yet this is precisely what numerous civil governors of Russia were driven to do in the years after the fall of Sevastopol. In so doing, they demonstrated clearly the pluralism of interests that existed within the nominally unitary autocratic government.

That the governors faced particularly acute bureaucratic paralysis after the Crimean War is evident from a list of outstanding administrative problems in Vladimir province drawn up by order of the Senate in 1859. The astounded investigators filed a closely written list covering 260 pages and detailing literally thousands of unresolved matters including several score that had dragged on since 1849.[26] This extraordinary backlog was paralleled in most other provinces where civil administrators had fulfilled military functions during the war. Frustrated ministerial officials met this situation by demanding that the governors show a clean work sheet within a year after the coronation, a crude measure that had the deplorable consequence of alienating precisely those governors who took their duties most seriously.

Typical of this group was Peter Valuev, the talented career civil servant who had taken on the thankless task of representing the tsar's interests to the Baltic German nobility of Courland.[27] In an anonymous essay written as he left the gubernatorial post, Valuev asked rhetorically "Which of our governors or even of his subordinates can properly and accurately execute all of the duties entrusted to him by the legal code?"[28] Viktor Artsimovich, Governor of Tobolsk province, shared Valuev's feelings. After five years of frustration in office he bemoaned the fact that "The spirit of

[26] TsGIA-SSSR, f. 1281, op. 6, d. 39, pp. 36-170.
[27] TsGIA-SSSR, f. 1162, op. 6, p. 59, *Zasluzhnaia zapiska Valueva.*
[28] P. A. Valuev, "Duma Russkaia (1855)," *Russkaia Starina,* LXIX, March 1891, pp. 354-55. This remarkable testament, written in 1855, passed from hand to hand and received considerable attention from diverse figures. *Ibid.,* p. 359.

lifeless bureaucratism has penetrated deeply into all higher institutions. Everywhere one meets the same answers: 'It doesn't depend on us,' 'It's being seen to,' 'we need more information,' etc., and meanwhile important local questions remain unanswered for years. The essential work of a governor of a province disappears in a mass of details, and often he himself has trouble locating things amidst the chancelleries and clerks."[29] Unable to compel obedience from his own civil and police staff, Artsimovich had to choose between falsifying his annual reports—a common way out[30] —or appealing to his superiors in Petersburg for help. He chose the latter. This only increased Artsimovich's anger, for he discovered that in Petersburg ". . . little attention and respect are shown the governors of our provinces; from the capital they seem like nothing but department heads."[31] Only one level of appeal remained, the tsar. Neither Artsimovich nor Valuev took their case this far, but General Muraviev, the Governor-General of Siberia, did, and vowed to resign unless he received "an expression of special trust from the tsar; I feel that I must be secured against those

[29] *Viktor Antonovich Artsimovich—vospominaniia—kharakteristika,* St. Petersburg, 1904, p. 155.

[30] See Valuev, "Duma Russkaia," p. 354: "Look at the annual reports. Everything possible is done everywhere; successes are everywhere; everything is being seen to, if not immediately, at least shortly, and in proper order. Glitter above; below—clay." A more concrete example of falsification in annual reports can be found in comparing the 1858 report of the Vladimir governor (TsGIA-SSSR, f. 1281; op. 6, No. 49) with the *reviziia* by Lebedev ("Iz zapisok . . . ," pp. 116-17), and Karger (TsGIA-SSSR, f. 1389, op. 3, d. 11) of the same province in 1859 and in 1862. In 1859 it was reported that "procedure in the civil government is quite satisfactory" (p. 15) and that no work was outstanding. Two years later the 260-page list of unfinished affairs alluded to above was drawn up.

[31] . . . *Artsimovich* . . . , pp. 155-57. Valuev complained that he was subordinated "not to Messrs. the Ministers but to the clerks of this or that ministry." Valuev, "Duma Russkaia," p. 356. In TsGAOR, f. 647, op. 1, ed. khr. 53, pp. 10-13, there is a memorandum "Duma russkogo grazhdanina" by N. N. Nezvanov (pseud.) proposing elaborate procedures whereby governors' reports might be more thoroughly and swiftly reviewed and acted upon by the ministers themselves.

unpleasantnesses to which I have been subjected. They will either kill me or force me to become a blind executor of the *letter* of the law."[32]

The fact that such letters were being written is evidence of the widespread malaise among the governors by 1856. Ineffective locally and isolated from their superiors, they turned to analyzing the administrative system itself in hopes of discovering alternative structures. Valuev wrote various critical analyses of "centralization"; Artsimovich, a regular reader of the *Revue des Deux Mondes*, analyzed the French *préfecture*; and the Governor-General of Siberia allowed his subordinates (with both Bakunin and Kropotkin among them) to discuss the chances "of establishing a United States of Siberia, federated across the Pacific with the United States."[33] At the same time, they all endeavored to improve their own staffs as a necessary preparation for achieving greater administrative autonomy from their superiors.

The first step toward realizing this objective was to fill all the vacancies left by retirement and resignation during the Crimean War. But during the years from 1855 to 1857 a partial freeze on hiring was imposed. Baron Haxthausen, who was familiar with the agencies which collected such data, stated in 1857 that governors required twice as many new civil service recruits as the treasury would permit them to employ.[34] Nor was money the only source of the difficulties. It became increasingly difficult to fill even those places

[32] Ivan Barsukov, *Graf Nikolai Muraviev-Amurskii* (*Materialy dlia biografii*), 2 vols., Moscow, 1891, I, 471.

[33] Valuev, "Duma Russkaia," p. 356; . . . *Artsimovich* . . . , pp. 40, 151-57; P. Kropotkin, *Memoirs of a Revolutionist*, Boston, 1899, p. 162; also M. Bakunin, *Correspondence, 1860-1874*, Michael Dragomanov, ed., Paris, 1896, pp. 103-06.

[34] TsGIA-SSSR, f. 1180, d. 81; Baron Haxthausen, "Zamechaniia o razvitii i ustroistve uchrezhdeniia gubernii v Rossii v otnoshenii ego k unichtozheniiu krepostnogo sostoianiia," p. 388. The manuscript is not dated but from the date of other papers in the same folder we can assume that it is from the summer of 1857, when Haxthausen met the Grand Duchess Elena Pavlovna at Bad Kissengen.

for which salaries were available. In 1859, for example, the Governor-General of Kiev reported that at least 500 new scribes would be required merely to stabilize the personnel situation in his province.[35] The central staff of the Ministry of Internal Affairs was horrified; Nikolai Miliutin, who read the report for the government, penciled in the margin the rhetorical query "Where could we find five hundred reliable, honest, responsible, and industrious people?"[36]

If the situation regarding semiskilled posts was bleak, the short supply of educated men to fill more responsible posts presented a truly alarming problem. An anonymous correspondent reported that "Every time a position falls vacant in the higher governmental apparatus extreme difficulties arise in filling it."[37] An official study of the pool of skilled bureaucrats revealed that every year 3,000 positions in the civil service fell vacant out of a total of approximately 80,000; at the same time, however, the graduating classes at institutions of higher learning, excluding medical schools, remained constant at only 400.[38] Governors seeking to enhance their independence through better staffs reached an impasse. In Vladimir a Senate investigator found the governor wringing his hands over his staff of ". . . civil servants drawn from one hundred eighteen offices of the navy, from the sabre corps and even from the artillery. Almost the entire office staff of some agencies is composed of seminarians. . . . It is amazing that there is any government left here at all."[39] Even in Petersburg province the picture was deplorable by 1856. In his annual report for that year the military governor openly admitted that the personnel problem had assumed crisis proportions and announced his intention of issuing an appeal to young men in the province's official newspaper. In a dignified but anxious tone, the official

[35] TsGIA-SSSR, f. 869, op. 1, d. 393. Extracts from the report of Count I. I. Vasilchikov, 1859.
[36] *Ibid.*, pp. 14-16.
[37] TsGAOR, f. 647, op. 1, ed. khr. 55, p. 104 (1856-57).
[38] Nikitenko, *Dnevnik*, II, 243.
[39] Lebedev, "Iz zapisok . . . ," pp. 108ff.

argued the case for a career in the provincial service and especially in the districts immediately adjacent to the capital. He attempted to convince young men of fashion that they would not be divorced from society by serving in the royal estates of Tsarskoe Selo, Peterhof, or Gachina, and that their abilities would be more highly esteemed there than in Petersburg itself. He capped the appeal with the ludicrous claim that any farsighted young man should disdain the life of the capital anyway since the lack of fresh air there would be injurious to his health.[40]

The recruitment drive collapsed. Similarly, the efforts of other provincial governors to achieve greater independence for their local administrations by creating efficient staffs broke down. There were exceptions, to be sure, but most governors found themselves thwarted by the sheer impossibility of forging an adequate apparatus from bands of poorly trained novices. Like it or not, they were therefore forced to appeal to Petersburg and to mount a campaign for more money, personnel, and wider prerogatives—i.e., for administrative deconcentration. And like the gentry in its later campaigns for provincial self-government, the governors found themselves in the paradoxical position of seeking reform from the very ministers whose grip they were trying to escape!

This may explain why provincial governors emerged as an interest group when they did and also the uneven mixture of goodwill and rancor with which they received the news from Lanskoi that decentralizing reforms were being contemplated in Petersburg. Had Lanskoi not himself already taken the initiative by broaching a program of decentralization to the tsar, the governors' demands might well have taken a more intractable form than they did. But Alexander's announcement of October 21, 1856, helped preempt the governors' movement. From that date forward the function of the activist governors was not to force the gov-

---

[40] This article was reprinted in an abbreviated form in *Otechestvennye Zapiski*, 1857. *Sovremennaia Khronika* (January 1857), 8.

ernment to undertake a policy that it might not otherwise have followed but to lend support to Lanskoi against those who opposed him within the government.

The channels through which the support of governors for the October 21 policy reached the government were the annual reports and the governors' responses to official rescripts for information and data. Only rarely, as in the case of Valuev's manuscript essay, "A Russian Thought," did the ferment spill over into public modes of communication. As a result, the entire movement was virtually unknown to the public at large. Only in 1862 did the official *Northern Post* (*Severnaia Pochta*) publish an article on the confidential circulars issued by Lanskoi to the governors between 1855 and 1861. Prior to that date they had received no publicity.[41] The fact that the reformist activities of the governors were unknown to contemporaries in no way diminishes their importance though, since they broaden our conception of the political forces at work during those critical years of Russia's development. Two years before the gentry formed itself into an interest group (or groups), the governors had become a force that could not be disregarded. Never organized in a formal manner, the governors nonetheless campaigned together for a single program of administrative reform.

The event which imparted to the governors a consciousness of participating in a movement was the Lanskoi circular of October 1856. In a successful effort to mold the contours of the interest group with which he would have to deal, he chose a group of twenty-four governors and the five governors-general to receive the request for reform ideas. The basis on which Lanskoi made his selection reveals his purposes. Neither age, length of tenure in office, nor geographical considerations appear to have played a part. Rather, the Minister of Internal Affairs chose those

[41] *Severnaia Pochta*, No. 13 (January 17, 1862), 50. *Kolokol* ceased to follow the administrative debate as early as September 15, 1859, No. 52, "Komissiia dlia sostavleniia polizhenii."

governors whose previous reports indicated a concern for administrative reform.[42] Conspicuously underrepresented on the list of twenty-four were those governors of military background; only four former officers received the circular and all these had demonstrated an interest in reforming the civil bureaucracy.[43] The fourteen military men who held joint appointments as civil and military governors were excluded entirely.

Having carefully screened his field, Lanskoi waited for the replies. A preliminary reading of the responses revealed that "They almost all agreed on one point, namely, the necessity of broadening the gubernatorial power at the expense of the sphere of action of the Ministries and the Main Departments. Many append to this the view of the true meaning of the governor of a province as its 'full steward,' finding this concept stated in the dicta of the [original] *Nakaz* on civil governors."[44] Of the many demands of the governors, Lanskoi named the reform of the Provincial Directorates as the most pressing. The governors hoped that they could be rendered more efficient, their staffs reduced, and the salaries of the remaining members increased. But these changes alone would not suffice. Sweeping beyond the earlier program of the Committee on Reducing Correspondence, the governors proposed that the Provincial Directorates be given full control over all administrative agencies in the province, regardless of the central ministry to which they were presently subordinated.[45]

---

[42] Many contemporary reformers, however, took a dim view of the abilities of governors. Iakov Soloviev wrote in his memoirs that only fifteen of the forty-six governors of provinces with serfs had come up through the civil service; that two or three more were of unknown backgrounds, and the remaining two-thirds were military men. Of the fifteen civil employees, Soloviev counted nine who were graduates either of the Aleksandrovskii Lycee or the Law School in St. Petersburg, but of the remainder he could recall none with a university education. (Soloviev, "Zapiski . . . ," October 1882, p. 135.)

[43] Lt. Gen. Hesse, Kiev; Maj. Sinelnikov, Voronezh; Lt. Gen. Zhukovskii, Tauride; Lt. Gen. Baratinskii, Kazan.

[44] *MSVUK*, I, otd. 3, p. 6.   [45] *Ibid.*

129

In his complete digest of the replies Lanskoi detailed the governors' views on the local agencies of each central ministry in turn. The program of the governors' movement is most clearly revealed in this section of the document. Regarding the Ministry of Finances, they demanded advisory and even executive power over the local treasury offices, as well as "personal influence in the appointment, penalizing and rewarding of civil servants and members of the treasury offices and of agencies subordinate to them."[46] Most governors wanted the Ministry of Finances to grant them an annual sum of money for use in emergencies, but several went further: one requested the right to withdraw funds from the provincial treasury without authorization from Petersburg;[47] another thought that this could be accomplished better by establishing a discretionary fund in each province from which governors could draw freely without central restraints;[48] a third proposed an elaborate system whereby a governor could effectively override the objections of the local treasury officials;[49] and still another called for power to punish individuals with sizable tax arrears.[50] All assumed that reports to the Ministry of Finances on such operations would be abolished.

The most extreme plan for deconcentrating treasury affairs came from Governor Semenev of Viatka. First, he mildly suggested that provincial treasuries should be obliged to submit budgets and reports to the governor's office rather than to Petersburg; then, however, he claimed for the governor the right to approve or stop the implementation of any decision by the local treasury without prior consultation with the Ministry of Finances or any other central

---

[46] *Ibid.*, pp. 7-8.
[47] *Ibid.*, p. 117. These views were summarized in the 1862 study by M. N. Popov, *Osobaia zapiska po voprosu ob otnosheniiakh gubernatorov k vedomstvu palat kazennykh i gosudardarstvennykh imushchestv i k gubernskim pochtovym kontoram," ibid.*, I, otd. 5, pp. 78-135.
[48] *Ibid.*, I, otd. 3, p. 120.   [49] *Ibid.*, p. 119.
[50] *Ibid.*, p. 113.

agency.[51] This effectually divorced the Ministry of Finances from all direct control in the provinces and made it wholly dependent upon powerful governors wielding localized authority. Semenev took care to note that he was not seeking simply to increase his personal power but to decentralize the overly congested operations of the Ministry of Finances.[52]

No less far reaching were the governors' proposals for the Ministry of State Domains, which controlled the lives of the thirteen million serfs inhabiting government lands. Ex-Governor Valuev of Courland began his comments on this ministry with the observation that "bureaucrats of the [provincial] agencies of the Ministry of State Domains have no understanding of the degree of independence . . . which should and actually does exist between their agency and the general government of the province."[53] Nine governors boldly proposed "to expand the governors' rights to investigate [the functioning of] the agencies and to penalize errors and omissions, as well as to decide several of the most important affairs of the agencies; to increase the influence of provincial governors on hiring, setting salaries and firing of members and civil servants, both of the agencies and of their subordinate offices."[54] These governors expressed the view that decentralization should be total. Instead of turning for authorization to the Ministry of State Domains or to the Senate, the provincial agency would simply file in Petersburg a year-end report on its work "for [the Ministry's] information." Minor taxes could be levied with the sole authorization of the governor, and public buildings and grain stores would be maintained and controlled entirely at the provincial level.[55] T. S. Bakunin, Governor of Tver and cousin of the federalist-anarchist Mikhail Bakunin, concluded his suggestions by applying the same standard for determining the sphere of local initiative that

[51] *Ibid.*, pp. 114-15.   [52] *Ibid.*, p. 120.
[53] *Ibid.*, pp. 124-50.   [54] *Ibid.*, p. 8.
[55] *Ibid.*, I, otd. 5, pp. 127-28.

Andrei Tsie had evolved in the Committee for Reducing Correspondence: all matters not specified as directly ministerial would be included among the residual powers of the provincial administration.[56]

The governors were no less forthright in their demands in the military sphere. One wanted a general equalization of powers between the military and civil administrations and two others went so far as to seek control over troops.[57] The objective of these men was to extend their power over the local garrison commanders who, like the ministerial agency heads, were directly subordinate to Petersburg.[58]

Neither the Ministry of Crown Lands nor the Ministry of Enlightenment came in for serious criticism from the provincial officials, though minor changes were proposed that would affect each. In contrast to their mildness on these matters, the interest shown by the governors in the postal department is surprising both for its intensity and for the radicalism of the proposals they advanced. They demanded nothing less than control over the mails. Three governors insisted on the power to hire and fire all postal employees, to inspect the post office, and to institute whatever changes or improvements their investigations should indicate to be warranted.[59] A fourth, while making essentially the same demands, appeared willing to settle for the right merely to approve the appointments made by the central Postal Department.[60]

The stated aims of these measures proposed by the governors were: "1) to escape from the false position in which the Governors are now placed by being removed from all

[56] *Ibid.*, pp. 134-35.

[57] *Ibid.*, pp. 18-20. Governors Muraviev of Pskov, Fabre of Ekaterinoslav, and Governor-General Stroganov of New Russia.

[58] Privy Councillor Panchulidzev, governor of Penza province, revealed his own motives for joining the campaign when he asked to be granted the right to have a military guard placed at the gate of his residence to symbolize his authority. *Ibid.*, pp. 9-10.

[59] Governors Muraviev of Pskov, Semenov of Viatka, Rosset of Lithuania. *Ibid.*, pp. 27-32.

[60] *Ibid.*, p. 27. Governor Hesse of Kiev.

influence in the post offices . . . 2) to give the governors the opportunity of watching over the maintenance and improvement of these institutions. With the yearly development of commercial and industrial relations, which give the province a greater meaning in the life of the populace, the post office is naturally connected with all aspects of provincial government."[61] By demanding provincial control over the postal system, the four governors placed themselves beyond the range even of most federalist thought of the period which was at least willing to grant the central power administrative supervision of the mails. That they would go to this extreme indicates the degree of radicalization which decentralizing sentiment could reach when provoked by a malfunctioning bureaucracy.

So far did the governors go in their demand for administrative decentralization that it must be asked whether their campaign was for absolute stewardship over the provinces rather than merely for an efficient realignment of functions.[62] Yet not one governor sought power to interfere with the functioning of public and estate bodies, and for every one prone to abuse decentralized authority, there were half a dozen who expressed their consciousness of just this danger. Far from seeking to establish a satrapy and to stamp out public initiative, the reforming governor characteristically aimed only to institute efficient procedures that would overcome the woeful undergovernment of his region. After all, provincial governors had been put on the defensive by the excessive demands of the ministries and had been criticized publicly for being unable to provide needed services.[63]

---

[61] *Ibid.*, p. 10.

[62] The governor of Vologda proposed to operate a decentralized system of censorship, and also sought authorization to fire elected officials. The governor of Voronezh requested authority to inflict bodily punishment on townspeople without trial. *Ibid.*, pp. 210-11.

[63] TsGAOR, f. 647, op. 1, ed. khr. 32, pp. 10-11. Address of the Moscow gentry, criticizing the governor's "unsatisfactory handling of local affairs."

However benign their campaign was on one level, on another the reforming governors posed a serious challenge to the provincial system of Nicholas I. Reversing the tendency of Russian legislation since the founding of the ministries, they adhered more or less consistently to Tsie's doctrine that residual administrative power belonged in the provinces. Why then, did the Ministry of Internal Affairs and its chief, Sergei Lanskoi, choose to champion the governors' cause? As we have seen, the ministry faced a breakdown in its provincial offices, and the decentralists offered the only financially feasible solution. But rivalry with other ministries was no less important a factor. In meetings of the Committee on Reducing Correspondence, representatives of the Ministry of Internal Affairs found themselves contending with other ministries for the loyalties of field personnel in provincial and district capitals.[64] Recognizing the trouble that might arise within his ministry if he ignored the governors and aware, too, that the governors' disloyalty could drastically reduce the power of the Ministry of Internal Affairs vis-à-vis the other ministries, Lanskoi resolved to champion them.

In a message to Alexander II on February 28, 1858, Lanskoi summarized the governors' proposals with tact and restraint. He concluded with a seemingly innocent plea: "I would like to make bold humbly to request permission from Your Highness to forward to the other ministers all of those outlines which relate to the affairs of other ministries, along with the proposals from the provincial governors; this will serve to direct their attention to the goal . . . which you, Sir, have set."[65] Alexander approved without hesitation and a week later Lanskoi sent the proposals around to the other ministers. To avoid giving the appearance of promoting only the interests of his own ministry Lanskoi wrote the

[64] On the competition among central government agencies over local agencies, see Herbert A. Simon, *Administrative Behavior*, pp. 309-10.
[65] *MSVUK*, I, otd. 5, p. 4.

cover letter on the stationery of the Committee for Reducing Correspondence. But the replies from the five ministers to whom the governors' proposals had been forwarded indicate that they realized full well that their own ministerial power was at stake.

The other ministers submitted their opinions during the spring and summer of 1858. The defensive tone of their memorandums indicates the extent to which they feared self-aggrandizement by the Ministry of Internal Affairs. Alexander Kniazhevich, Minister of Finances, found the governors' accusations "baseless" and their demands "irrelevant," since several of these same issues were being discussed in the State Council.[66] Prince Viktor Vasilchikov, Minister of War, was highly incensed by the fact that the prerogatives of his ministry in the provinces were being challenged by men without military training.[67] He pointed out that already military commanders had no legal grounds for refusing to honor a request from the civil authorities, and that further legislation would be redundant.[68] Much more moderate in its tone was the response of Egor Kovalevskii, Minister of Public Enlightenment, who suggested that all the proposals be carefully studied, except those affecting his own ministry, which were unnecessary.[69] Regarding the crown lands, Count Adlerberg, the elderly Minister of the Imperial Household, declared categorically that the existing gubernatorial powers were quite adequate, a view which the Minister of State Domains echoed.[70]

Of all the responses to the governors' assault on the ministries by far the most interesting was submitted by the Director of the Postal Department, Alexander Priashnikov.[71] He began by aligning himself with the decentralizing governors. All provincial agencies of the central government,

[66] *Ibid.*, pp. 12-17. [67] *Ibid.*, pp. 18-24.
[68] *Ibid.*, p. 23.
[69] *Ibid.*, pp. 15-26. April 27, 1858.
[70] *Ibid.*, pp. 35-36. April 16, 1858.
[71] *Ibid.*, pp. 26-35.

he wrote, have a defined sphere of action involving the life of the people, the interests of the treasury, and also the welfare of each individual province. Consequently, it is possible to localize most functions "without the general participation of those same agencies in other provinces." But, he asked, did the Postal Department belong in the same category as the other provincial agencies to which the governors' proposals were directed? "The post office, serving as a channel for governmental and private relations not only within Russia but also with foreign states, has an exceptional character and does not fall under the heading of administration. Constituting a single general and thereby indivisible concern, working at the same time within Russia and abroad [the postal service], cannot be split functionally into separate regions."[72] In other words, he argued that postal affairs would necessarily have to remain under central control, even in an otherwise deconcentrated system.

Taken together, the reactions of the ministers to the proposals of the provincial governors were cool to the extreme. As early as 1856 the Committee on Reducing Correspondence had felt this opposition and had warned in its annual report that "everything would be lost if all the governmental organs do not cooperate."[73] But the relations among the ministries only worsened. The Minister of Justice, Count Viktor Panin, and the Minister of Finances deliberately undermined the committee's projects. Panin singlehandedly killed a measure affirming the governors' power to confirm punishments and rewrote another proposal to free certain agencies run by the gentry from the obligation of semi-annual reporting.[74] Lanskoi finally accused Panin of not cooperating either with the other ministers or with the tsar.[75] Panin shot back a bristling note listing examples of his support for the committee and pointing out to Lanskoi that

[72] *Ibid.*, p. 26.
[73] TsGIA-SSSR, f. 1314, op. 1, ed. khr. 27, pp. 7-8.
[74] *Ibid.*, pp. 1ff.   [75] *Ibid.*, pp. 14-15.

only three proposals referred to Panin had remained unanswered.

At stake in this stiff exchange of veiled insults was the fate of administrative decentralization in Russia. And behind that lurked the question of which ministry's agents should gain control of the countryside. However little support existed for his position on the former issue, Lanskoi was fully isolated in his support of the agents of the Ministry of Internal Affairs, the governors. Except for the postal director, none of the ministers accepted the governors' proposals as evidence of a cleavage between central and local agencies of state; and instead they all interpreted them as proof of a fundamental incompatibility among the interests of the various central agencies themselves. They believed that to countenance the demands of the governors and the expressed wishes of the tsar on this issue they would not merely have to support the principle of administrative decentralization but, far more important, would have to abdicate the authority of their own agencies in favor of the Ministry of Internal Affairs.

In another country this might not have been a serious cause for concern. In Russia, however, where there was no prime minister to preside over the other top administrators, suspicions continually arose among the ministers that their colleagues were motivated by lust for self-aggrandizement. Especially in this crucial period from 1857 to 1858, when a broad slate of reforms was contemplated, the relative importance of ministries became a very real issue. To its enemies, the program of administrative decentralization envisaged by Lanskoi and the tsar seemed an entering wedge for expanding the powers of the Ministry of Internal Affairs. The objections raised to it in the ministerial comments on the governors' memorandums were a warning for the future. They showed Lanskoi that the ideal of decentralization could never be realized unless he could override the vested interests of his ministerial rivals.

DECENTRALIZATION AND EMANCIPATION

Until the summer of 1857, advocates of administrative decentralization in the Ministry of Internal Affairs had one decided advantage over their opponents. However distasteful the proposed reforms may have been to the leaders of other ministries, no one could deny that that organ was the only ministry with the right to initiate changes in the rules defining the powers of the governors. In the summer of 1857 this strategic advantage was nearly lost or, at the very least, seriously qualified. This turn of events was caused neither by the revision of reform procedures nor by the emergence of leaders who altered the balance of power in Petersburg. Rather, a new factor intruded on the ministries from without: the opening of discussion in the so-called Secret Committee on how to liberate the twenty-four million Russian serfs.

Compared to the resounding conflicts of 1858 to 1859, the sessions of the Secret Committee seem bland indeed. No blueprint for emancipation was produced, and even Alexander II became disgusted with the apparent inactivity of the committee. But neither the tsar nor subsequent scholarship recognized that the emancipation issue unleashed strong new pressures for concentrated forms of administration and that it was in the Secret Committee that these pressures were first registered and dealt with. At the very time the emancipation issue *per se* seemed to have been tabled, members of the Secret Committee were locked in fundamental disagreement as to the relation of the serf question to the proposed administrative reforms. In the midst of this conflict several ministers challenged Lanskoi with their own centralizing programs for institutional reforms in the provinces. Until this threat was removed, the fate of the decentralist movement remained in the balance.

Alexander II founded the Secret Committee at the end of 1856 to plan "the improvement of the lot of the peas-

THE POLITICS OF DECENTRALIZATION

ants."[76] In purpose, procedure and even personnel this committee closely resembled the seven groups convoked by Nicholas I over the previous three decades to consider the same issues.[77] Its members were drawn from the same top court and ministerial circles to which Nicholas had turned for advice; their average age was almost sixty, and five of the twelve were older than sixty-five.[78] With the exception of Lanskoi, none of the members showed any great interest in the abolition of serfdom *per se* and two of them actually sought the tsar's permission to decline appointment.[79] Even before its opening session on January 3, 1857, the Secret Committee seemed marked for difficulties.

The first task to which the committee addressed itself was to read and evaluate over a hundred projects for improving the lot of serfs. Of the three members of the committee chosen to evaluate them, one opposed emancipation outright, one sought emancipation without land, and the third

---

[76] On the Secret Committee see *Zhurnaly sekretnogo i glavnogo komitetov po krestianskomu delu*, 2 vols., Petrograd, 1915; P. A. Zaionchkovskii, *Otmena . . .* , pp. 76-81; *Materialy dlia istorii uprazdneniia krepostnogo sostoianiia . . .* , I, pp. 121-37; Soloviev, "Zapiski . . . ," February 1881, pp. 235-46; E. I. Vishniakov, "Nachala zakonodatelnykh rabot," *Velikaia reforma*, IV, pp. 138-44; the most competent monograph on the committee is that of the economist, P. I. Liashchenko, *Poslednyi sekretnyi komitet, po materialam arkhiva gos.-a soveta*, St. Petersburg, 1911.

[77] Count Bludov, Baron Modest Korf, and Count Kiselev had all served on earlier committees. The other members were Prince Orlov, Lanskoi, Muraviev, Brok, Adlerberg, Chevkin, Gagarin, Rostovtsev, Butkov, and Dolgorukov. The previous committees had been convened in 1826-30; 1839-42; 1840; 1844; 1846; 1847; 1848. V. A. Alekseev, "Sekretyne komitety pri Nikolai I," *Velikaia reforma*, II, pp. 194-208.

[78] D. N. Bludov, 72; V. F. Adlerberg, 67; P. O. Gagarin, 68; A. F. Orlov, 69; S. S. Lanskoi, 72.

[79] It had been claimed that Baron Korf was disappointed at not being named to head the group. Kornilov denies this (*Obschestvennoe dvizhenie . . .* , p. 736), but, in view of the fact that Korf was engaged at the time in writing a biography of the great reformer Speranskii, such a leadership role may well have held an attraction for him. Iakov Rostovtsev wished to resign because of his total unfamiliarity with the serf problem.

wanted the government to supervise emancipation with land. To break this stalemate Lanskoi submitted his own proposal,[80] but no sooner was it received than the group adjourned for the summer, its members dispersing to their provincial estates and favorite foreign spas.[81] It was at this point that Alexander II intervened. To speed the pace of work (the committee had heretofore met only on Saturdays) the tsar appointed as chairman his activist brother, Konstantin Nikolaevich, and urged the members to proceed at a more rapid pace.

By the time Grand Duke Konstatin assumed office in August 1857, the committee was evaluating a series of important memorandums submitted by members in response to a set of eight questions raised earlier in the summer.[82] These questions pertained largely to the specific form that emancipation might take in Russia: the future role of the peasant communal organizations; the amount of land to be retained by the gentry; and the pace of implementation of the reform. The final question, however, bore directly on the problem of administrative reform, and received far more attention from members of the Secret Committee than any of the others. Was it necessary, it asked, to strengthen the local powers—particularly the governors and police—before the promulgation of the emancipation manifesto?

Only two members of the Secret Committee thought that emancipation could be achieved without altering existing provincial institutions. General Rostovtsev conceded that if emancipation had to come it should be planned and

[80] TsGIA-SSSR, f. 1180, 1857, op. xv. d. 13, pp. 7-15. Introduced on July 26 with a letter by Lanskoi, the Levshin project is described in detail in Kornilov, "Gubernskie komitety . . . ," No. 1, 1904, pp. 155-57. It envisaged emancipation without land but it required lords to loan land to peasants for their permanent use. It also included a system of redemption and a gradual process of emancipation, beginning in the western provinces. The three members who received the project were Rostovtsev, Gagarin, and Korf.

[81] Soloviev, "Zapiski . . . ," February 1881, pp. 241ff.

[82] TsGIA-SSSR, f. 1180, 1857, op. xv, d. 13, pp. 4-6.

executed by the government, with adjustments to accommodate local conditions.[83] After emancipation had been achieved, though, provincial institutions would remain unaltered, with the gentry still in charge of police functions on their estates and the governors responsible for their accustomed round of duties, including supervision of the police. Talk of further institutional reform, he thought, was simply a device for delaying the unwelcome necessity of emancipation.[84] Prince Gagarin shared these views, except that he wanted the entire emancipation to be conducted by the gentry.[85] Both men opposed administrative decentralization for the same reason that they would have opposed further centralization of the bureaucracy: they feared that it would imperil the traditional balance of power between the gentry and the state.

Compared to this consistent opposition to reform, the views of Mikhail Muraviev were far more subtle, and from the standpoint of administrative reform, more dangerous.[86] As Minister of State Domains he was more closely involved with peasant affairs than any other minister and his views were bound to carry considerable weight.

Muraviev's response to the question of whether administrative reforms should precede emancipation was founded on precisely the same insight that motivated the reforming governors, namely, the awareness that the local civil administration wielded only fictitious power.[87] Emancipation, he believed, constituted a fundamental threat to civil authority because it would unleash millions of peasants from age-old habits of submissiveness. Any failure to increase the degree of authority wielded by local civil administrators would

[83] *Ibid.*, p. 79.   [84] *Ibid.*, p. 80.
[85] *Ibid.*, pp. 54-55.
[86] For an unflattering picture of Muraviev see "Kak Muraviev vzyskival v Kurske nodoimki," *Russkii Arkhiv*, xii, 1885. An even less favorable picture is presented by P. Dolgorukov in his brochure, *Kn. M. N. Muraviev*, London, 1864.
[87] TsGIA-SSSR, f. 1180, 1857, op. xv, d. 13, p. 224.

therefore expose Russia to destruction by a "rural proletariat."[88] Such fears were shared by six other members of the Secret Committee.

Historians have followed contemporary memoirists in seeing the substitution of Muraviev's form of administrative reform for emancipation as an attempt to sidetrack emancipation into a maze of administrative details and hence to bury the issue.[89] Doubtless, Muraviev and several of his backers were not eager to undertake full emancipation of the serfs under any circumstances; when he toured the provinces in the summer of 1857 Muraviev went so far as to assure local gentry that the serfs would never be freed. But on the other hand, the Minister of State Domains did not personally belong to the "planter" faction of the Committee,[90] and he eventually lent his support to a proposal of Lanskoi's for a governmentally managed reform to begin in the western provinces.[91] His primary concern, then, was with the problem of domestic security rather than with emancipation *per se*.

That Muraviev's anxiety was genuine cannot be doubted. Fear of peasant disorders figured large in the consciousness of Russian statesmen at the time, regardless of the actual frequency or severity of outbreaks.[92] An anonymous essayist had voiced this fear as the Crimean War commenced and had translated it into a call for tightened local security. "There are the bold ones," he wrote, "who consider the first necessity to be the reform of serfdom on the landlords' estates." But, given the miserable condition of the courts and local gendarmerie, "Russia cannot withstand the shock

---

[88] *Ibid.*, pp. 59-61. The others were Count A. Orlov; Gen. A. Adlerberg; Count V. Dolgorukov; P. Brok; Baron M. Korf and Count D. Bludov.

[89] Zaionchkovskii, *Otmena* . . . , pp. 77-78. Soloviev "Zapiski . . . ," February 1881, pp. 241-42.

[90] Soloviev, "Zapiski . . . ," February 1881, p. 241.

[91] TsGIA-SSSR, f. 1180, 1857, op. xv, d. 13, p. 225.

[92] See for example, Nikitenko, *Dnevnik*, II, 26.

which would come from changing the status of the ten million ignorant people."[93]

To ward off the threat of violence, Muraviev and his followers wanted the entire system of security and executive police strengthened. Loosely organized police at the local level had existed since Muscovite times, but in the eighteenth century had been structured into bodies which exercised judicial, executive, and administrative power in the provinces, districts, and cities.[94] The lowest police with officer rank (*zemskie ispravniki*) were elected by the gentry while the rest were state appointees. Since the eighteenth century the scarcity of personnel had caused a wide range of functions to agglomerate to the police, including fire fighting, the control of certain philanthropic work, and supervision of sectarian groups.[95] Although the chain of command was frequently broken in practice, the formal line of authority in police matters went straight to the governors and then to the tsar and Minister of Internal Affairs; only on a few exceptional matters did the police report to other ministries. This fact presented Muraviev with a challenge. Would it be possible to strengthen the police through administrative concentration and at the same time utilize that issue as a means of deflating the pretensions of the Ministry of Internal Affairs to hegemony in the countryside?

This convenient possibility faced an immediate impediment from the Ministry of Internal Affairs, which had al-

[93] TsGAOR, f. 722, op. 1, ed. khr. 610, pp. 27-28. "O neobkhodimosti reform tsentralnogo i mestnogo upravleniia." The plan proposed by this anonymous essayist was strikingly similar to that proposed later by Muraviev: to divide Russia into ten vast regions in which representatives directly subordinated to the tsar would wield nearly absolute authority, cutting across all other chains of command.

[94] On the police function see I. Andreevskii, *Leksii po istorii politseiskogo prava i zemskikh uchrezhdenii v Rossii*, Moscow, 1883; I. Tarasov, *Politsiia v epokhe reform*, Moscow, 1885; "Predely politseiskoi vlasti," *Russkii Vestnik*, No. 5 (1858). See also Abbott, "Police Reform. . . ."

[95] *Polozhenie o politsiiakh* (text and commentary), St. Petersburg, 1837.

ready begun to consider police reform on its own initiative. The director of that Ministry's Department of Executive Police complained to Lanskoi that the excessive burden of work left his local agents "unable to protect one and all."[96] To remedy this situation he appealed to Lanskoi personally to lead the reform of the police agency. Another unsigned but official proposal indicates that the Ministry of Internal Affairs had early resolved to retain and expand its control over the local police: "At the present time it is more necessary than ever to provide this ministry with the possibility of having in the localities its own agents who would follow its orders exclusively."[97]

Muraviev viewed all reforms pertaining to local government introduced by the Ministry of Internal Affairs with high suspicion. He reflected the fear, common to top administrations of today's developing nations, that a single branch of the state would set itself up as a "department of local government" and dictate policy on social and economic change.[98] In the Russian case during the nineteenth century there was some ground for this fear. Not only were rumors of decentralization spreading, but, as was well known, Lanskoi had recently introduced a rule whereby governors (who were the nominal heads of the local police) were to submit their reports not to the tsar first but to the Minister of Internal Affairs! Clearly, the time had come to strike back.

In a flurry of strategic maneuvers, Muraviev propounded two schemes which would strengthen local security in preparation for the liberation of the serfs and at the same time curtail the designs of the Ministry of Internal Affairs. Both proposals called for far-reaching extension of administra-

---

[96] TsGIA-SSSR, f. 869, op. 1, d. 520, p. 28. Report of S. Zhdanov, October 5, 1857.

[97] TsGIA-SSSR, f. 869 (N. A. Miliutin archive), op. 1, d. 395, pp. 6-8.

[98] Maddick, *Democracy . . .* , p. 133.

144

tive control and concentration in all security functions. First, he called for a new system of military governors-general. A law of 1852 had abolished these offices throughout Russia except in border regions where they were retained for international defense.[99] Opponents of decentralization sought to reverse this ruling and extend the system of governors-general to cover all the central Russian provinces. The new governors-general would wield supreme authority in the countryside and would be competent to overrule any decisions by local police or civil governors. Directly responsible to the tsar rather than to the Ministry of Internal Affairs, they would be charged with implementing the emancipation of the serfs.

Related to, but distinct from, the governor-generalship scheme was Muraviev's plan to establish an unprecedented network of representatives of the central authorities in each district of the fifty provinces. These officials would enjoy all the powers of governors but at the district level. Similar "district governors" had in fact been introduced temporarily in the western provinces in 1830 as a means of quelling revolt but had been abolished at the insistence of provincial governors.[100] Now the Muraviev faction saw the proposed district officials as valuable pawns in the battle being waged against the Ministry of Internal Affairs. Muraviev insisted that they be subordinated not to the local governors or the Ministry of Internal Affairs but directly to the tsar.

The proposals to establish military governors-general and district governors had much in common. Both would have strengthened substantially the government's security forces in the countryside. And either would have undermined the power of the existing governors to such an extent that they would have been left as minor functionaries. Most impor-

---

[99] In 1856 the governor-generalship of Vitebsk and Kharkov was abolished. The capitals, of course, retained their governors-general. Soloviev, "Zapiski . . . ," September 1882, p. 642-43.

[100] *Ibid.*, March, p. 567 refers to these offices.

tant, both schemes would have reinstituted the old goal of administrative concentration at the moment when it was under attack from all sides.

Muraviev began his campaign immediately, focusing his energies first on his plan to create eight huge civil and military districts under new governors-general. He could well afford to be optimistic since he had the support of all but two members of the Secret Committee, Lanskoi and the Grand Duke Konstantin.[101] These two men had stood alone in insisting that general administrative reforms be instituted only after the success of emancipation was assured. The attempt to introduce administrative reforms and emancipation simultaneously, Grand Duke Konstantin argued, would jeopardize the welfare of both programs, leaving an unsettled peasantry and an ever more rigidly centralized bureaucracy.[102]

An essential step in the Russian legislative process was to gain the support of the tsar for the measure at hand. Naturally, partisans of Muraviev's scheme hoped to elicit support from Alexander for their administrative program. At length the tsar yielded to heavy lobbying by his secretary, State Councillor Butkov, and announced that he backed the proposal for new governor-generalships. So fearful was Alexander of peasant unrest that he willingly backed a plan that directly contradicted the decentralization program that he himself had earlier supported.[103] Ignoring the inconsistency, he sided with the majority in the Secret Committee, and when the Main Committee was formed in January 1858, the tsar named an outspoken advocate of the governors-general plan, Iakov Rostovtsev, to be its chairman.

Meanwhile, an opposition movement was under way in the Ministry of Internal Affairs to save the governors and rescue the policy of decentralization. Nikolai Miliutin, whose influence was growing rapidly, expressed his categorical opposition to the proposed governor-generalships,

[101] *Ibid.*, p. 587.   [102] *MSVUK*, I, otd. 5, pp. 23-26, 31-33.
[103] Cf. Dzhanshiev, *Epokha* . . . , pp. 41-44.

labeling them "satrapies with their pashas."[104] A similar view was expressed in an anonymous tract that passed through Lanskoi's office at this time. The new officials, the pamphleteer declared, would succeed only in ravaging the provinces as the central emissaries had done under the Muscovite tsars.[105] In still another critique of the proposal, Iakov Soloviev of the Ministry of Internal Affairs admitted the faults of the existing governorships but insisted that these would best be corrected by granting them more initiative rather than by transferring their powers to Petersburg or to new governors-general.[106]

With this support Lanskoi made a stand against the tsar and against the entire Main Committee when it met to consider Muraviev's proposal on May 16, 1858.[107] Earlier, in the same month the chairman, Rostovtsev, had asked Lanskoi to draft a letter of instructions to be sent to the new governors-general upon appointment. Lanskoi stubbornly disobeyed this request, though he knew full well that it was supported by Alexander. At the meeting of May 16 he calmly announced that he had not prepared the instructions. Denied even the support of Grand Duke Konstantin, who was out of the country, Lanskoi was left to face the wrath of the Committee alone.[108] Fortunately for Lanskoi, he received valuable aid from the young reformist Governor of Tobolsk province, Viktor Artsimovich, who had just arrived in the capital. In Siberia, Artsimovich's tenure of office had been plagued with constant conflict with the ministries in Petersburg and especially with the governor-gen-

[104] Anatole Leroy-Beaulieu, *Un Homme d'état Russe* (Nicholas Milutine), Paris, 1884, p. 24n.
[105] TsGAOR, f. 647 (archive of Grand Duchess Elena Pavlova), op. 1, ed. khr. 51, pp. 3-4.
[106] Soloviev, "Zapiski . . . ," March 1882, pp. 575-79. Prince Cherkasskii mocked the plans as "half-comic, half-tragic," O. Trubetskaia, *Materialy . . . Cherkasskogo*, I, 109.
[107] The full stenographic account of this important meeting is not extant in TsGIA-SSSR or TsGAOR. Soloviev, "Zapiski . . . ," March 1882, pp. 576-79, contains the best secondary account of this incident.
[108] *Ibid.*, p. 587.

eral of the region.[109] Utterly frustrated, he finally quit his post to seek a less hamstrung governorship in Great Russia. On June 10 he presented Lanskoi with a strongly phrased note castigating the governors-general and the central ministries and pleading the governors' case once more.[110] Lanskoi immediately recognized in the young governor a sympathetic and capable ally and commissioned him to draft a detailed critique of the Muraviev-Rostovtsev proposal. Though Alexander seemed firmly in the camp of the centralizers, Lanskoi hoped that Artsimovich could persuade him of the correctness of his earlier commitment to decentralization and reform of the governorships.

By June 21 the Artsimovich brief was on Lanskoi's desk. With its general attack on the theory of centralization and specific critique of the Muraviev-Rostovtsev plan, it was ideally suited to its purpose.[111] But it failed to convert the tsar, who in a curt reply of August 5, 1858, informed Lanskoi that the tract had produced "a sad impression" on him. Faced with a blank wall Lanskoi had no further resort but to offer his resignation, which he did. The young Alexander seems to have been stung by this personal rebuke from a distinguished statesman who had served both his uncle, Alexander I, and his father, Nicholas I. With an abject apology he persuaded Lanskoi to stay at his post. And yielding to the Ministry of Internal Affairs' counterlobby, the tsar reversed his ground once more and prevailed upon the Main Committee to drop the centralization project.[112] Though the governors-general plan continued to be dis-

---

[109] . . . *Artsimovich* . . . , pp. 74, 88.   [110] *Ibid.*, p. 48.

[111] Due to a careless remark by the wife of N. A. Miliutin it has been widely believed that Miliutin, rather than Artsimovich, was the author of this memorandum. Miliutina, "Iz zapisok . . . ," *Russkaia Starina*, xcii, January 1899, p. 272. Evidence presented by the author of "Krestianskaia reforma v Kaluzhskoi gubernii pri V. A. Artsimoviche," . . . *Artsimovich* . . . , p. 159n, refutes this. This memorandum was subsequently published and attributed wrongly to Lanskoi; Soloviev, "Zapiski . . . ," September 1882, pp. 641-69.

[112] A version of this conversation is reported in Dzhanshiev, *Epokha* . . . pp. 41-43.

148

cussed for another year, the threat of Lanskoi's resignation, as well as the apparent passivity of the peasantry—the fear of disturbances had given rise to the scheme in the first place—caused the issue gradually to die; by the autumn of 1858 it was Rostovtsev's and Muraviev's turn to be completely isolated.

After the scheme for establishing governors-general was checked, the old majority in the Secret Committee—now the majority in the Main Committee—turned to the second strategy, to establish a concentrated system of "governors" at the district level.[113] The cloak under which these new officials were to enter the administrative system was the one heretofore worn by the district police inspectors (*zemskie ispravniki*), who were elected by the gentry. These local police officials were under scrutiny because as the gentry's representatives they could not be expected to act impartially in settling differences between lords and peasants after emancipation. It was therefore proposed to transfer the police inspectors' functions to government appointees who would become for all practical purposes district governors, inheriting a series of judicial and civic functions as well as responsibility for peace-keeping.

In the spring of 1858 Alexander affirmed his support for this police reform[114] and in the latter part of February his secretary wrote to the ministers of Internal Affairs, Justice, and State Domains requesting them to prepare projects for the reform of district institutions "as soon as possible."[115]

---

[113] It is possible that this proposal was an adaptation of a law introduced in Prussia after the suppression of the Revolution of 1848. Ministerial opponents of decentralization in Prussia, like their counterparts in Russia in the 1850's, worked indefatigably to establish field agents at the lowest level and to subordinate them directly to the central ministries; cf. Heffter, *Die Deutsche Selbstverwaltung . . .* , p. 296. Volkstumliche Kreisverwaltung law of April 10, 1849, introduced by Minister of Internal Affairs Bekk.

[114] Soloviev, "Zapiski . . . ," March 1882, p. 562.

[115] TsGIA-SSSR, f. 1291, 1858, op. 123, d. 22, February 18, 1858, Butkov to Lanskoi, pp. 1-4; February 24, 1858, Butkov to Muraviev, pp. 5-6; February 24, Butkov to Panin, pp. 7-9.

The tsar's sole concern in this was to strengthen local security in preparation for emancipation, but he had unwittingly placed his authority behind the centralizing district governorships as well. He seems not to have anticipated the opposition of those interested in administrative decentralization, nor, for that matter, did he foresee the wrath of these gentry and other advocates of public self-government. At the same time, his own position was firmly supported by all the ministers except Lanskoi and by all those centralists concerned about the "inadequate concentration of governmental authority in the districts."[116]

The support which the district governorship scheme received in rival ministries threw the Ministry of Internal Affairs into full retreat. Only a few months earlier Lanskoi had attempted to use his governors as agents for the reform of local offices of all other ministries. Now a coalition was maneuvering to reform the Ministry of Internal Affairs in such a way as to cripple the gubernatorial power in the provinces and to create in the districts new officials whose considerable powers could be activated only from Petersburg. And all this was being proposed in the name of police reform which was supported in principle by Lanskoi and by his director of the police department.

Once more Lanskoi was saved by the emergence of new forces from his own staff. While the elderly trio of Muraviev, Rostovtsev, and Panin was laying the groundwork for its final campaign, subordinate members of the Ministry of Internal Affairs quietly prepared a counterthrust. The two chief figures in this defense of administrative deconcentration were Iakov Soloviev and Mikhail Saltykov, the latter of whom was soon to establish himself as one of Russia's greatest prose satirists. Both were young men, aged thirty and thirty-eight respectively, and had entered the Ministry of Internal Affairs at the end of the Crimean War. Soloviev now worked as director of a subsection

[116] *Ibid.*, p. 14.

of the Main Committee and Saltykov had been put in charge of a temporary police reform board in the Ministry of Internal Affairs in 1856.[117]

The first task assigned to Saltykov was to work out the details of the proposal submitted by Muraviev and approved by the tsar. Unlike Lanskoi earlier, Saltykov was in no position to ignore an order backed by the throne. But at the same time that he fulfilled it he drew up his personal views on district government and circulated them within his ministry. These views were the fruit of years of thought. Saltykov had written tales on bureaucratic themes in the 1840s and had worked in the office of the Governor of Viatka, after having been exiled there for his involvement with the Petrashevskii circle in 1848.[118] In addition to performing his official duties in Viatka he translated long passages on centralization from Tocqueville's *Democracy in America,* from Vivien's *Études administratives,* and from Sherieul's *Histoire de l'administration monarchique en France.*[119]

[117] TsGIA-SSSR, f. 869, op. 1, d. 520, pp. 29-37. Saltykov began work on police reform in the autumn of 1856. His first proposals were for a very limited modification of the existing police structure and were submitted in December 1856.

[118] See Saltykov's "A Confused Affair" (*Zaputannoe Delo*); on Saltykov and the Petrashevskii group see P. E. Shchegolov, ed., *Petrashevtsy v vospominaniiakh sovremennikov; sbornik materialov,* 2 vols., Moscow and Leningrad, 1926, I, 45, 54; A. S. Nifontov, *Rossiia v 1848-om godu,* Moscow, 1952, p. 235; and Francis M. Bartholomew, "The Petrashevskii Circle," Ph.D. diss., Princeton University, 1969, Chap. I.

[119] Though these translations are not so much as mentioned in Soviet editions of Saltykov's works (*Polnoe sobranie sochinenii M. E. Saltykova,* Moscow, 1941, I, 59) and are not preserved in the Saltykov-Shchedrin archive in TsGIA-SSSR, f. 445, they are significant for our understanding of the antibureaucratic movement in Russia. Among the passages recorded by the only person to have seen them was the following, from Tocqueville: "Central power, however enlightened it might be, cannot embrace all the details of the life of a great people; when it seeks by its own means to control the diverse manifestations of popular life it wastes its time in fruitless effort." (K. Arseniev, "Materialy dlia biografii M. E. Saltykov," in *Polnoe*

In his substitute proposal, Saltykov linked the entire administrative problem with reformist ideology, advancing a solution which, though appearing radical in 1858, was to be adopted within a year.[120] Centralization, he claimed, was "the primary question" in Russian life.[121] By forcing a diverse population into a single procrustean bed, the Russian government was following France's example in paving the way for revolution.[122] To prevent revolutionary violence he considered it essential to redraw all the internal boundaries so that they would correspond to genuine regional differences and then to restructure authority within them along federative lines like those proposed by Prince Cherkasskii. Having defended administrative decentralization, Saltykov then took steps to assure that the government's local agents would not arrogate to themselves functions that properly lay beyond the purview of state interference. "What essential need is there for the government to know how I conduct my domestic affairs if I accurately fulfill all the duties entrusted to me as a citizen," he asked. The solution, he believed, lay in local self-government, which he promoted with a convert's zeal. To distinguish between matters of an administrative, as against a "public" character, Saltykov adopted the same standard as Vladimir Tsie had used in his memorandum to the Committee on Reducing Correspondence: the local administrative authorities had only to coordinate local interests with one another and with overall state policies; otherwise, all matters were to be conducted locally by the populace itself.

---

sobranie sochinenii M. E. Saltykova, 12 vols., St. Petersburg, 1905-06, I, 35.)

[120] The only known copy of this memorandum was cited at length by Arseniev in *Polnoe sobranie sochinenii . . .* , I, pp. 45-55. Arseniev first hypothesized that the project dated from 1860, but then corrected himself. The document must be dated between February and March 1858, because (a) Alexander did not request a full project on police reform before February 18, and (b) in March, Saltykov was named vice-governor of Riazan province.

[121] *Ibid.,* pp. 45-49. [122] *Ibid.,* p. 45.

From this Saltykov concluded that the proposed police reform was a grievous error. Centralization had led to a broad interpretation of the police function and the new proposal, he felt, would broaden that definition still more. Decentralization would have the reverse effect, while self-government would strip from the administration its excess functions. Saltykov proposed to embody these principles in new institutions. The cornerstone of his system would be all-class elective councils at the district and provincial levels, which would supersede all existing organs and assume general control of local affairs. At the end of his memorandum Saltykov appended an outline of the makeup of these councils (or *zemstvos*).[123] The members were to be elected by their estates rather than directly by the entire populace and would include representatives of the peasantry and urban class as well as the gentry. Though he differed from practically everyone else in 1858 by making a place for the peasantry in the local government, Saltykov was equally outspoken in his defense of the rights of the gentry against the administration; in an earlier memorandum on the police he had defended gentry-elected *ispravniki* against those who wanted to replace them with crown appointees.[124] Now Saltykov proposed that the district and provincial marshals of the gentry be appointed the presidents of the new councils *ex officio*. Like the historian Shchapov, he showed himself receptive to any proposal that would shift responsibility from Petersburg to the province and from the administration to the public.

This then was the conception of reform held by the chairman of the Police Commission in the Ministry of Internal Affairs. Rather than merely call in the public to watch over the proposed district governors as Muraviev's more cautious opponents had proposed, Saltykov swept away the plan entirely and replaced it with a complete system of administrative decentralization and public self-government at

[123] *Ibid.*, pp. 51ff.
[124] TsGIA-SSSR, f. 869, op. 1, d. 520, pp. 24-27.

153

the district and provincial levels. This proposal was immediately taken up by Iakov Soloviev who, as a member of the Main Committee, transmitted it to the inner circle of legislators planning the emancipation.

That Soloviev, a son of a minor Petersburg gentry-bureaucrat and cordially hated by the provincial lords whose cause he now seemed to advocate, should become the champion of local self-rule requires some explanation.[125] He had advanced in the civil service by playing the part of a gadfly, feeding on the foibles of Nicholas' bureaucracy. Now, confronted by a solid phalanx of men who most epitomized that reign, Soloviev was bound to oppose them, even though it meant supporting the cause of the gentry who resented him so deeply. Apparently he had convinced himself that the Ministry of Internal Affairs and its local agents were simply too weak an interest group to thwart the forces for administrative centralization unleashed by the projected emancipation. To block the plan to set up district governors, Soloviev proposed an alliance with the local public by which certain gubernatorial powers would be granted to all-class representative assemblies in exchange for the preservation of the remainder of gubernatorial rights. During the following months he vigorously pursued this policy.

The first confrontation between the two forces took place in the office of the Minister of Justice, Panin, who had invited Soloviev to discuss the forthcoming reform after the tsar's announcement of February 18, 1858.[126] Soloviev made it clear in conversation that he would oppose the district governor plan and that the Ministry of Internal Affairs was committed to strengthening the power of the governors and

---

[125] D. N. Tolstoi, "Zapiska grafa Dmitriia Nikolaevicha Tolstogo," *Russkii Arkhiv*, xxiii, No. 2, 1885, p. 59. Among the causes of Soloviev's stance must be included his genuine, though academic, attachment to the tradition of provincial government and life. See his "Pamiatniki i predaniia Vladimirskoi gubernii," *Otechestvennye Zapiski*, cxii (May 1857), 521, 551. On Soloviev see also Semenev, *Epokha osvobozhdeniia krestian* . . . , iii, 24-27.

[126] Soloviev, "Zapiski . . . ," March 1882, pp. 565ff.

establishing self-governing elective councils instead. Panin listened in stony silence, convinced that Russia was on the brink of a peasant uprising and could be rescued only by the immediate installation in the district capitals of semi-military officials responsible directly to the tsar. The two men parted coldly and for several months the rival parties they represented contended in overt clashes and more subtle tests of strength.[127]

During April the "fundamental principles" for district reform were drafted on the basis of Saltykov's official report and the comments of Minister of Justice Panin.[128] Dissenters from the Ministry of Internal Affairs, including Lanskoi, were barred entirely from the drafting process. Soloviev relates that this was achieved only through intrigue, with Muraviev, Rostovtsev, and Panin going so far as to prevent the aged Lanskoi from communicating with supporters within his own ministry.[129] Whether or not matters reached this extreme, Lanskoi and his aides were helpless to oppose them effectively when they came to a vote on May 16. In a crushing roll call, the establishment of virtually unrestricted governorships at the district level was approved.[130] Centralization carried the day.

But the issue was not dead. The vote completed, the Min-

[127] During this period Muraviev urgently requested that the Ministry of Internal Affairs send him whatever data they had at hand on police reform and was told by Lanskoi that hardly any precise material existed. TsGIA-SSSR, f. 869, op. 1, d. 520, pp. 16-17, Muraviev to Lanskoi, February 27, 1858 and Lanskoi to Muraviev, March 1, 1858. Lanskoi must be accused of attempting to put off Muraviev, for he claimed that the only material regarding police reform in his ministry's possession was a memorandum by August von Haxthausen and the projects which Muraviev and Rostovtsev had prepared. He failed to mention that a committee of his own ministry was presently collecting volumes of precisely such data.

[128] TsGIA-SSSR, f. 869, op. 1, d. 520, pp. 42-45.

[129] Soloviev "Zapiski . . . ," March 1882, pp. 575-76.

[130] *Ibid.*, February 1884, p. 244. The only modification considered at this session was a suggestion from the Ministry of Internal Affairs to place the new district heads under the control of the existing provincial governors. No decision was taken. TsGIA-SSSR, f. 869, op. 1, d. 520, pp. 44-45.

ister of Internal Affairs modestly requested permission to submit copies of the legislation to the governors, along with a report on the plan for introducing governors-general. With their guard down in the mood of overweening self-confidence that engulfed them after their victory, the centralizers readily consented. This letter to the governors proved to be a fatal concession to Lanskoi. The papers of the Main Committee provide no clue as to why Panin, Muraviev, and Rostovtsev committed this blunder, but Soloviev claims that everyone assumed that the matter was settled on May 16 and that any communication on the subject with the governors in the field would be a mere formality.[131] The governors, accustomed to the decentralizing mood of the Ministry of Internal Affairs, were shocked to learn that the opposite tendency held sway in Petersburg. Of the forty-six who responded to the circular, only three mustered the slightest praise for the proposed district governships.[132] Four more confined themselves to bland statements in favor of the general principle of police reform. The remaining thirty-nine governors greeted the plan with "terror and alarm" and fulminated against the inability of the Main Committee to comprehend the concrete needs of the provincial administrators.[133] Indeed, their responses to the circular of May 16, 1858, far surpassed in intensity, unanimity, and sheer hostility all other communications to Petersburg from the provinces before the years 1860 to 1861. Only in the last stages of the emancipation debate did the gentry equal the gubernatorial outcry of 1858.

[131] *Ibid.*, pp. 78-79. Butkov to Lanskoi, May 14, 1858, notes that even before the May 16 meeting the tsar was speaking as if the plan would definitely be approved.

[132] Soloviev notes that all of these had been graduates of the elite Corps de Pages and had spent their careers in the military ("Zapiski . . . ," February 1884, p. 253). The support of the governors-general for the plan is more perplexing, though a major factor was doubtless the fact that at the time the Vasilchikov program for thoroughgoing reform was still in the first planning stage.

[133] *Ibid.*, pp. 244-45. (The full texts of the replies are not available in either TsGIA-SSSR or TsGAOR.)

156

To protect themselves from the Main Committee, the governors fought to undercut the prerogatives of the proposed district heads. Two lines of attack were open. On the one hand, most governors invoked the principles of the division of powers to reclaim from the proposed district governors control over the economic and administrative functions which lay outside their security duties.[134] This would introduce a greater degree of functional specialization into the Russian administration than had ever before existed, which was highly desirable at a time when local institutions were called upon to execute an unprecedented number of tasks. On the other hand, a few governors proposed to call in the local public as a means of heading off the plan for creating district governors. This plan, too, would increase functional specialization, but unlike the solution of the majority of the governors, it required no new administrators since the public would manage those civic functions which public officials would otherwise have discharged. Needless to say, this option won the overwhelming support of the gentry who learned of it, and scores of them added their letters to those coming from the governors.

Members of Soloviev's committee may well have wondered how the gentry had become involved in the issue since only the governors were authorized to submit comments. The answer lay in the fear on the part of some of the governors that their voices alone would be too weak to prevail against the centralizers in Petersburg. Preferring to grant power to the public rather than turn it over to officials empowered only to be mouthpieces for Petersburg, they followed Soloviev's course and turned to the gentry. Most gentry opposed the district governorship plan anyway because, like the reforms that were later introduced, it would deny them their traditional control over rural police. Egged on by governors who supplied them with confidential information, groups of gentry denounced the high cost of the

---

[134] *Ibid.*, March 1884, pp. 566-68.

157

proposed district governorships[135] and the expansion of bureaucracy that would inevitably follow. For the moment
provincial administrators and the local public stood firmly
together in opposition to the central administration. As
Soloviev later recalled: "One may say without exaggeration
that except for those who drew them up, there existed no
defenders of the principles sent to the governors; everyone
opposed them. . . . Extreme planters agreed with extreme
abolitionists and so-called 'reds'; adroit district bureaucrats were of one mind with the governors."[136] The gentry
of Smolensk summed up the feelings of all these groups: the
plan for establishing district governors with combined police and administrative functions was "unjustifiable in both
political and administrative terms."[137] And so it was.

Against such unanimous opposition the centralist faction
in the Main Committee was helpless. By the early autumn
of 1858 it was evident to all that the extreme administrative
concentration embodied in the district governor plan and
the new governor-generalships was unacceptable to the
present governors and the gentry and hence infeasible. The
final demise of the centralists' proposal came some months
later, in October 1858. Faced with the reports from the governors and the Ministry of Internal Affairs, Alexander II
admitted defeat: "I see that all are opposed to my view," he
said. "I shall therefore withdraw it, though I am convinced
that I am right."[138] Politics was an illegal enterprise in tsar-

---

[135] TsGIA-SSSR, f. 1291, op. 123, d. 23, pp. 81-83. Report of
Nikolai Verbleskii, Smolensk province. See also Soloviev, "Zapiski
. . . ," February 1884, pp. 24-26.

[136] Soloviev, "Zapiski . . . ," February 1884, pp. 24-26; also
TsGAOR, f. 649, op. 1, ed. khr. 51, p. 7. "Mysli po povodu vnov
predpolozhennogo administrativno-politseiskogo ustroistva," May 24,
1858.

[137] *Ibid.*, Nikolai Ogarev called the proposal a "Bysantino-Germano
Chinese system." "There is now no salvation from bureaucracy," he
wrote, "instead of one governor there will be tens of them, i.e., Russia
will be pilfered ten times worse than she is now." *Kolokol* (August
15, 1858), 171.

[138] Soloviev, "Zapiski . . . ," March 1884, p. 600.

ist Russia; nevertheless, in this instance pressure from interest groups within and outside the autocracy succeeded in reversing an autocratic decision.

In light of the tsar's later support after 1865 for the reconcentration of administrative authority and restriction of elective agencies, it is revealing that at this point Alexander II was the last to hold out for the district governorships and the governors-general plan. In so doing he suggested that two of the three main recipes for reorganizing political authority at the time—to deconcentrate the bureaucracy or to share authority with the gentry through independent elective bodies—would not be fully acceptable to the Russian autocracy. But the events of 1858 provided only the barest hints at this verdict, hints that the tsar himself was as yet unable to perceive. Consequently, these two alternatives continued to be promoted with full vigor while the third—to exert more authority from Petersburg through appointed or elected officials—went into temporary eclipse.

The demise of the Muraviev program in the spring of 1858 did not automatically open the way for the implementation of the original reform proposals based on administrative deconcentration. Disinterest cannot be blamed for this, though governmental leaders were admittedly preoccupied with planning the emancipation of the serfs; nor can it be attributed to the absence of a general plan of action, for Saltykov, Soloviev, and the provincial governors had already set forth a fairly clear program of reform. Rather, the further delay after the summer of 1858 stemmed first from the fact that reforms in several distinct areas were still being dealt with under one heading and second from the absence of governmental organs empowered to draft the actual reform legislation.

The centralizers had blithely ignored the first problem. Their dual scheme for district governors and governors-general endowed single officials with a host of judicial, administrative, civic, and peace-keeping powers. Pressure for functional specialization was so great, however, that a major concern of the reformers was to crack this atomic mass into its individual components. They wanted to turn security affairs over to the police, judicial matters to the courts, civic issues to the local public, and purely administrative concerns to professional administrators. Before any one of these areas could be improved through reform, it had first to be isolated. Lanskoi made the first move in this direction by proposing to the tsar in a memorandum of October 24, 1858, that police and judicial powers henceforth be separated in Russia.[139]

This was an important step toward administrative reform but not a decisive one, for the police were still competent to meddle in a large number of civic affairs that had no bearing on peace-keeping and security. To whom should these matters be entrusted? Though they agreed that the gentry should lose its police role, neither Soloviev nor his colleagues wanted civic matters to fall into bureaucratic hands if they pertained to purely local interests. They proposed instead to take such civic functions from the police and local bureaucrats and turn them over to self-administered bodies of the local public. After consulting with Lanskoi, Soloviev on November 28, 1858, laid before the Main Committee a sketch to provide "the [elective] government of the district with greater unity, more independence and greater trust."[140]

Was Soloviev's desire to turn the civil functions of the police over to elective organs prompted by the need to compensate the gentry for the loss of its police jurisdiction?[141]

[139] *Ibid.*, pp. 594-95.

[140] TsGIA-SSSR, f. 1291, op. 123, ed. khr. 23, p. 2. In his "Zapiski . . . ," Soloviev describes the reading of the projected memorandum to Lanskoi, with N. A. Miliutin present. According to Soloviev, Miliutin commented that "It's hardly likely that you will succeed in getting this through," to which Lanskoi smiled "goodheartedly and sarcastically, with the look of an extreme liberal," and Soloviev replied "God will help us." Soloviev, "Zapiski . . . ," March 1884, pp. 601-03.

[141] The lords did not actually lose all their control over the local

Though this popular interpretation is plausible, two pieces of evidence contradict it. In the first place, Soloviev explicitly denies it, claiming that he was motivated "by the desire to strengthen the police" and to make them more efficient.[142] Second, had he been concerned merely to compensate the gentry, Soloviev no doubt could have transferred the civil functions of the police directly to the gentry's assemblies rather than to all-class bodies. This was not done and, in fact, he called for further study "to define the degree of participation of *each estate* in the government of the district's economic affairs."[143] Thus, this important act must be seen as a deliberate measure for clarifying and strengthening local authority, and no crude ploy to repay the gentry for lost powers.

By these means the spheres of local administrative and public authority were isolated from the judicial and security functions and from each other.[144] But until late in 1858 there existed no organ with responsibility for drafting the final administrative reforms. In March, Lanskoi had constituted a special *"Zemskii"* ("land" or "local") Section in his ministry to supervise "the public economic organization of the Empire."[145] That the Ministry of Internal Affairs organized this group was itself something of a victory, for members of the Main Committee had wanted the group to be divorced from the interests of any particular ministry, with members drawn equally from three other ministries in addition to Internal Affairs.[146] For the time being, this re-

---

peasantry, as had been pointed out by Zaionchkovskii, *Otmena . . . ,* p. 143. Zaionchkovskii sees this residue of police power as a part of the same effort at compensation as the establishment of self-government.

[142] Soloviev, "Zapiski . . . ," March 1884, p. 601.

[143] *Ibid.*

[144] TsGIA-SSSR, f. 572, op. 6, ed. khr. 7574, pp. 51ff.; also, *Ministerstvo vnutrennykh del,* pp. 132-33.

[145] *Materialy dlia istorii uprazdneniia krepostnogo sostoianiia,* I, 264.

[146] Levshin, "Dostopamiatnye minuty . . . ," p. 554.

161

mained a Pyrrhic victory for Lanskoi, though, because for five months after its foundation the *Zemskii* Section had only two permanent members.[147] To make matters worse the entire work of organization was left to the more subordinate member, Iakov Soloviev.

Working as a committee of one, Soloviev began by compiling all further replies from the governors to Lanskoi's circulars. To deal with the important circular of May 16, 1858, he divided his small staff into two groups, one to examine comments relating to organs of district government and the other to study peasant institutions. In so doing, he created in the first group the germ of the future Commission on Provincial and District Institutions which was to prepare both the final reform of local government and the new *zemstvo* organs.

At this juncture Lanskoi and his co-workers had carried their decentralization plan over several hurdles. They had led it safely through heavy attack from the centralizers, had neatly distinguished its sphere from all other reforms affecting local life, and had entrusted it to the care of a vital central agency of their own ministry for final drafting. Moreover, Alexander had himself declared that the success of the forthcoming emancipation would hinge on the smooth implementation of local administrative reforms.[148] Emboldened by this favorable turn of events, Lanskoi decided to bring into the open a plan that had long been hatching within his ministry. In February of 1859 he submitted to the Committee of Ministers a sweeping proposal for administrative reform to be conducted on a trial basis in the province of Kiev. As approved in March it embodied most of the principles of reform under discussion since 1856.[149] Within weeks, local administrators were implementing this experiment in decentralization in the province of Kiev.

[147] Soloviev, "Zapiski . . . ," February 1883, p. 286.

[148] TsGIA-SSSR, f. 1281 (1858), op. 123, d. 22, pp. 1-2. Butkov to Lanskoi, February 28, 1858.

[149] *MSVUK*, I, otd. 4, p. 9n.

THE KIEV EXPERIMENT

It seems strange that an important administrative innovation should have been unveiled in a non-Russian province 600 miles from the capital. The landholding classes there were notoriously committed to the old order. Though serfdom had arrived late in the Ukraine, it became a more integral factor in the local black-soil economy than in many industrial provinces in the North and members of the local gentry were anxious to preserve it as nearly intact as possible. They fought first to bring about a landless emancipation and when they lost on this attempted to minimize the acreage allotted to the peasants in order to preserve as much of their capital in land as possible.[150] Such intractability on the part of the gentry caused the governor of neighboring Poltava province secretly to petition the tsar to have the entire emancipation debate conducted in St. Petersburg.[151]

The prospect of emancipation aroused the five and a half million peasants of the Ukraine more than their northern counterparts. Thousands had fled to the war zone in 1855 in the hope that military service would gain them freedom; those who stayed behind raised a series of revolts more numerous and extensive than any within Great Russia.[152] The prevailing tension also found expression in the crime rate of Kiev province. According to statistics—obviously approximate—submitted to the secret police, the incidence of murder in Kiev province exceeded the levels of both

---

[150] A. Z. Baraba and others, eds., *Otmena krepostnogo prava na Ukraine: sbornik dokumentov i materialov*, Kiev, 1961, p. 13, and pp. 106-08 for a report of Lanskoi to the Main Committee on emancipation concerning the assemblies of gentry in the Ukraine in 1857.

[151] TsGIA-SSSR, f. 1291 (1856), op. 33, d. 2, pp. 99ff. Letter to Lanskoi, January 25, 1857. The governor feared that the influence of rumor and gossip would adversely affect the discussions if they were to be held in Podolia, *ibid.*, p. 104.

[152] Baraba, *Otmena . . . na Ukraine*, p. 15, pp. 69ff.; also P. Kopoliuk, G. Marakhov, eds., *Obshchestvenno-politicheskoe dvizhenie na Ukraine, 1856-1862*, 2 vols., Kiev, 1963, I, iv.

Petersburg and Moscow provinces with their large metropolitan centers; and compared to such northern provinces as Tver and Pskov, the Kiev murder rate was two and three times greater, respectively.[153]

Added to these difficulties was the double-barreled nationality problem. Ukrainian federalism did not become a matter for serious concern until the early months of 1860, though provincial officials had kept partisans of the movement under surveillance for years.[154] The Polish radical movement attracted the attention of the Governor-General of Kiev in October of 1858, when he alerted civil governors to the activities of Polish secret societies and immigrant organizations.[155] Less revolutionary but more dangerous than the secret societies were the Polish landlords who dominated the serf-owning class on the right bank of the Dnieper. Authorities in Kiev could not be blind to this separatist threat; the governor-general gathered ancient acts and documents to "prove that Poles had no valid historical claims to Ukrainian land," and even established a newspaper in Kiev to spread anti-Polish propaganda.[156]

Reports from his agents familiarized Lanskoi with conditions in the Ukraine but did not deter him from conducting his administrative experiment in Kiev province. Looming large among his reasons for doing so was the fact that he had in the Governor-General of Kiev one of the most reliable civil servants in the empire, Prince Ilarion Vasilchikov. Vasilchikov had advanced rapidly in the military thanks to frequent special peace-keeping assignments in the prov-

[153] Figures computed from Rashin's population data, pp. 28-29, and from murder reports contained in the archive of the IIIrd Section, TsGAOR, f. 109, op. 85, ed. khr. 27, "Otchet o deistviiakh III otdeleniia sobstvennoi ego imp. velichestva kontsiliarii, 1862," p. 317.

[154] Kopoliuk and Marakhov, eds., *Obshchestvenno-politicheskoe dvizhenie* . . . , I, xii, xiii, 7.

[155] *Ibid.*, I, 17-18; also 31-34, 37ff. on mass arrests early in 1860.

[156] TsGIA-SSSR, f. 769, op. 1, d. 401, pp. 2-3; f. 1180 (1858-62), op. xv, d. 88, pp. 265-69.

inces given him by Nicholas I.[157] Then, when war broke out in the Crimea, Nicholas appointed him Chief of Staff of the army,[158] and after the conclusion of peace, Alexander II called on him to conduct an investigation into the corrupt practices and profiteering which had accompanied the national sacrifice.[159] Thus, by the time he was named to the post of Governor-General of Kiev, Podolia, and Volhynia, Vasilchikov enjoyed a solid reputation as a military man and as an expert administrator, skilled in handling civil disorders but devoted to reform.[160]

Even if Vasilchikov had been less well recommended, the administration of Kiev province could not long have escaped official notice. For, as he pointed out in his reports to the Minister of Internal Affairs, conditions there were forcing reform upon him. In the first three postwar years,

[157] As a Flügel-Adjutant in 1839 he was dispatched to provinces where peasant revolts were occurring, and in 1842 his expertise on civil disturbances earned him a place on a ministerial committee studying an uprising in Volhynia. A. V. Predtchenskii, ed., *Krestianskoe dvizhenie v Rossii v 1825-1849 gg.*, Moscow, 1961, pp. 426-31, 674n.

[158] S. S. Tatishchev, *Imperator Aleksandr II, Ego zhizn i tsarstvovanie*, 2 vols., St. Petersburg, 1903, ı, 164-65, E. V. Tarle, *Krymskaia Voina*, 2 vols., Moscow, 1950, ıı, 309.

[159] Tarle, ı, 207-08. This commission is not to be confused with the better known Riediger Commission of 1855-56, of which Vasilchikov was not a member. P. A. Zaionchkovskii, *Voennye reformy 1860-1870 gg. v Rossii*, Moscow, 1952, pp. 45-46.

[160] Among the many family dynasties which dominated Russian civil and military life in the prereform era, none were more successful than the Vasilchikovs. Ilarion's father had been president of both the State Council and the Committee of Ministers under Nicholas I. His younger brother, Victor, had commanded the beleaguered garrison during the siege of Sevastopol. Through a rapid series of promotions, he became a top aide in the Ministry of War in 1857 and, in the following year, was appointed Minister. Another brother, Alexander, served the state as a leader in provincial administrative life and became an early convert to the idea of self-government. In his monumental work. *On Self-Government (O Samoupravlenii)*, of which mention has been made, he showed himself to be a no less adamant champion of regional public service than his brother was of administrative improvement.

for instance, the number of separate problems considered by his underlings rose from 24,490 to 26,144 and the quantity of individual papers sent out grew from 227,851 to 275,176.[161] The building commission had long grumbled about being overworked and by 1858 was too overwhelmed with petty affairs even to build itself a headquarters.[162] Meanwhile, the provinces were "extremely ill-prepared against fires, floods, livestock diseases, epidemics and other misfortunes."[163]

Vasilchikov candidly exposed to the tsar all the faults of the administration which he controlled: "With extreme contrition . . . I am compelled to report with all frankness that the principal administrative and judicial institutions do not fulfill their designated purposes. They are . . . in an entirely unsatisfactory condition."[164] Underlying the monotonous list of difficulties Vasilchikov found that the provincial apparatus suffered from a lack of "independence" (i.e., from the central authorities) and a consequent inability to exercise power commensurate with the needs of the situation. In other words, Kiev was undergoverned. To remedy this and to establish "true local government,"[165] Vasilchikov appended an outline for reform to his report for the years 1858 and 1859. His six proposals were:

1. To unite in a single Provincial Directorate its disjointed parts, including the present Provincial Directorate, the Building and Roads Commissions, the Office of Public Charity, the Medical Directorate, the Committees on Local Duties, Health, Smallpox, Jails, Jewish Landworkers, Public Provisioning, etc.

---

[161] TsGIA-SSSR, f. 869, op. 1, d. 393, pp. 8-10, 12.
[162] *Ibid.*, pp. 24-27. [163] *Ibid.*, p. 52.
[164] *MSVUK*, I, otd. 4., p. 1.
[165] This expression was not used in the first proposal, but in the report he submitted in 1861 on the experiment. TsGIA-SSSR, f. 869, op. 1, d. 401, "Obzor polozheniia gub. Kievskoi, Podolskoi i Volynskoi . . . v 1858 i 1860," pp. 9ff.

2. To form Sections of the Provincial Directorate from these, by combining several of them into one unit according to the similarity of the issues with which they deal . . .

3. To combine the offices of all these institutions, together with the Governor's office, into one general Chancellory of the Provincial Directorate . . .

4. To abolish forever written communication among those branches and to eliminate published proceedings except for the most important issues . . .

5. To combine all district committees and commissions into a District Directorate . . .

6. To free the provincial governments . . . of the duty of reviewing judicial affairs . . .[166]

Lanskoi's Committee on Reducing Correspondence brought these recommendations to the tsar's attention. Eager to strengthen administration in the provinces, Alexander approved the Vasilchikov proposals and forwarded them to the two ministries affected, Internal Affairs and Justice, both of whose directors responded favorably.

The plan which Alexander finally approved embodied contradictory tendencies. Undeniably it represented a certain retreat from the extreme reformism of the governors' responses to the Committee on Reducing Correspondence in 1857 and 1858. Vasilchikov and Lanskoi could mollify the centralists by pointing out that their new proposal left largely intact the much criticized collegiate system established in the provinces by Catherine.[167] At the same time the plan did abolish collegiate relations *within* local agencies of the Ministry of Internal Affairs, and once that ministry dismantled its clumsy collegiate structure the local of-

---

[166] *MSVUK*, I, otd. 4, pp. 6-7. (On point "4" see also TsGIA-SSSR, f. 869, op. 1, d. 394, for an unsigned project submitted to Nikolai Miliutin with the same end.)

[167] *Ibid.*, p. 2.

fices of the other ministries would be placed in a relatively disadvantaged position, and by the natural processes of institutional change, would find their functions slowly gravitating toward those bodies which were able to handle them more efficiently.

Vasilchikov did not so much as mention the word "decentralization." But in reality the "independence" which he sought for the provincial head was identical to that advocated by the governors in 1856. The governor would preside over the consolidated directorates and the staffs of these agencies would be merged with the governor's chancellery. The governors and their aides would thus be endowed with genuine power and competence. Evidence of the governor's new freedom of action is his right, confirmed by Lanskoi, to hire and fire staff members.[168] Another example of autonomy is the distinction which Vasilchikov drew between those decisions which could be approved by a committee, those which had to be referred to the vice-governor, and those which the governor alone could pass on. Conspicuously absent from this list was a category of decisions which could be undertaken only with the consent of the central authorities.[169] Yet another manifestation of the trend toward deconcentration was the call for a fund to be placed at the governor's disposal. Lanskoi readily consented to this, and suggested that 7,000 rubles be granted annually to the governor to be used at his own discretion.[170]

Finally Vasilchikov designated the Provincial Directorates to be centers of a network of District Directorates where functions would be consolidated on the same lines as at the provincial level. To these district offices would be transferred a wide range of functions presently controlled

[168] *Ibid.*, p. 23. This was to be tested on an experimental basis for three years.

[169] *Proekt uchrezhdeniia Kievskogo gubernskogo upravleniia*, Kiev, 1860, pp. 11-12.

[170] *MSVUK*, I, otd. 4, p. 24.

by provincial officials, including management of grain storage, toll roads, medicine, prisons, fire fighting, and the quartering of troops. But final control in all district matters would be retained by the governor and his agents, to whom the new District Directorates would be directly subordinated. Not only would the governor become more independent of the central agencies but he would acquire substantial new means for acting directly on the life of his provinces at the most local level.

So strong was Vasilchikov's desire to extend the powers of the provincial governor to its ultimate limits that he invaded areas properly reserved for the local "societal" organization. His usurpation of public powers was evident in his treatment of the Offices of Public Charity.[171] Catherine II's provincial statute of 1775 denied that these were administrative organizations at all. As "societal" institutions they were controlled jointly by officers elected by the gentry and by local officials. In addition to managing philanthropy, the Offices of Public Charity served the local gentry as credit institutions, issuing loans to which many an estate owed its long-term survival. Vasilchikov's plan to place them under gubernatorial jurisdiction would certainly have fortified the province as an autonomous administrative unit but would also have placed an important element of gentry self-rule under administrative surveillance. Nikolai Miliutin detected this conflict between decentralization and gentry self-government in the Vasilchikov reform and penciled in the margin, "This measure would destroy the societal institutions."[172] This feature disturbed Lanskoi as well, who in disavowing it pointed out that to unite the charity funds with the provincial treasuries would adversely affect the former.[173]

The reason Vasilchikov so blithely placed institutions of public self-rule under local administrative control was that

[171] *Ibid.*, p. 16.
[172] TsGIA-SSSR, f. 869, op. 1, d. 393, p. 11.
[173] *MSVUK*, I, otd. 4, p. 16.

however skeptical he may have been of the ability of centralized ministries to function effectively in the provinces, he had boundless faith in the capacities of a deconcentrated administration. This conviction led him so far as to internalize the function of inspection and control within the governor's own office. Like the French Saint-Simonians, he proposed to appoint specially trained *tekhniki*, or administrative technicians, to check on local agencies. These locally based specialists, with the help of the governor, would take over the heretofore centralized system of revision and control.[174]

Taken as a whole, the proposal of Governor-General Vasilchikov for the province of Kiev closely paralleled the demands of the governors. And it was persuasive. The evidence he mustered to the cause of decentralization might, had it come from a less respected administrator, have been interpreted as evidence of Vasilchikov's own incompetence, or, at the very least, as proof that effective central control was required to save the day. The fact that nobody drew these conclusions attests both to the esteem in which the governor-general was held and to the prior commitment of the Ministry of Internal Affairs to the principle of administrative decentralization.

On March 3 and 17, 1859, the Committee of Ministers acceded to all the proposals advanced by Prince Vasilchikov with the exception of the localization of prison administration and the usurpation of "societal" functions by the provincial bureaucracy.[175] Vasilchikov then prepared a final draft of the project and during August and September of 1859 introduced deconcentrated administration into Kiev province.

How did the Vasilchikov program actually function in

---

[174] *Proekt . . . upravleniia*, pp. 49-50. Cf. P. Polezhaev's proposals from the same year, "O gubernskom nadzore," *Zhurnal Ministerstva Iustitsii*, No. 5, 1859.

[175] *MSVUK*, I, otd. 4, pp. 28-30. ("Vypiski iz zhurnalov Komiteta Ministrov, 3 i 17 Marta 1859 goda sostoiavshikhsia.")

Kiev? In his first annual report following the changeover, Vasilchikov spoke openly of the virtues of "decentralized administration" and advocated its adoption everywhere. "Internal correspondence between the agencies no longer exists," he gloated.[176] The local governor, Hesse, eliminated numerous secretarial jobs at an annual saving of 1,350 rubles. These funds he applied to raising the salaries of the remaining civil servants, from the provincial architect through the senior councillors. Unresolved administrative issues declined from 10,535 to 6,962 and Vasilchikov anticipated that the remaining backlog would soon vanish.

Upon reading Prince Vasilchikov's enthusiastic report, Alexander penciled on it his hope that the Kiev experiment "would serve as an example and guide for the other provincial governors."[177] Not delaying a minute, Vasilchikov immediately prepared an identical proposal for the provinces of Podolia and Volhynia, which were both under his control as governor-general of the entire region.[178] These reforms received royal authorization at once and by the spring of 1860 were being introduced in practice; the following year the same reforms were extended to the province of Lithuania.[179]

Thus, in 1859 to 1861 the Ministry of Internal Affairs succeeded in realizing at least a part of the program for decentralization advocated by the provincial governors and by the Committee on Reducing Correspondence. But unless it could be generalized and applied to the other forty-seven provinces the Vasilchikov experiment would leave no deeper mark on Russian provincial administration than the Balashov experiment in regionalization had in the 1820s. Several distinct inadequacies flawed the Kiev program and

---

[176] *Ibid.*, pp. 9-10.   [177] *Ibid.*, p. 1.
[178] *Proekt uchrezhdeniia Podolskogo gubernskogo upraveleniia,* Kamenetsk-Podolsk, 1861. *Proekt uchrezhdeniia Volynskogo gubernskogo upravleniia,* n.p., 1861. Lithographed copies of both are in the Leningrad Public Library.
[179] TsGIA-SSSR, f. 908, op. 1, d. 310, p. 38. Report of Prince Urusov, 1869.

had to be corrected before it could serve as a model for a general deconcentration of provincial agencies. First, the Vasilchikov reforms made no provisions for the participation of elective bodies in provincial and district affairs; since he considered the gentry to be a threat to the orderly administration of the region, he simply excluded them and the public in general from any share in his local reforms. Nor was the Kiev program integrated with the other social and institutional conditions soon to be introduced by the emancipation of the serfs; Vasilchikov cannot be faulted for this, but full coordination between reforms was essential if deconcentrated administration was to succeed. Third, Vasilchikov had cautiously avoided interfering in the affairs of local organs of the powerful Ministries of Finances and State Domains. Unless deconcentration was to be limited, the reforms would have to encompass the local agents of these bodies as well.

The only suitable organ for resolving these crucial problems was the *Zemskii* Section, to which the tsar entrusted the matter on March 25, 1859.[180] By then, however, most of that body's staff was occupied with other issues. Accordingly, Alexander elevated the subgroup already dealing with administrative matters to the status of a legislative body and renamed it the Commission on Provincial and District Institutions. Though Soloviev promptly emerged as the most active member of the new group, Lanskoi selected his newly appointed assistant minister, Nikolai Miliutin, as chairman.[181]

The fate of administrative reform for all of Russia now resided in the hands of Miliutin's commission within a section under the Ministry of Internal Affairs. This should have rendered the body relatively secure from influence by other ministries. Lanskoi, however, was not content with this clear advantage and pressed Alexander at once for permis-

[180] TsGIA-SSSR, f. 1291, op. 123, d. 23, p. 61.
[181] TsGIA-SSSR, f. 869, op. 1, d. 398, invitation of March 30, 1859; Miliutina, "Iz zapisok . . . ," p. 48.

sion to place on the commission as many of his provincial governors as possible and also to limit further the influence and participation of other ministries.[182] By seizing the initiative, he managed to gain seats for eight of his appointees. But Lanskoi had overplayed his hand. Other ministries became suspicious, and they retaliated by demanding seats for three representatives from the Ministry of the Imperial Household, two from Justice, one from State Domains, and one from the Second (legal) Section of the Imperial Chancellery.[183] The gains Lanskoi scored by stacking the commission with his own men were further qualified when his own bureaucracy kept governors from the capital for months while they corresponded over authorization to travel and for money to cover expenses on the road.[184] Still further vexations were experienced when several conscientious governors declined to serve for fear of missing local gentry assemblies at which the emancipation of the serfs was being debated.[185]

Before the new commission could take up the administrative reforms it had to draft a final text for the reform of district and town police. This should have been done with dispatch since the character of the proposed reforms had earlier been discussed and settled in principle. But now the gubernatorial bloc, ever suspicious of moves against their office, compelled the commission to solicit the local governors once more for their views on the territorial division of police functions.[186] This maneuver antagonized those concerned with domestic security and delayed the promulgation of police reform, and hence of the other administrative reforms as well. In 1862 police reform finally was sent to the

---

[182] TsGIA-SSSR, f. 1291 (1859), op. 123, d. 37, pp. 3-5, 12, Lanskoi to Alexander, March 27, 1859; also, f. 1405, op. 57, d. 207, Lanskoi and Soloviev to Panin.

[183] TsGIA-SSSR, f. 869, op. 1, d. 392.

[184] TsGIA-SSSR, f. 1291 (1859), op. 123, d. 37, p. 50.

[185] *Ibid.*, p. 34. The governors of Kaluga, Samara, and Tauride provinces all refused for this reason.

[186] TsGIA-SSSR, f. 1316, op. 1, d. 126.

173

Senate for its formal approval.[187] This legislation went far toward converting the police—in theory at least—into a specialized security force, formally depriving them of the dominant role in local administration which they had enjoyed for a century. One firm stroke excluded them—again, in theory—from such diverse affairs as conducting lotteries, sponsoring lecture series, organizing processions of the cross, founding clubs, organizing commercial undertakings, and managing philanthropic bureaus.[188]

Doctrinaire partisans of English self-government, including the Soviet scholar Garmiza, complain that all this was achieved only through "the extreme centralization of the autocratic state power and not through decentralization."[189] In one sense this is certainly correct, for an important element of English rule before Peel had been the localization of what little police function did exist. But this can hardly be the cause of Garmiza's concern. Rather he is taking note of the fact that even though the new legislation granted to the localities control over the levying and auditing of certain taxes, the actual collection remained in the hands of the police. And though police functions were reduced, the reform led directly to a 9 percent increase in the total number of police in Russia.[190] On the other hand, the police power was now defined in negative as well as positive terms. Because the legislation excluded police from areas in which they had heretofore enjoyed free rein, it opened to local administrative and elective bodies a broad new sphere of activity to be organized in accordance with the reformist principles of the era.

---

[187] TsGIA-SSSR, f. 572, op. 6, ed. khr. 7574, pp. 51ff.; see also, *Ministerstvo vnutrennykh del* . . . , pp. 132-33. Alexander had signified his approval earlier, on April 12, 1860. TsGIA-SSSR, f. 1291, op. 123, d. 23, p. 149.

[188] TsGIA-SSSR, f. 1386 (1863), op. 24, d. 1142.

[189] Garmiza, *Podgotovka* . . . , p. 138.

[190] Police pay was also somewhat augmented: TsGIA-SSSR, f. 573, op. 6, ed. khr. 7574, October 24, 1863.

COMPLETING THE LEGISLATIVE PROCESS

The translation of administrative intentions into policies is never simple, and Russia in the reform era was no exception. Alexander II himself articulated the decentralizing goals of the Commission on Provincial and District Institutions when, quoting Soloviev, he urged the group to grant local administrative bodies "as much unity, independence and trust as possible."[191] Lanskoi, too, considered the commission as above all a tool for achieving his program of administrative decentralization.[192] Yet in spite of this clear mandate, the commission failed to meet the tsar's request that the new local institutions be promulgated simultaneously with the liberation of the serfs. When the emancipation statutes were issued on February 19, 1861, Miliutin's commission had existed for a year and a half but had not yet presented final drafts for any major legislation. Another year was required to ready the police reform for promulgation, and the equally crucial administrative reorganization had to wait until 1865 to be fully instituted. Given the enormous change of temper which Russian society and government underwent in the interim, this delay is of more than passing importance. By the time the decentralization reforms were instituted, few of their original partisans remained in office and the domestic conditions of Russia cast deep shadows over the entire reformist program.

Lanskoi in 1860 did not anticipate this great delay,[193] and the impatience of the press suggests that the public at large expected it no more than Lanskoi did. It was caused pri-

---

[191] *Sbornik pravitelstvennykh rasporiazhenii po ustroistvu byt krestian* . . . , I, 46-47; *Materialy po zemskomu obshchestvennomu ustroistvu*, 2 vols., St. Petersburg, 1885, I, 1-2; *Trudy komissii o gubernskikh i uezdnykh uchrezhdeniiakh*, 6 vols., 2 pts., St. Petersburg, 1860-63, I, 7ff.

[192] TsGIA-SSSR, f. 1291 (1859), op. 123, d. 387, p. 90.

[193] *Trudy komissii o gubernskikh i uezdnykh uchrezhdeniiakh*, I, p. 15.

175

marily by the restiveness of the local gentry, which forced the planning of the self-governing *zemstvo* institutions to take precedence over purely administrative reforms. In addition, the "petty bureaucratic formalism" which the commission was supposed to abolish impeded reform at every step. Not until mid-1860, for example, did the Commission on Provincial and District Institutions receive funds to cover its expenses.[194] Likewise, important working papers of the Commission on Reducing Correspondence were not made available to the legislators until a year after Lanskoi ordered them transferred.[195]

True to the meticulous procedures of the Petersburg ministries, Miliutin's commission began by gathering data. It availed itself of all the reports from governors over the past half-decade and prepared its own digest of their more outspoken proposals.[196] Also, the group commissioned a weighty historical study of provincial institutions in west European nations and a compilation of all existing legislation on local administration in the more developed states.[197] Armed with this flood of data, and much outright propaganda for decentralization, the commission drew up its first "Considerations" on administrative reform. It declared that the focal point of local administrations should be the Provincial Directorates under the governors. During 1860, this principle was developed concretely in a much more detailed draft written largely by Iakov Soloviev.[198] At this

[194] *MSVUK*, I, otd. 4, pp. 1-2, October 23, 1858; the original is preserved in TsGIA-SSSR, f. 1291 (1859), op. 123, d. 37, pp. 83-84.

[195] TsGIA-SSSR, f. 1291 (1859), op. 123, d. 37, pp. 92-93; also TsGIA-SSSR, f. 1314, op. 5, d. 55, pp. 5-6.

[196] *MSVUK*, I, otd. 4, p. 36.

[197] *Ibid.*, pp. 35-36. (*Otdel dlia nachertaniia nachal preobrazovaniia gubernskikh uchrezhdenii, Doklad No. 1.*)

[198] *Ibid.*, p. 18, this draft is usually referred to as the Miliutin project because N. A. Miliutin turned it over to Valuev when Valuev took charge of the ministry; Soloviev, "Zapiski . . . ," February 1884, p. 272. The text was printed in *MSVUK*, *otdel administrativnyi*, I, otd. 5, pp. 18-25; it was signed by Nikolai Miliutin,

point, the commission benefited from the experiment in administrative deconcentration being conducted in Kiev, Podolia, and Volhynia. Following the Vasilchikov reforms, the commissioners planned such independent organs as the Provincial Committees for Public Health, the Provincial Committees for Vaccinations, the Road Commissions, and the Building Commissions to function only as consultative bodies to the Provincial Directorates, which, with the governors, would make all administrative decisions. In order to free the governors from all trifling affairs and to enable them to fulfill their stewardship function, the commission entrusted day-to-day control over the directorates to the vice-governors.

Through the reform of the directorates, provincial administrations would receive greater unity but little more power than they had previously enjoyed. To increase their power vis-à-vis the central ministries in Petersburg, entirely new Provincial Councils (*gubernskie sovety*) were to be created. These bodies would be composed of the heads of subsections of the directorates, the marshals of the gentry, directors of the agencies of self-government, and local representatives of the Ministries of Finances and State Domains. The Councils would be empowered "to decide, in order to eliminate excess concentration of work in the higher [i.e., central] state institutions, several administrative matters which exceed the power of the local Provincial Directorate as stated in the existing legislation."[199] Thus, special provincial superagencies of all bureaucratic and elective administrative leaders would become the vehicles for deconcentration.

Soloviev readied his project for the entire commission to examine in the spring of 1861. Then, just as it was coming up for debate, Alexander summarily relieved both Lanskoi

Konstantin Grot, Nikolai Stoianovskii, Konstantin Marchenko, and Iakov Soloviev.

[199] *Ibid.*, p. 24.

and Miliutin of their posts.[200] And though the reforming minister was seventy-four years old and his health had been faltering for some time, there seems to have been no effort made to groom a successor. Passing over all members of the Editing Commissions and the State Council, the tsar finally selected the relatively little known ex-governor of the Lithuanian province of Courland, Peter Valuev, to succeed both Lanskoi as Minister of Internal Affairs and Miliutin as chairman of the Commission on Provincial and District Institutions. Whatever qualities Valuev possessed that had impressed Alexander, charity toward top officials was certainly not one of them. In his diary, Valuev vindictively described Lanskoi as obtuse,[201] Panin as "simple-minded,"[202] State Councillor Count Gurev as "stuck in the past,"[203] Minister of Finance Reutern as "intellectually obese,"[204] and both Baron Korf of the Legal Department and State Councillor Bakhtin as "naive."[205] In return for his dispeptic attitude toward his colleagues Valuev was not infrequently snubbed by Petersburg society; as if to spite his drawing-room critics, the widowed Valuev married a Polish Catholic noblewoman in the midst of the Polish uprising.[206] Proud to the point of arrogance, Valuev was at the same time an almost pathological introvert. "I know why I have no friends and why I cannot have any," he wrote, "and I know that I am not at fault."[207]

In spite of Valuev's abrasive personality, Alexander's choice was a wise one, for Valuev had demonstrated an unbending devotion to the government. During the historical debates of 1856 to 1858, Valuev had sided with Boris Chicherin's argument that the peasant commune was a cre-

---

[200] The reasons for their dismissal were connected solely with the emancipation issue; see page 242.

[201] Valuev, *Dnevnik*, I, 57.   [202] *Ibid.*, pp. 83-84.

[203] *Ibid.*, p. 57.   [204] *Ibid.*, p. 135.

[205] P. A. Valuev, "Dnevnik za 1847-1860 gg." *Russkaia Starina*, LXX-LXXI, April-August, 1891, p. 270.

[206] Miliutina, "Iz zapisok . . . ," pp. 59-60.

[207] Valuev, *Dnevnik*, I, 78.

ation not of the people but of the Russian state.[208] Throughout the nationalities crisis of the sixties, he stood firmly for what he termed "the state principle" and, like Katkov, with whom he carried on a lively correspondence, sought an ideology that could unite the Russian people under the throne. At the same time, Valuev was known as a man able to win the confidence of suspicious provincial gentry, a quality that was particularly needed after the divisive confrontations over emancipation. Most important from the standpoint of administrative reform, he was among those civil servants who had earned their reputations by expressing hostility to bureaucratism and at the time of his appointment was a firm partisan of administrative decentralization.

A decisive factor in his appointment as Minister of Internal Affairs was the lengthy memorandum which he submitted to the Committee on Reducing Correspondence in compliance with the circular of October 2, 1856. Indeed, next to Vasilchikov's project for Kiev, Valuev's report was the most thoroughgoing reform program advanced by a provincial official during the reform period. In his memorandum Valuev voiced most of the same demands raised in the other twenty-two reports received by Lanskoi, but Valuev's essay was distinguished by a fluency and precision that was exceedingly rare even among top administrators.[209]

The new minister stamped his views on the administrative reform immediately after his appointment. On July 28, 1861, the Commission on Provincial and District Institutions met under his chairmanship to examine the Soloviev-Miliutin project. Valuev and other members presented critical comments and counterproposals and, by the end of the session, agreed that the draft would have to undergo considerable revision before promulgation.[210] Their keenest discontent was with the petty tasks still assigned to gover-

[208] Valuev, "Dnevnik . . . ," p. 607.
[209] *MSVUK, otdel administrativnyi*, I, otd. 4, pp. 197-206.
[210] *Ibid.*, pp. 276-85.

nors and the still "far from satisfactory" powers granted to them. The Governor of Petersburg submitted a strongly worded demand that the governors be freed from time-consuming bureaucratic procedures,[211] while another member turned in a counterproject relieving governors of the need to watch over every move by city and town authorities.[212] With respect to the governors' sphere of authority, the early draft had reaffirmed their control over agencies of the Ministry of Internal Affairs but failed to extend it to offices of other ministries (other than the local Road and Building Commissions, under the Main Directorate for Channels of Communication). Now Valuev ordered all agencies of both the Ministry of Finances and State Domains to be decentralized and subordinated to the governor and directorates.

Word of this bold measure reached both ministries in question within hours. Since the Ministry of State Domains would no longer exercise wardship over state peasants, the minister, Muraviev, was now surprisingly amenable to Valuev's idea.[213] This was decidedly not the case, however, with the Ministry of Finances. In his early months in office Valuev had tactfully required his governors to consult with the Ministry of Finances every time a major case of unpaid taxes arose.[214] Soon, however, Valuev began what was to be a protracted campaign against that ministry. The response of the Ministry of Finances to Valuev's proposals came in a letter from the talented economist and future minister, Mikhail Reutern. In it he stated his ministry's categorical refusal to consider any decentralization that would benefit the governors: "In the case of disorder or irregularities in the treasury offices the governor has already been given the right to inform those agencies and to demand that the error or illegality be righted. However, he cannot touch on

211 *Ibid.*, p. 279, proposal by Count A. Bobrinskii.
212 *Ibid.*, pp. 69-77, proposal by A. Giers.
213 *Ibid.*, pp. 283-84.
214 TsGIA-SSSR, f. 1287 (1861), op. 22, d. 1041, p. 4.

the internal decisions of an office or the method of disbursing Treasury monies, which depends wholly on the Ministry of Finances."[215] In the face of this clash of interest, Valuev refused to withdraw his proposal, just as his rival ministry refused to comply with it.

Returning to the Commission on Provincial and District Institutions, members criticized the failure of the Soloviev-Miliutin draft clearly to distinguish administrative concerns from those matters to be handled by the future *zemstvo* organs of self-government. Several commissioners singled out the apparently capricious assignment of road building and local public works to administrative rather than public elective bodies,[216] while one member proposed that medical facilities be publicly controlled.[217] Most concurred with Valuev on the need "to define in the most precise manner the relation of governors to the new institutions."[218]

The last area of criticism of the Soloviev-Miliutin plan was that it left intact the remnants of the system of governors-general. "In accordance with the contemporary demands of decentralization,"[219] Valuev wanted this office to be completely reformed or abolished. Once provincial police and administrative institutions were reorganized, the commission felt, "the sphere of activity not only of the remaining governors-general but also of the administrative agencies subordinate to them diminishes of its own accord." It was accordingly proposed that they be stripped of their role in the conduct of urban affairs except in the two capitals,[220] that they relinquish to the governors all responsibility for tax matters including the collections of arrears, that they be excluded from attending meetings of the gentry assemblies, that they likewise give up all their judicial functions and influence over the hiring and firing of local

[215] *Ibid.*, pp. 283-85.
[216] *Ibid.*, p. 278, K. Marchenko; Count Bobrinskii.
[217] *Ibid.*, pp. 47ff. A. Giers.
[218] *MSVUK*, I, otd. 5, pp. 279-80.
[219] *Ibid.*, otd. 6, pp. 1-2.   [220] *Ibid.*, pp. 47-48.

officials—the provincial authority thus freed could be completely localized to the benefit of both provincial administrations and public agencies. Pruned of their civil and judicial functions, the governors-general would retain power to act only in questions of security affecting two or more provinces, and in extraordinary times of crisis within a single province.

REFORM WITHOUT COORDINATION

In the summer of 1861 a five-man subcommittee was designated to revise the Soloviev-Miliutin draft in accordance with these criticisms.[221] By November 18, 1861, this group was able to report that nearly all the suggestions raised in the Commission on Provincial and District Institutions had been incorporated into the text. The result was a document which substantially satisfied the demand for administrative decentralization first raised in the Committee on Reducing Correspondence. Not only were the local administrative apparatus shorn of unnecessary procedures but they were to be reorganized along rational and functionally specialized lines. The question of domestic security, which had not been raised in the Committee on Reducing Correspondence but which had nearly wrecked the hopes of the reformers in 1858, had been successfully resolved by separating the centralized police system from the rest of local administration. These changes alone should have enhanced the ability of the state's representatives to respond positively to the increasingly complex local situations. To this same end, the powers of the governors within the provincial bureaucracies were enlarged and extended to cover local representatives of other ministries in addition to the Ministry of Internal Affairs. Most important, the central administration consented to allow its top local officials a greater

[221] This group consisted of A. Giers, N. Kolesov, K. Marchenko, Ia. Soloviev, and, surprisingly, D. Tolstoi.

sphere of autonomy and more initiative in all matters relating to local government.

Side by side with these achievements must be recorded the several areas in which the administrative reform was incomplete and ill-coordinated with existing institutions and projected reforms. Valuev's battle with the Ministry of Finances had resulted in changes of which that ministry did not approve and which its representatives had no intention of honoring; as long as this clear conflict of interest remained, the two chief arms of local rule—administrative and financial—would be poorly articulated with one another. The commission's failure to coordinate the various branches of local rule is more glaringly evident in the slight attention it paid to the proposed *zemstvo* institutions. Notwithstanding the warnings of several commissioners, Valuev's group allowed the administrative reforms to be published before working out the fine points of contact between governors and *zemstvos*, an oversight that was bound to foster confrontations between administrative and elective organs. If the mutual rights of the governors and public agencies were left undefined, the relations of both governors and *zemstvos* to the proposed "Provincial Councils" were wholly ignored. So poorly were these projected super-agencies coordinated in theory with other powerful local institutions that it was immediately doubtful whether they could even be established.

The eventual fate of the administrative reforms hinged in part on these legislative flaws but in equal measure on practical considerations. The proposals advanced by the reformers, for all their apparent simplicity, required greater numbers of reform-minded administrators than had emerged by 1861. They demanded that deeply ingrained patterns of authority be routed out in one stroke. And they expected men with years of experience within one system suddenly to transform themselves into competent practitioners of another quite different system, a system in which all their political education and expertise would be useless. Even if these metamorphoses could somehow be affected, decentralization would not have proven itself. After all, any system can function without breakdown when not subject to stress. But how would the reformed governor act when faced with major insubordination within his administration or hostility from the public? Would he coolly assert his now deconcentrated authority, or would instinct prevail as he invoked the might of his remote superiors? And how would that central administrator in Petersburg behave? Would he stand by passively as his local agents took actions different from what he himself might do in the same circumstances? Or would he wade into the fray, suspending decentralized procedures in order to save the day for decentralization? If the latter were to occur, decentralization would be reduced to a hollow ideal.

These considerations were far from the minds of reforming statesmen in 1861. Regular reports from governors in Kiev, Volhynia, Podolia, and Lithuania encouraged Valuev and his colleagues to believe that the worst abuses of Nicholas I's era had been eradicated. So confident were they that a workable solution for administrative malfeasance had been devised that there grew up a substantial movement to transplant the entire program into the tumultuous Polish provinces; in fact, over the next months several leaders of the administrative reforms found their way to Russian Poland![222] Fresh and powerful pressures for the centralization of provincial administration were soon to be felt, but in 1861 they were scarcely perceived. Hence those appraising the ability of the Russian government to reform its administrative apparatus at the time of the emancipation had ready cause for optimism. It seemed that a new era in Russia's internal governance was soon to begin with the establishment of administrative decentralization.

[222] A. Kornilov, *Zemskoe i gorodskoe samoupravlenie v tsarstve Polshi v 1861-1863 gg.*, Petrograd, 1915.

IV | The Politics
of Self-Government

It has long been customary to categorize nineteenth-century tsardom as an autocracy, in which a single ruler and his close advisers initiated and planned all change. This is certainly as Nicholas I would have had it. The official ideology propagated by his regime declared Russia to be founded on the triple pillars of Orthodoxy, Nationality—and Autocracy. Yet it is not accidental that this ideology was devised in the 1830s and 1840s, just as the tsar's bureaucracy was undergoing an unprecedented expansion. One-man rule, if it had ever existed, was giving way to bureaucratic rule and the politics of autocracy to the politics of bureaucracy. Autocracy was enshrined as an ideal precisely at the moment it was being diluted in reality.

The decentralization debate revealed the degree to which autocratic policy could be molded by individual bureaucrats at and below the ministerial level. But it revealed more. For as bureaucratic organizations became larger and more complex, clusters of individuals conscious of their common interests emerged within the system. Provincial governors constituted one of these groups, and they pressed their schemes for administrative reform as a lobby. To the degree that they succeeded they demonstrated that factions and interest groups within the state apparatus had come to play an important role in decision-making. Bureaucratic politics were already being diluted by the politics of interest groups.

The issue of self-government was to prove clearly that provincial governors were by no means the only significant interest group nor the sole politicized one in Russia. The chief proponents of that program were once more to be individual activists working from the gold leaf and green felt *milieu* of Petersburg chancelleries. These administrators were able practitioners of bureaucratic politics and not merely innovating advisers to the autocrat. As in the campaign for decentralization, an essential element in the reform alliance was local forces banded together as a loose interest group. On this issue, however, the provincial component was composed not of governors but of organized bands of reformist gentry.[1] Habits of subordination in the civil service had minimized friction between local governors and the Petersburg reformers on whom they had to rely for actual legislation. The gentry also felt such constraints but gradually overcame them to the point that the alliance of central and provincially based partisans of self-rule was left quite fragile. The history of the establishment of self-government in Russia is the story of joint efforts by

---

[1] Competent studies of the activities of these groups in the reform era are readily available. The classic source of material is A. Kornilov, "Gubernskie komitety . . . ," *Russkoe Bogatstvo*, Nos. 1-5, 1904; *Materialy dlia istorii uprazdeneniia krepostnogo sostoianiia* . . . , contains much valuable information in Vol. ii, as does *Krestianskoe delo* . . . A. I. Skrebitskii, ed.; of the many attempts at synthesis the short and superficial monograph by N. I. Iordanskii, *Konstitutsionnoe dvizhenie 60-kh godov*, St. Petersburg, 1906, reflects the traditional liberal view in the clearest form. Far more scholarly is Terence Emmons' *The Russian Landed Gentry and the Peasant Emancipation of 1861*, Cambridge, 1968; numerous studies of specific provincial assemblies have appeared and will be cited at appropriate times.

bureaucratic politicians in the capital and by an interest group of gentry activists in the provinces and of their mutual relations with the rest of the autocratic state. Through the unfolding of these intricate relations, the imported concept of self-government was given definition in legislative terms.

Those who joined the drive for reform knew all too well that Russia's provinces were undergoverned and discounted the ability of the civil administration to improve the situation. Long before they discovered political outlets for their views, such people provided leadership for public and local self-help projects. The result was an astonishing proliferation of private organizations serving public ends. The Imperial Free Economic Society of Petersburg served as a clearinghouse for fledgling schools of trade and agriculture and for the small but proud public libraries opening in provincial centers. Reports on such institutions appeared regularly in the society's publications.[2] Primary education provided a useful outlet for the energies of other would-be reformers. Typical was the young Leo Tolstoi who in 1858 traveled abroad to gather ideas for a school which he eventually set up at his estate in Tula province. Zeal for nongovernmental organizations burst forth in the capital as well, where it led to the foundation of the Commissions on Literacy and Political Economy in the Imperial Geographic Society, scores of Sunday schools, and the Petersburg Conservatory. The Russian public took the problem of underinstitutionalization into its own hands.

Pessimists charged that the gentry and the rest of local society were at least as inept at administration as officialdom. As evidence, critics—including the gentry themselves —cited the record of the provincial militias which the gentry had been authorized to form during the gloomy days

[2] The activities of the Imperial Free Economic Society in stimulating local initiative are an important development of this period. See TsGIA-SSSR, f. 91 (Archive of the Imperial Free Economic Society), 1861, op. 1, d. 304, pp. 80ff.

of 1854.[3] So prevalent was mismanagement that the government designated several commissions to investigate these bodies; these commissions had little difficulty in collecting shocking data on the extent of profiteering and outright thievery.[4] Even honestly managed militias had been riddled with problems. Few provinces could provide enough educated gentry to staff an officer corps and those that could were never able to muster a staff of doctors. So serious was the medical problem that at length the Ministry of Internal Affairs intervened to allow any person with training to be elected to the militia, regardless of his class origin.[5]

If the militias provided an argument for the detractors of local self-government, they were a vital factor in the development of the movement in its behalf. By making the provincial gentry collectively responsible for a matter of vital significance, they stimulated local feeling to an unprecedented degree. Under pressure of war, the gentry eagerly undertook to rally their provinces. For once they could not escape consulting the interests of the entire local public and in the process thrashed out many of the vexing technical problems of self-rule. All militia officers were elected, but was a man obliged to serve if chosen for a staff position? In other words, should participation in local government be considered a privilege or a duty? The militias had to raise substantial sums through local levies to clothe and equip their forces. The scale of the financial operation can be judged from the fact that Moscow's militia alone operated on an annual budget of 700,000 rubles.[6] What control, if any, could the central organs of state exercise over the levying and expenditure of such funds which the law

---

[3] Miliutina, "Iz zapisok . . . ," pp. 108-09. During the Polish uprising of 1863, many gentry expressed their desire to reassemble the Crimean militias. *Severnaia Pochta*, No. 82 (April 16, 1863), 329. There exists no study of these important institutions.

[4] GPB, f. 781 (I. I. Tolstoi archive), ed. khr. 1632, "Gosudarstvennoe podvizhnoe opolchenie."

[5] *Ibid.*, p. 50.　　　　　　　　　　[6] *Ibid.*, p. 60.

classed as "estate" monies but which clearly promoted the public interest? Peasant enlistees in the lower ranks of the militia frequently expected the state to reward them with freedom at war's end.[7] Was the potential danger sufficient pretext for the state security system to assert police control over militia organs?

With the conclusion of peace many former militia officers sought new outlets for their awakened public spirit. In Nizhnii Novgorod province these men aroused interest in liberating the serfs.[8] Elsewhere the gentry proposed to make service in provincial and district public agencies compulsory and to provide salaries for a large number of elected officials to open self-administration to the less wealthy gentry.[9] With the same end in mind, a Chernigov lord suggested that all property qualifications for public service be abolished and that double voting, which offended the spirit of provincial representation, be outlawed.[10] And in a move directly parallel to the governors' movement, provincial marshals of the gentry endeavored to increase their authority over public agencies. As militia officers during the war they had frequently been frustrated in their patriotic efforts by bureaucratic formalities. By 1856 the marshals of the gentry had raised a widespread movement. From Tambov province came a well-argued case for broadening the number of public functions executed by elected nonprofessionals at the provincial level,[11] and the gentry of a remote district of Chernigov province drafted a memorandum favoring direct elections for pro-

[7] S. B. Okun, ed., *Krestianskoe dvizhenie v Rossii v 1850-1856*, Moscow, 1962, pp. 15-16, 431-52, 472-510.

[8] F. Chebaevskii, "Nizhegorodskii gubernskii dvorianskii komitet, 1858 g.," *Voprosy Istorii*, No. 6, 1947, p. 87.

[9] TsGIA-SSSR, f. 869, op. 1, d. 404, p. 6. Report of V. O. Ignatiev to S. S. Lanskoi, June 1859.

[10] *Ibid.*, p. 8. Proposal of Lieut. Dobolevskii, a lord of Chernigov province, January 11, 1857.

[11] *Ibid.*, p. 10. Letters of Kozlov, a lord of Borisogleb district, Tambov province, September 15 and December 29, 1857.

vincial officials so as to eliminate the spirit of party in local affairs.[12] These proposals were complemented by the intense journalistic campaign for self-government.

For dramatic purposes it would be tempting to juxtapose this political effervescence among certain members of the provincial gentry to a fearful opposition from the side of the government. But in the first place, we have already had ample evidence of the inaccuracy of employing such categorical terms as "the government" and "the bureaucracy" in speaking of the reform era; rarely, if ever, did the unity which these terms imply actually exist. And in the second place such an opposition simply did not exist, at least in the form ascribed to it by those scholars who, following Sergei Witte, have insisted upon viewing the establishment of the *zemstvos* merely as a concession to gentry opinion.[13] To be sure, there were the Muravievs and Panins in the government who could on occasion act with draconian ferocity, as they did in 1858 when the Petersburg City Council dared to publish a minor protocol without permission from the central authorities whose offices were scarcely a mile distant.[14] But if this behavior showed what was possible when elderly bureaucrats were offended by local public initiative, it cannot be taken as representative. For at the very time the government is purported to have been working to remove the influence of the gentry on local administration, the Committee on Reducing Correspondence labored to enhance the sphere of local self-government. It dropped the requirement that public organs submit semiannual reports to the Provincial Directorates, empowered district marshals

---

[12] *Ibid.*, p. 9. Also A. Kizevetter, "Nikolai Aleksandrovich Miliutin," *Istoricheskie otliki*, p. 242.

[13] S. Iu. Witte, *Samoderzhavie i zemstvo. Konfidentialnaia zapiska ministra finansov stats-sekretaria S. Iu. Witte (1899 g.)*, St. Petersburg, 1907, pp. 63ff.; cf. Emmons, *The Russian Landed Gentry . . .*, p. 416.

[14] A. Leroy-Beaulieu, *Un Homme d'état Russe . . .*, p. 22. A. Kizevetter, "Nikolai Aleksandrovich Miliutin," p. 242.

of the gentry to enter contracts with private firms for public works, and proposed in 1856, that many judicial and
educational offices presently filled by civil servants be
turned into elective posts.[15]

A neglected but astute writer on the period observed that
the reform of provincial institutions was taken up at almost
the same time, but independently, by both the central government and the local public.[16] The reasons that some state
officials advocated the devolution of functions during these
years are implicit in what has already been said. First, there
was the overwhelming necessity of reducing the cost of the
civil administration—a short-lived Commission on Reducing the Civil Service Lists under the Ministry of Internal
Affairs worked out a plan in the late fifties for transferring
functions to other agencies and to the public in order to reduce the ministerial budget.[17] Second, there was the scarcity of manpower, which prompted Alexander II to remark
that though the country needed reforms, the government
"lacks the men to carry them out."[18] Finally, the Ministry
of Internal Affairs had an interest in local self-government
because it found in it a means of thwarting the administrative centralization that was being advanced so diligently by
the Ministers of State Domains and Justice. Reasons such
as these prompted V. O. Ignatiev, Governor-General of
Petersburg, to write Lanskoi in 1859 that in reforming local
government "the opinions of the gentry are essential and
thus should precede the views of the government."[19] Indeed, concluded Ignatiev, to alter the role of elective offi-

[15] TsGIA-SSSR, f. 1314, op. 1, d. 55, p. 6.

[16] S. V. Svatikov, *Obshchestvennoe dvizhenie v Rossii, 1700-1895*,
Rostov-on-Don, 1905, p. 47.

[17] TsGIA-SSSR, f. 1286, op. 24, d. 1142. Commission on Reducing
the Civil Service Lists. *Soobrazheniia o preobrazovanii departamenta
politsii ispolnitelnoi.*

[18] Leroy-Beaulieu, *Un Homme d'état Russe* . . . , p. 16n.

[19] TsGIA-SSSR, f. 869, op. 1, d. 404, pp. 11-13. V. O. Ignatiev to
S. S. Lanskoi.

191

cials at the provincial and district level "without the participation of the gentry itself would not be in the general spirit
of our administration."[20]

It was precisely this attitude which prevailed in the Ministry of Internal Affairs during the autumn of 1857 when
Sergei Lanskoi was locked in combat with the security-conscious faction of the Secret Committee. With the prospect
of watching the plans of his ministry wrecked, Lanskoi
turned to the provincial gentry for support. He did not,
however, desire support for emancipation, as that issue was
progressing on the impetus imparted to it by Alexander, the
Grand Duke Konstantin, and Levshin. Rather, Lanskoi welcomed an alliance with the provincial gentry as a means of
promoting his program of self-government. A timely petition forwarded by Governor-General Ignatiev from the
gentry of Petersburg province seeking permission to form
a committee to consider problems of tax reform served as
an excuse for contracting such an alliance.

THE PETERSBURG EXPERIMENT

The province whose gentry submitted the petition was by
no means impoverished. A well-managed estate could still
bring 6 percent annually and during 1857 not one estate
was sold for mortgage arrears.[21] In addition, the many factories in the capital and district towns were considered excellent investments and their number was being augmented
annually.[22]

In sharp contrast was the provincial administration,
which in 1857 was on the brink of fiscal collapse.[23] After an
initial drop in 1856 the level of tax arrears rose again in

[20] *Ibid.*, p. 13.
[21] TsGIA-SSSR, f. 1281, op. 6, d. 47, p. 8. "Otchety Sankt-Peters-
burgskogo gubernatora 1857 g."
[22] *Ibid.*, p. 10.
[23] *Ibid.*, d. 46, pp. 8, 17. "Otchety Sankt-Peterburgskogo gubernatora 1856 g." See also Petr Struve, *Krepostnoe khoziaistvo*, St.
Petersburg, 1913, Chap. I.

1857 by 91 percent.[24] That the fault lay not in the economy but in the tax system is shown by the fact that by the end of 1857, 8,342 rubles had yet to be collected from the prosperous royal estates. This inability to collect taxes impeded the execution of all public services. The province's highways were miserable; fire fighting equipment was virtually nonexistent; the district jail at Tsarskoe Selo, close by the most splendid of royal palaces, rotted in complete disrepair; and a mere fifty-seven doctors served a population of three-quarters of a million people.[25]

During the Crimean War the gentry of the province had formed committees to study the problem of public services and taxation. They blamed the breakdown on officials who were so preoccupied with other matters that they could not exercise adequate controls (*nadzor*) over taxation and expenditures and therefore frequently spent beyond their means. The groups formed in 1853 and 1855 concluded their study with what were already fully developed arguments for devolving functions to the public. They spoke of: "the necessity of entrusting these affairs exclusively to the estates, so that they would supervise the taxes. Since they have a direct interest in these matters, they can manage them with great convenience, at the same time saving the men in the Provincial Directorate the necessity of busying themselves with these issues."[26]

Experience in the militia confirmed the belief of the Petersburg lords that they could see to the province's business more efficiently than the state administration.[27] During the summer of 1857 they therefore petitioned the Minister of Internal Affairs for permission to form a commission to reform the local tax and public works administrations. The request was enthusiastically approved by Lanskoi who was

[24] TsGIA-SSSR, f. 1281, op. 6, d. 47, p. 14.
[25] *Ibid.*, pp. 20, 25.
[26] TsGIA-SSSR, f. 869, op. 1, d. 395, pp. 26-27.
[27] Particularly active in the Petersburg militia was Prince Grigorii Shcherbatov, marshal of the gentry, 1861-64; see *Russkii biograficheskii slovar*, XXIV, 94-97.

working at the same time to deconcentrate his administration. Because such a nongovernmental commission was quite unprecedented it was necessary to obtain authorization from the throne. In view of traditional assumptions on the autocracy's attitude toward public initiative in "political" matters, the wording of the tsar's reply of November 1, 1857, is of interest, for it granted permission to the gentry of Petersburg to form a special commission "to work out *in detail* the project proposed by them for a new organization for the management of provincial affairs."[28] Thus, as late as 1857 Alexander could assent to a plan initiated by a corporate group of provincial lords for working out "in detail" a reform touching the conduct of all provincial affairs.

A striking aspect of the Petersburg experiment is that the men who conducted it can scarcely be included in the ranks of the "liberal gentry" as that group is generally defined. Especially in regard to the emancipation issue the gentry of Petersburg were unusually defensive of their aristocratic prerogatives. Many owned estates in the productive South and were reluctant to part either with their serf labor force or particularly with any portion of their land in the form of farm plots for peasants.[29]

Count Peter Pavlovich Shuvalov, marshal of the Petersburg gentry, shared these views completely. It was he who led the movement in his province to take advantage of the offer implied in the rescript enabling Governor-General Nazimov of the western provinces to form committees to explore the serf problem. On December 5, 1857, Alexander issued a second rescript to the Petersburg gentry and within days a committee on peasant affairs had been formed with Shuvalov at its head. This became the first provincial committee to begin work, preceding that of Nizhnii Nov-

[28] TsGIA-SSSR, f. 869, op. 1, d. 395, pp. 19-20.
[29] In the 1840s the Petersburg gentry had briefly discussed but rejected the controversial "inventory" system, by which land could be put at the peasants' disposal without transferring title. Henceforth, they advocated the Baltic "Bauerland" system. *Materialy dlia istorii uprazdeneniia krepostnogo sostoianiia*, II, 315-17.

gorod province by a month and that of Tver province by seven months.[30] The intent of its members was not to promote abolition but to preserve for the gentry as great a part of their property as possible, a position which attracted friends of the *status quo* from across Russia to the salons of Shuvalov and other Petersburg grandees.[31]

Though stubbornly opposed to change in the economic sphere, the gentry of Petersburg showed itself to be extremely receptive to alteration of the provincial administration. When the Special Commission on Provincial Reform began work on November 1, 1857, its first task was to examine the existing charter on local taxes.[32] After some study it concluded that the trouble lay not in the legislation but in the execution: "if the goals of the charter are not realized in practice, then the cause is the difficulty experienced at present by the local provincial government in seeing to the public interest as it should be done, and this is due to the burden of other duties."[33] Further, control of major functions had been splintered among eight different agencies controlled by "an infamous group of book-keepers and bureaucratic controllers."[34] The remedy proposed for these problems strikingly anticipates that suggested by Governor-General Vasilchikov for Kiev province: "to form from all of the above committees and commissions a single institution for the governance of all of Petersburg province."[35] The gentry commissioners thought that the new agency should take over the management of all public affairs of a local na-

---

[30] Kornilov, "Gubernskie komitety . . . ," No. 1, pp. 107-08, 123n; No. 2, p. 205. Soloviev, "Zapiski . . . ," No. 2, 1881, p. 245; *Sbornik pravitelstvennykh rasporiazhenii* . . . , pp. 4, 34.

[31] Semenov-Tian-Shanskii, *Epokha osvobozhdeniia krestian* . . . , III, 291.

[32] TsGIA-SSSR, f. 869, op. 1, d. 395 (*Proekt Polozheniia ob uchrezhdeniiakh po delam zemskikh povinnostei Sankt Peterburgskoi gubernii*), p. 21. The complete papers of this body have not been preserved in the archive of the Petersburg Gentry Assembly at GALO (Gosudarstvennyi Arkhiv Leningradskoi Oblasti), but its activities can be reconstructed from the detailed report just cited.

[33] *Ibid.*   [34] *Ibid.*, p. 27.   [35] *Ibid.*, pp. 28-29.

195

ture. It would apportion general as well as local taxes and would supervise the district agencies which would collect them. In order to strengthen the public's ability to expose and prosecute irregularities, a series of ombudsmen were to be added at the district level; these elected troubleshooters would work to reduce correspondence and promote the public interest through economy and efficiency.[36] Moreover, district elective councils would be created to control local matters presently administered by the police and professional civil servants, including surveying, the gathering of statistics, and the promotion of trade and agriculture. An elective provincial council and five-man directorate (*uprava*) would bear final responsibility for the execution of all local decisions. In effect, the governor would be relieved of all functions relating exclusively to the locality.[37]

Surprisingly, the Petersburg lords rejected the notion that the gentry could manage the province's affairs alone and opted instead for the principle of all-class representation. They proposed to call forth delegates from all local classes that paid taxes, not excepting merchants, traders, and peasants, who, they pointed out, paid "incomparably" more taxes than other classes.[38] Representation would be set at a ratio proportionate to assessed values, i.e., on a property standard. By establishing property rather than class as the chief criterion for election and by extending local government to urban dwellers and even the peasantry, the Petersburg gentry went beyond the views of their governor-general, Ignatiev, who felt that: "To expand election to these agencies to the commercial guilds and peasant communes . . . is impossible . . . as shown by the lack of education among people of these estates who have been elected for service in the city of Petersburg."[39] In 1857-1858 the propertied gentry of Petersburg were more interested in

---

[36] *Ibid.*, pp. 30, 32.   [37] *Ibid.*, p. 58.   [38] *Ibid.*, p. 42.
[39] *Ibid.*, p. 20. The reference is to the 1845 Statutes for the Petersburg city government introduced by Nikolai Miliutin.

joining forces with all other classes of society to protect the provincial interests from bureaucratic mismanagement than in asserting the absolute dominance of the gentry over the rest of local society. And even though the Petersburg assembly of gentry was to press for absurdly high property qualifications in 1862, it never abandoned its theoretical adherence to the principle of all-class representation based on property rather than birth. This principle was eventually embodied in the *zemstvo* statutes of January 1, 1864.

This sweeping plan for administrative reform was submitted in the spring of 1858, fully a half year before the more famous but considerably less thoroughgoing plan of Alexander Golovachev of Tver province.[40] Unlike the Golovachev program and the later demands for reform issued in the form of manifestos, the Petersburg proposal was made with the full consent of the Ministry of Internal Affairs. And while the manifestos of 1859 and 1860 were known by the names of the few deputies bold enough to sign them, the earlier and more detailed Petersburg proposal received the support of an entire provincial assembly and one not noted for its abolitionism.

Whatever the long-term impact of the Petersburg proposals, the commission which drafted them was beset by serious internal differences. One faction, led by Alexander Platonov, marshal of the gentry in Tsarskoe Selo district, advocated a maximal program which would turn over a large number of functions to the new all-class elective organs and set up a federal relationship between them and the central administration. Shuvalov and the largest property owners proposed a minimal program that would confine the competence of provincial councils to matters of a purely local character. They wanted to exclude the building and road commissions, which received most of their

---

[40] Emmons, *The Russian Landed Gentry* . . . , pp. 134ff. Although it is quite likely that the Petersburg *zapiska* served as the basis for Golovachev's plan, no direct evidence for this exists.

197

funds from national taxes and were responsible for the maintenance of national as well as local roads.[41] By strictly defining the competence of self-administration, they endeavored to establish an area in which the provincial councils would enjoy virtual autonomy; otherwise, the minimalists claimed, the councils would continually feel pressures from the national tax system. The Shuvalov group also feared that by overextending their powers the councils would invite outside interference in provincial self-rule; they therefore decided to drop the promotion of trade and agriculture.[42] Finally, Shuvalov himself urged the commission to reconsider the question of salaries for councilmen. In the initial project it had been proposed to have all elected officeholders paid from the receipts of local levies, with wages high enough to attract the most competent people, however poor they might be.[43] After a second review the tight-pursed commission decided to have the estates themselves pay their representatives' salaries and to limit public salaries to the five directors.[44]

Working under pressure of time, the commission settled on a hastily written compromise report which kept the sphere of self-rule substantially as proposed but restricted salaried positions. This document was submitted to the tsar and Ministry of Internal Affairs, at which point the Petersburg gentry turned its energies fully to influencing emancipation legislation. The committee on emancipation with Shuvalov at its head advanced to the center of the local political stage.

This new body acted in everything with the self-possession to be expected of the lords of Russia's capital. It immediately probed to see whether the broad freedom enjoyed by the Special Commission on Provincial Reform extended also to the committee on emancipation.[45] Other pro-

---

[41] TsGIA-SSSR, f. 869, op. 1, d. 395, p. 37.
[42] *Ibid.*, p. 39.   [43] *Ibid.*, pp. 33-34.   [44] *Ibid.*, pp. 47-49.
[45] *Materialy dlia uprazdneniia krepostnogo sostoianiia,* I, 323.

vincial committees had also been testing the bounds of their competence and had written to Petersburg for advice. The Main Committee, as the Secret Committee had been renamed in January of 1858, faced a dilemma: should it allow the provincial committees to deliberate without rigorous guidelines or a coordinated timetable or should it lay down both at the risk of offending the local gentry? Alexander II supported the latter course and on April 21, 1858, the Main Committee issued a three-stage timetable for all reforms.[46] During a preliminary period, data would be collected; a second stage would be devoted to drafting short-range rules governing relations between lord and peasant; and in a concluding period all outstanding administrative questions would be dealt with, including the long-range restructuring of provincial administrations. The Main Committee accordingly banned all formal discussion of local government until after emancipation.

This decision has been widely hailed as an attempt by the Main Committee to squelch local initiative.[47] Certainly there are reasonable grounds for such views, for the April 21 order coincided almost exactly with the triumph—albeit temporary—of the proposal to institute centralized governors-general and district governors throughout Russia. But contemporaries who censured Lanskoi for supporting the order of April 21 were ignorant of his opposition to the centralizers and were equally unaware of his vigorous denunciation of those who sought to exclude the local gentry from a role in preparing the emancipation.[48] Un-

[46] The text of the program was published by Skrebitskii, *Krestianskoe delo* . . . , I, xxxviff. An earlier order of March 20, 1858 had explicitly prohibited discussion of district administrative organs, *Sbornik pravitelstvennykh rasporiazhenii* . . . , I, 66.

[47] Kornilov, "Gubernskie komitety . . . ," No. 3, pp. 110-11.

[48] TsGIA-SSSR, f. 1180. 1875, op. xv, d. 13, pp. 31-34. Grand Duke Konstantin held this view because he believed, rightly as it turned out, that the majority of gentry would oppose emancipation. Count Kiselev shared this position, while Lanskoi cited Baron Hax-

aware of the subtleties of Lanskoi's position, they saw the command only as an act of irresponsible centralization.

Stripped of the gentry's polemics against it (which are unfortunately reflected in the historiography), the order of April 21 appears simply as an attempt to coordinate what would otherwise have been a maze of conflicting processes and proposals. The command was directed in part against privileges granted earlier to the Petersburg Special Commission on Provincial Reform which were now incompatible with the timetable set down by the Main Committee.[49] It was entirely consistent with the already well-established Central European tradition of serf emancipation through state legislation. Nonetheless, it stifled the spirit of participation in a common endeavor that permeated earlier relations between the Petersburg reformers and the Ministry of Internal Affairs; thereafter the gentry of Petersburg became staunch critics not only of the emancipation but of the administrative reforms which they had done so much to mold.[50]

The great scope and freedom of action granted to the Petersburg Special Commission on Provincial Reform in 1857 and 1858 suggests that tsarist bureaucracy could respond positively to new needs when it did not see them as constituting a threat to itself. These needs did not change substantially with the emancipation of the serfs. But that event profoundly transformed the disposition of forces on

---

thausen to show that it was possible for local gentry and central ministries to work together harmoniously. *Ibid.*, pp. 22-23.

[49] In fact, the Petersburg group continued to exercise its privilege of meeting well into 1859, but with no results. TsGIA-SSSR, f. 1291, op. 123, ed. khr. 23, p. 146.

[50] The hostility generated by the emancipation issue remained for some years among the Petersburg gentry. In 1862 the Commission on Provincial and District Institutions refused even to consult the Petersburg lords, who, outraged, tried unsuccessfully to remind the commission of its indebtedness to them. "Zapiska Sankt Peterburgskogo predvoditelia dvorianstva," with penciled notes by Valuev, TsGIA-SSSR, f. 908, d. 34, pp. 2-22.

the issue of local institutional reform because it drove a wedge between the perceived interests of gentry activists and bureaucratic reformers. Just as the program of administrative decentralization barely passed the test of fire imposed by the emancipation-related issue of security, so now the establishment of local self-government was to occur as much in spite of as because of the abolition of serfdom.

An examination of the state of affairs between the issuance of the order of April 21, 1858, and the promulgation of the emancipation edict in 1861 reveals how the self-government program spread through the provinces and came to be seen as opposed to official policy.

SELF-GOVERNMENT AND EMANCIPATION

There is no development in educated Russian society in the late 1850s more stunning in its novelty than the tumultuous appearance of organized groups of gentry on the political stage. For four years, large and small landowners castigated the government to which they owed their existence as gentry. By forcing the government to reckon with them, they made themselves a factor in all legislative work including the reform of provincial institutions.

The gentry's political activities before the promulgation of the emancipation may be divided into three phases. During the first, the tsar issued a rescript to form local committees and provincial capitals hummed with the work of collecting data. In the second phase the Main Committee summoned deputies from these committees to confer in Petersburg in two groups, the first between August and October 1859, and the second between February and April 1860. The last phase was marked by unsolicited addresses by gentry assemblies to the tsar criticizing the work of the Editing Commissions and seeking to save the reform from the reformers.

Relating this chronology to the broader debates on administrative decentralization and local self-government, the

201

first of these periods began just as the commission of Petersburg gentry was completing its work and corresponds to the months in the spring of 1858 when Lanskoi fended off the campaign of the centralizing ministers. During these same months the *Zemskii* Section accepted in principle the Saltykov-Soloviev program for local reform. The second phase coincided with the issuance of Alexander II's decree calling for the reform of local rule and with the founding of the Commission on Provincial and District Institutions. The third and final phase was concurrent with the efforts of Miliutin's commission to complete police reform and its first detailed examination of the principles of administrative decentralization and public self-government.

With this chronology in mind let us turn to the activities of the provincial gentry committees. Notwithstanding the anger evoked by the April 21, 1858 decree, all gentry groups with the exception of Tver's chose to honor it. Until well into 1859 the gentry of Petersburg and Tver provinces remained the only corporate bodies to give their collective support to any program for governmental reorganization at the provincial levels or even to consider local reform.[51]

A major cause of the reticence of provincial gentry to air their concerns over local government was their long conditioning in rigidly hierarchical power relations. Hundreds had received political baptism through militia work during the Crimean War, but most of them considered a *ukaz* from Petersburg to be the end, rather than the beginning, of controversy. For this majority, the tradition-rocking form of confrontation that arose on the eve of emancipation was unsettling, bewildering, and something to be approached gradually through experience, if at all. The plea of a provincial lord to the Ministry of Internal Affairs for permission

---

[51] On Tver see Dzhanshiev, "Rol Tverskogo dvorianstva v krestianskoi reforme," *Epokha* . . . , pp. 126-27; and Emmons, *The Russian Landed Gentry* . . . , Chap. 4. Individuals and minority factions who expressed their views on local reform before 1859 were to be found in Simbirsk, Kaluga, Nizhnii Novgorod, Kharkov, and Riazan provinces.

to submit ideas on police reform epitomized the response of this group to the times. Though eager to enlighten officialdom with his opinions, he did not venture to do so until he had received a proper mandate.[52]

Bound by old habits, provincial leaders struggled with new conditions. A contemporary to these frenzied times recalled later that most speeches that he heard in local assemblies were nothing but essays from Petersburg journals, encrusted with high-flown but rustic rhetorical flourishes. Autocratic practice had not encouraged the political finesse demanded by the situation. "We were masters at quarreling," the avuncular memoirist reminisced, "and at shouting in private conversation."[53] Not surprisingly, such political amateurs frequently failed to calculate their actions in terms of defined objectives and instead struck out blindly against real or imagined foes.

The gentry overcame its reticence to campaign actively for institutional reform only gradually and at varying rates from province to province. In general, the intensity of the campaign for self-government in a given region shows little correlation with the geographic or economic circumstances of the locality. Rather, the principal factor affecting the political mobilization of the gentry was the exertions of barely a score of energetic and articulate local leaders who were sharply distinguished from their fellow committeemen in education, experience, and attitude toward change.

Take, for example, a group of eleven activists who spearheaded the drive for self-government in five of the earliest provincial committees to consider local reform.[54] All the younger members of the group were university graduates

[52] TsGIA-SSSR, f. 1291, 1856, op. 33, d. 2, p. 158.
[53] A. A. Antonov, "Chetvert veka nazad; vospominaniia stepnogo pomeshchika," *Sankt-Peterburgskii Istoricheskii Vestnik*, xxx, 1887, p. 372.
[54] P. N. Svistunov, G. S. Batenkov, N. S. Kashkin, E. P. Obolenskii (Kaluga province); Iu. F. Samarin, A. I. Koshelev (Riazan province); A. I. Evropeus, A. A. Golovachev, A. M. Unkovski (Iver province); D. P. Khrushchev (Kharkov province); D. P. Gavrilov (Vladimir province).

with lawyers predominating; all but one had held important posts in the provincial civil service; four of the eleven were working concurrently with the central government or were conducting studies for central commissions to serve as the bases for reform; three were among the handful of qualified experts on tax problems in Russia; while one, G. S. Batenkov of Kaluga, had actually served as secretary to Speranskii while the administrative reforms of 1822 were being carried out in Siberia.[55]

In training and experience in practical affairs these reformers far outshone their fellows on the provincial committees. Further, the proclivity of this minority for ideological solutions to problems sets them off clearly from the others. No less than seven of them had involved themselves directly in the leading intellectual movements of the era— three had served sentences for their complicity in the Decembrist uprisings in 1825 and had not received royal reprieve until 1856; two had received sentences for their involvement with Mikhail Petrashevskii's circle in 1848; and two were a part of the last flowering of Slavophilism.[56] Together, these seven men all made direct contact with the highly ideological reformism that existed as a submerged continuum through the first half of the nineteenth century.

Few provincial gentry could ignore the difficulties which beset administration in their localities. As late as 1858, though, most of them simply did not perceive their self-interest in terms of the reorganization of the provinces. They

[55] The lawyers in the groups were Golovachev, Khrushchev, Unkovskii, and Gavrilov; Golovachev was the author of the tax studies cited above, Section I, while Unkovskii also was a tax expert; Koshelev and Samarin, who had received their posts not by election but gubernatorial appointment, were also working concurrently on projects for Petersburg; Khrushchev had helped reorganize the local government of Petersburg after N. A. Miliutin's reforms of 1845; and Svistunov had earlier reorganized the Provincial Directorate of remote Kurgan.
[56] The Decembrists were Batenkov, Svistunov, and Obolenskii (see his *Souvenirs d'un Exilé en Siberie*, Leipzig, 1862); the *Petrashevtsy* were Evropeus and Kashkin; the Slavophiles were Koshelev and Samarin.

looked for leadership to their better educated and ideologically more sophisticated fellows, whoever they were, entrusting even their dearest interests to be represented by men once condemned as political criminals and wholly divorced from local life through years of exile. Through the efforts of this minority, the majority came to see that the proposed program for self-government, however alien in origin, presented an attractive remedy for misrule and underinstitutionalization.

These figures in the provincial committees sketched their program in terms that were at once less detailed than that of the Petersburg gentry and less far-reaching than the Saltykov-Soloviev plan. Chronologically, the first proposal from the ranks of a provincial emancipation committee came from Tver, where a plan by Alexander Golovachev served to crystallize a group of twenty-two supporters, including both abolitionists and antiabolitionists.[57] This scheme stressed the lower units of administration, the subdistrict (*volost*) and the district, with no plan for organization on the provincial level at all. It placed heavy emphasis on the separation of judicial, police, and administrative affairs, and thus reflected the primary point of contention in 1858 between the *Zemskii* Section and the centralizing ministers. But delays in communication denied to the Golovachev program the supporting role which it might have played in the governmental debate; before the final vote was taken in Tver the separation of provincial functions had been agreed upon in the capital.

In regard to the social content of the new institutions and their sphere of action the "liberal" Tver gentry did not move beyond the thinking of the grandees of Petersburg. In spite of protestations against artificial divisions among estates and classes, the Tver majority granted the right of participation in district assemblies to all hereditary gentry regardless of the extent of their holdings, set up separate

[57] TsGAOR, f. 109, 960 (Third Section), *Zapiska A. A. Golovacheva i A. M. Unkovskogo*, 1858.

property standards for merchants and nonhereditary lords, and allowed peasants to participate only through representatives. The specific prerogatives of the district assembly were not defined, and, no less important, the relation of that assembly to the state administrative structure at the provincial level remained unspecified. Here the lords of Tver as much as planned head-on conflicts between public and state administrative orders by granting to the governor the right to name district police commandants but giving the districts control over the local police budget.[58]

Whatever its inadequacies, the program approved in Tver became a model for discussion in other provinces and brought together the emerging gentry reform coalition. In Vladimir a five-man minority paraphrased it in a brief report of 1858-1859;[59] a memorandum from Simbirsk province was still more roughly sketched than the Vladimir proposal and, like it, did not include a reform at the provincial level.[60] Isolated reformers in Riasan, Kharkov, and Tula provinces failed to sway even strong minorities to their views, but did lay foundations on which they could later build.[61] In Kaluga province the core of reformers extended beyond the emancipation committee, which provided support for a group of five members who called for public agencies at the provincial and district level to handle all "economic" affairs of the region.[62] Firmly supporting them was the governor, V. A. Artsimovich, who had just arrived in Kaluga after turning over to Lanskoi his fiery critique of

[58] *Proekt polozheniia Tverskogo komiteta*, cited by Emmons, *The Russian Landed Gentry . . .* , p. 144.

[59] V. G. Zimina, "Krestianskaia reforma 1861 g. vo Vladimirskoi gubernii," diss., Moscow University, 1956. The leaders of the Vladimir minority were D. P. Gavrilov and I. S. Bezobrazov.

[60] For evidence of bolder spirits in Simbirsk province, see *Materialy dlia istoriia uprazdneniia krepostnogo sostoianiia . . .* , II, 167-80.

[61] In Riazan province: Iu. F. Samarin, A. I. Koshelev; in Kharkov province: D. P. Khrushchev, A. Schreter; in Tula province: Prince V. A. Cherkasskii.

[62] A. Kornilov, "Krestianskaia reforma v Kaluzhskoi gubernii pri V. A. Artsimovicha," *. . . Artsimovich . . .* , pp. 142ff.

administrative concentration.[63] Though initially offending local gentry with his lack of concern for public agencies, he quickly won their support by backing their drive for public self-government.[64]

This short list does not exhaust the number of those provinces where organized factions of gentry registered their concern over the issue of local government by 1858 or 1859, but only these committees drafted concrete programs of self-government. In Nizhnii Novgorod province, for example, an active militia during the war and a local tax commission patterned after the Petersburg group did much to heighten local consciousness.[65] But without leaders to articulate self-government as an ideological and institutional program, the committee was not moved to vocal protest.

The mobilization of the gentry for self-government was in part a function of communications.[66] Local activists brought the reform program to a few discontented gentry but only the government could make possible its communication to the entire estate by inviting representatives of every provincial committee on emancipation to convene in Petersburg in 1859. These sessions enabled reformers to coordinate their positions and pass them on to the remaining delegates, who then carried them back to the majorities in the provinces.

The primary administrative issues in the air at the time of the arrival of the gentry deputies in Petersburg related to the subdistrict or *volost* level. The Administrative Section of the Main Committee had spent some months debating means for replacing the lords' patrimonial power over the

---

[63] *Ibid.*, pp. 166, 173.

[64] See *Moskovskie Vedomosti*, No. 108 (1858), for an attack on Artsimovich as a "despot from the Siberian tundra."

[65] Chebaevskii, "Nizhegorodskii . . . komitet," pp. 87, 92.

[66] On this problem Samuel Huntington writes "Political mobilization . . . may result simply from increases in communication, which can stimulate major increases in aspirations that may only be partially, if at all, satisfied. The result is a 'revolution of rising frustrations.'" "Political Development and Decay," *World Politics* (April 1965), 405-17.

peasantry with alternatives adapted to the new conditions. Since the government could ill afford the expense of a new bureaucracy at the *volost* level and since it was out of the question to leave the peasantry again in a state of wardship to the gentry, the Administrative Section opted for a peasant *volost* to be ruled by a communal assembly (*mirskii skhod*) and its elders.[67] This decision was reached by late June and forwarded to the Main Committee.

The first group of gentry deputies arrived in Petersburg at the end of August, after the Administrative Section had submitted its report to the Main Committee. When they became aware of the fact that the Main Committee was already committed to the views of the Administrative Section they were outraged. Most deputies, oligarchic and blindly committed to the *status quo*, opposed the substance of the decision. A reformist minority supported the decision in principle but was angered by the manner in which it had been made. For the first time since Catherine II's Legislative Commission of 1767 the government was bringing representatives of the entire gentry to the capital and many deputies nourished the belief that they had been invited in the capacity of legislators to plan the reform. This belief was not supported by any recent pronouncement of the government or by any legislative precedent,[68] but it existed nonetheless and led to considerable frustration. Yet what sort of system of balloting would have satisfied the reformist deputies among them? By any method of voting then functioning in western Europe, their program would have gone down to crushing defeat. They were in the uncomfortable predicament of having to choose between the spe-

---

[67] A thorough discussion of this issue is in Semenov-Tian-Shanskii, *Epokha osvobozhdeniia krestian . . .* , III, 240ff.

[68] Some delegates claimed that the tsar, in a speech to the nobility of Tver province in August of 1858, had ceded them legislative powers when he referred to "meetings in the Main Committee for a general study of the projects." Tatishchev, *Imperator Aleksandr II . . .* , pp. 308-09; Semenov-Tian-Shanskii, *Epokha osvobozhdeniia krestian . . .* , III, 283ff.

cific program to which they were committed and their interest in establishing a representative form of government. Politically they could not have both—yet psychologically they could not reject either. So with equal fervor they supported their program and opposed the bureaucratic politicians who alone could get it instituted. In a single stroke, illogical but masterful, they revealed the dilemma of Russian reformism.

Thus, official actions prodded both opposed factions of delegates to a peak of indignation with the Main Committee.[69] On this basis, a curious *mariage de convenance* was effected, bringing together parties which disagreed fundamentally on the liberation of serfs, but which could agree that somehow the voice of the provinces should be treated with greater deference in the capital. Like all such marriages, this one tolerated considerable infidelity so long as the working compact was preserved; like all such marriages, too, a small but real possibility existed that the partners so rudely thrown together could find a basis for a more enduring union. Before six months had passed, this change had become a reality.

During the early sessions with the Main Committee, open dissension appeared among gentry delegates as the abolitionists flirted with the reformers from the Ministry of Internal Affairs. This cooperation became unnecessary when the Main Committee made known its general commitment to abolitionism. Meanwhile, the planters were forced to acknowledge that their unlimited authority over the peasantry was soon to end. Thereafter both factions could turn to the broader questions of administration above the *volost* level, and here they discovered substantial common ground between them. Deeply outraged by the central bureauc-

[69] The government, "defending itself against its opponents [i.e., planters] had unceremoniously dealt with its loyal [i.e., abolitionist] friends. Dzhanshiev, *Epokha* . . . , p. 143. For other discussions of this problem see Garmiza, *Podgotovka* . . . , pp. 57-59; Ivaniukov, *Padenie* . . . , pp. 178-83; and especially Semenov-Tian-Shanskii, *Epokha osvobozhdeniia krestian* . . . , III, 286ff.

209

racy, both now advocated provincial and district self-government. This new union of interest was revealed in the commentaries submitted by thirteen individual delegates as they were leaving the first Petersburg convocation in October 1859.[70] The thirteen, representing both abolitionists and planter interests, declared their support for public self-rule and suggested institutional means for achieving it.[71] Ignoring the peculiarities of each proposal, certain common features can be readily discerned: all believed that any form of local control would be preferable to a bureaucratic administration dominated by central appointees; all preferred to see the major burden of local responsibility borne by the gentry with other local residents participating as representatives of their estate rather than as individuals;[72] all envisaged three levels of local assembly: the province, district, and *volost* (or for Koshelev, *okrug*); and all

[70] *Materialy dlia istorii uprazdeniia krepostnogo sostoianiia* . . . , II, 172-75; *Prilozheniia k trudam redaksionnykh komissii* . . . , II, 1860; Iordanskii, *Konstitutsionnoe dvizhenie* . . . , pp. 75ff.; N. P. Semenov, *Osvobozhdeniia krestian v tsarstvovanii imp. Aleksandra II*, St. Petersburg, 1890, II, 935-37; Skrebitskii, ed., *Krestianskoe delo* . . . , II, 761-69; Barsukov, *Zhizn . . . Pogodina*, XVII, 121ff; Garmiza, *Podgotovka* . . . , pp. 60-63; other related addresses and materials are to be found in TsGIA-SSSR, f. 1180 (1859), op. sv, d. 227, 228.

[71] The deputies were Unkovskii and Kardo-Sysoev of Tver; Dubrovin and Vasiliev from Iaroslavl; Khrushchev and Schreter of Kharkov; Kosogovskii of Novgorod; Volkov of Moscow; Bezobrazov of Vladimir; Volkonskii, Ofrosimov, and Koshelev from Riazan; and Shidlovskii of Simbirsk. The pattern for these statements was a memorandum by A. Unkovskii of Tver, as has been demonstrated by Garmiza, *Podgotvka* . . . , p. 59. The Unkovskii plan was published by Iordanskii, *Konstitutsionnoe dvizhenie* . . . , pp. 75ff. An earlier version of the same program was published by Dzhanshiev, . . . *Unkovskii* . . . , pp. 173-79. This earlier draft dates only from February 1859, and is thus considerably later than either the Soloviev or Saltykov programs, to which it bears a strong and probably not coincidental resemblance.

[72] Koshelev's comments were not an exception to this, for, although he emphasized the all-class character of the public assemblies, he did not deny that purely estate organs would continue to function. *Prilozheniia k trudam redaksionnykh komissii* . . . , II, 196; Garmiza, *Podgotovka* . . . , pp. 58-59.

defined the sphere of public self-government as limited to "economic" functions. On the negative side, few of the brief comments specified which functions would be turned over to public control and which would remain in bureaucratic hands; none had anything more specific to offer on the precise relations of elective and administrative authorities except that the former would be "independent"; all set property qualifications for voting at a very high level while allowing hereditary lords to participate without election.[73]

The Editing Commissions did not respond to these proposals or to any of these documents. Perhaps its members realized that although the various deputies shared certain common objectives, they were too poorly organized as an interest group as yet to stand together behind a single and unified program. Tempers sharpened at this rebuff, and a group of five reformist deputies drafted a call for judicial, press, and administrative reform which they sent directly to the tsar. Still the government took no repressive action.[74]

The only threat that could bring forth reprisal was that of an oligarchic conspiracy. The Russian system functioned best when the state could itself choose the interest groups to which it would respond. Oligarchy meant that one faction demanded the right to be institutionalized as a permanent lobby functioning in the capital, and however narrow the social perspective of tsarist policy may actually have been, the men who led the government in the reform era

[73] The most specific of these commentaries was that presented by Kosogovskii of Novgorod and signed by the abolitionists Bezobrazov, Khrushchev, and Schreter, but even this project stayed safely within the confines of the official but unpublished Saltykov-Soloviev proposal of 1858. Skrebitskii, ed., *Krestianskoe delo . . .* , I, 763-66.

[74] This "Address of the Five" became a bulwark of reformist ideology in Russia and its signers (Khrushchev, Schreter, Dubrovin, Vasiliev, Unkovskii) became heroes to the late nineteenth-century liberal movement. See Semenov, *Ozvobozhdenie krestian . . .* , II, 935-37; *Materialy dlia istorii uprazdeniia krepostnogo sostoianiia . . .* , II, 172-75; Garmiza, *Podgotovka . . .* , pp. 61-63. On Dubrovin and Vasiliev see TsGIA-SSSR, f. 1180 (1859), op. sv, d. 228, pp. 286-322.

conceived state power as a force serving the whole Russian people.[75] Having stood fast in the face of criticism of the emancipation and demands for self-government, Alexander II and Lanskoi finally lost patience when two antiabolitionist deputies pleaded pathetically for the tsar to call the gentry to the throne to consult.[76] Overreacting to a pitiable deed of questionable political significance, they severely reprimanded all deputies who had included general propositions in their memorandums.

Contemporaries interpreted this as a cavalier insult to the gentry and a slap in the face of advocates of self-government, and thus it has been viewed ever since. But this was not the intention of Alexander or of Lanskoi. In their statement they alluded only to the danger posed by opponents of emancipation and oligarchists seeking permanent representation in the capital. Together these groups certainly constituted a numerical majority of the gentry in 1859, numbering some of the wealthiest grandees of the empire. But whatever their numerical strength together, oligarchists and opponents of emancipation were by no means identical groups that were unified on all issues, particularly that of local government. In fact, those who *both* opposed emancipation *and* spoke out for oligarchic centralization constituted a far smaller group, and one poorly organized at that. By failing to draw this distinction, the stern government policy backfired disastrously, driving the various gentry factions yet closer together. Doctrinaire interpretations notwithstanding, this development was due not to evil design but to bad politics arising from the traditional insecurities of the Russian state.[77]

[75] "The tsar expressed to [Lanskoi] his desire that the role of the deputies, as representatives of only one estate, would be limited in working out the peasant issue." Semenov-Tian-Shanskii, *Epokha osvobozhdeniia krestian* . . . , III, p. 285.

[76] Dmitrii Shidlovskii (Semenov-Tian-Shanskii, *Epokha osvobozhdeniia krestian* . . . , III, pp. 346ff.) and Mikhail Bezobrazov.

[77] In August 1859 Miliutin and Soloviev analyzed the views of

The doctrinaire view of this incident must be rejected, but several of its assumptions require closer examination for, if substantiated, they must color our understanding of the movement for devolving bureaucratic functions onto elective bodies. These assumptions, common to the writing of Soviet and prerevolutionary liberal historians alike, are that the governmental agencies were doing nothing on their own initiative to establish public organs, that they were uninterested in and even opposed to doing so,[78] and that the disenchanted deputies posited a program more radical than anything under consideration in the ministries.[79] Together, these assumptions underlie the conclusion that self-government was a program evolved by Russian "society" and accepted by the state only reluctantly and under duress.

These assumptions, widely held at the time, significantly misrepresent the actual state of affairs. Returning to the 1858 debate on administrative deconcentration, it will be recalled that the Soloviev faction finally achieved a *modus vivendi* with the security-conscious centralizers by separating the "economic" functions of the police from their security role. This appeased Muraviev's group and opened the way both for the deconcentration of administrative function and the devolution of other local duties to the public. The Commission on Provincial and District Institutions was formed for the explicit purpose of planning reforms

---

the gentry in a joint memorandum to Alexander II, dividing them into three groups: a few who favored the abolition of serfdom, those who opposed emancipation categorically, and those who would consent to it if it would lead to some form of oligarchy. Iordanskii, *Konstitutsionnoe dvizhenie* . . . , pp. 44-46.

[78] Garmiza's version of this view is scarcely to be distinguished from that of turn-of-the-century liberal historians. *Podgotovka* . . . , Chap. III.

[79] Iordanskii assumes this in his *Konstitutsionnoe dvizhenie* . . . , pp. 54ff., as does Garmiza, *Podgotovka* . . . , pp. 138ff. Both of these scholars extend their arguments to the point of suggesting that a governmental conspiracy against self-government existed in 1859.

which would give local powers "more unity, trust and confidence," as the published decree of foundation made plain to anyone who cared to read it. The commission was dominated by the most conspicuous advocates of decentralization and self-rule in the bureaucracy and was led by Nikolai Miliutin who, though an abolitionist, had nonetheless made St. Petersburg the only self-governing city in Russia. An early declaration of the commission made explicit this commitment. "The Commission finds that at the present time, with the fundamental alteration of the juridical and economic status of the greater part of the population of districts [i.e., emancipation] . . . the introduction of a properly structured organization for economic affairs in the districts, based on the elective principle, would be completely timely and would correspond to the needs of society."[80]

In light of these declarations, accessible to any gentry deputy, the question arises as to why they felt compelled to submit their proposal as if the Commission on Provincial and District Institutions had issued no commitments. Were they ignorant of the Commission's intentions?[81] Or, since this is scarcely possible, was it that they knew and simply refused to believe them? If so, gentry delegates could have nodded knowingly as the commission worked to centralize local security functions. Those inclined to do so could readily interpret this act as an antireformist stratagem.[82] Many deputies did just that, revealing vividly that a disastrous breakdown of trust had occurred on both sides, which is confirmed by memoirists reflecting on the psychological temper of the capital at the time.[83]

[80] *Trudy komissii o gubernskikh i uezhdnykh uchrezhdeniiakh*, I, Bk. 2, pp. 133-34.

[81] See Skrebitskii, ed., *Krestianskoe delo* . . . , I, 766, letter of Nikoforov and Petrovo-Soloviev asking whether the economic institutions would be run by the public or by the bureaucracy.

[82] That this was not an antireformist stratagem and was a practical necessity was acknowledged by Alexander II on May 10, 1860, TsGIA-SSSR, f. 1162, No. 1, pp. 1-3, *Dela otdeleniia zakonov*.

[83] See, for example, Nikitenko, *Dnevnik*, II, 100; Barsukov, *Zhizn . . . Pogodina*, XVII, pp. 120, 130-31.

Given this state of mind, further communication between even reformist officials and gentry delegates could only exacerbate their differences. The mood of mutual suspicion and distrust gripping both groups created a wall between them and led each to the unshakable conviction that what the other was *not* doing and saying was of far greater import than what it was. Gentry leaders could not be dissuaded from their certitude that the government was waiting only for them to depart from the capital to institute a sinister program of bureaucratic centralization. Government leaders closed their eyes to genuine similarities between their own and gentry views on local government and they suspected the gentry of conspiring against emancipation. Lanskoi, the bureaucratic innovators, and the tsar as well were all affected by this general mood and, fearing that the departing leaders would return to their provinces and inflame all the gentry against the reform program and emancipation in particular, they summarily issued on November 9, 1859, a ban on all further discussion of the government projects.[84]

Alexander and his minister decided not merely to ignore gentry pressure but temporarily to abolish it, as if blocking off channels of expression would cause the sentiments that might have been communicated to evaporate. They did not. Instead, the ban spurred communication on all matters pertaining to reform. During the winter of 1859-1860 a number of provincial assemblies convened to elect officers for the forthcoming three-year term, and at these meetings the gentry of all factions vied with each other in exorcising this new *bête-noir*.[85]

Everywhere the pattern was the same; first the deputies

---

[84] *Materialy dlia istorii uprazdeneniia krepostnogo sostoianiia*, II, 260; also, see Lanskoi's two memorandums to Alexander II, Semenov, *Osvobozhdenie krestian . . .*, I, 826-34. GBL, f. 327, 1/22/6, pp. 1-10.

[85] *Ibid.*, II, 277-347; *Kolokol*, No. 71 (1860), 592, reviews these meetings; also *Sankt-Peterburgskie Vedomosti*, No. 36 (February 17, 1860); and A. Povalishin, *Riazanskie pomeshchiki i ikh krepostnye*, Riazan, 1903, pp. 380ff.

returning from Petersburg were warmly welcomed and invited to report on what they had seen; then would follow a free-wheeling discussion of the Main Committee program, in which the bitterness of the deputies would be transmitted to the entire gathering; finally the assembly would draft indignant addresses to the throne. Often, as in Tver, serious friction developed between the gentry and local officials.[86] In the end, a handful of ringleaders were exiled, but it was evident that the great number of protesters against the ban exceeded the government's ability to apply punishment.

When a year later, in December of 1860, the assemblies of provincial gentry again convened for their annual meetings, Alexander and Lanskoi faced a difficult choice. It was evident that their ban on discussion had done more than any other single measure to weld the gentry into an interest group spanning divisions that had only a year before prevented common action. Should they now reaffirm the ban on discussion, or should they instead attempt to correct their tactical blunder? They eagerly took the latter course and announced that gentry assemblies were free to consider fully any aspect of reform *except* the abolition of serfdom. To structure these discussions, Alexander and his minister set five questions on which they would particularly welcome the opinions of the corporate gentry: (1) the organization of institutions providing credit in the countryside (2) the structure of the provincial tax system (3) the extent to which affairs should be managed by elected officials and the method by which they should be selected (4) the organization of medical service in Russia, and (5) the use of hired labor.[87] Broadly interpreted, the first four of these questions embraced all the major issues connected with self-government.

[86] Dzhanshiev, *Epokha* . . . , pp. 135ff., and Emmons, *The Russian Landed Gentry* . . . , pp. 266-81, as well as *Materialy dlia istorii uprazdneniia krepostnogo sostoianiia*, II, pp. 273-94.
[87] TsGIA-SSSR, f. 908, d. 34, pp. 40-43.

Did the government retreat in the face of interest group pressure? This was certainly the case, but at the same time the policy reversal contained its own inner logic. In part, the tsar and Lanskoi sought to capture the highly politicized issue of local rule within the orderly molds of administrative procedure. In part, too, they wanted to choose the interest groups with which they would deal and to specify the grounds of contact. It is important to note that on this point the positions of the autocrat himself and of the leading bureaucratic politicians were identical. Lanskoi's successor, Peter Valuev, expressed this well in a categorical opinion handed down a year after the event: "This measure was taken primarily with the aim of avoiding as far as possible the appearance of statements not corresponding to the views of the government, and especially to ward off statements in the form of addresses to the throne."[88] Still another factor underlying the issuance of the five questions is suggested by the contents of the addresses of 1859-1860. When the 1859 ban on discussion was levied it was assumed in Petersburg that the gentry's primary hostility toward the provisions of the emancipation would spill over into other issues. Alexander and Lanskoi therefore did not bother to distinguish between debate on emancipation and consideration of other reforms, including the restructuring of provincial government. The addresses actually submitted, however, while attacking the ban, revealed at the same time a preoccupation with these "other problems" that contained little of the oligarchism that officialdom so feared. Calls for self-rule in various areas of local life came from five assemblies. To the gentry of Tver and Riazan this required the establishment of autonomous provincial land banks;[89] the Vladimir and Iaroslavl gentry sought judicial reform so that

[88] TsGIA-SSSR, f. 1275 (Archive of the Council of Ministers), d. 22, pp. 85-86.
[89] On the Tver bank see Unkovskii, "Zapiska," *Russkaia Mysl*, No. 7, 1906, pp. 89-90; for the Riazan bank project see Povalishin, *Riazanskie pomeshchiki . . .* , pp. 380-86.

217

the public organs would not be subject to administrative review;[90] in Tver province tax reform was considered essential;[91] and in Petersburg, Iaroslavl, Tver, Riazan, and especially Vladimir province self-government entailed the establishment of elective organs at the district and provincial levels.[92] In short, gentry activists of all stripes had finally concentrated their interest on a broad program for local reform rather than on the details of emancipation *per se*.

This interest must have come as a welcome surprise to Sergei Lanskoi who had devoted his old age to achieving these measures and had long encouraged bureaucratic subordinates who would back them. He realized that he had erred in not distinguishing between gentry oligarchism and opposition to emancipation on the one hand and gentry interest in practical reform at the local level on the other. The substance of their resolutions apparently convinced him that on the issue of local governance he could again cooperate with provincial interests.[93]

The effect of this momentous reversal of policy was to push public discussion beyond the extremely divisive question of emancipation to problems of local government. Differences of opinion persisted here, of course, both between bureaucratic reformers and gentry and within each of these groups, but they were not so sharp as to diminish the value

[90] TsGIA-SSSR, f. 1180, No. 37, pp. 59ff.; *Materialy dlia istorii uprazdneniia krepostnogo sostoianiia*, II, 299, 306-07.

[91] *Materialy dlia istorii uprazdneniia krepostnogo sostoianiia*, II, 299, 306-07.

[92] *Ibid.*, pp. 295-321.

[93] This explanation should be contrasted to that presented by Garmiza, *Podgotovka* . . . , pp. 63-68, and by Emmons, *The Russian Landed Gentry* . . . , p. 333. According to their argument, the issuance of the five questions was little more than a concession to gentry opinion necessitated by fear of further manifestos to the tsar. Evidence is taken from the passage of Valuev's cited above. Actually, the only point on which Lanskoi acknowledged the need of a policy of concession was on the social composition of the *zemstvos*; see Iordanskii, *Konstitutsionnoe dvizhenie* . . . , p. 52.

of the legislators consulting with local leaders. Serious consideration of the problems of local taxation, credit, medicine, and the new elective bodies could now take place.

COMMUNITY CONTROL OF PUBLIC FINANCES

In the early stages of the debate on local government, administrative malfeasance figured much larger in the concerns of reformers than did any economic considerations. True, both Prince Cherkasskii and the Petersburg gentry commission had considered finances to be important, but they were exceptions. Only in 1859 and 1860 did the economic dimensions of provincial life force itself upon the attention of those concerned with reform. Once this happened, debate shifted from the definition of rights to the acquisition of powers.

Credit and finances would have come up for consideration under any circumstances since they were inextricably tied with the abolition of serfdom.[94] But the event which suddenly thrust the problem of provincial finances to the fore was the sudden demise of the State Bank in 1859. Warnings had sounded earlier. Beginning in the last months in 1856 a worldwide credit squeeze seized the money markets of Europe and America.[95] In a sudden decline in business activity the value of Credit Mobilier shares shrank in six months by 45 percent, and that of the respected Darmstadt Kredit-Bank by 51 percent. A wave of bank closures originating in the American Midwest rolled along the well-worn channels of trade to Europe, reaching Hamburg and Paris by November and affecting Petersburg and Moscow by New Year's Day, 1858. Their impact was

[94] This relation is the subject of an excellent study by P. Kovanko, *Reforma 19 fevralia 1861 g. i ego posledstviia s finansovoi tochki zreniia*, Kiev, 1914.

[95] The European financial crisis is analyzed in detail by H. Rosenberg, *Die Weltwirtschaftskrisis von 1857-1859*, Berlin and Stuttgart, 1934.

219

immediate.[96] Withdrawals from treasury banks exceeded deposits by 11 million rubles in 1857, by 52 million in 1858, and by 104 million in 1859.[97] Annual deposits in the State Bank plummeted from 412 million to 318 million in less than two years.[98] Never had a crisis originating abroad so gravely affected Russian credit institutions.

Russian government bankers had watched a brief postwar boom in savings with apprehension and cut the interest rate in July of 1857 in an attempt to temper it.[99] A series of desperate steps to stem the looming crisis followed in 1858 and 1859, including a ban on the formation of new joint-stock companies, but to no avail. With the sharp rise in bankruptcies and the imminent collapse of Russia's main credit institution, the malaise spread. "Our position is frightful," Grand Duke Konstantin wrote in his diary. "I hope to God that finally our eyes are opened and that we stop reacting in our usual way with half-measures."[100]

Finally, on April 29, 1859, Alexander II hurriedly established a state commission for the purpose of remodeling the entire credit apparatus. Within weeks this body recommended that the State Bank be closed and its assets liquidated. Then, shortly after this, the tsar called on the Minister of Finances to set up a second commission to study the tax system with the explicit aim of increasing the government's revenues.[101]

By their very nature, both the Commission on Banking

[96] A. F. Iakovlev, *Ekonomicheskie krizisy v Rossii*, Moscow, 1955, pp. 61-77; S. Ia. Borovoi, *Kredit i banki Rossii (seredina XVIII v.—1861 g.)*, Moscow, 1958, pp. 275 ff.

[97] I. Kaufman, *Iz istorii bumazhnykh deneg v Rossii*, St. Petersburg, 1909, p. 6, cited in Borovoi, *Kredit i banki . . .* , p. 277.

[98] Brockhaus and Efron, *Entsiklopedicheskii slovar*, iv, p. 920. See also Borovoi, *Kredit i banki . . .* , p. 278.

[99] It was the opinion of V. Lamanskii, a member of the Banking Commission, that this action made the crisis more acute in Russia than it would otherwise have been by overstimulating the outflow of deposits. *Trudy Imperatorskogo Volnogo Ekonomischeskogo Obshchestva*, Vol. 2, No. 4 (April 1862), pp. 1-7.

[100] TsGAOR 722 (Marble Palace archive), op. 1, ed. khr. 91, p. 61.

[101] TsGIA-SSSR, f. 572, op. 1, ed. khr. 9, p. 28.

and the Commission on Taxes and Duties were intimately involved with provincial finances. Formed at the moment that provincial deputies were drawing up hostile manifestos and the Commission on Provincial and District Institutions was beginning its work, these new groups were plunged headlong into the midst of agitation for provincial autonomy. Surprisingly, though, the invective which marred the emancipation debate left little mark on relations between these commissions and the public. Temporarily, government and society each perceived its interest in mutually compatible terms.

Tax Reform and Self-Administration

As earlier in the case of Petersburg province, tax arrears were the immediate cause of consternation over finances among gentry and state officials. An 1861 survey revealed that several provinces owed the government over a million rubles each.[102] Although the worst offenders were in the south, even northern Novgorod owed a quarter of a million rubles and showed no inclination to pay.[103] Local gentry knew well that the greatest deficits were in funds that reverted to the provinces themselves, the state levied "local taxes" (*zemskie sbora*), which averaged 306 to 402 thousand rubles arrears per province surveyed.[104] To the pleas and threats of the Ministry of Finances, provincial officials and gentry leaders responded with helpless silence.[105] In Orel province a special commission formed in 1862 to study the tax problem affirmed what the Petersburg gentry had

[102] TsGIA-SSSR, f. 1287, d. (1861), op. 22, d. 1023, pp. 1-40.
[103] *Ibid.*, p. 28.
[104]

Province	Rubles	Province	Rubles
Mogilev	1,098,694	Kostroma	80,428
Penza	82,490	Samara	377,828
Kaluga	143,427	Vologda	52,119
Vitebsk	742,803	Iaroslavl	99,465
Tver	49,308	Novgorod	213,544
Poltava	437,436		

[105] TsGIA-SSSR, f. 1287, op. 22, d. 1023, p. 40.

221

long known: that the trouble lay as much in the inefficiency of collection and accounting procedures as in the inability of the local economy to sustain the taxes.[106]

Government specialists watched in alarm as the national debt soared to unprecedented heights and the state's credit plunged downward, rendering the treasury less able than ever to float the loans that alone could rescue it.[107] To make the picture darker still, the emancipation promised to rob the state of the precious yield on the soul tax.[108] No sooner was the Commission on Taxes and Duties functioning than its members set about devising means of squeezing every free kopek from the economy. They carried out extensive investigations to determine how far upward they could push duties on trade,[109] pored over land tax legislation from western Europe,[110] proposed further luxury taxes,[111] and seriously considered an income tax.[112] Their arguments on behalf of sweeping change readily convinced Alexander II who, on March 31, 1860, authorized a complete reform of the tax system.[113]

The Commission on Taxes was fortunate to have as its

[106] This was glaringly evident in cases where expenditures not anticipated by the tax estimates were incurred. The ministries systematically refused to allow these to be covered directly from local levies, though this would have been the simplest means of solving the problems. TsGIA-SSSR, f. 1287 (1861), op. 22, d. 1041, p. 19. Requests of gentry of Perm, Podolia, and other provinces; also, p. 46 for response of A. Troinitskii, aide to the minister of finances.

[107] Lebedev, "Iz zapisok . . . ," p. 10.

[108] TsGIA-SSSR, f. 572, op. 1, ed. khr. 9, *Zhurnal komissii podatei i sborov*, October 7 and 14, 1861, p. 5.

[109] *Trudy komissii vysochaishei uchrezhdennoi dlia peresmotra sistemy podatei i sborov*, v, "O Poshlinakh za pravo torgovli i drugikh promyslov," St. Petersburg, 1863.

[110] F. G. Terner, *Svedeniia o pozemelnom naloge v inostrannykh gosudarstvakh*, St. Petersburg, 1863. The countries studied were Prussia, Austria, France, England, and the United States.

[111] Lebedev, "Iz zapisok . . . ," p. 96.

[112] TsGIA-SSSR, f. 908, op. 1, d. 161, pp. 26ff. Report of the First Division of the Commission on Taxes and Duties, 1862; see also TsGIA-SSSR, f. 572 (1859), op. 1, p. 8.

[113] TsGIA-SSSR, f. 572, op. 1, d. 13, p. 1.

chairman Iulii Hagemeister, a man who had never suc-
cumbed to the antigentry suspicions so strong in government circles in 1859 and 1860. Now, in 1861, he enthusiastically proposed to expand his commission with the
introduction of elected advisers from the provinces.[114] The
new Minister of Internal Affairs, Valuev, praised the plan
warmly and suggested that the commission invite not only
gentry but delegates from all the nation's taxpayers, including urban residents and Jews.[115] In other words, at the very
time that the government as a whole is said to have worked
to prevent any articulation of gentry opinion, two prominent officials appeared eager to convoke a second, expanded
group of provincial representatives. The State Council approved this and, on December 4, 1861, Alexander II signed
the measure, allowing elected representatives from sixty-
five provincial tax agencies and fifty cities to come to Petersburg and present their proposals.[116]

Some time after its enactment this plan was drastically
curtailed to the point that only a half dozen gentry delegates sat on the commission. No sinister intent lay behind
this, however; as in the earlier attempt of the Ministry of
Internal Affairs to bring governors to Petersburg for consultation, bureaucratic impediments simply proved too
time-consuming and the expense too great. Broad channels
for indirect participation remained, nonetheless, in the right
to respond to the five questions,[117] of which at least twenty
provincial assemblies availed themselves.

[114] TsGIA-SSSR, f. 572, op. 1, d. 7, p. 1-b, letter to unknown
person by A. Kniazhevich, Minister of Finances, June 20, 1861.

[115] TsGIA-SSSR, f. 572, op. 1, d. 7, pp. 8-10. Valuev to Kniazhevich, December 3, 1861.

[116] TsGIA-SSSR, f. 572, op. 1, ed. khr. 9, pp. 8, 20.

[117] Short extracts from thirteen replies are published in *Materialy
po zemskomu obshchestvennomu ustroistvu*, I, 381-409. Full texts
of these and other responses are in TsGIA-SSSR, f. 1287, op. 22,
d. 1065, 1066. The total list of known proposals includes Nizhnii
Novgorod, Kharkov, Voronezh, Kursk, Smolensk, Tula, Moscow, Tambov, Simbirsk, Petersburg, Orenburg, Vladimir, Orel, Kherson, Poltava,
Kaluga, Ekaterinoslav, Iaroslavl, Riazan, Vitebsk, Saratov; opinions

Of gentry opinion one thing is certain: by 1862 the "political" demands of the provincial elite were proposals for tax reform written large. The Poltava lords expressed the dominant theme that the existing tax system was "completely unsatisfactory for the needs of our times."[118] Means for rectifying the situation varied. For some, the compelling if mundane need to save money could be met by minimal structural alterations. Thus, the gentry of Orel submitted a plan to enable local residents to take over the auditing of records,[119] while from Kazan province came a yet milder suggestion simply to introduce the right to petition the tsar directly on tax matters.[120]

Most assemblies were not content with such palliatives and proposed instead to turn tax affairs over to strong elective bodies, even to a local *Zemskaia Duma*,[121] which would control fully its own autonomous sphere of taxation. Variants on this line of reform were championed by the majority of gentry in Kaluga, Kharkov, Kostroma, Kursk, Novgorod, Orenburg, Pskov, Riazan, Smolensk, Tambov, Iaroslavl, and Voronezh provinces.[122] The authors of these proposals in-

---

from other provinces which were not asked to submit proposals, including Tver, can be deduced from indirect evidence. Garmiza, *Podgotovka* . . . , p. 68, and Emmons, *The Russian Landed Gentry* . . . , p. 333n, err in claiming that only thirteen provinces were asked to submit responses.

[118] TsGIA-SSSR, f. 1287, op. 22, d. 1065, pp. 510-54, 13 April 1863.

[119] TsGIA-SSSR, f. 1287, op. 22, d. 1065, pp. 34-42, 1862. A similar plan came from Saratov, TsGIA-SSSR, f. 1287, op. 22, d. 1037 (June 1861), pp. 1-3, 7. Valuev expressed his approval of this plan, *ibid.*, p. 8. See also TsGIA-SSSR, f. 572, op. 1, d. 361-69.

[120] *Ibid.*, f. 1287, pp. 64-65. The heretofore volatile gentry of Vladimir submitted only a list of means by which economies might be achieved. TsGIA-SSSR, f. 1287, op. 22, d. 1066, *Zhurnal dvorianskogo sobraniia Vladimirskoi gubernii* (June 10, 1861).

[121] TsGIA-SSSR, f. 1287, op. 22, d. 1065 (April 13, 1863), pp. 51-54. Ekaterinoslav province.

[122] KALUGA: TsGIA-SSSR, f. 1287, op. 22, d. 1065, p. 61; Garmiza, *Podgotovka* . . . , p. 69.

KHARKOV: TsGIA-SSSR, f. 1287, op. 22, d. 1065 (December 1861), sisted on two points: that all funds spent locally should be considered provincial duties, and that national and provincial budgets should be completely divorced from one another. At the same time, they did not agitate for the state to spend a greater percentage of the total tax budget for provincial development. They reasoned that local control would assure the effectiveness of every ruble spent locally and thereby create a budgetary expansion which would be actual, if not real in accounting terms.

The gentry of a few provinces wanted the government to increase its total expenditures in the provinces and were willing to abolish the distinction between national and local levies if necessary.[123] Most recoiled from this solution and proposed instead that more money be spent in the province while retaining a sharp distinction between national and local budgets. This view was adopted as a majority position in Poltava, Simbirsk, Tula, Kaluga, Kharkov, Kostroma,

---

pp. 1-3. *Materialy dlia istorii uprazdneniia krepostnogo sostoianiia . . .*, I, 383-85.

KOSTROMA: TsGIA-SSSR, f. 1143, 1863, op. vi. d. 82, p. 694.

KURSK: TsGIA-SSSR, f. 1287, op. 22, d. 1065 (March 1862), pp. 16-20; *Materialy dlia istorii uprazdneniia krepostnogo sostoianiia . . .*, I, 390-94.

NOVGOROD: *Ibid.*, I, 409.

ORENBURG: *Ibid.*, I, 408-09.

PSKOV: *Ibid.*, I, 395, 398.

RIAZAN: TsGIA-SSSR, f. 1287, op. 22, d. 1065, p. 77.

TAMBOV: *Materialy dlia istorii uprazdneniia krepostnogo sostoianiia . . .*, I, 399-400.

IAROSLAVL: TsGIA-SSSR, f. 1287, op. 22, d. 1065 (April 1863), p. 77.

VORONEZH: *Ibid.* (January 1862), pp. 12-16; *Materialy dlia istorii uprazdneniia krepostnogo sostoianiia . . .*, I, 388-90.

SMOLENSK: TsGIA-SSSR, f. 1287, op. 22, d. 1065, pp. 9-12. *Materialy dlia istorii uprazdneniia krepostnogo sostoianiia . . .*, I, 395-97.

123 TsGIA-SSSR, f. 1287, op. 22, d. 1065, pp. 4-7, 66-72. Also *Materialy dlia istorii uprazdneniia krepostnogo sostoianiia . . .*, I, 397-98.

Kherson, Petersburg, Tver, and Nizhnii Novgorod provinces.[124]

In order to see what was entailed by all these proposals, the evidence compiled by a gentry-sponsored Commission on the System of Taxation in Nizhnii Novgorod province is instructive.[125] According to its statistics, the value of taxes collected annually from the province in 1858-1860 totaled 1,168,753 rubles. Of this sum, 563 to 586 thousand accrued from the soul tax on peasants and 476,077 was from national-local taxes; purely local levies generated only 129,676 of the total.[126] Under the unreformed system, in other words, the provincial public had control of only 11 percent of the funds collected locally.

These figures must be balanced against the expenditures within the province by central authorities in the same period. From the soul tax, vodka tax, and trade tax the province received back a mere 220,711 rubles, or less than half the yield on the soul tax alone. Only 55,595 of the 476,077

---

[124] Poltava: TsGIA-SSSR, f. 1287, op. 22, d. 1065 (April 1863), pp. 51-54.

Simbirsk: *Ibid.* (February 1862), pp. 22-29. *Materialy dlia istorii uprazdneniia krepostnogo sostoianiia . . .* , I, 400-01.

Tula: TsGIA-SSSR, f. 1287, op. 22, d. 1065 (December 1861), pp. 398-99.

Kherson: TsGIA-SSSR, f. 1287, op. 22, d. 1065 (April 1863), pp. 48, 50.

Petersburg: *Materialy dlia uprazdneniia krepostnogo sostoianiia . . .* , I, 401-07. See also *Severnaia Pochta*, No. 60 (1863), 238.

Nizhegorod: TsGIA-SSSR, f. 1143, 1863, op. vi, d. 82, pp. 532-587. The Tver proposal was not solicited by the government. TsGIA-SSSR, f. 1287, op. 47, pp. 20-21, Garmiza, *Podgotovka . . .* , p. 80.

[125] On the background to the formation of this powerful body see TsGIA-SSSR, f. 1287 (1860), op. 21, d. 1872, pp. 3-22. "Vypiska iz vysochaishei utverzhdennoi smety gubernskikh zemskikh povinnostei Nizhegorodskoi gubernii na trekhletie s 1860"; this commission was under the strong influence of federal systems in western Europe (Switzerland) and America, as well as of the earlier Petersburg Commission. (TsGIA-SSSR, f. 1143 [1863], op. vi., d. 82, pp. 533, 568). See also Chebaevskii, "Nizhegorodskii gubernskii dvorianskii komitet . . .," p. 92.

[126] *Ibid.*, pp. 572-74. The total does not include excise taxes on vodka, etc., nor the tax on trade.

rubles of national-local duties came back to the province in any form. Purely local duties, of course, could not be expended outside the province. Thus, of the sum paid into the central treasury by the province, only 33 percent (389,828 rubles) reverted to the locality. Of this, the provincial agencies controlled less than a third while the rest was controlled from Petersburg, unaffected even by local administrators! The province was being bled.

To rectify this imbalance, the gentry of ten provinces including Nizhnii Novogord proposed first that the national-local duties now returned to the province through the bureaucracy would in the future be levied and disbursed locally by elective public agencies. Second, they proposed that all "natural duties" now paid in labor and managed by officials be converted to taxes in currency and transferred to the control of elective agencies. By these means the budget of Nizhnii Novgorod's elective agencies would increase at least by a factor of six, from 113,522 R. to 660,492 R. Third, and most important, they requested the national government to pare down its own budget for the sake of locally controlled provincial development.

In the Russian context, such a proposal must rank as a utopian dream. Even the reformers in Petersburg had never doubted that the central state would continue to play a dominant role in the economy. At the same time, the plan was undeniably grounded on common sense. Most provinces whose gentry advocated this reform had all achieved eminence as manufacturing or commercial centers. Local leaders there would have realized that, as relatively developed regions, their national-local tax payments were subsidizing the maintenance of more backward provinces. For them, this extreme form of self-government presented a simple means of benefiting from the development which had already taken place in their localities. However unrealistic the actual proposal may have been, it attests that the new ideology of the mid-1850s had become tightly interwoven with concrete problems a half decade later.

227

No member of the commission charged with examining these proposals was firmly committed to any one method of applying self-government to taxation and even the two most active members, the ubiquitous Iakov Soloviev and the ambitious young economist, Fedor Terner, did not arrive at the first meeting with a ready plan of action.[127] In 1860 tax reform was an open issue.

Like most legislative bodies of the era, the Commission on Taxes and Duties refused to entertain documents from any interest group until it had first worked out its own tentative pattern for reform. To this end, some members reviewed the experience of Belgium, Prussia, Austria, and Italy,[128] while others sought to extract guidance from the perennial contrast of England and France. All waited eagerly to examine the four studies of Russia's own tax situation drawn up at the commission's request.

Even the most cautious of these studies, that of the efficient-minded bureaucrat B. E. Trutchenko, called for deconcentrated control of taxation. But he argued that "in ten years experience [elective representation of the estates] has not at all realized the hopes of the government."[129] Expanded local power must therefore be wielded by com-

[127] TsGIA-SSSR, f. 572, op. 1, d. 7, p. 6. Also, Lebedev, "Iz zapisok . . . ," p. 230. Among the members were V. P. Bezabrazov, D. P. Gavrilov, A. A. Golovachev, K. K. Grot, N. A. Malashev, M. Kh. Reutern, V. A. Tatarinov, B. E. Trutchenko, A. P. Zablotskii-Desiatovskii. The chairman, Iu. A. Hagemeister, was esteemed for his knowledge of local financial affairs. Bezobrazov used material on this subject gathered in an extensive tour of the country in 1860 for a series of published essays, and Hagemeister's *Teoriia nalogov, primenennaia k gosudarstvennomu khoziaistvu,* St. Petersburg, 1852, was long a basic text in the field of taxation.

[128] *Kratkii ocherk sistem pravitelstvennogo nadzora za obshchestvami ili zemskimi delami v glavnykh evropeiskikh gosudarstvakh,* St. Petersburg, n.d. Although this was printed, this interesting document is not preserved either in the Lenin Library or the Public Library in Leningrad. A single copy exists in TsGIA-SSSR, f. 572, op. 1, d. 39, pp. 19ff.

[129] *Materialy ob ustroistve upravleniia zemskimi povinnostiami,* B. E. Trutchenko, ed., St. Petersburg, 1861, p. 3.

228

mittees of provincial officials and civil servants, and not by "society."

The weighty memoir by the gentry-expert of Vladimir province, D. P. Gavrilov, amplified the decree of Alexander II to the Commission on Provincial and District Institutions and urged that the proposed elective organs be given "greater independence, trust, and a larger burden of power in all matters regarding taxation."[130] This theme was expanded upon by Alexander Golovachev of Tver who proposed that local elective bodies be given *exclusive* control over all civil expenditures affecting only their territory.[131] Furthermore, any irregularities in the collection and disbursal of tax funds should be prosecuted not by the central administrative organs but by the soon to be formed courts of law.[132]

The Gavrilov and Golovachev memorandums faithfully represented the views of the local gentry of Kaluga, Kharkov, Kostroma, etc. A fourth study by N. A. Malashev presented a curious variant on the argument of those who insisted on the need to expand the number of areas under public control. To achieve this he did not follow Golovachev in drawing the central-local dichotomy yet more sharply but urged instead that it be discarded.[133] In its place Malashev invoked the concept of a national public, or the "*zemstvo* of the entire empire."[134] He called for the formation of a national elective body representing all prop-

---

[130] D. P. Gavrilov, *Materialy i svedeniia o sushchestvuiushchem poriadke i sposobakh otpravleniia naturalnykh zemskikh povinnostei v tsentralnykh guberniiakh imperii*, St. Petersburg, 1860, pp. 102ff.

[131] Golovachev, *Materialy . . .* , pp. 29, 30, 39.

[132] *Ibid.*, pp. 32, 38.

[133] Malashev, *Materialy . . .* , p. 9. For earlier views on this see *Trudy komissii . . . podatei i sborov; Poiasnitelnaia zapiska o robotakh po soglasheniiu otsenkov gosudarstvennykh imushchestv mezhdu guberniiami*, St. Petersburg, 1862, Section I.

[134] Cf. M. Bezobrazov's proposals of 1859: TsGIA-SSSR, op. 1, d. 7. See also his *Zapiska o sobrannykh deputatov ot gubernskikh komitetov*, TsGIA-SSSR, f. 908, op. 1, d. 101 (later published: St. Petersburg, 1860).

229

erty-owning citizens, with deputies elected by province. To this central elective body would be entrusted control over all those taxes which by their nature would fall unequally on different provinces, while the provincial public bodies would control only matters of a "purely local" character. "Again, we repeat that the inadequacy of means in the State treasury . . . is sufficiently great in our view to transfer all expenditures for such general matters to the public of the *entire* empire."[135]

Malashev's centralism and his failure to distinguish between national and provincial matters evoked a strenuous rebuttal from Golovachev. This second memorandum, though studied by the Commission on Taxes and Duties, was barred even from internal ministerial publication by the red seal of censorship.[136] Golovachev insisted that public control was absolutely incompatible with central rule in any form. To achieve both an equitable division of taxes among provinces and a high degree of self-rule, Golovachev followed the path first cut by Vladimir Tsie and later by so many gentry groups: he turned the existing principle of allocation upside down. Instead of defining local taxes as those covering expenditures unique to each province, he declared that provincial taxes should be considered precisely as those that are everywhere equal.[137] This, he cogently argued, would reduce the national government's share in taxation from its present nine-tenths to only a quarter of the total. Such diverse matters as education, health, public buildings, the quartering of regular troops, and even postage would be financed entirely by provincially levied taxes. In effect, the country would become a federation of publicly controlled and administratively independent provinces.

---

[135] Malashev, *Materialy* . . . , p. 25.

[136] TsGIA-SSSR, f. 572, op. 1, d. 7, pp. 1-33, "O zemskikh povinnostiakh."

[137] TsGIA-SSSR, f. 1287 (1860), op. 21, d. 1972, p. 42. The ministries agreed that this proposal was "admirable." *Ibid.*, pp. 29-41.

Armed with these memorandums and having also digested some twenty detailed reports by gentry assemblies, the Commission on Taxes and Duties could be assured that it had a thorough sample of gentry and official opinion. The first steps of the commission were cautious, though indicative of an awareness of the provincialist cause. Typical was its approval of the Nizhnii Novgorod proposal for public control of taxation at the district level.[138] In the same spirit, the commission supported the gentry of Saratov in its eminently moderate request for the right to audit local tax estimates and apportionments.[139]

The first evidence of the commission's endorsement of a tax system based clearly on a division between national and provincial levies came in October of 1861, when two members were deputized to draw up a detailed plan assigning taxes to these categories.[140] The significance of this step should not be underestimated, regardless of its ultimate consequences. For the first time in its history, the Russian government was considering a tax system which would grant to the public an area of *exclusive control* rather than merely the privilege of assisting local administrative officers. And, whereas in the past public participation had been confined to the gentry estate and its corporate agencies, it would now be expanded to embrace "all of the people of each province." This was precisely the sense in which reports of the commission employed that elusive word *zemstvo* in 1861-1862.

The pride of the commission members in their work is suggested by the eagerness with which they distributed copies of the proposal embodying provincial tax autonomy to governors and gentry leaders throughout Russia.[141] The negative side of their accomplishment at once struck pro-

---

[138] TsGIA-SSSR, f. 572, op. 1, d. 36, pp. 2-60.
[139] TsGIA-SSSR, f. 572, op. 1, d. 7, p. 6. Protocol of the First Section of the Commission on Taxes and Duties, October 19, 1861.
[140] *Ibid.*, Report No. 7, p. 2.
[141] *Ibid.*, Journal of the Commission on Taxes and Duties, December 8, 1861, p. 2.

vincial leaders, both officials and gentry, who detected that in the same move the legislators had transferred to the central treasury over 18 million rubles of annual income heretofore labeled as national-provincial duties and managed jointly—if wastefully—by central and local officials. In endowing the localities with political *competence*, the commission denied them the requisite economic *power*.[142]

It did not take long for the self-congratulatory euphoria to dispel itself, as the two local interest groups—gentry and governors—combined to attack the centralizing character of the initial proposal. By unanimous vote, the commission agreed to append to its 1862 report a statement expressing the hope that the sphere of provincial tax power would soon be broadened: the small figure projected at first, it announced, did "not fully reflect the scale which provincial duties will assume after being restructured along the lines proposed."[143] The commission then set to work preparing a fresh plan under which autonomous public agencies would be given broader tax powers. This was drawn up and debated in the autumn of 1862.[144] Though national-provincial duties were still converted largely to national taxes, in many provinces the volume of public money spent locally showed an increase over current levels. At the same time, the quantity of capital controlled exclusively by local public bodies increased sharply and the firm demarcation between national and provincial duties remained intact.[145] Finally, the new legislation established procedures whereby natural duties could readily be converted into cash payments, which opened to self-government a large area for future expansion. In short the second draft embodied the essential principles advanced by the more moderate gentry in their responses to the five questions.

This document was virtually ready for promulgation by

---

[142] *Ibid.*, pp. 14-15, 17-18.   [143] *Ibid.*, Report No. 7, p. 28.
[144] The final draft was published: *O glavnykh nachalakh preobrazovaniia zemskikh povinnostei*, St. Petersburg, 1863.
[145] TsGIA-SSSR, f. 572, op. 1, d. 7, p. 109.

232

the end of 1862. Yet for another year the plan underwent continual alteration and revision, not at the hands of the Commission on Taxes and Duties or its patron, the Ministry of Finances, but rather of the Commission on Provincial and District Institutions and its new chairman, Valuev. That the focus of reform should change was logical enough, for the financial provisions had to be coordinated with institutional plans being worked out by Valuev's group. At the same time, the shift back to the Ministry of Internal Affairs implied a transition from economic to more frankly political concerns.

Local taxpayers were justifiably piqued at the length of time required to transform the tax proposals into legislative terms. Their ire might have been considerably greater, though, had it not been for the speed with which the Commission on Banking acted to dispose its assigned duties.

Banking Reform and Self-Administration

The task before the Banking Commission was to restructure the entire system of local credit. During the reign of Nicholas I, Count Kankrin had devised a geographically concentrated system of land credit with the transparent motive of subsidizing the landed classes through cheap mortgages.[146] Conservative in that it assumed that credit would be used to satisfy existing needs rather than to expand the economy, the Kankrin system was now dead. Should it be replaced with another centralized mortgage bank? Iulii Hagemeister, chairman of the Commission on Banking, framed the problem in the following terms: "The main problem demanding solution by the Commission is *whether or not there will be a system of centralized land credit*, i.e., whether there will be a single central bank and all the other banks established throughout the empire become its offices or branches, or will there be allowed the establishment of many local banks completely independent

[146] Walter McKenzie Pintner, *Russian Economic Policy under Nicholas I*, Ithaca, New York, 1967, pp. 35-44.

of one another?"[147] The only advantage of a centralized bank that the members of the commission could adduce was that it might more readily list its stock issues on foreign exchanges, a compelling argument at a time of scarce domestic credit. On the other side, locally based banks would have the triple advantage of being more responsive to local needs, of being more trusted by local residents and of being free of "all the disadvantages of centralized rule, the large staff of officials, complexity of procedures and the volume of correspondence."[148]

Although the commissioners preferred to bulwark their own predilections against centralization in banking with foreign examples, particularly from the works of the French economist Charles Royer,[149] it would have been possible to garner the same arguments from statements of earlier Russian political figures, of contemporary Russian journalists, and of provincial gentry. Decades before, the distinguished financial expert, Admiral Nikolai Mordvinov, had stood staunchly against Kankrin's Petersburg-based credit organs.[150] Since Mordvinov's day the case against centralized credit had been further developed because the factors influencing mortgage credit varied according to the locale. As an anonymous pamphleteer in Kiev put it in 1860: "It is difficult to make general rules for any sort of administrative activity in our broad land. Everyone recognizes this as be-

[147] *Trudy komissii vysochaishei uchrezhdennoi dlia ustroistva zemskikh bankov*, St. Petersburg, 1861, I, xxxi, *Proekt polozheniia o zemskikh kreditnikh obshchestvakh*.

[148] *Ibid.*, pp. xxxiii-xxiv.

[149] Charles Eduard Royer (1811-1847) was Chief Inspector of Agriculture under Louis Philippe and was a frequent contributor to the *Journal des économistes* where he denounced the centralized credit institutions of Germany and Belgium. After the establishment of the Credit Foncier in 1852, Royer's ideas became accepted as the financial credo of the anti-Napoleonic opposition. See *Journal d'agriculture pratique*, No. 23, 1859.

[150] Helma Repszuk, "Nicholas Mordvinov (1754-1845)," Ph.D. diss., Columbia University, 1962, pp. 289-309.

ing especially true in regard to private credit, whose needs are so different in various localities.[151] The same concern occupied overseers of the Imperial Free Economic Society when they announced a prize essay contest on the theme "The Organization of Credit Institutions," for which they refused to accept proposals embracing the entire country since such arrangements were "obviously unworkable."[152]

Both of the above statements implied that the monolithic Russian state had to be regionalized and saw the fractionalization of credit institutions as a tool for achieving this objective. The man who developed this idea most fully—and thereby set the pattern for utopian populists for decades to come—was the émigré publicist Nikolai Ogarev. He stressed the political dimension of regional land credit banks, and concluded his essay in *The Bell* on the banking system of the future by defining the federal division of Russia for whose creation the credit reform would serve as a catalyst.[153]

This federative view of banking institutions was widely shared among provincial gentry of all casts of opinion. By 1861-1862 detailed proposals for provincial banks had been drawn up in the provinces of Nizhnii Novgorod, Vladimir, Kostroma, Tver, Kherson, Petersburg, Simbirsk, Lithuania, and the western Ukraine.[154] In addition to these, other less detailed projects appeared from those gentry assemblies that responded to the five questions. Vladimir Bezobrazov, who reviewed the projects for the Commission on Banking, characterized them all as "provincial" in that they "limit[ed] the sphere of banking operations to one area and

---

[151] I. D. *Neskolko slov po voprosu o zemskikh bankakh*, Kiev, 1860, p. 16.

[152] *Trudy Imperatorskogo Volnogo Ekonomicheskogo Obshchestva*, IV, No. 11 (December 1859), *prilozhenie*, pp. 7-13.

[153] "Na Novyi God," *Kolokol*, IV, No. 89 (January 1, 1861), 750-51.

[154] *Sovremennaia Letopis* (supplement to *Russkii Vestnik*), Nos. 24, 25 (1861), 26-32; No. 5 (1863), 13-16.

in most cases even to one province and are completely opposed to the proposals for building a central bank for the whole empire."[155]

The "provincial" projects unanimously advocated localized banks and, except in Moscow, all preferred an organization of landowners, whatever their class, to joint-stock companies. As the Commission on Banking noted, joint-stock companies were discredited in the eyes of the Russian public after the stock market crisis of the late 1850s,[156] and were rendered impractical because the requisite free capital with which to form them did not exist. Also, should joint-stock banks be founded, the general public would still exercise no more actual control over them than it had over the centralized Land Bank due to the small number of investors. For these reasons the gentry of Russia rejected stock companies and resoundingly endorsed landowners' mutual credit organizations.

A conspicuous aspect of the entire debate over credit institutions is the close similarity between projects emanating from the assembled gentry to those drawn up by the government. But questions of influence in this area are easier to pose than resolve. On the one hand, the Commission on Banking was exceedingly well informed of gentry attitudes: a few gentry representatives were invited as members when Bezobrazov toured the countryside for the explicit purpose of gathering gentry views on the issue; the other commissioners conferred conscientiously with gentry spokesmen by mail. On the other hand, many groups of provincial gentry did not draft their proposals until after the commission had published its guiding principles.[157] The gentry of Tver, for example, met first in 1859 to plan a local bank but took no positive steps until the principles were in hand. The

---

[155] *Ibid.*, No. 5 (1863), 15.

[156] V. P. Bezobrazov, *Otchet o deistviakh komissii . . . dlia ustroistva zemskikh bankov*, pp. 45ff., 122.

[157] *Materialy dlia istorii uprazdneniia krepostnogo sostoianiia . . . ,* II, 293; Unkovskii, "Zapiska . . . ," *Russkaia Mysl*, No. 7, 1906, pp. 89-90.

same occurred in Vladimir province,[158] in Riazan,[159] and in Petersburg,[160] where local groups did not gather until 1862, by which time the reports of the Commission on Banking were published and available as models. The only permissible conclusion, then, is that gentry interests and reformers within the government cooperated effectively in this effort, each influencing the other.

The commission members joined provincial landlords in opposing joint-stock companies as unable to brook the "dangerous . . . artificial increases in credit,"[161] and wholly unsuited to Russia's needs. This was not the case with landowners' mutual banks: "An extremely important property of landowners mutual banking for the totality of the economy is that . . . the banks are formed in the same locality in which the actual need for credit arises."[162]

In Denmark, Prussia, and the Baltic provinces, landowners' mutual banks existed exclusively to serve the interests of the hereditary nobility. Did the Commission on Banking reject a broader view of financial self-government for a narrowly aristocratic organization? The hope expressed by the gentry of Tver and elsewhere that the new banks would bear the burden of emancipating the local serf population would certainly suggest that this might have been the commission's aim. In fact, this was not the intention of the Commission on Banking and it took pains to counter the accusation. Its chairman acknowledged that the chief function of the new institutions would be to provide mortgage credit, but pointedly specified that all property-owning classes in the province, including urban residents and peasants, could avail themselves of this service.[163] Since the peasantry would own land collectively, the communes would be encouraged to join as full participants and their

---

[158] *Ibid.*, pp. 312-14

[159] Povalishin, *Riazanskie pomeshchiki* . . . , pp. 380-86.

[160] *Severnaia Pochta*, No. 66 (1863), 262-63. Proposed charter for the Petersburg Land Credit Society.

[161] *Trudy komissii . . . dlia ustroistva zemskikh bankov*, I, xiv.

[162] *Ibid.*, I, xx.   [163] *Ibid.*, I, 5.

leaders could be elected to posts of leadership in the banks.[164]

These arguments notwithstanding, subsequent critics have claimed that the Commission on Banking went farther than political circumstances required toward satisfying the demands of the landed gentry.[165] In this context it is curious to note that there were only two major landowners on the commission, Prince Cherkasskii and Alexander Koshelev, both of whom shared a keen interest in the localizing doctrines of western political writers such as Tocqueville. This being the case, we may trace the commission's desire to assure for the landed class a prominent role in the banks to the assumption of several members—Konstantin Grot, Victor Artsimovich, and Nikolai Miliutin in particular—that no local institution could survive without steadfast gentry support.

If the ideal of self-government found expression in the all-class composition of the new banks, it was also manifested in their relation to the government. The landlords' mutual banks of western Europe that served as models for the Commission on Banking jealously protected their private and unofficial status. Members of the commission respected this to the extent that they excluded central authorities from interfering in local bank activities. At the same time, they were unwilling to accept the "completely private" definition and modified the western pattern to such a degree that the planned credit organs were all but identical to the proposed *zemstvos*. The main governing body was to be a general assembly of members, from which a board of directors would be elected.[166] Like the later *zemstvo* organs, the general assembly was to meet once every three years, and was bound by decisions of the directorate at other times.[167] Also similar to the *zemstvos*, the

[164] *Ibid.*, I, xxviii.
[165] Borovoi, *Kredit i banki* . . . , pp. 266-74.
[166] *Trudy komissii . . . dlia ustroistva zemskikh bankov*, I, 140.
[167] *Ibid.*, I, 140, 146.

directors could be removed only through court action and the proceedings were to be freely publicized and subject to "the judgment of the public."[168]

Reviewing these provisions, one senses that what the commission had in mind was not a private body at all but something more akin to what in America would be called a "public corporation." How else can one account for the fact that the provincial mortgage banks would be exempt from the paper tax, granted the right to frank mail, and given the obligation to publish their accounts in the press of the provincial government? Similarly, their relation to the governors was not that of a private corporation but rather of a branch of local self-government.[169] It is little wonder that a prominent figure on the Commission on Banking used the terms "private" (*chastnoe*) and "public" (*obshchestnoe*) interchangeably and contrasted them both to the state (*kazennoe*).[170] Clearly, the provincial mortgage banks were conceived as being arms of the same provincial self-government of which the *zemstvos* would be the head.

These principles were compiled in a single proposal approved by the Commission on Banking at the end of 1861. When the commission announced its preliminary proposals, the educated public welcomed them with overwhelming enthusiasm. Provincial gentry especially vied with one another in praising the draft project, penning essays with titles such as *A Few Words Regarding the New Basis of Trust*.[171] To be sure, there were critics as well. Some felt the proposal did not go far enough in the direction of independence from the state,[172] yet no one had a feasible alter-

---

[168] *Ibid.*, I, 164.   [169] *Ibid.*, I, 26, 158, 166.

[170] V. P. Bezobrazov, *Pozemelnyi kredit i ego sovremennaia organizatsiia v Evrope*, St. Petersburg, 1860, pp. 199-200.

[171] Iu. Mikshevich, *Neskolko slov o novoi osnove doveriia*, Kazan, 1862.

[172] *Trudy Imperatorskogo Volnogo Ekonomicheskogo Obshchestva*, No. 7, 1861, II, 21ff. and No. 8, 1861, II, 59ff. See also Golovachev's earlier *Mysli, vozbuzhdennye pri chtenii proekta Polozheniia o zemskikh kreditnykh obshchestvakh*, St. Petersburg, 1860.

native to propose. Until the economic conditions of Russia changed, localized credit based on land appeared as the most promising means of meeting provincial needs.

However great the public enthusiasm for the work of the Commission on Banking, a network of self-governing provincial credit institutions did not yet exist. Until they were actually operating, a gnawing question hung in the air: would they work? Since nothing of this sort had ever been given a fair test in Russia before, the question was by no means frivolous. At least one critic flatly denied that Russians could manage such alien institutions.[173] At the very least, economic self-government in the provinces was a highly contingent policy. Its success hinged on the existence of at least five factors. First, it assumed that the local economies and land values upon which localized taxes and banking foundations relied would reach and surpass old levels. Should the local tax base diminish or the value of land decline substantially, then both public agencies and banks would have to look to the capitals for aid. Second, it assumed that the government would not endorse a policy of massive economic development to be sponsored by central institutions. Such a policy would tend to channel tax funds from local services into high priority national ventures and to encourage landowners to convert marginal investments in land into capital for industry. Third, it assumed that ambitious Russians would stake their hopes on "making it" in a nonbureaucratic and provincial environment. Fourth, it assumed that entrenched traditions of subordination to the capitals had actually been broken in fact as well as in rhetoric. And, finally, it assumed that the principal institutions of self-administration, the *zemstvos*, would emerge from their legislative womb viable and vigorous.

[173] I. N. Shill, *Predpolozhenie ob uchrezhdenii Russkogo gosudarstvennogo ili zemskogo banka*, St. Petersburg, 1861, pp. 56ff.; *Aksoiner*, No. 15 (1861); see also "Razbor komissii . . . ," *Sovremennik*, No. 7 (1860), where the need for a central fund of development capital is discussed.

In 1861-1863 it was impossible to determine whether any of the first four of these conditions would materialize, for they depended on the general health of the economy and on other factors beyond the reach of immediate legislation. The only nearly independent variable in the equation was, therefore, the fifth, the establishment of local self-government in its institutional aspects. This remained, as before, an open political issue to be resolved in the Commission on Provincial and District Institutions. Given this situation, attention turned naturally once more to that organ and to the preparation of the *zemstvo* reforms.

PLANNING THE ZEMSTVOS, 1861-1862

When we left the Commission on Provincial and District Institutions it was enacting administrative decentralization in an attempt to increase the efficiency and decrease the cost of the Romanov government. The president of the commission, Nikolai Miliutin, resolved to carry this project to conclusion before dealing with the more delicate problem of public self-rule and during the entire year of 1860 turned a deaf ear to those who would have him act otherwise. Meanwhile, the Minister of Internal Affairs, Lanskoi, took upon himself the frustrating task of mollifying impatient gentry; with considerable tact this veteran statesman negotiated with gentry representatives, listened sympathetically to their proposals on "preserving and developing self-government," and giving them a field for positive action in the form of the five questions.[174]

By the spring of 1861, Miliutin was ready to fulfill Alexander II's call for the establishment of provincial and district elective organs. But before starting what he knew would be a lengthy legislative process, Miliutin provided stop-gap agencies to carry on public affairs until the *zemstvos* were introduced. To this end he temporarily

[174] TsGIA-SSSR, f. 1275 (archive of the Council of Ministers), op. 93, d. 6, p. 1, Lanskoi to A. F. Orlov, April 1, 1860.

241

shored up the old three-man Public Economic Offices (*Zemskie prisutstviia*), a step that aroused perturbation in a few provinces where the gentry mistakenly took it to be the final administrative reform.[175]

Having provided transitional institutions, the commission turned to drafting the first detailed version of the code which would govern the *zemstvos*. It proposed to expand the old Public Economic Offices into elective assemblies managed by an executive committee elected from the membership.[176] The assemblies, composed of representatives of all three estates, would meet annually to review the apportionments for provincial taxes (but not for national taxes), to audit the books of the welfare and provisioning agencies, and to draw up proposals "on the needs of the localities" for presentation to the throne.[177]

Scarcely had the commission sketched in these broad outlines than Lanskoi and Miliutin were relieved of their posts. This was possible by April of 1861 because neither Lanskoi's patience nor Miliutin's vigor was required further on the peasant reform and both men, especially Miliutin, had become targets of acrimonious criticism from opponents of emancipation. As Miliutin noted, "The spirit of reaction simply claimed its own."[178]

The eclipse of Miliutin at this moment has given rise to considerable controversy among historians over the authorship of the first draft of the *zemstvo* legislation, a document which framed all governmental debate on the problem of self-government in 1862. Unfortunately, published and archival editions of the text are both undated and un-

[175] *MSVUK, otdel administrativnyi*, I, otd. 5, pp. 276-80; *Trudy komissii o gubernskikh i uezdnykh uchrezhdeniiakh*, I, 133-37; these agencies were abolished when the *zemstvos* were introduced.

[176] TsGIA-SSSR, f. 908, op. 1, d. 123, report of Valuev, February 22, 1862, pp. 4-6.

[177] *Ibid.*, p. 5.

[178] GBL, f. 265, Samarin archive, No. 193, Miliutin's to Samarin. Essentially the same message was contained in Miliutin's note to Cherkasskii in Trubetskaia, *Materialy dlia biografii . . . Cherkasskogo*, II, 277.

signed.[179] Faced with this lacuna, scholars have claimed it either for Miliutin or for his successor, Valuev, as if the act of composition would bring either credit or discredit to one or the other of the "progressive" administrators.[180] However pedantic this debate, it has a significant side, for if the first draft came from the pen of Miliutin he would have had to prepare it during or before the spring of 1861; had that been the case, it might have been a factor leading to the purge of the Ministry of Internal Affairs and the subsequent realignment of policy. If, on the other hand, it was the work of Valuev, then it would mean that the important modifications in the text introduced shortly afterwards by Valuev himself were the result of a fundamental change of heart.

In fact, neither of these men was the author. In his annual report for 1861 Valuev spoke at length of the steps being taken to decentralize the government apparatus but said nothing about local self-government.[181] The tsar, puzzled by Valuev's silence, questioned him explicitly on self-government in a note written in early February 1862, and the minister's reply indicates that he was as yet poorly informed on the issue.[182] Given Valuev's apparent laxity on this matter it is the more surprising that only two weeks later, on March 10, he was able to turn over to the Council of Ministers a complete draft of laws to govern the *zemstvos.*

Where had this draft come from and who was its author? In his diary, Valuev noted that on the evening of March 9, 1862, the day before he was supposed to defend the conclusions of the Commission on Provincial and District Institutions before the State Council, he "called for the project for the statutes on provincial economic institutions worked out

[179] *Materialy po zemskomu obshchestvennomu ustroistvu,* I, 129-74.

[180] Tseitlin, "Zemskaia Reforma," pp. 199ff.; Kizevetter, ". . . Miliutin," *Istoricheskie otliki,* pp. 50ff. Garmiza, *Podgotovka . . . ,* pp. 139ff.

[181] TsGIA-SSSR, f. 1274, d. 22, pp. 40ff.

[182] TsGIA-SSSR, f. 908, op. I, d. 123, pp. 1-22, February 11, 1862.

under the supervision of Soloviev";[183] this he proceeded to study, apparently for the first time. Since the report of February 22 indicates that no legislative act had appeared by that time, we can infer that Soloviev's was the first draft which can therefore be identified as the *Considerations* ascribed by the Russian and French scholars Kizevetter and Leroy-Beaulieu to Miliutin and by the Soviet specialist Garmiza to Valuev. Evidently, Valuev had been so preoccupied with orienting himself in his new post that he had focused his attention on completing the measures for administrative decentralization already before the commission.[184] Meanwhile, the bureaucrat-politician Soloviev seized the initiative, combining his own ideas with the broad guidelines approved by Alexander II in 1859.

During the spring of 1862, Soloviev's draft began its passage through the long process of emendation that threatened to emasculate every Russian legislative act. Before it emerged as law, virtually every government politician and societal interest group had a chance, direct or indirect, to modify it. The first channel through which these pressures were brought to bear was an *ad hoc* committee which scrutinized the statutes at six sessions early in 1862.[185] Led by the reformist Grand Duke Konstantin and consisting of heads of ministries and chancellery departments, this body stood completely outside normal legislative agencies. During its month-long existence, the committee dwelt on the social composition of the *zemstvos*. Valuev dominated discussions of both issues, presenting the need to modify the Soloviev draft to assure a dominant place in the proposed organs for the gentry.

It may appear that Valuev was motivated in this campaign solely by the desire to grant timely concessions to a

---

[183] Valuev, *Dnevnik*, I, 152.

[184] TsGIA-SSSR, f. 908, op. 1, d. 123, p. 8.

[185] *Istoricheskaia zapiska o khode rabot po sostavleniiu i primeniniiu polozheniia o zemskikh uchrezhdeniiakh*, St. Petersburg, n.d., p. 3. Its members were P. A. Valuev, Baron M. A. Korf, K. Chevkin, V. N. Panin, M. Kh. Reutern, A. A. Zelenyi, and A. V. Golovnin.

restive gentry.[186] The sheafs of adroit letters he sent to the provinces,[187] his relief at the receipt of moderate proposals,[188] and his confession to the tsar that his decision to allow certain gentry to form committees to plan self-government may "have predecided the question of establishing provincial assemblies"[189]—all these may be interpreted to support such a conclusion. But Valuev's motives for strengthening the hand of the gentry were more complex, embracing domestic and internal politics, and economic factors as well.

In the first place, six gentry assemblies had requested that a national parliamentary body be created in Petersburg or Moscow to legislate basic changes in the emancipation statutes that bureaucrats allegedly refused to introduce. The earliest such proposal came from Tula province in December 1861,[190] to be followed by others from Tambov, Petersburg, and Voronezh.[191] In Moscow, the indefatigable Nikolai Bezobrazov led a spirited drive for the formation of a central body representing principally—but in the end not exclusively—the gentry.[192] Then, just as these affairs were subsiding, the Tver gentry announced its readiness to abdicate all its class privileges and to join a national assembly to correct errors in the emancipation provisions.[193]

In all these statements, two common themes stand out. On the one hand, many gentry wanted to register their gen-

[186] Cf. Emmons, *The Russian Landed Gentry* . . . , pp. 415-17.

[187] TsGIA-SSSR, f. 1282, op. 2, d. 1108, pp. 55ff.

[188] *Ibid.*, d. 1110, p. 4.   [189] *Ibid.*, d. 1108, p. 7.

[190] TsGAOR, f. 109, op. 85, ed. khr. 27, p. 78; Valuev, *Dnevnik*, I, 135.

[191] TsGIA-SSSR, f. 1282, no. 1091, pp. 17-18. A similar statement was penned in Riazan and would probably have been approved had the marshals of five districts not walked out of the meeting in protest as the voting began. Valuev, *Dnevnik*, I, 381.

[192] N. A. Bezobrazov, *Predlozhenie dvorianstvu*, Berlin, 1862, pp. 3-40; the full draft is in TsGAOR, f. 678 (Alexander II archive), op. 1, d. 609. On the meetings themselves, see TsGAOR, f. 111, d. 109, p. 1, especially d. 33, Chap. 1, pp. 35-37, "O dvorianskykh vyborakh v Moskve."

[193] Emmons, *The Russian Landed Gentry* . . . , pp. 334-49.

eral dissatisfaction with the "Great Reform" of February 19, 1861. Clearly, the Editing Commissions had failed to satisfy anyone, and now these local lords proposed to rework the entire body of statutes to right the errors. On the other hand, the entire Russian gentry was undergoing a collective crisis of identity following the abolition of serfdom. Some, like the Tver group, wished simply to renounce their privileged status,[194] while others sought to define their role by turning back to Catherine's original Charter to the Nobility.

Valuev exhibited no alarm at the more outspoken statements by the gentry at this time, probably because he realized that the moderate majority of that class strongly approved of the plans for tax and banking reform, as well as for local self-rule.[195] At the same time, he acknowledged that the emancipation left many gentry feeling that "they have nothing to do,"[196] to which he responded by proposing that the gentry become the government's first co-worker in the reforms being undertaken, and especially in the final resolution of the peasant question and the establishment of a new administrative order that would provide greater scope for them in matters of local rule.[197]

The second factor affecting Valuev's turn to the gentry was the intensification of the radical movement in Russia. The punctilious minister watched in horror as student unrest, ever the bane of administrative minds, succeeded in closing Petersburg University late in 1861:[198] inflammatory

[194] The Pskov gentry also followed this course, TsGAOR, f. 109, op. 85, ed. khr. 77, pp. 77ff, as did a strong faction in Kherson province, Zelenyi, "Khersonskoe dvorianstvo . . . ," pp. 65ff.

[195] The gentry's overall moderation in 1862 is acknowledged by both prerevolutionary and Soviet historians. Cf. Garmiza, *Podgotovka* . . . , p. 71, who cites Veselovskii approvingly.

[196] TsGAOR, f. 544, op. 1, d. 15, pp. 6-7. Also, K. L. Bermanskii, "Konstitutsionnye proekty tsarstvovaniia Aleksandra II," *Vestnik Prava*, No. 9 (1905), 11.

[197] *Severnaia Pochta* (January 17, 1862); Valuev, *Dnevnik*, I, 140.

[198] Valuev, *Dnevnik*, I, 130-31, 151; Sergei Gessen, "Petersburgskii universitet oseniu 1861 g." in *Revoliutsionnoe dvizhenie 1860-kh godov*, Moscow, 1932, pp. 9-27.

handbills distributed on Nevskii Prospect eventually came to rest on Valuev's desk; the censorship committee sent him a copy of Afanasii Shchapov's essay "Regional Political Assemblies and Councils" that was so democratic in tone as, in Valuev's words, "to smell for miles of Pugachev";[199] and the telegraph lines to the Ministry of Internal Affairs carried daily reports from that smoking political tinderbox, Poland.[200] Valuev responded to these alarming conditions just as Catherine II did after Pugachev's uprising and sought a firm alliance with Russia's upper class and to bar "communists and men of low morality" from the zemstvos.[201]

A third factor in Valuev's decision to support the gentry in the zemstvos was financial in character. Though himself an advocate of administrative deconcentration, Valuev found that the fiscal deficit and resultant wage freeze caused many competent men to refuse appointments as governors.[202] Unwilling to entrust the welfare of the provinces to incompetents, Valuev turned to the responsible gentry to stabilize conditions locally. Accordingly, he sought to modify the Soloviev draft to the gentry's benefit. While it was still under consideration by the Commission on Provincial and District Institutions he successfully defended an amendment to prohibit provincial governors from attending zemstvo meetings even as observers,[203] and a second alteration to enable district councils to lodge complaints di-

---

[199] Valuev, *Dnevnik*, I, 138.

[200] *Ibid.*, p. 219. At the same time the Grand Duke Konstantin had already begun Polish lessons, anticipating being sent there as an emissary of his brother, the tsar. Grand Duke Konstantin Nikolaevich, "Iz dnevnika . . . ," p. 218; Valuev, "O vnutrennom sostoianii Rossii," p. 141ff.

[201] M. Katkov, cited by Nevedenskii, *Katkov . . . ,* p. 233.

[202] Valuev, *Dnevnik*, I, 148, reports on two such cases in February, 1862.

[203] Soloviev had introduced this after being impressed by the fact that the English Lords Lieutenant enjoyed a comparable right, *Materialy po zemskomu obshchestvennomu ustroistvu*, I, 169.

rectly to the Senate rather than through the provincial administrators.[204]

Valuev then went on to suggest means of limiting the franchise in the provinces.[205] Grand Duke Konstantin was openly hostile toward members of the provincial gentry and saw no need to reward them through a regressive franchise.[206] Valuev, however, knew that the surest way to win the support of the upper ranks of the gentry was to minimize the power exercised by those countless petty land-holders whose privileges existed only by virtue of their civil service rank. On this point Alexander II backed his minister.[207] Soloviev's text had granted the right to participate in the curiae that would elect gentry to provincial assemblies to all those who owned land equal to fifty of the maximum allotments (*vyshye nadeli*) as established in the locality at the time of emancipation; for nongentry the figure was set at one hundred allotment units.[208] To Valuev these figures seemed perilously low for they could conceivably have enabled minor property holders to outvote the great planters. To prevent this he raised the minimums from fifty and one hundred to one hundred and two hundred units of land, respectively. These revised figures, it should be noted, are identical to the property qualifications proposed earlier by the special commission of Petersburg lords,[209] and also to the high standards advocated by Valuev's friend Mikhail Katkov in his widely read *Russian Messenger*.[210]

At the same time that Valuev was working to disen-

204 *Ibid.*, I, 185; *Zhurnal komissii . . .* , March 10, 12; in these sessions Dmitrii Tolstoi led an unsuccessful effort to have a crown representative in the *zemstvo* assemblies.

205 Garmiza, *Podgotovka . . .* , pp. 173-92 has dealt with this issue in great detail.

206 Grand Duke Konstantin Nikolaevich, "Iz dnevnika . . . ," p. 218.

207 Valuev, *Dnevnik*, I, 153, 158.

208 *Istoricheskaia zapiska . . .* , p. 23, Statute 13a; *Materialy po zemskomu obshchestvennomu ustroistvu*, I, 154.

209 *Russkii Listok*, No. 12 (March 24, 1863), 231-33.

210 *Sovremennaia Letopis* (supplement to *Russkii Vestnik*), No. 46 (1862). Nevedenskii, *Katkov . . .* , p. 422.

franchise small landholders, he opposed all attempts to strengthen peasant representation. Soloviev's project made peasant delegates *ex officio* the *starshina* and *starosta* of the *volosts* and communes,[211] but the possibility of having them elected especially to the post was raised both in the Commission on Provincial and District Institutions and in the Grand Duke's committee. Valuev strongly opposed this policy of politicizing the peasantry through provincial self-government and took steps to divert their political interests into ineffectual channels. This was the aim of a scheme which he introduced in the Grand Duke Konstantin's group to establish miniscule territorial units, called *vyty*, within the districts.[212] These lowest units would syphon off the public activity of peasants from the district and provincial *zemstvos*, thus leaving the major local institutions more securely than ever in the hands of the great lords.[213] The Grand Duke's faction succeeded in blocking this cynical attempt to aggrandize the gentry, but the plan was far from dead, and within the space of two years it was to be revived as a tool for fortifying the state administration directly.

In his amendments to the Soloviev draft, Valuev's main interest was to alter the social composition of the *zemstvos*. The relations of the *zemstvos* to the central government interested him only secondarily, and their sphere of action scarcely at all. Grand Duke Konstantin and his supporters from the Ministries of Public Enlightenment and Finances, however, ascribed particular meaning to these last two issues but were long ineffectual in promoting their cause. Only an unexpected maneuver by Nikolai Miliutin succeeded in shifting the balance of power in their favor.

[211] *Materialy po zemskomu obshchestvennomu ustroistvu*, I, 182-83.
[212] GPB, f. 379, No. 210, pp. 1-2.
[213] TsGIA-SSSR, f. 1162, op. xvi, d. 1, pp. 3-29. This plan is the subject of an article by Peter Czap, Jr., "P. A. Valuev's Proposal for a *Vyt'* Administration, 1864," *Slavonic and East European Review*, XLV, No. 105 (1967), 391-407. Czap's analysis is done from the standpoint of the *volost*; the discussion of the proposal here emphasizes its relation to the *zemstvo*.

249

In the summer of 1861, Miliutin had gone to Europe to recover from the crushing effects of his loss of position and power. While abroad, all his correspondents were foes of Valuev and all fervently sought to mobilize Miliutin's reformist spirit behind their battle with the Ministry of Internal Affairs.[214] Miliutin was equally impatient to become involved again and when the *zemstvo* question came to the fore he jumped into the fray with a thorough critique of the revised Soloviev draft; it arrived in Petersburg from Paris in May 1862. According to Miliutin, the purpose of *zemstvo* self-government was to enable the state to

relieve itself of moral responsibility for minor and remote abuses, a responsibility that is incompatible with the true dignity and meaning of governmental authority. At the same time, the activity of our society will be given a practical direction which will serve to oppose the anarchic intellectual ferment. Thus, I am deeply persuaded that the highest interests of the state, with which all the future developments of Russia is bound up, insistently demand that the new *zemstvo* institutions, which are destined to attract to themselves a significant part of the active elements of society . . . be given as genuine and serious a role as is possible. . . . For this it will not be necessary to restrict . . . the rights and prerogatives of the central authority, for the *zemstvos*, as purely local organs, cannot and must not in any way touch upon matters of state, neither the interests of the national treasury or the court, nor of the executive police, that prime organ of the central institutions.[215]

[214] Sterling Library, Yale University, Miliutin Collection, II, pp. 1-4; other letters are in BIL, Miliutin archive.

[215] N. A. Miliutin, "Zapiska o gubernskikh i uezdnykh uchrezhdeniiakh," in Garmiza, *Podgotovka* . . . , p. 144. This document was partially published also by S. M. Seredonin, *Istoricheskii obzor deiatelnosti komiteta ministrov*, 3 vols., St. Petersburg, 1902, III, 70-72; the archival original is in TsGIA-SSSR, f. 1275, d. 33, pp. 105-11.

Miliutin, then, committed himself fully to the idea of devolving functions to the public while at the same time recognizing that the central institutions would lead the process of modernization. This perspective, identical to that expressed by the banking and tax commissions, provided a standard by which to assess the resources at the *zemstvo's* disposal.

> The [present] figure for "provincial duties" is scarcely a fifth of the total amount of taxes collected locally . . . even in this insignificant budget a substantial amount consists of salary payments and petty expenditures that require no managerial skill. Given only this, the work of the *zemstvo* institutions will be purely mechanical and, of course, will not satisfy the goals of their foundation.[216]

He saw competence and control over taxation as inseparable. Accordingly, he proposed to broaden the Valuev program so as to transfer to the *zemstvos* full responsibility for the construction and maintenance of all local public buildings and roads except turnpikes and even of postal facilities and services; he also proposed to grant the power to levy taxes for these functions.

To enable the *zemstvos* to execute these new duties, Miliutin insisted that agencies of self-government be as free as possible from the restraints arising from distrust:

> I cannot but repeat my personal conviction, derived from many years' experience, that the application of the elective principle to administration will work only when the elected figures are empowered by law to act seriously and independently. Otherwise they will be turned into tools of the caprice of secondary administrators. . . . I consider it my special duty, then, to insist on the necessity of giving the greatest possible [sphere and independence] to the economic activities of the new institutions.

[216] Quoted by Garmiza, *Podgotovka* . . . , pp. 147-48.

251

Under present circumstances this need is all the more felt. . . . The proposed institutions cannot and must not have a political character; their meaning is entirely *administrative*, and for this reason there is no basis, I am emboldened to think, for founding the new law exclusively on suspicion and exaggerated apprehensions.[217]

Miliutin's eloquent statement perfectly suited the needs of a man eager to reestablish his credentials as a reformer, for it set down principles but left legislative details to sympathetic followers. These details were considered by the Council of Ministers which met to review the *zemstvo* laws in May and June of 1862.[218] Here Miliutin's position was represented by the Grand Duke, Minister of Public Enlightenment Golovnin, Minister of Finances Reutern, and the Director of Channels of Communications, Chevkin. The aim of their effort was to broaden and to define the powers of the *zemstvos*.

To this end they now put the *zemstvos* in full charge of the development of local trade and industry.[219] And whereas Soloviev had cautiously dealt largely with *zemstvo* powers at the provincial level, the revised draft extended all provincial rights down to district *zemstvos* as well.[220] Finally, the revised draft specifically granted the right to petition the governors directly on all regional concerns[221] and also to manage the local affairs of the postal system.[222] These new powers were accompanied by a sharper definition of what the *zemstvos could not* do and what they *must* do. The revised law explicitly forbade all forms of activity

[217] *Ibid.*, pp. 148-49.
[218] Seredonin, *Istoricheskii obzor . . .*, iii, Pt. 2, pp. 69-70.
[219] *Istoricheskaia zapiska . . .*, p. 236, Statute 2, vi. Soloviev's draft gave them only the right to help other agencies in this area.
[220] *Ibid.*, p. 243, Statute 40 of Soloviev draft, Statute 42 of revision. This was first applied in the case of fostering trade and industry.
[221] *Ibid.*, p. 236, Statute 2, ix.
[222] *Ibid.*, Statute 2, vii; *Severnaia Pochta*, No. 62 (1863), 247.

involving more than one province and defined closely the right to tax and to issue legally binding decrees.[223] In the new draft only a few minor functions of a national character were left to the *zemstvos*, and in general every function was weighed in terms of the concepts of national versus provincial and district responsibilities.

With these modifications the draft of the laws governing the *zemstvos* was approved by Alexander II on June 2, 1862.[224] Beyond question the code represented a victory for advocates of self-government: it established provincial and district councils based on territorial rather than estate divisions;[225] the decisions of the bodies would have the force of law,[226] and the organs themselves would be subject to control by public opinion rather than bureaucratic caprice; they were endowed with the power to levy taxes to finance their work, and were given a substantial role in the local apportionment of national taxes. No wonder then that the tsar, expecting that the *zemstvos* would be opened at once, requested the Commission on Provincial and District Institutions to draw up a final draft of the legislation and in October of 1862 proudly published the revised document for the public to see.[227]

This was not to be the end of the story, however, for an interministerial battle of epic proportions was to delay the promulgation of the *zemstvo* reform for fully a year. At one level, the *cassus belli* was the failure even of the revised text to reckon with the most advanced partisans of self-government, both within the government and in educated society. No sooner were the contents of the legislative act known than critics demanded that the short period allotted

[223] *Istoricheskaia zapiska* . . . , p. 238, Statute 7; p. 235, Statute 11; p. 237, Statute 4.
[224] *Materialy po zemskomu obshchestvennomu ustroistvu*, I, 211-12.
[225] *Ibid.*, I, 135.
[226] *Istoricheskaia zapiska* . . . , p. 248.
[227] *Materialy po zemskomu obshchestvennomu ustroistvu*, I, 244; *Severnaia Pochta*, No. 212 (1862).

to annual *zemstvo* assembly sessions be lengthened, that the president of the *zemstvo* directorate be elected by the public organs themselves rather than appointed by the governor, and that *zemstvo* functions be expanded still further to include what actually became two of the most important areas of provincial activity: education and health.

On another level, the battle arose from the fact that the draft approved by the tsar would have made conflict between *zemstvos* and local administrators all but inevitable. Both Miliutin and Valuev, it will be remembered, were professional bureaucrats who had, of course, long advocated administrative deconcentration, but who had, for different reasons, also come to support elective self-government. Their past remained with them, however, to the extent that neither chaffed at the provision that governors could veto any *zemstvo* act deemed contrary to the interests of the state. When advocates of community control discovered this flaw they attacked it with all the political resources at their disposal.

The ensuing struggle eventually caused Valuev's downfall. But long before that occurred, external events forced him to reassess completely his views on local government. In the process Valuev crossed his Rubicon, and, by the early months of 1863, he had all but abandoned his faith that administrative decentralization and public self-government were compatible with and even essential to the interests of the autocracy.

SELF-GOVERNMENT UNDER ATTACK, 1862-1863

Our imperial mastadon should pass away. . . . Moscow yielded before the organization of Petersburg; now Petersburg should give up its place to a federation of provinces.

Nikolai Ogarev[228]

[228] N. Ogarev, *Essai sur la Situation Russe: Lettres à un Anglais,* London, 1862, p. 148.

254

Is Russia not perishing? Am I called upon to serve her in her final moments?

Peter Valuev[229]

Interest in administrative deconcentration and community control of public functions was closely intertwined with the mood of lyrical optimism that stirred Russia after 1856. On the surface this seemed merely the natural state for a nation freed from a stern but unsuccessful militarism and eager to attack old problems afresh. But public optimism was compounded of other elements as well, or rather, by the absence of other conditions which, if present, might have muted the prevailing hopefulness.

In the first place, the post-Crimean years were for Russia a period of withdrawal from international affairs. Since 1812 the educated Russian had believed implicitly that his nation was the savior of Europe. This faith demanded enormous expenditures of psychic and physical resources. With the Crimean collapse Russia emerged briefly from the self-deluding displays of national might. Foreign contacts continued, but diplomacy ceased temporarily to dominate national policy considerations.[230] Energy and resources were released for internal development.

In the second place, the anticipation of reforms had erased what little radical sentiment had existed before 1856. Outbursts against bureaucratism during the period rarely exceeded legal bounds and no significant movement toward the organizing of radical opposition existed. In spite of the gentry's rapid politicization, the government could turn to "society" with fewer fears in the years from 1856 to 1862 than at practically any subsequent period in Russian history.

---

[229] Valuev, *Dnevnik*, I, 178.
[230] Professor Rieber's convincing argument that the tsar's advocacy of emancipation was due to military considerations does not alter this, for, whatever Alexander's motives, most educated Russians viewed the step in more parochial terms; see *The Politics of Autocracy* . . . , pp. 22ff.

Events in the autumn and winter of 1862 to 1863 destroyed these prerequisites of reform. International concerns once more seized Russia and claimed primacy over
domestic affairs. Radical activity increased at home, reaching levels unknown since 1825. The effect of the new conditions was felt at once among those drafting the *zemstvo*
institutions. Assertions about self-government that had been
readily accepted for half a decade now required substantiation. Criticisms that had earlier seemed carping now attracted rapt attention. And well they might, for new conditions of international and domestic life now existed and
were to characterize Russian life for generations to come.
They imparted to the final stages of the *zemstvo* debate a
peculiar significance. As one of Russia's greatest historians
observed: "already in its embryo there are visible the diverse and mutually contradictory tendencies which in the
course of the succeeding half century fill the internal and
ideological life of the *zemstvo* institutions."[231] Ironically, the
campaign for public self-administration culminated at the
very moment that self-government as a theory of political
development ceased to answer the most pressing needs, real
and imagined, of the Russian state.

The keystone in the overarching series of events leading
to this change of temper was the insurrection in Russian
Poland. In terms of lives lost this explosion of national feeling surpassed all internal disorders in the empire between
the Pugachev rebellion and the Revolution of 1905. Yet its
relevance to Russia's internal policy does not derive from
this fact so much as from the bitter experience of Russian
leaders with the Polish reforms that preceded the
insurrection.

Tension had been compounding throughout the five Polish provinces since the late 1850s. After Russian serfs received their freedom in 1861 the clamor for reform in

[231] Kizevetter, "Borba za zemstvo . . . ," *Istoricheskie otliki*, p. 271.

Poland rose to a dangerous pitch, accompanied by elemental peasant rebellions. Finally, Marshal Weilopolski, a Pole and a conciliator by temperament, promulgated what he optimistically hoped would be a compromise between Russian and Polish interests. Weilopolski's program was instituted between March and December of 1861, and it followed closely the more cautious of the many lines of reform propounded in Petersburg.[232] He abolished labor service for peasants but did not grant complete emancipation. He instituted district and provincial self-administration but at the same time fixed property qualifications for electors so high that out of a population of nearly 5,000,000 barely 25,000 received the franchise.[233]

However half-hearted the Weilopolski program, the Russian government had backed it with the expectation that it would usher in an era of normal relations. What followed instead was a second wave of rebellion. This time the "Reds" of the streets were joined in opposition to the rule of Petersburg's emissaries by a rising number of "White" landowners (*szlachta*). "Reds" and "Whites" were so fundamentally opposed to one another that a state of virtual civil war was created within Poland, but at the same time both sides had cut or were cutting their remaining bonds with Russia, which came as a bitter shock to Alexander and his leading officials.

Bitterness soon turned to alarm when it was learned at Tsarskoe Selo that sixty-six officers of the Russian garrison in Poland actively sided with the Polish cause.[234] In a second and final effort to save the situation, Alexander II appointed his reformist brother, Grand Duke Konstantin,

---

[232] R. F. Leslie, *Reform and Insurrection in Russian Poland, 1856-1865*, London, 1963, Chap. iv.

[233] J. Struminski, "Rady miejskie i powiatowe w Królestwie Polskim (1861-1863)," *Czasopismo prawo-historyozne*, 1952, iv, 328, cited in Leslie, *Reform and Insurrection . . .*, p. 122.

[234] V. A. Diakov, I. S. Miller, *Revoliutsionnoe dvizhenie v Russkoi armii i vosstanie 1863 g.*, Moscow, 1964, pp. 28-84.

Viceroy of Poland on May 22, 1862. It was hoped that the privileged status thus conferred on Poland would halt the headlong plunge toward insurrection. The Grand Duke tried his best, even giving his infant son a Polish Christian name, but within forty-eight hours after arriving at Warsaw he lay wounded by an assassin. In a state of alarm, the Russian government foolishly attempted to call up young Poles to military service, thus driving the radical youth into full defiance. In the first weeks of 1863 the last barriers to full-blown insurrection were broken. The Russian government had to garner all its forces just to maintain its presence in Poland. More alarming, it became evident that the government had even to defend its rule at home. In September of 1862, 249 leaders of the largely Polish gentry of Podolia province in the Ukraine shocked official Petersburg with the following declaration:

> Our region is in a grim condition; the populace is unedu-
> cated, the middle schools are unsatisfactory in respect
> both to the quantity and the quality of teaching; indus-
> try is denied capital and burdened with excessive taxes;
> the grain trade is cut off from foreign markets due to
> poor communication; landed property is without credit
> due to the closure of loans from state credit institutions
> and the absence of a mortgage system; the laws are re-
> pugnant to our customs, traditions and to the degree of
> progress of social thought; the execution of law is ren-
> dered ineffectual by a bureaucracy alien to the land; ad-
> ministration focuses on needs and interests outside the
> locality; and finally, the region is without organs elected
> from its midst for managing its public undertakings. The
> situation arising from our dissociation from the Kingdom
> of Poland hinders the final resolution of the peasant prob-
> lem. The province is threatened with decisive collapse if
> there is not established administrative unity with that re-
> gion with which it shared identical needs, the same tradi-

tions, identical conceptions of civil and religious freedom and a common course of future development.[235]

In short, the Podolia gentry borrowed arguments used heretofore to justify self-government within Great Russia and twisted them to justify separatism on the borderlands. Polish gentry in other western Russian provinces followed suit, forwarding similar claims to Petersburg.[236] The result was that the label of sedition was pinned on the entire movement for control of civic functions by the local public.

Simultaneously with the development of the Polish crisis symptoms of internal disruption cropped up on Russian soil. The summers of 1861 and 1862 were exceptionally dry in eastern Europe, turning parched wooden villages into tinderboxes which everywhere erupted in flames. The suspicion of arson was already abroad before May of 1862 but in that month an enormous holocaust in Petersburg gutted the central offices of the Ministry of Internal Affairs and Valuev's own chambers.[237] In high circles it was agreed that the disaster was "undoubtedly" the work of arsonists.[238] To curb terrorism, a special Committee of Public Safety was set up and endowed with military authority. A rumored attack by the English and French fleets added to this body's extraordinary powers and fanned tensions in the capital to a still higher pitch.

The contents of journals appearing in Petersburg gave further cause for alarm,[239] and the censors struck out with

[235] TsGAOR, f. 111, otd. 109, d. 33, Pt. 10, 1862, pp. 47-48; also TsGAOR, f. 109, op. 85, ed. khr. 27, p. 77; published in part by Zaionchkovskii in Valuev, *Dnevnik*, I, p. 394, n183. Valuev hid this address from Alexander II, to whom it was addressed, *Dnevnik*, I, 191-92.

[236] See letter of unknown person to Count I. I. Vorontsov-Dashkov in which the identical argument is applied to all the western provinces. TsGIA-SSSR, f. 869, op. 1, d. 400, p. 1, n.d.

[237] A vivid description of this event is in Kropotkin, *Memoirs . . .* , Pt. I, Sec. 10.

[238] Valuev, *Dnevnik*, I, 172.

[239] See, for example, N. Kostomarov's essay "Dve Russkie narod-

force, here banning an article, there closing a publication. To the degree that these repressive efforts succeeded they were responsible for a spate of illegal manifestos such as *The National Assembly* (*Zemskaia Duma*) which appeared in April of 1862 over the evocative signature "Young Russia." Others which found their way to the files of the Ministry of Internal Affairs bore titles such as *What Should the Troops Do?*, *What Do the People Want?*, and *To the Entire Orthodox Russian People; a Bow and a Charter from Those Loyal to It*, and *Romanov, Puguchev, or Pestel?*.[240] The forces behind such proclamations gained credibility when police agents uncovered evidence of an apparently widespread undergound organization, "Land and Liberty."[241]

Radicalism and the Polish revolt triggered a collapse of optimism that verged on ideological bankruptcy. As Valuev confessed in his diary, "[the Poles] have ideas on their side. On ours there is not one."[242] Policy hardened. The revered journalist, Chernyshevskii, was arrested; university unrest was dealt with simply by closing many institutions; armed force was called out against the insurgents in Poland. Such acts reveal the change that had been wrought in many offi-

---

nosti" (Two Russian Nationalities) in the pro-Ukrainian sheet, *Osnova* (March 1, 1861), 33-80. A radical cooperative journal had also been founded and, though actually ephemeral, its table of contents alone had considerable shock value. In *Vek* (*The Century*), Shchapov published his boldest essays on "The *Zemstvo*"; "*Zemskie Sobory* of the 17th Century"; and "Urban Communal Councils." V. P. Kozmin, "Artelnyi Zhurnal *Vek* (1862 g.)," *Iz istorii revoliutsionnoi mysli v Rossii*, Moscow, 1961, pp. 68-98.

[240] R. A. Taubin, "Iz istorii propogandy revoliutsionnoi partii sredi krestian i soldat v gody revoliutsionnoi situatsii," *Revoliutsionaia situatsiia . . .* , 1960, pp. 380-422; M. A. Bakunin, *Narodnoe Delo*: *Romanov, Pugachev ili Pestel?*, London, 1862.

[241] L. Linkov, *Revoliutsionnaia borba A. N. Gertsena i N. P. Ogareva i tainoe obshchestvo "Zemlia i Volia" 1860-kh godov*, Moscow, 1964; M. V. Nechkina, "Vozniknovenie pervoi 'Zemli i Voli,'" *Revoliutsionnaia situatsiia . . .* , 1960, pp. 238-98; F. Venturi, *Roots of Revolution*, New York, 1964, pp. 253-84; *Gertsen I Ogarev*, I, 521, provides evidence on the federative program and organization of this otherwise innocuous group.

[242] Valuev, *Dnevnik*, I, 258-59.

cials' conception of "society." Back in 1857 they had debated various means for tapping the expertise of gentry interest groups, little fearing that they would thereby activate any radical forces. Now "society" seemed riddled with threatening elements and those advocating independent public initiatives were easily tarred with the brush of subversion.

The partial suppression of the Imperial Geographic Society and of the Imperial Free Economic Society reflects the amount of pressure exerted on all nonstate enterprises.[243] In 1861 both societies had created statistical committees that included among their members many leaders of the self-government movement in Petersburg, including Soloviev, N. Miliutin, Terner, Hagemeister, and the Grand Duke Konstantin—as loyal a group of subjects as anyone could want.[244] The committees rapidly evolved into forums where the issues of the day were debated by national leaders without concern for official formalities. Though all the members were closely connected to government circles, this semipublic initiative caused concern among those already shaken by events in Russia and in Poland. One aged bureaucrat swore that the two committees were planning a revolution,[245] and Valuev, who regularly attended meetings, denounced the Geographical Society group as "a symptom of our disorganization."[246] To be sure, some evidence exists that ideas incompatible with the imperial system were discussed in the Committee on Political Economy of the Geographical Society.[247] Yet Valuev's con-

[243] P. P. Semenov-Tian-Shanskii, *Istoriia poluvekovoi deiatelnosti Imperatorskogo russkogo geograficheskogo obshchestva, 1845-1895,* 3 vols., St. Petersburg, 1896, i, 169ff. TsGIA-SSSR, f. 91 (Archive of the Imperial Free Economic Society), op. 1, d. 304, p. 186.

[244] Semenov-Tian-Shanskii, *Istoriia poluvekovoi . . . ,* i, 171; TsGIA-SSSR, f. 91, op. 1, d. 304, p. 9.

[245] TsGAOR, f. 728, op. 1, ed. khr. 2538 a, Diary of A. S. Menshikov, 1858-1865, p. 185 (October 23, 1862).

[246] Valuev, *Dnevnik,* i, 70-71.

[247] See the debate over the position of Australia within the British Empire as reported in *Ekonomist,* iv, No. 9 (1861). "Zapiski o

cern was not so much with subversive ideas as with the fact that neither of the new committees had any organic tie with the public interest as defined by the government.[248] A six-month campaign against them in late 1862 left the Geographical Society group disbanded and the work of the Free Economic Society greatly restricted.[249]

Such suspicion of all public groups and institutions not directly under the guidance of the state had the gravest implications for the *zemstvo* legislation. Uneasy administrators at once proposed limitations on the new institutions.

The restrictions were in part a blind reaction to the deteriorating national situation, but they were just as much a reasoned response to the apparent radicalization of demands for governmental reform in the provinces. Specifically, this final drive to alter the *zemstvo* statutes arose as a direct answer to the threat posed by the so-called constitutional movement of 1862-1863.

Constitutionalism and Federalism

"There is no doubt that we are moving towards a constitution," a senator wrote in 1863—"Poland is leading us there, freedom of the press is, and so are the reforms themselves."[250] As early as 1861 the Minister of State Domains, Muraviev, was readying himself to join a constitutional ministry,[251] and Alexander II had declared, not without bravado, that "If a constitution is the desire of Russia and if the country is prepared for it, I'm ready."[252] At least twenty-five reform projects entitled "constitutions" were penned in the early 1860s, and many of them represent the views of sizable groups. In addition to those who presented

---

zasedaniiakh komitita politicheskoi ekonomii v Geograficheskom Obshchestve."

[248] Valuev, *Dnevnik*, I, 201.

[249] TsGIA-SSSR, f. 91, op. 1, d. 304, pp. 43, 50ff.; Semenov-Tian-Shanskii, *Istoriia poluvekovoi . . .* , I, 172ff.

[250] Lebedev, "Iz zapisok . . . ," p. 551.

[251] Valuev, *Dnevnik*, I, 117.

[252] Nikitenko, *Dnevnik*, II, 98. Statement to A. F. Orlov.

schemes for "constitutional" government, there were those, equally numerous, who penned counterarguments. It is safe to say that between 1860 and 1863 nearly all of those most active in Russian social thought, both in the public and in the bureaucracy, expressed themselves on the question of constitutionalism.[253]

Just what do all these calls for a "constitution" signify? One recent specialist on the period defines a constitution as providing public representation on all legislative undertakings, presumably through a central assembly,[254] while another defines the words so broadly as to include the *zemstvo* as a constitution.[255] These usages are justified by contemporaries who often employed the term so loosely as to embrace a variety of phenomena, including the judicial reforms![256] Clearly, it is now essential to reach a satisfactory definition or to reject completely the term "constitution" as an analytical category.

The problem may be traced to the diverse sources of "constitutional" rhetoric in Russia. The greatest earlier flowering of such notions occurred during the reign of Alexander I. Knowledge of constitutional projects by Mikhail Speranskii and others of the first decades of the nineteenth century was communicated to the reform era through laudatory biographical works by Baron Korf and others.[257] At the same time, the reading public was inundated with studies of the constitutions of western European states. The

---

[253] Baron M. Korf, head of the Legal Section of the tsar's chancellery, summarized the movement throughout the nineteenth century in *Istoricheskii ocherk konstitutsionnykh nachinanii v Rossii*, TsGAOR, f. 728, op. 1, ed. khr. 2748.

[254] Emmons, *The Russian Landed Gentry . . .* , pp. 368-69.

[255] Leonard Krieger, "Nationalism and the Nation-State System," *Chapters in Western Civilization*, New York, 1965, II, 137.

[256] Lebedev, "Iz zapisok . . . ," p. 414. N. Ogarev denied that the word had any precise meaning; "Konstitusiia i zemskii sobor," *Kolokol*, No. 164 (June 1, 1863), 1351.

[257] Baron M. A. Korf, *Zhizn Grafa Speranskogo*, St. Petersburg, 1861; cf. N. G. Sladkevich, "Polemika vokrug knigi M. A. Korfa, 'Zhizn Grafa Speranskogo,'" *Revoliutsionnaia situatsiia . . .* , 1960, pp. 509-21.

best of these, *A Digest of Contemporary Constitutions* by Alexander Lokhvitskii, detailed the structure of a half dozen of what Russians believed to be the most developed states of the West.[258] The availability of descriptive, historical, and theoretical studies of the "constitutions" of western Europe and Russia enabled those interested in the problem to find good precedents for whichever of the many notions they might prefer.

The numerous constitutional proposals from the period group themselves into four more or less distinct currents of thought. The first sense in which the term "constitution" was employed referred to the *status quo*, to "what is." This is what Lokhvitskii meant in his survey of constitutions. Under the rubric "our Russian constitution," the historian Shchapov spoke of all the "historical, juridical, geographic, and ethnographic conditions and elements,"[259] and criticized the absence of an organic tie between them and the *political* structure. Mikhail Katkov used a related definition to oppose written constitutions. True constitutionalism exists, he felt, only when the political order is in complete accord with the organic forms of society, a state which legislative action was incapable of establishing.[260]

The second sense in which the word "constitution" was used posited an order in which public life would be managed according to standards of rationality, efficiency, and internal consistency. Baron Korf, director of the legal section of the tsar's chancellery and Mikhail Speranskii before him held this view, and believed that only positive legislation could endow a state with the ability to govern successfully.[261]

---

[258] A. V. Lokhvitskii, *Obzor sovremennykh konstitutsii*, 2 vols., St. Petersburg, 1862.

[259] Shchapov, *Neizdannye sochineniia*, p. 1.

[260] "Chto nam delat s Polshei," *Russkii Vestnik*, No. 3 (1863), 469, 506; Joseph Backor, "M. N. Katkov, Introduction to His Life and His Russian National Policy Program," Ph.D. diss., Indiana University, 1966, p. 300.

[261] Korf, *Istoricheskii ocherk* . . . , p. 45. On Speranskii's constitu-

The third interpretation of the word "constitution" involved the familiar formula of a central representative organ governed by a written system of laws. The proposals noted above from four gentry assemblies in the winter of 1861-1862 were for such a "constitution." Subsequently, the gentry of Nizhnii Novgorod, Ekaterinoslav, Novgorod, Smolensk, Kherson, and Orenburg also petitioned the throne to convoke a consultative assembly in the capital.[262] Among the advocates of central representation were many sincere advocates of rule by law and also a few who followed the inflammatory proposal of Ivan Aksakov and the Tver gentry that the landed class abdicate its privileges in favor of democratic representation.[263] But exclusive class interest continued to guide the majority of this kind of constitutionalist, who saw in the central assembly a tool for rewriting the emancipation statutes to the gentry's advantage and thereafter a means of preserving their waning influence in Petersburg. To the extent that this third view of constitutionalism was frankly oligarchic and centralist in spirit, its best representatives were the brothers Mikhail and Nikolai Bezobrazov. Themselves far removed from the spirit of provincial life, these two *Kammerherren* harbored a bitterness toward officialdom that suggests that they knew full well that the court gentry was being displaced by a new professional service corps.[264] Their program included an

---

tionalism see the persuasive analysis by Marc Raeff, *Michael Speransky: Statesman of Imperial Russia*, The Hague, 1957, pp. 49ff.

[262] TsGIA-SSSR, f. 1287, op. 22, d. 1065, pp. 66ff.; *ibid.*, f. 1341, No. 59, pp. 17ff.; *ibid.*, f. 1282, op. 2, d. 1108, pp. 103, 107; Zelenyi, "Kherskonskoe dvorianstvo . . . ," p. 43; TsGAOR, f, 109, Nos. 11-13, pp. 5ff.; see Iordanskii, *Konstitutsionnoe dvizhenie . . .* , pp. 132-44; Emmons, *The Russian Landed Gentry . . .* , pp. 334, 370-81.

[263] I. S. Aksakov, *Sochineniia I. S. Aksakova*, v, 217ff., reprinted from *Den*.

[264] ". . . the power of the lords is the best and strongest support for the state, the gentry's land property provisions the state and gives material and moral strength to its defense." TsGIA-SSSR, f. 982, No. 1, ed. khr. 60, p. 17, Mikhail Bezobrazov, "Zapiska o sobrannykh deputatakh ot gubernskikh komitetov," October 15, 1859; another

element of local self-rule,[265] but from pessimism or realism they placed their hopes in thwarting the ministerial apparatus at its center, Petersburg.[266]

The structural reforms championed by the Bezobrazovs have generally been taken as the very essence of Russian constitutionalism in the 1860s. But by no means all of the great lords adopted this narrow class program, and in more than one provincial assembly in the Black Earth region their memorandums were read before unresponsive audiences.[267] At the same time, some form of central representative body was the expressed goal of Russia's most articulate writers who could by no means be considered oligarchists; for example, Nikolai Turgenev, Peter Dolgorukov, Alexander Koshelev, and Nikolai Ogarev, all of whom published tracts demanding the establishment of a popular elective organ in the capital.[268] Several clandestinely printed manifestos made essentially the same points, but in the thoroughness of their argument and breadth of their readership, the books of these four men best represent the fourth and most influential group of constitutionalists of the period.[269]

---

copy is in TsGIA-SSSR, f. 908, op. 1, d. 101. Since both of these differ slightly from published versions, I have cited the original; see also Nikolai Bezobrazov, *Predlozhenie dvorianstvu*, Berlin, 1862; and Semenov, *Osvobozhdenie krestian . . .* , II, 940ff.

[265] TsGIA-SSSR, f. 908, op. 1, d. 101, p. 146.

[266] Cf. the essay by A. P. Platonov, marshal of the gentry of Tsarskoe Selo, Petersburg province: "Zapiska o neobkhodimosti sozvaniia vybornykh zemli russkoi," *Svobodnoe Slovo*, I, No. 3 (1862); *Vest*, No. 3 (1862), 179; *Otechestvennye Zapiski*, No. 3 (1863), 35.

[267] TsGIA-SSSR, f. 1282, op. 2, d. 1110, pp. 8-9; confidential memorandum from N. Nikoforov, marshal of the gentry of Tambov province, to Valuev, May 18, 1862.

[268] Nikolai Turgenev, *Vzgliad na dela Rossii; Russkii zagranichnyi sbornik*, Pt. 5, Leipzig, 1862; Nicholai Ogarev, *Essai sur la Situation Russe . . .* , London, 1862; Nikolai Ogarev, "Konstitutsiia i zemskii sobor," *Kolokol*, Nos. 172, 174 (1863); Petr Dolgorukov, *O peremene obraza pravleniia v Rossii*, Leipzig, 1862. A. I. Koshelev, *Kakoi iskhod dlia Rossii ot nyneishei ee polozheniia?*, Leipzig, 1862; *Konstitutsiia, samoderzhavie i zemskaia duma*, Leipzig, 1862.

[269] All four of these men had for one reason or another settled in western Europe. The emigration of Turgenev dated to 1825 when

The central elective bodies envisioned by these men would have differed little from parliaments functioning in western Europe, or for that matter, from the assemblies proposed by other Russian "constitutionalists." Like the oligarchists, these four understood the purpose of the assembly to be to enact legislation which they thought the government itself would not undertake.[270] In other words, these spokesmen of constitutional parliamentarianism considered the central elective organ as a means more than as an end in itself. But what was the end toward which they were striving? What institutional forms would the central legislative body establish? What was implied by the word "constitution"? Alexander Koshelev expanded on his long-range ideal in a letter to his fellow liberal Slavophile Prince Cherkasskii: "Samarin says it is necessary to begin building from below, from the fundament, that is from social life; but how can local social life revive when bureaucracy won't allow even the arbiters of the peace and [provincial] leaders to meet for joint conferences? Whatever you say, local life cannot revive under a bureaucracy. In Russia we must snatch this from above, and then the rest will revive."[271] Dolgorukov was no less explicit in connecting the institutional goals of constitutionalism with the revival of local provincial life: "To establish regions in Russia and to endow them with local government is possible only under a constitutional order, that is to say, an order in which there

---

he fled abroad after the Decembrist revolt. Ogarev lived in Paris and Dolgorukov in London, and they circulated ideas that could not be printed freely at home. Koshelev had worked actively on the emancipation through its promulgation in 1861 and then set out to travel.

[270] For Turgenev see *Vzgliad* . . . , pp. 113ff.; also see his "De l'avenir de la Russie" in *La Russie et les Russes*, Paris, 1847, III, 208-10. For Turgenev's views on this subject in 1815, see V. I. Semevskii, *Politicheskie i obshchestvennye idei Dekabristov*, St. Petersburg, 1910, p. 389; for Koshelev, see *Konstitutsiia* . . . , p. 29; for Ogarev see "Konstitutsiia i zemskii sobor," *Kolokol* (June 1, 1863), 351; for Dolgorukov see *O peremene obraza pravleniia*, p. 8.

[271] Trubetskaia, ed., *Materialy dlia biografii . . . Cherkasskogo*, I, 352. Koshelev to Cherkasskii, March 20, 1862.

would exist in Russia a general *Zemskaia Duma* for the whole country, above the regional councils in each territory."[272] To attempt to achieve these supreme objectives through the existing bureaucratic administration would be tantamount "to condemning each territorial unit to serve as a sacrifice to the despotism of the governor-general and the thievery of the local [administrative] powers."[273] At times Dolgorukov goes so far as to equate constitutionalism with the formation of those territorial governments rather than with the establishment of a central elective legislature to institute them:

> . . . it seems to us that *under a constitutional order of things, under the decentralization that is desired by all reasonable men, in which the various parts of Russia would be provided with the power to conduct their own affairs and to manage their local interests so long as they do not conflict with the general interests of all Russia,* under such conditions it would be beneficial to divide Russia not into provinces as is now the case . . . but into territories of two, three, or even four provinces."[274]

At a minimum, constitutionalism was a means of achieving local community control of affairs; at a maximum, it was that system of self-government itself.

The extent to which provincial and regional concerns stood at the forefront of Russian constitutionalism of the period is evident from the western theorists whom Russian writers chose to emulate and to the manner in which they warped the arguments of the men whom they claimed as their mentors. For instance, the Prussian jurist Rudolph Gneist was revered in Germany for his views on the English constitution.[275] But since he considered the British con-

---

[272] Dolgorukov, *O peremene obraza pravleniia* . . . , p. 32.
[273] *Ibid.*
[274] *Ibid.*, pp. 70-71. Note that Dolgorukov here uses the term "decentralization" in the sense that others used the term "self-government."
[275] Dr. Rudolph von Gneist, *Das heutige englische Verfassungs und*

stitution to be embodied in its central parliament rather than in local councils, our four constitutionalists ignored him.[276]

Far more satisfactory from the Russian standpoint was John Stuart Mill, whose epochal *Considerations on Representative Government* came from the presses in 1861. In this work Mill posited a system balanced between publicly controlled local organs and a central parliament.[277] He accorded the administrative authorities their share of work as well, and assumed that bureaucratic agencies and elective assemblies could coexist peacefully within one polity provided their spheres of action were precisely deliniated.[278] All four of our Russian constitutionalists were avowed disciples of Mill and two of their constitutional tracts, those of Koshelev and Ogarev, were written under the direct inspiration of *Considerations on Representative Government*. In his foreword to *Constitution, Autocracy and Zemskaia Duma*, Koshelev lavished praise on Mill and on what he understood English parliamentarianism to be;[279] Dolgorukov did the same in various journal articles;[280] and

---

Verwaltungsrecht, Berlin, 1857-1863; and his more concise *Die Geschichte des Self-Government in England, oder die innere Entwicklung des Parlamentsverfassung bis zum Ende des achtzehnten Jahrhunderts*, Berlin, 1863; see *Vest*, No. 32 (1866).

[276] The first outline of Gneist's views appeared in Russia in 1864, with the translation of *Das constitutionelle Princep, seine geschichtliche Entwicklung und seine Wechselwirkungen mit den politischen und socialen Verhältnissen der Staaten und Völker*, August von Haxthausen, ed., Leipzig, 1864. (Translated, St. Petersburg, 1864.)

[277] John Stuart Mill, *Considerations on Representative Government*, New York, 1882, pp. 157, 304.

[278] In this context see his remarks on central and local power in Russia. *Considerations on Representative Government*, pp. 88, 286.

[279] Koshelev, *Konstitutsiia . . .* , pp. 26ff.

[280] *Listok*, No. 2 (1863). He attacks Baron Korf for misapplying Mill's principles. Leonid Blummer, editor of *Vest*, of whom Dolgorukov wrote, "My political program is identical to Blummer's," *Listok*, No. 6 (1863), 2; he wrote a lengthy appreciation of *Considerations on Representative Government* in *Svobodnoe Slovo*, No. 1 (1863), 10-27.

Ogarev went so far as to initiate a correspondence with Mill, which culminated in his sending the Englishman a first copy of his *Essai* on Russia.[281]

The Russians admired Mill but at the same time upset his delicate balance of central and local powers, thus turning his entire parliamentary machine into a tool for achieving the provincial self-rule they demanded above all else. Dolgorukov, for example, scarcely sketched out the organization of the two houses of his parliament before turning to the more important territorial councils.[282] Koshelev also linked constitutionalism with local public rule,[283] and Ogarev passed quickly over the central council to expound on the territorial divisions and local institutions of the future federated state, an emphasis which Mill remarked upon to his Russian disciple.[284] Federalism so dominated Turgenev's constitutional project that it caused even Dolgorukov to fear for its lopsidedness![285]

This fourth concept of constitutionalism, then, proposed to create a central elective organ which would in turn shift the political center of gravity from the capital to the provinces. In this respect it was frankly federative in intent, harking back to the constitutionalism of such earlier French liberals as Benjamin Constant.[286] Several leading reformers accepted the federative implications of local control of public functions but balked at creating another centralized organ—even an elective one—to achieve it. They wanted

[281] *Gertsen i Ogarev*, 1953, i, 895-96, Ogarev to Mill, June 1862.

[282] Dolgorukov, *O peremene obraza pravleniia* . . . , pp. 66ff.

[283] Koshelev, *Konstitutsiia* . . . , p. 30.

[284] *Letters of John Stuart Mill*, H.S.R. Elliot, ed., 2 vols., London, 1910, i, 266-67. Mill to Ogarev, November 7, 1862.

[285] Dolgorukov, "O knizhke N. I. Turgeneva *Vzgliad na dela Rossii*," *Pravdivyi-La Véridique*, No. 4 (May 21, 1862).

[286] "I do not hesitate to say that there should be introduced into our internal administration as much federalism as possible, but a federalism different from that which has heretofore existed." Henri Benjamin Constant de Rebecque, *Cours politique constitutionelle*, 3rd edn., Brussels, 1837, p. 61; for Constant in Russia, see Semevskii, *Politicheskie i obshchestvennye idei Dekabristov*, pp. 209-39.

the authorities "simply to give the country good and free local institutions,"[287] and rejected as "child's play"[288] the idea of constructing it from the center. At the same time, most critics of the plan, while critical of its strategy, agreed with the importance of its final objective—self-government.

To summarize, constitutionalism connoted not one but many currents in the 1860s. Of these, two predominated: the oligarchic view, which took as its goal the capture of certain functions of the central state by gentry representatives; and the federative view, which looked to a new elective body to set up semiautonomous local governments and to devolve upon these public bodies as many state functions as possible. Because of its narrow appeal to the prosperous gentry, the oligarchic program held little attraction for most of those supporting other forms of constitutionalism. By contrast, the program of the federative constitutionalists absorbed the leading tendencies of contemporary reformism, particularly its urge toward the localization of power and its faith in community control of that power. Because of this, the federative form of constitutionalism could and did influence the other three and, in fact, came to dominate the entire constitutional movement.

Valuev and Constitutionalism

It is impossible to estimate what impact the constitutional movement might have had on the *zemstvo* legislation had it not coincided with the Polish revolt and internal disorders within Russia. These events left Valuev on the defensive, and by the time he addressed himself to the constitutional movement he was suspicious not just of public initiatives but of everyone around him. He suspected Grand Duke Konstantin of using his position as Viceroy in Poland

---

[287] Prince Cherkasskii, cited by Trubetskaia, ed., *Materialy dlia biografii . . . Cherkasskogo*, I, 110. Konstantin Kavelin considered the "constitutional" strategy an overly circuitous route to local rule: *Sobranie Sochinenii K. D. Kavelina*, 4 vols., St. Petersburg, 1904, II, 139-42.

[288] Iurii Samarin, cited in Veselovskii, *Istoriia zemstva . . .*, III, 31.

to mount a secession movement there.[289] He read hearty attestations of undying loyalty from the provincial gentry as a trick to reconstitute the local militias that earlier had so spurred the movement for self-rule.[290] He even accused his own subordinates of flagging loyalty as this comment on a provincial governor reveals: "He's a characteristic man of our times. . . . He talks about the government as if it were a certain unknown inhabitant of Petersburg and not a complex organism embracing the entire empire and of which he himself, as a governor, is a part."[291]

Racked by these suspicions, Valuev struggled to make sense of the constitutional movement. A lengthy essay published anonymously in the newspaper of the Ministry of Internal Affairs presented the definitive opinion of that agency on constitutionalism and its bearing on the *zemstvo* reforms.[292] Thanks to a manuscript copy preserved in Valuev's archive, we may be certain that it came from his pen.[293] He began by setting forth his general view of the *zemstvos*:

> . . . there is applied as the basis of the draft bill on *zemstvo* institutions the idea of decentralization; but this is not intended to weaken the existing ties between the parts and the common center. The state authority is not dividing the *zemstvos* from itself. . . . In transferring to the *zemstvos* issues within certain bounds the government does not diminish the totality of its rights but rather relieves the burden resting upon itself. . . . It is essential to bear in mind the form and inviolability of our state unity. The mutual tie between the various parts of the organism is possible only by preserving the firm bounds between the various units and the center.[294]

[289] Valuev, *Dnevnik*, I, 228-29.

[290] TsGIA-SSSR, f. 1275, op. 93, d. 6, p. 2.

[291] Valuev, *Dnevnik*, I, 193.

[292] *Severnaia Pochta*, No. 140 (June 26, 1863), 505; No. 141, June 27, 569; No. 142, June 28, 573.

[293] TsGIA-SSSR, f. 908, op. 1, d. 175, pp. 126-56.

[294] *Ibid.*, p. 130, marginal note in pencil by Valuev (subsequently

Valuev accepted the fact that the creation of *zemstvos* would further the process of specialization in the autocratic state structure, and that the new organs would mobilize substantial groups of the population for public decision making. What, then, was his objection, since he, like Lenin later, conceived the local organs as two-way "transmission belts" between government and local society?

THE POINT AT ISSUE HERE IS BETWEEN A UNIFIED PRINCIPLE OF STATE STRUCTURE AND THE PRINCIPLE OF FEDERALISM. IT FOLLOWS THAT ON SUCH AN ISSUE THERE CAN BE NO QUESTION. In other countries it had been recognized and is still acknowledged that unity is the cornerstone of the might and welfare of the state. One of the principal orators of the Prussian liberal party, Mr. Beckerath, said in the united Landtag in 1847 that he does not advocate a centralization "which obliterates the peculiar differences among provinces" and that "the unity of the state does not exclude diversity in its composition," but that he is the enemy "of any provincialism that juxtaposes itself to this unity." A profound truth is expressed therein.[295]

Significantly, the Prussian Beckerath to whom Valuev referred was an avowed constitutionalist, but one who defended German unity against provincial particularism.[296]

---

published). Valuev repeated this statement in 1863 (TsGIA-SSSR, f. 908, d. 34, marginal pencil note on memoir by Marshal of the Gentry Shuvalov, p. 181) and in the meetings of the combined Departments of Law and Economy, where he added that: "Under the proposed reform there can be no thought of a complete division of the *zemstvos* from the general system of rules and institutions and of providing it with unconditional independence, for that would be to establish within the state two independent powers based on different principles—*a state within the state*." (TsGIA-SSSR, f. 1160, op. 1, d. 134, *Zhurnal soedinennogo prisutstviia departamentov prava i ekonomii*, pp. 343ff.)

[295] TsGIA-SSSR, f. 1160, op. 1, d. 134, *Zhurnal soedinennogo prisutstviia . . .* , pp. 343ff.

[296] Hermann von Beckerath (1801-1870), see *Allgemeine Deutsche Biographie*, Leipzig, 1875, I, 231-35.

Concluding his attack on Russia's federalist constitutionalism, Valuev lashed out at writers who had imported the theory in the first place:

> A publicist will hold up the governmental project for the *zemstvo* reform as something abstract, existing outside of time and place, and measure it against another ideal which he has created in his own head or borrowed [from foreign writers]. Under the influence of this fantasmagoria one publicist is ready to set up quarter sessions of the justices of the peace, another demands a general assembly, a third wants to create . . . some kind of New York State. . . . With such an attitude no governmental reform at all is possible.[297]

From our earlier conclusions on the character of the constitutional movement, it is plain that Valuev had hit the mark in accusing its partisans of federalism. The influential *Contemporary Chronicle* disseminated the same analysis, setting it in the context of contemporary state development and particularly of the American Civil War:

> The unity of the United States is being destroyed before our eyes as an obvious consequence of the inadequacy of their state structure. . . . Because of the conviction that the interests common to all were so strong, the separate states were given the character of independent units. . . . If in America a federal structure does not work, then what can be expected if it is tried in Europe where the position of each state is 1,000 times more perilous, and where the dangers are not only internal but external?[298]

Valuev prepared to take the bull by the horns. With the support of the chief of gendarmes and the tacit backing of the tsar he proclaimed his willingness to make a concession by introducing 120 representatives elected by the *zemstvos*

[297] TsGIA-SSSR, f. 908, op. 1, d. 175, pp. 126-56.
[298] *Sovremennaia Letopis*, No. 37 (1861), 13.

into the State Council as nonvoting members.[299] This Valuev "constitution" has been seen variously as a response to the revolutionary movement,[300] to the discontented gentry, to the growth of Russian nationalism, and to the Polish revolt.[301] All of these interpretations are well-founded and were corroborated by Valuev himself.[302] In the background of the broader constitutional movement, however, its meaning is inescapable. Its purpose was to impress upon local leaders the immediacy of their tie with the national polity. He sought to co-opt the oligarchic constitutionalists' central representative body and use it to defuse the *zemstvo*-based federative constitutional movement. Indeed, when the threat to Russia's unity began to subside toward the end of 1863 Alexander conveniently dropped the project.[303]

Valuev's State Council scheme was only one of many moves in a concerted counterattack against federalism and self-government as it had been understood since 1858. Of much greater moment was the legislative onslaught which Valuev directed against the 1862 *zemstvo* statutes in the Commission on Provincial and District Institutions. The first objective of this attack was to redefine the relation of the *zemstvos* to the central government. As originally conceived, they were to be *societal* organs which could not exercise *governmental* authority. Indeed, they were considered "as two completely distinct spheres of life."[304] Accordingly, the judiciary would alone be empowered to review actions by the local bodies and, in the wording of the 1862 draft, "No *administrative* penalties whatsoever can be levied against the *zemstvos*."[305] At the same time and in flat

---

[299] Iordanskii, *Konstitutsionnoe dvizhenie* . . . , p. 146.
[300] Tseitlin, *Zemskaia reforma* . . . , p. 217.
[301] Zaionchkovskii, "P. A. Valuev," p. 34.
[302] Bermanskii, "Konstitutsionnye proekty . . . ," pp. 227-28; Valuev, *Dnevnik*, I, 349.
[303] Valuev, *Dnevnik*, I, 261.
[304] Kizevetter, "Borba za zemstvo . . . ," *Istoricheskie otliki*, p. 303.
[305] *Istoricheskaia zapiska* . . . , p. 253, Statute 76.

contradiction to this principle, the draft of 1862 left the *zemstvos* subject to general administrative law. Worse, it included the controversial paragraph 49 empowering governors to suspend temporarily the promulgation of any *zemstvo* act deemed contrary to "the laws and general interest of the state"; the suspended legislation was to be reviewed by the Ministry of Internal Affairs rather than by the law courts.[306] Aside from reinstituting the ministerial review that was elsewhere denounced, this clause invited the ministry to hold any *zemstvo* decisions in limbo for up to two years. A localist faction in the commission decried these dangerous provisions. Yet the effort to rectify them failed because it ran afoul of Valuev's doctrine that "no power can establish institutions that are hostile to itself."[307] Indeed, Valuev succeeded in deleting the important paragraph protecting the *zemstvos* against administrative penalties. This stroke, so significant for the future of local institutions meant that the *zemstvos* were scarcely to be distinguished from the general state administration.

Valuev reduced the competence of the *zemstvo* organs in his second assault on provincial self-government. Though the Minister of Internal Affairs concurred with the desire of the gentry commission in Petersburg to restrict the *zemstvos'* sphere of competence, his motive was not to assure their independence but to remove any possibility of their pretending to be territorial governments within a federation. In light of the severe administrative controls being imposed on the *zemstvos* anyway, it would appear that this move was redundant. After all, if there were "no provincial *zemstvo* affairs that do not also affect the [central] government," state control of them would be complete, and it would be unnecessary to confine them to "busy-work."

[306] TsGIA-SSSR, f. 1316, op. 1, d. 148, Protocol of the Commission, February 25, March 4, 11, 18, 1863, pp. 7ff.
[307] TsGIA-SSSR, f. 908, op. 1, d. 175, d. 136. The minimal successes scored by this faction are discussed by Kizevetter, "Borba za zemstvo . . . ," *Istoricheskie otliki*, pp. 309ff.

Notwithstanding this, Valuev worked to emasculate the executive power of the *zemstvos*.

The 1862 edition of the *zemstvo* statutes had stated that the provincial organs would control "the properties, capital, and incomes of the entire provinces,"[308] but Valuev managed to have this clause dropped from the 1863 version. The statutes approved by the tsar in 1862 also provided the provincial bodies with control over measures to facilitate and support local trade and industry,"[309] but Valuev and his allies had this removed a year later. Finally, Valuev transferred control of welfare functions and the keeping of grain reserves for famine relief from elective control back to the administration.[310] All these changes were also applied to the district level.[311] It now appeared that the *zemstvos* were to come into being stripped of important functions that the tsar himself had confirmed in 1862.

The third flank of Valuev's assault on the 1862 legislation entailed reducing the financial powers and resources of the *zemstvos* to such a level that it would be impossible for local interest groups to use them as a staging ground for federalist schemes. These questions lay within the formal purview of the Commission on Taxes and Duties in the Ministry of Finances. Until the autumn of 1862 Valuev was unable to intervene successfully in either agency, notwithstanding his continued contempt for Reutern, whom he inconvenienced in every way possible.[312] Gradually, though, he gained the upper hand in this ministerial battle. Finally, in October of 1862, Valuev asserted his authority over the Commission on Taxes and Duties, aiming at two points in the proposed tax plan. First, having already denied the *zemstvos* any *executive* control over the functions of welfare and provisioning he wanted to assure that they would

---

[308] *Istoricheskaia zapiska* . . . , p. 239, Statute 40, 1.
[309] *Ibid.*, p. 240, Statute 40, v.
[310] *Ibid.*, p. 240, Statute 40, iii, iv.
[311] *Ibid.*, p. 241, Statute 41.
[312] TsGIA-SSSR, f. 572, op. 1, d. 7, pp. 15-17, 77-99.

277

have no *financial* control over them either. The provisioning agencies and the welfare boards together controlled a substantial pool of credit. Traditionally these funds had been controlled by the governors and executive police with the advice of elected gentry. Now Valuev argued that they were in no sense "local" or "public" monies, since they were collected at the instigation of the state.[313] Further, the government had a natural interest in their expenditure just as it does in such local matters as trade fairs, bazaars, and banks.[314] Hence, Valuev concluded, the governmental interest must be maintained by keeping financial control over these matters in state hands.

Second, he wanted to quash all talk of local interest groups participating through self-governing bodies in the apportionment and collection of national (*gosudarstvennye*) duties. Taxation had been the worst managed area of Nicholas I's chaotic provincial system. The first positive steps toward creating locally controlled provincial taxes had been prompted by the discontent of the Petersburg gentry with existing tax policy. Subsequently tax reform had been the aim of projects advanced by the gentry and members of the Commission on Taxes and Duties. As a consequence of this many-sided campaign, the commission conceded to provincial *zemstvos* a sphere of autonomy in tax matters without involving them in the apportionment and collection of the all-important national taxes. Reutern strongly favored such participation as a step to greater efficiency and hence larger tax yields. He resented the blindness of the Ministry of Internal Affairs to this fiscal consideration and scorned it for viewing the issue of national taxes in narrowly political terms.[315]

Extreme partisans of the "localist" or "societal" view of the *zemstvo* organs—notably former members of the

[313] *Ibid.*, d. 39, p. 15.
[314] *Severnaia Pochta*, No. 62 (1863) 247; *Istoricheskaia zapiska* . . . , p. 293.
[315] TsGIA-SSSR, f. 572, op. 1, d. 39, p. 15.

Petersburg gentry's Special Commission on Provincial Reform—opposed Reutern because they did not want to involve the *zemstvos* in collecting funds over which they exercised no control.[316] Valuev opposed Reutern but for entirely different reasons. If the government were to relinquish the power to apportion taxes between Russian provinces, would this not have to be extended to the non-Russian provinces as well? And would this not build pressure for democratizing and federalizing the state structure? In a letter to Reutern, Valuev wrote: "Maybe I fail to grasp the issue correctly, but it seems to me that at the bottom of the system of self-apportionment of taxes there lies the principle of democracy. [If the tax reform is adopted] there is good reason to fear the growth of democracy, growth in precisely the sphere which least of all answers the demands of our government, that is, in the federative sphere."[317] This was no crude ploy to scare Reutern into compliance but Valuev's honest assessment of the issue. He was bent on safeguarding the interests of the central government at all cost.

THE FINAL DEBATE, 1863

Valuev launched his attack on public and provincial autonomy behind closed doors. The earlier squabbles over decentralization had reverberated to obscure district centers, but these debates took place in such privacy that few traces of it are to be detected even in the private papers of well-informed Petersburg gossips. The press aired a heated debate over the *zemstvos*, but its concern was still with the draft published in 1862 without any of the subsequent revisions.[318] Bureaucratic secrecy created a situation in which

[316] *Severnaia Pochta*, No. 62 (1863), 247; *Istoricheskaia zapiska* . . . , p. 293.

[317] TsGIA-SSSR, f. 908, pp. 2-3, Valuev to Reutern, October 9, 1862, copy of No. 2722; partially cited in Garmiza, *Podgotovka* . . . , p. 196.

[318] See for example, the incisive essays by Iurii Samarin, "O proek-

the only point from which criticism of Valuev's stand could emerge was from within the government itself.

Here the situation was complicated to the extreme, for who could forcefully express the views of the opposition? Grand Duke Konstantin was in Warsaw, as were Miliutin, Samarin, and Cherkasskii, while the more subordinately placed Soloviev was now too isolated to successfully challenge a man of ministerial rank. Of the ministers, Reutern was the obvious center of opposition but in his relations with Valuev he had proven to be so much the weaker that he, too, was searching for a champion. By process of elimination, leadership of the opposition fell to the quite unlikely figure of Baron Modest Korf.

It would be hard to find another man in the highest court and administrative circles who embodied the ideal of faithful service to the autocracy more perfectly than did this Baltic German. In 1859 he had been a guest of honor at a magnificent feast commemorating his fifty years in the Russian administration.[319] He had served three tsars and had advised two of them, had written an official history of the beclouded debut of Nicholas I's reign,[320] and had participated dutifully in the "Era of Censorship Terror" following the revolutions of 1848. On the other hand, he was the reigning heir of the reformism of the 1820s, and was known to have been described by Speranskii as "my golden pen."[321] From his mentor he inherited an antipathy toward ministerial oligarchy which he now directed against Valuev.

Korf was director of the Second (legal) Section of His Majesty's Imperial Chancellery. In January 1862, Alexander II had ordered this body to examine the various proposals

takh zemskikh khoziaistvennykh uchrezhdenii," published in *Den*, Nos. 29, 30, 35 (1863).

[319] GPB, f. 380, No. 15.

[320] Baron M. A. Korf, *Vosshestvie na prestol imperatora Nikolaia I*, St. Petersburg, 1857.

[321] GPB, f. 827 (N. P. Sobko archive), No. 22 contains information about Korf's opposition to the Ministry of Public Enlightenment in 1850.

for local reform prior to sending them to the State Council for final approval.[322] This gave Korf the chance he needed to bring together all the opponents of the Valuev project. After meetings with Reutern and with former members of the Petersburg gentry's tax commission, Korf completed his critique of the *zemstvo* project by May of 1863. But he did not pass it on to Valuev at once. Instead, he carefully paved the way for the tsar to approve his critique *before* Valuev saw it. To accomplish this, he presented Alexander with a short note innocuously seeking royal approval to turn his commentary over to Valuev. In his note Korf claimed to agree with the main principles of Valuev's project, "but thought it advisable to enter a few changes."[323] He then enumerated these "few changes" and the unsuspecting autocrat gave the quite unnecessary authorization for Korf to pass them on to Valuev. Thus far, Korf assumed the role of the honored house servant, deferential, meticulous, and plodding, while Alexander gladly acted the part of the *grand seigneur*, dispensing largess and nodding his approval. In fact, the tsar had been used.

Protected against royal displeasure, Korf turned on Valuev, presenting him not with the modest note that had been used to obtain royal support but with a 150-page brief on the proposed *zemstvo* statutes.[324] In this way Korf made it appear to Valuev that Alexander had no intention of approving Valuev's amendments to the 1862 draft and that Korf himself had been delegated to set the statutes right. Far from the "few changes" that Korf had suggested to the tsar, he now demanded that the statutes be completely overhauled.[325]

[322] TsGIA-SSSR, f. 1291 (1863), op. 5, II, d. 65, p. 1.

[323] *Ibid.*, pp. 2-3. Korf to Alexander II, May 2, 1863.

[324] *Ibid.*, pp. 5-82. Korf to Alexander II, May 2, 1863 and reply May 6, 1863. A somewhat contracted version of this text was published in *Materialy po zemskomu . . . ustroistvu*, II, 411-56; all citations will be from the full archival text with Valuev's notes.

[325] The extent of Korf's amendments was first appreciated by N. N. Avinov, "Graf M. A. Korf i zemskaia reforma 1864 g.," *Russkaia Mysl*, 1904, No. 2.

The essence of the reform, Korf maintained, was not to substitute one set of bureaucratic agencies with another but on the contrary,

> ... to change the most fundamental conditions of our system of local government, to destroy the old and to rebuild on a new principle almost diametrically opposed to that which has heretofore existed: decentralization and self-government. This task presents great difficulties. At the present time there is an extraordinary lot of talk of decentralization and self-government and in the science of state law the subject has in recent years occupied one of the most prominent spots. Yet very little has been accomplished up to now to solve the problem—especially in practical life. The history of all European states has led them to one of two extremes, either to excessive concentration of all activity in the center and the complete suppression of the independent public life in the separate localities, or to excessive independence of the regions and a weakening of the necessary bonds of union between them. With the exception, perhaps, of England, whose unique conditions do not present a suitable example for emulation, and also of several very recent attempts on which it is too early to pass judgment, not one of the great states of Europe has yet succeeded in finding a fully satisfactory middle course.[326]

This was Russia's task. To accomplish it Korf sought drastic changes in the composition, structure, sphere of action, and relation to the central government of the proposed provincial organs.

Korf's detailed critique opened with an attack on the labyrinthine rules governing the social composition of self-government. Agreeing that Russia's state of development required broader politicization, he objected to the curial system through which Valuev wanted to achieve it. The

---

[326] TsGIA-SSSR, f. 1291 (1863), op. 5, ɪɪ, d. 65, p. 39.

fractioning of the electorate into subgroups would surely lead to a situation in which elected representatives would feel bound to narrow constituencies rather than to the broad public interests of the region.[327] Accordingly, he proposed that Valuev's rigid distinction between gentry and nongentry landlords be abolished,[328] and that the polarity of city and country be softened. Russian cities are indistinguishable from large villages, he reasoned, and with a few obvious exceptions they needed no special representation. For peasants, he believed that the *ex officio* appointment of communal leaders would lead to disinterest, and suggested that instead special elective assemblies be established at the village level.[329] Finally, Korf pointed out that leasees need not be enfranchised as a special interest group since few major estates were actually rented.[330]

All of these amendments revealed an openness toward the political energies of Russian provincial society that by 1863 had become quite unusual in the imperial administration. But Korf's province was a static and socially conservative conception. Granted this characterization of the provincial "city" was accurate, it failed to anticipate the urbanization that had already begun. Granted, too, that little acreage was under lease in 1863, Korf did not suspect that by the 1880s up to two-fifths of the land would be leased or rented.[331]

In spite of its conservative features, Korf's attack on the curial system received the voting support of only two members of the Combined Departments of Law and State Economy, far too few to establish a single, all-class assembly to select *zemstvo* members.[332] At the same time the Combined Departments did endorse Korf's proposals to have peasant

[327] *Ibid.*, p. 16.   [328] *Ibid.*, pp. 8-9.
[329] *Ibid.*, p. 22.   [330] *Ibid.*, p. 9.
[331] N. A. Karyshev, *Krestianskie vnenadelnye arendy*, Dorpat, 1892, p. vii.
[332] General Suvorov and Nikolai Bakhtin, TsGIA-SSSR, f. 1149 (1863), op. vi, d. 82, p. 842. (*Zhurnal soedinennogo prisutstviia . . .*, August-September 1863.)

representatives elected rather than appointed *ex officio*. Valuev withstood the bid in the Combined Departments to take the vote from out-of-province leasees,[333] but he was overruled later in the State Council, thanks to the presence there of many ex-provincial administrators who considered nonresident lords an impediment to swift and efficient rule.[334] The same group carried through Korf's proposal to abolish the distinction between gentry and nongentry landlords.[335]

In his critique of Valuev's draft project Baron Korf brought to light a glaring lacuna, namely, the total absence of discussion on voting procedures and on the rules of order to be followed in the *zemstvos*.[336] Should voting be secret? Should minutes be published? Who would compile the lists of voters? How would they be checked? All of these issues were very much on Korf's mind in the spring of 1863 because he, too, had just perused Mill's *Considerations on Representative Government*.[337] Korf realized that if these questions were not resolved in advance the Minister of Internal Affairs could settle them by administrative fiat. To prevent this he proposed to adopt British rules on procedure and to borrow wholesale Mill's system of proportional representation.[338] This sophisticated scheme for assuring minority representation appealed to Korf as an antidote to the Valuev plan, according to which the members of the provincial assemblies (chosen from the members of district assemblies) would come largely from the landed classes. Proportional representation would

---

[333] *Ibid.*, p. 843.

[334] TsGIA-SSSR, f. 1159, op. 1, d. 215, pp. 209ff. *Memoriia sobraniia gos.-a soveta*, December 1863.

[335] Kizevetter, "Borba za zemstvo . . . ," *Istoricheskie otliki*, p. 278.

[336] TsGIA-SSSR, f. 1291 (1863), op. 5, II, d. 65, pp. 50, 64ff.

[337] *Severnaia Pochta*, No. 69 (1863), 273.

[338] TsGIA-SSSR, f. 1291 (1863), op. 5, II, d. 65, p. 68. *Severnaia Pochta*, No. 69 (1863), 35, 36, 36n. Citation from *Considerations on Representative Government*, Chap. VI.

doubtless have prevented the peasantry from being disenfranchised at the provincial level but, it need hardly be said, it required political skills quite beyond those possessed by the average Russian peasant. Again, Valuev succeeded in blocking it. The other procedural questions raised for the first time by Korf were debated in tedious detail but ultimately left to the decision of the *zemstvos* themselves.[339] Participatory government in Russia was still viewed more as a matter of structures than of day-to-day procedures.

Other practical aspects of the proposed legislation attracted Korf's attention. As constituted, the provincial assemblies would number twenty to thirty and, in the rarest cases, up to fifty members.[340] Baron Korf feared that such small bodies would be ineffective as counterbalances to the local administrative apparatus and proposed instead that their number be raised to forty or even sixty members.[341] This plan, too, was rejected out of hand as an unnecessary encouragement to those who already distrusted the central authorities. A similar fate befell an attempt by Korf and the Petersburg gentry to lengthen the sessions prescribed for district and provincial assemblies from seven and twenty days per annum to ten and thirty days, respectively.

No aspect of Valuev's assault on self-rule was more vulnerable than the support of bureaucratic control over *zemstvos* and the means by which he proposed to restrict their competence. Baron Korf singled out both points for strong criticism. In France, he declared, administrative control had a better chance of succeeding than anywhere else because of the small size of the nation and the absence of stark local peculiarities. But, Korf pointed out: "We Russians are in completely different circumstances. The huge expanse of our empire, the remoteness of the capital, the

[339] TsGIA-SSSR, f. 1143 (1863), op. vi, d. 82, pp. 758-67.
[340] *Istoricheskaia zapiska* . . . , pp. 13-15, Statutes 54, 55.
[341] TsGIA-SSSR, f. 1291 (1863), op. 5, ɪɪ, d. 65, pp. 127-28.

backwardness of communications and the diversity of our geographic, linguistic, and religious conditions, our customs and even our social systems, render things that would be merely difficult or inconvenient in France completely impossible here."[342] Valuev scratched a scornful question mark on Korf's brief at this point, but in the July 4 session of the Combined Departments and of the State Council he could not hide behind irony. On that date he was challenged with a firm demand to broaden the competence of self-government. Leading the attack with Korf was the curmudgeon Nikolai Bakhtin. Though his own friends considered him to be "dry, callous," and "extraordinarily cold and steadfast,"[343] he now stepped forth as an able bureaucratic politician.[344] It was Bakhtin who nearly broke up the sitting of the Combined Departments of Law and State Economy by flatly insisting that the *zemstvos* control local public health and jails.[345] Bakhtin then turned to the former Minister of Public Enlightenment, Egor Kovalevskii, who moved that the *zemstvos* be put in charge of public education as well. These rapid-fire moves caught Valuev off guard, but he was able to evoke the specter of imperial collapse with sufficient force to prevent an immediate vote.[346]

Shut off from direct public pressure, the two factions were stalemated over several weeks. And so long as this standoff persisted it remained an open question whether two of the most important local functions—education and public health—would fall under local public control. Only on July 25, 1863 did the situation break. Reutern and Kovalevskii mustered support for their proposal to permit provincial leaders themselves to submit their views on the questions of education, public health, and jails. Know-

[342] *Ibid.*, p. 42. [343] *Golos*, No. 87 (1869), 2.
[344] *Russkii Biograficheskii Slovar*, II, 607-08.
[345] TsGIA-SSSR, f. 1143 (1863), op. vi, d. 82, pp. 737ff.; an abbreviated version of these debates is in *Istoricheskaia zapiska . . .*, pp. 301ff.
[346] TsGIA-SSSR, f. 1143 (1863), op. vi, d. 82, pp. 737ff.

ing full well what the outcome of such a poll would be, Valuev acknowledged his position as untenable and backed down.[347] He realized that not even a powerful minister could brook the force of a bureaucratic opposition linked with the threat of interest group pressure. Just as the vote was about to begin he calmly announced that his staff was prepared to draft legislation to cover *zemstvo* activity in the areas of health, education, and jails. Valuev conceded reluctantly, and with utter contempt for his victors. "Almost nobody," he recorded in his diary, "has a close knowledge of what he is debating, what he wants and where he is going."[348] But he conceded.

This episode dramatically broadened the range of public life in the provinces for generations to come. But should *zemstvo* power be extended still further to include a role in the apportionment of national taxes? On the one side stood the enemies of bureaucracy who saw this as the sole means of achieving honesty in the national tax system. On the other side were those friends of self-government who feared that by assuming a role in these *national* affairs the *zemstvos* would leave themselves exposed to central control as well. Baron Korf now championed this latter position, first expounded by the Petersburg gentry.[349]

Valuev showed confusion and irresolution on this important point. In the sessions of the Combined Departments of Law and State Economy on July 25, 1863, he reiterated his conviction that: "There can be no talk of permitting the *zemstvos* to manage national (*gosudarstvennye*) taxes. To allow the *zemstvo* institutions to participate in affairs of general interest to the [national] government would be tantamount to parcelling out the single national-governing

---

[347] TsGIA-SSSR, f. 1143 (1863), op. vi, d. 82, p. 840. *Memoriia No. 7.*

[348] Valuev, *Dnevnik*, i, 236, 247.

[349] TsGIA-SSSR, f. 1291 (1863), op. 5, ii, d. 65, p. 41. This section of the Korf memorandum is published in *Materialy po zemskomu . . . ustroistvu*, ii, p. 436.

power among forty or fifty separate unities and to putting the social order and the state itself in jeopardy."[350] Notwithstanding this statement, when the final vote was taken he switched and voted with those seeking to give this power to the provincial public![351] Evidently, Valuev believed that to stand with Korf on this vote would leave the way open for the opposition to capture the policy for its own ends. But Valuev had outsmarted himself and was soundly defeated by a majority consisting of a curious alliance of Nicholaevan opponents of the reform and the outspoken *zemstvo* faction.

In its final stage the debate on local government returned to the question that had spurred the movement for self-government in the first place: the relation of local public agencies to local administrators. Throughout the legislative process, Baron Korf had impressed upon his colleagues that he "most of all desired the *zemstvo* institutions, however limited their sphere of activity, to enjoy complete independence."[352] His intention was to protect them from local administrators, armed as they were with more decentralized authority. To this end, Korf insisted that several clauses empowering the provincial agents of Valuev's ministry to review *zemstvo* decisions be deleted from the text.[353] He took special pains to warn the various bodies reviewing the legislation that if the prerogatives of the governors were not limited and the *zemstvos* placed under the general control of the courts, the entire system could and would be subverted administratively.[354] Korf's proposal was carried, thanks to the same majority that won education, jails, health, and provisioning for the *zemstvos*. In theory, at

[350] TsGIA-SSSR, f. 1143 (1863), op. vi, d. 82, p. 777. *Memoriia No. 7*, July 25, 1863.
[351] TsGIA-SSSR, f. 1159, op. 1, d. 215, pp. 322ff. *Memoriia sobraniia gos.-a soveta, 14, 16, 18 Dekabria, 1863.*
[352] *Istoricheskaia zapiska . . .* , p. 295.
[353] TsGIA-SSSR, f. 1291 (1863), op. 5, ii, d. 65, pp. 46, 62ff.
[354] *Ibid.*, p. 62.

least, self-government was now secure from overt administrative interference.

REFORM WITHOUT COORDINATION

The *zemstvo* statutes were now completed. The questions at issue had been precisely those which in western Europe traditionally formed the basis of domestic politics: the relative power of diverse groups in civil life; the powers of local bodies; and the means of expanding or checking the authority of the state administration in public affairs. In western Europe these momentous issues dominated party conflict in parliaments, assemblies, and other elective councils. In Russia, though, the legislative process in its final stages was monopolized by a small group of men, all of them professional bureaucrats. It is characteristic of Russian development that these considerations of the limits of administrative power and its harmonization with local public initiatives received their fullest exposition at the hands of the bureaucracy and were in fact resolved by the very administration that was supposedly to be restricted.

The amended *zemstvo* statutes were a battle-scarred monument to the debates of 1859 to 1863. For generations to come the *zemstvos* bore the mark of the peculiar circumstances of these years, both to their detriment and to their benefit. On the negative side, important issues remained unresolved. At no point in the debate did the tsar personally underwrite fully the basic notions upon which provincial public self-rule was grounded. Nor had partisans of this program worked out satisfactorily all the theoretical aspects, particularly the means for distinguishing central from local functions and state from public responsibilities. This failure was the more glaring because of the extensive consideration that had been accorded proposals for administrative deconcentration; until potential rivalries between up-graded local administrators and newly formed societal agencies could be erased it would be naive to believe that the institutional problems of the Russian province were solved.

On a more human level, the proposed *zemstvos* demanded a new type of local administrator. Just as the decentralization reforms required old habits to be broken instantly, so now the self-government reforms assumed that local bureaucratic agencies would be directed by governors sufficiently restrained and self-confident to stand by without interfering when the public bodies pursued policies which, though fully legal, were inconsistent with the governors' estimation of the needs of the situation. Similar restraint was required of the ministers.

Even more subtle transformations were required of the local public if it were to exercise its new prerogatives effectively. For centuries, unilateral initiatives by any interest group in Russian society other than the state administration had been viewed with suspicion, even by those engaging in such action. Throughout the reform era one senses that the gentry and even "radical" publicists who expressed positions not explicitly condoned by the state did so only after undergoing searching self-examination. Indeed, the need of educated Russians to convince themselves that an action was not disloyal is scarcely less striking in retrospect than the independent act itself. *Zemstvo* members, in order to meet the compelling need to develop provincial institutions, had to overcome these doubts. At the same time they had to remain free of the exaggerated sense of autonomy which so frequently saps the power of local agencies in developing nations.[355]

Turning to the positive side of the achievement, it must be acknowledged that the Russian state underwent a major constitutional crisis without bloodshed or the use of major force. After 1856 its leading ministers came quickly to recognize the need for broader involvement of the populace

[355] See Maddick, *Democracy* . . . , p. 243.

290

in public life—for "politicization" in the proper sense of the word—and accurately pinpointed the underinstitutionalization of the province as the most appropriate sphere for such engagement. Moreover, Lanskoi, Soloviev, Saltykov, the Miliutins, Korf, and even Valuev acknowledged the practical necessity for decision-making to be diffused through more social groups and geographical areas than it had been previously. Consciously or unconsciously, all of these men and the tsar as well acknowledged that normal functions of public life would have to be divided among a greater variety of agencies than had ever before been required in Russia. In short, they accepted institutional growth and change as a fact. The capacity of the Russian autocracy to absorb these lessons without significant backlash and to translate criticism into seriously conceived innovations attests to a greater vitality than might generally be ascribed to it.

V | New Reforms, Changed Conditions, Old Habits, 1864-1870

Government commissions charged with reforming Russia's provincial institutions had largely completed their work by 1864. True, serious disputes stalled the judicial code for another year and plans for new urban institutions lay on ministerial tables for another half decade.[1] But the concerted effort to improve local administration by enhancing the governors' sphere of initiative and by excluding the executive police from purely local affairs had received formal expression. Similarly, the text of statutes establishing regional elective bodies free from overt bureaucratic interference were published for all who could read. Though the notions had been softened and even transmuted through years of debate, some forms of administrative decentralization and provincial self-government existed as legislative realities by 1864. Only one question remained to be answered: how would the reformed institutions function in practice? Firm conclusions, of course, demanded the experience of generations. Over the remaining years of the

[1] G. I. Schreider, "Gorod i gorodovoe polozhenie 1870g.," *Istoriia Rossii v XIX veke*, VI, 13-16.

decade, though, the new organs were sufficiently tested to allow us now to gain some perspective on the reforms which had fostered them.

UNDERGOVERNMENT AND THE ZEMSTVOS

Few legislative acts of the reform era met with such general approval as the *zemstvo* statutes promulgated on January 1, 1864. In Petersburg, Moscow, and provincial centers local publicists vied with one another in lauding the commission's work.[2] Joining in this paean were many provincial governors, stirred to benevolence by the confidence that they too would soon receive new independence thanks to programs of deconcentration in the administration. Astonishingly few observers voiced scepticism and those who did generally spoke from the standpoint of one or another unsatisfactory west European model which they accused the Russian legislators of having borrowed wholesale. Thus, *The Bell* criticized the *zemstvo* statutes by drawing parallels between them and the French code of 1852,[3] as had the *Odessa Messenger* somewhat earlier.[4] Such reservations met with little sympathy. To all appearances 1864 was indeed "the year of the *zemstvo* institutions," as a contemporary journalist dubbed it.[5] At last impediments to local civic action had been abolished and, in the words of a later Russian historian, the gates opened to "years of peaceful development."[6]

However genuine, such buoyancy cannot be taken as a full description of the situation. For, on the one hand, it was frequently based upon an overly sanguine reading of the legislative documents—when they were read at all; by

[2] For an exhaustive analysis of the press reaction to the *zemstvo* reform see Kirshman, *Pechat Peterburga i Moskvy* . . . , pp. 1-229.

[3] *Kolokol*, No. 185 (May 15, 1864), 1517-20.

[4] *Odesskii Vestnik*, No. 6 (January 15, 1863), 24-25.

[5] *Vestnik Evropy*, No. 4 (1867).

[6] For this interpretation see S. S. Tatishchev, *Imperator Aleksandr II* . . . , II, Bk. 4.

ignoring qualifying statutes enthusiasts convinced themselves that the state had devolved more powers on local communities than it had actually intended to do. On the other hand, such optimists assumed wrongly that legislative prescriptions could be actualized without the slightest alteration within a highly unsettled and at the same time tradition-bound society. Events proved otherwise. It is my contention that programs for devolution and administrative deconcentration underwent substantial changes when introduced in practice after 1864 and that these alterations were the natural consequences of conditions both internal and external to the local institutions themselves. The internal factor that altered the reforms was the continuity of prereform attitudes and habits that were carried over into the new situation. The external circumstances that contributed most to the reshaping of local government in Russia after 1864 was the further sharpening of the political and economic tensions that had been felt since 1862. Together, these two elements stamped their indelible mark on local institutions and, while leaving the reforms largely intact, transformed many of their most visible and important aspects.

The first eighteen *zemstvos* were formed in the spring of 1865, over a year after the promulgation of the statutes. Each year thereafter several more were founded until a total of thirty-four was reached by 1870. Since considerable preliminary work by commissions of local administrators had to be undertaken before a *zemstvo* could open,[7] bureaucratic factors rather than local ardor determined the speed with which any particular province or district received the new agencies. It fell to the governor to inaugurate the provincial assembly, usually with an avuncular oration on the unity of interest between *zemstvos* and the

---

[7] These commissions consisted of the marshals of the provincial and district gentry, the police *ispravniki*, town heads, administrators from the Ministry of State Domains, and the governor; "Pravila o poriadke privedeniia v deistvie Polozhenie o zemskikh uchrezhdeniiakh," TsGIA-SSSR, f. 1282, op. 2, d. 1801, p. 2.

administration. The meetings that followed frequently lasted as long as ten hours, providing time for all to test their forensic skills. Since delegates were forbidden to bind themselves beforehand to any particular position, they were more free to practice politics at the *zemstvo* meetings.[8] No matter what the agenda, though, it seems rarely to have interfered with the essentially social character of the annual sessions. From the outset great banquets and receptions added color to *zemstvo* gatherings at all levels, attracting many who would not otherwise have attended. No wonder that decades later veterans of *zemstvo* conflicts looked back on these founding sessions as a time of promise when it was expected that, in Boris Chicherin's words, "Russia would be renewed by her provinces."[9]

Such optimism and conviviality was engendered in large measure by the fact that most early *zemstvo* leaders had long known one another through gentry assemblies and had merely transferred their venue of meeting to the new bodies. Gentry spokesmen in the *zemstvos* included such distinguished activists from the post-Crimean years as Alexander Unkovskii, Alexander Golovachev, Vladimir, Cherkasskii, Alexander Koshelev, Iurii Samarin, Boris Chicherin, Alexander Platonov, Fedor Ofrosimov, and Count Orlov-Davydov. Former opponents of emancipation were at least as well represented as the reformers and received support for a class program from scores of new members.

That the gentry dominated the actual proceedings is attested by several contemporary observers, both Russian and foreign.[10] As the British traveler Mackenzie Wallace noted, however, this was due not so much to aristocratic disdain for the peasantry as to the numerical preponderance of the former masters. During the early years after 1864, the

[8] *Ibid.*, p. 14.

[9] Boris Chicherin, *Vospominaniia Borisa Nikolaevicha Chicherina:* . . . *Zemstvo i Moskovskaia Duma*, Moscow, 1934, p. 20.

[10] *Ibid.*, p. 24; D. Mackenzie Wallace, *Russia*, New York, 1887, p. 216.

gentry and civil servants accounted for fully 74 percent of the total membership in the provincial assemblies, while peasants numbered slightly under 11 percent. At least one provincial assembly contained no peasants at all.[11] In the provincial directorates the peasantry fared better, with 18 percent as against the gentry's 66 percent.[12] The district assemblies included the strongest peasant representation since election was direct from the communes. For the period from 1866 to 1871 peasant representation in district assemblies equaled that of the gentry (41 percent each) which, given the fact that district *zemstvos* together numbered about six times more members than the provincial assemblies, is by no means inconsequential.[13] Indeed, this condition caused more than a few leading oligarchists to turn against the *zemstvos* by 1867,[14] in spite of the fact that even in district assemblies the gentry could and did dominate discussions.

This situation was precisely what had been predicted by those who in 1862 had argued for low property qualifications for delegates—at best the *zemstvos* lacked a firm solidarity between the gentry and peasantry, even when interclass relations were outwardly cordial.[15] At the worst, the *zemstvos* might dwell on legislation of a narrow class character. Typical was the effort launched in several provincial and district assemblies to reverse the 1863 rule which forbade the wealthiest landholders to participate in *zemstvos*

[11] Chicherin, . . . *Zemstvo i Moskovskaia Duma*, p. 24; *Obzor tsarstvovaniia gosudarstva Imperatora Aleksandra II i ego reformy 1855-1871*, St. Petersburg, 1871, pp. 371-72.

[12] *Obzor tsarstvovaniia . . .* , pp. 371-72.

[13] *Ibid.*, p. 370, cf. Svatikov, *Obshchestvennoe dvizhenie . . .* , p. 202; Veselovskii, *Istoriia zemstva . . .* , III, p. 49. The remaining 18 percent was made up of urban residents and other representatives, some of whom had been added unofficially at the discretion of local authorities.

[14] G. B. Blank, "Novgorodskaia gurbernskaia zemskaia uprava," *Vest*, No. 3 (1866); Kirshman, *Pechat Peterburga i Moskvy . . .* , pp. 194, 204.

[15] TsGIA-SSSR, f. 651, op. 1, d. 704, p. 9.

without election.[16] More sinister was a scheme to introduce work books for the peasants to reduce the inconvenience experienced by the gentry in hiring labor. Both were finally rejected out of hand.[17]

Probably the most ambitious of the many pro-gentry measures of the early period was the nearly universal attempt to found landlord mutual mortgage banks. As conceived by the Commission on Banking these were to have been truly *zemstvo* banks for the entire populace, including the peasant communes. As actually proposed, though, they assumed an exclusively gentry orientation, generally requiring individually owned land as collateral. Such exclusionary practices were more objectionable because the initial funds for the proposed institutions were to have been drawn from the former accounts of the local provisioning agencies, a reserve that had everywhere been built as much from communal peasant contributions as from gentry deposits. Scarcely half a dozen such proposals actually reached fruition, however,[18] and of these only one, that sponsored by the energetic Kherson *zemstvo*, attained any measure of success.[19] The others collapsed under a barrage of pressures, among which the most crippling proved to be a governmental ruling forbidding the use of provisioning funds for such purposes and the scarcity of alternative capital.

The debate over local mortgage banks revealed another striking—and in this case, enduring—characteristic of the new *zemstvo* organs: their general antiurban cast and their tendency to reflect and intensify rural-urban divisions. The level of urban representation—6 percent in district assemblies and 10 percent in provincial assemblies was just and corresponds roughly to the level of urbanization at that time.[20] As a result of their minority status, however, urban

[16] Veselovskii, *Istoriia zemstva . . .* , III, 52ff.

[17] *Ibid.*, II, 107-10.

[18] See *Moskovskie Vedomosti*, No. 170 (1870).

[19] Veselovskii, *Istoriia zemstva . . .* , I, 31-34.

[20] Figures are for the period of 1865-70. *Obzor tsarstvovaniia . . .* , pp. 370-72.

dwellers could not effectively resist the various mortgage bank proposals. Occasionally, town representatives struck back effectively at the rural interests. The refusal of urban delegates in several *zemstvos* to support proposals that would provide services to rural areas commensurate to their tax contribution is a case in point. An embittered contemporary observed that "Odessa, to which the neighboring districts annually give millions of *puds* of grain for which they pay in sweat exceeding even the *puds* of gold saved in the metropolis, gives those districts back only two or three thousand rubles for schools."[21] This sum, he noted, was less than the "mercantilists, burghers and *meschane*" of Odessa would gamble away on cards after *zemstvo* meetings. Such attitudes reflect the growing rivalry between the town merchants, who comprised 76 percent of urban delegates to the *zemstvos*, and the rural gentry.[22] Though natural in a developing economy such as Russia's, this rural-urban conflict in the early *zemstvos* aroused more hostility than it would have under purely bureaucratic rule and discredited self-rule in the eyes of critical officials.

At the same time, the *zemstvos* inherited many attitudes from the old gentry assemblies, even while the latter bodies continued to meet. Acknowledging this, the ministries from the outset showed a strong inclination to treat the new organs as they had formerly treated the provincial lords. Though in hindsight it is easy to condemn officialdom for its inflexibility, several events that occurred as the *zemstvos* were being established had the effect of blurring in administrative minds the line between the new bodies and the old. Among these the address delivered at the Moscow gentry assembly in 1865 calling for an oligarchic national *zemstvo* was the most important.[23] At once the Ministry of Internal

[21] Anon., "Pervoe desiatiletie zemstva," *Otechestvennye Zapiski*, ccxxi, No. 10 (1875), 424ff.

[22] Veselovskii, *Istoriia zemstva . . .* , iii, 52.

[23] TsGIA-SSSR, f. 1341 (First Department of the Senate), op. 182 (1865), d. 1, pp. 795ff.

Affairs reprimanded the gentry, closed the journal which had used a government press to publish the address,[24] and informed all provincial governors that any similar calls for a national *zemstvo*—whether from a gentry assembly or one of the new all-class bodies, should be met with the utmost severity.[25] The *zemstvos* were served notice that, to cite the governor of Petersburg's strictures to his local assembly, "Only a strictly law-abiding self-government can be strong; only such a *zemstvo* can have the respect of authority."[26]

It proved easier to declare that *zemstvos* should be law abiding than to delineate in practice their sphere of activity. During the years from 1865 to 1870 each *zemstvo* assembly had to repeat for itself many of the debates held earlier in the governmental commissions on the question of competence. For example, in 1856-1858 several governors had urged that certain postal functions be transferred to local administrative bodies. Then eight years later the *zemstvos* of Kherson and Novgorod requested the right to maintain postal horses and stations on their account rather than on that of the wasteful local administration.[27] When the Postal Department acceded to this, several other *zemstvos* submitted similar requests, by 1870 going so far as to inquire about setting up provincial postal systems for private use. Though flatly contradicting earlier decisions, the government allowed such localized mail services to be established everywhere in 1871 and to remain in operation until 1917.

A second area requiring practical definition was the old problem of *zemstvo* participation in the allocation of national taxes. The State Council had voted in 1863 to exclude

[24] *Vest* (January 14, 1865); the text was later published by Iordanskii, *Konstitutsionnoe dvizhenie . . .* , pp. 141ff.

[25] On this issue see Valuev, *Dnevnik*, II, 13-15; Kornilov, *Obshchestvennoe dvizhenie . . .* , p. 172; and Veselovskii, *Istorii zemstva . . .* , III, 96ff.

[26] A. A. Suvorov-Rumynskii, quoted in Veselovskii, *Istoriia zemstva . . .* , III, 99.

[27] Veselovskii, *Istoriia zemstva . . .* , II, 684.

the *zemstvos* from any role in the national tax system. Then in the autumn of 1864 the Minister of Finances, Mikhail Reutern, asked the tsar to reconsider this decision.[28] He now doubted the ability of provincial administrations to carry out the apportionment of national levies in an efficient manner and continued to resent the enhanced power of the governors. Though supported strongly by *zemstvo* petitions, Reutern's argument failed, largely because Valuev had meanwhile swung back to the other side. The bill died in 1866.[29]

A jurisdictional problem that the drafters of the *zemstvo* statutes had completely neglected to consider concerned the construction and operation of railroads. During 1865 the outspoken *zemstvo* organ *The Petersburg News* (*Sankt-Petersburgskie Vedomosti*) and Katkov's *Moscow News* both called for *zemstvo*-sponsored rail lines, and their pleas were echoed by *zemstvo* assemblies in Kazan, Kaluga, Kherson, Novgorod, and elsewhere.[30] Yet in spite of widespread interest, only one such proposal actually materialized—a short line running between Saratov and a neighboring district capital.[31] By 1867 the ministries were rejecting out of hand all *zemstvo*-sponsored railroad projects and a short while later even the Saratov *zemstvo* assembly split over whether the requisite capital outlays should be sustained by local resources. Beyond this lay still another point of contention: whether such local undertakings should be managed at the provincial or district level. During the 1860s the provincial *zemstvos* were rarely in overt competition with the district groups, but already the

[28] TsGIA-SSSR, f. 572, op. 1, d. 7, pp. 149-57. *Ob uchastii zemskikh uchrezhdenii v mestnykh rasporiazheniiakh nekotorykh gosudarstvennykh raskhodov,* October 30, 1864.
[29] TsGIA-SSSR, f. 572, op. 1, d. 67, pp. 95-96, Panin to Reutern, June 26, 1866. After its demise Valuev published the defunct bill "for those that might be interested." *Ibid.,* p. 99.
[30] See especially *Moskovskie Vedomosti,* No. 33 (1865).
[31] "Pervoe desiatiletie . . . ," No. 10 (1875), 430-34.

beginning of tension between the two and the rise of the "Districtists" (*uezdniki*) can be detected.

So frequently did such jurisdictional questions as these arise during the initial phase of *zemstvo* operations, and the process of adjudication with the administrative hierarchy was so time-consuming that many assemblies felt intimidated. The case of the Smolensk delegates in 1872-1873 arguing earnestly whether the statutory phrase "the improvement of life" referred to provincial or national measures is perhaps a ludicrous extreme.[32] But after having once transgressed, if only unintentionally, the line between national and local affairs, a *zemstvo* assembly tended to become cautious to the point of timidity—more concerned, as Alexander Koshelev complained, with staying within its powers than in doing its work.[33] Here the continued hold of traditional patterns of subordination to the capital is particularly evident, even among those who had proclaimed their independence from such attitudes. Such were the origins of the "small deeds" reformism that characterized so much local initiative in Russia through the end of the nineteenth century.

Side by side with their small deeds, the early *zemstvos* carried out numerous programs whose scope and social value more than fulfilled the hopes of early advocates of public self-rule. The importance of some of these, such as the singing classes for peasants in Nizhnii Novgorod province, lay mainly in the social intercourse and goodwill they engendered.[34] Others, such as the all-out measures taken against the widespread cholera epidemic of 1871, affected the lives of millions of persons and convinced even impassive government inspectors of the *zemstvos'* effectiveness.[35]

[32] *Ibid.*, No. 7 (1875), 341.
[33] A. Koshelev, *Golos iz zemstva*, Moscow, 1869, p. 15.
[34] "Pervoe desiatiletie . . . ," No. 7 (1875), 136.
[35] S. R. Count Leuchtenberg, "Svod otzyvov o neudobstvakh sushchestvuiushchei sistemy politseiskogo upravleniia," *MSVUK, otdel politseiskii*, iii, otd. 2, p. 43.

The first *zemstvo* responsibility to which assemblies directed their attention was the execution of the so-called natural duties: road building, the quartering of troops, etc. The 1864 statutes had specified that these should henceforth be conducted on the basis of hired labor rather than direct corvée; the additional cost, advocates of self-administration had argued, would be more than offset by the efficiency introduced by the new system. But after much discussion *zemstvos* generally decided to ignore the statutes and continue to levy such duties in labor rather than money. As the Kharkov delegates reasoned, it would be unjust to force a peasant to pay a tax which he could not bear when he would willingly pay in labor.[36] Such arguments prevailed in all but forty districts of Russia,[37] and continued in force until the turn of the century when more peasants were spending part of each year in cities and were unable to pay in labor. Notwithstanding this complication, when an official observer checked the roads of Iaroslavl and Kostroma provinces a few years after the *zemstvos* assumed responsibility for their maintenance he acknowledged a marked improvement. Nor did the military find much to criticize in the *zemstvos'* execution of another "natural duty," the quartering of troops.[38]

In a nation whose chief building material was wood, the quality of fire insurance available becomes a prime gauge of civil well-being. Prior to 1864, the only Russians having access to this essential service were those living in Petersburg where it existed thanks to the self-government reform of 1844, and those few state peasants for whom it had been provided by the Ministry of State Domains. The rest of Russia's rural and urban dwellers of all classes depended on sporadic operations by the bureaucratic Offices of Public

[36] S. A. Olkhin, *Svod suzhdenii i postanovlenii zemskikh sobranii o zemskikh povinnostiakh*, St. Petersburg, 1868, pp. 118ff.; Veselovskii, *Istoriia zemstva . . .* , I, Chap. 10.

[37] Veselovskii, *Istoriia zemstva . . .* , I, 182.

[38] Leuchtenberg, "Svod otsyvov . . . ," p. 53.

Provisioning. The successful entry of the provincial *zemstvos* into this neglected area was therefore warmly received. Thanks to supplemental legislation of April 7, 1864, *zemstvo* fire insurance became a compulsory service for inhabitants of a province.[39] Though technical problems of assessment and premiums were not everywhere resolved in the most expert fashion, by 1870 the *zemstvos* of thirty-one of the provinces of European Russia were providing Russians with a security they had never before enjoyed.[40]

Many services executed by the Russian *zemstvos* would in the more developed institutional environment of western Europe have been performed by private corporations or philanthropic societies.[41] Fire insurance fell into this category, as did the livestock insurance programs initiated by eight provincial *zemstvos* in the 1860s, the publication of basic statistical and ethnographic studies by the Kherson *zemstvo*,[42] and numerous other undertakings pioneered by the provincial bodies after 1865. As we have seen, however, the underinstitutionalization of the Russian countryside extended into areas that had traditionally been under the nominal jurisdiction of the state. Such were road building, supervision of forests, the management of credit institutions, the administration of vaccinations, and the planning of measures against epidemics. In all of these spheres the *zemstvo* organs worked to achieve what neither private initiative nor state sponsorship had accomplished: the development of agencies free from bureaucratic inertia and endowed with the power to act. Even before 1870 it was evident that they had achieved a measure of success. The growth of *zemstvo* receipts from a total of 10,309,000 rubles in 1868 to 20,656,000 in 1871 indicates this, as does the steady rise in the percentage of funds devoted to activities instituted by the *zemstvos* themselves rather than assigned

[39] Veselovskii, *Istoriia zemstva* . . . , II, Chap. 28.
[40] Leuchtenberg, "Svod otzyvov . . . ," p. 48.
[41] See Vasilchikov, *O samoupravlenii*, II, 90ff.
[42] "Pervoe desitiletie . . . ," No. 10 (1875), 433-34.

them by the state.[43] In 1871 nonobligatory expenditures reached 43 percent of the total, in 1875, 50 percent, and in 1901, 85 percent. Clearly, organs of regional self-rule had gone far to provide needed services to the undergoverned Russian countryside.

Had this been the complete record of the early *zemstvos* they would have justified the brightest hopes for the future. But from their foundation the new bodies were plagued by complications so serious as to lead sober-minded Russians to cast doubt on their chances of success and the *Times* of London to announce their failure.[44] In some cases these difficulties prevented district and provincial assemblies from initiating programs for which their own members had fought successfully during the legislative battles and which were now well within the competence of the *zemstvos*. Medicine, for example, had been cited by Alexander Vasilchikov in his book, *On Self-Government*,[45] as an area demanding particular attention from the new agencies. Yet even the Tver *zemstvo* of which Vasilchikov was a member furnished only a modest level of medical services for the first half-decade, doing little prior to the organization of the first congress of doctors there in 1871.[46] By comparison to other provinces, though, Tver's record in medicine was brilliant. As late as 1868, 50 district *zemstvos* had allocated no money at all to medicine, and another 126, while earmarking a few rubles to this purpose, refrained from hiring doctors.[47] In the years before 1870 the picture was anything but encouraging.

A similar condition existed with schools. When the journal *Notes of the Fatherland* sent a reporter out to inspect the nation's *zemstvos* in 1874 he discovered that few prov-

---

[43] See Veselovskii, *Istoriia zemstva* . . . , I, pp. 14, 251.
[44] Cited by Nikitenko, *Dnevnik*, III, 70-71.
[45] Vasilchikov, *O samoupravlenii*, II, 465.
[46] *Sbornik materialov po istorii Tverskogo gubernskogo zemstva, 1866-1886*, Tver, 1887, 4 vols., III, 1, 18ff.
[47] Veselovskii, *Istoriia zemstva* . . . , I, 327, 361.

inces had any serious intention of fulfilling their statutory mandate in this area and that most, in fact, were shirking their responsibilities.[48] This reporter's impression is sustained by data on expenditures for education; by 1871 the total educational budget of all but four provinces was less than 80,000 rubles each, the average expenditure per capita for the thirty-four provincial *zemstvos* being as low as 3.03 kopeks per annum.[49] Throughout Russia before 1870 the *zemstvos* commonly sought to pass responsibility for education either to the local arbiters of the peace, to church institutions and parish priests, or to the very peasant communes which presumably were the object of the campaign for enlightenment.[50]

In many provinces road building fared little better than medicine and schools, notwithstanding the substantial gains cited above. Livestock insurance programs were not instituted beyond the eight provinces that pioneered in them, and with some notable exceptions veterinary services failed to touch the "deaf" villages where they were most needed. Something was clearly amiss.

On the most obvious level the problem was the primordial one of personnel. Insurance programs required agents; road building required surveyors and draftsmen; schools required teachers; medicine required doctors; and all *zemstvo* activities required directorates staffed with secretaries, accountants, and controllers. Together these specialists and functionaries constituted what a journalist later dubbed the *zemstvos'* "Third Element." In the 1860s,

[48] "Pervoe desiatiletie . . . ," No. 7, July 1875, pp. 344, 368.

[49] Figures derived from data in Veselovskii, *Istoriia zemstva . . . ,* I, 567-68.

[50] On arbiters of the peace see F. Shcherbina, *Voronezhskoe zemstvo za 1865-1889 gg.: Istoricheskii-statisticheskii obzor,* Voronezh, 1891, pp. 495-529; on clergy see *Sbornik postanovlenii Vladimirskogo zemskogo sobraniia 1865-1895 gg.,* 4 vols., Vladimir, 1896, I, 5-15; on communal schools see A. K. Reingardt, *Istoriia nachalnoi shkoly v Orlovskoi gubernii; ocherk deiatelnosta mestnykh zemstv, 1866-1895.* Orel, 1896. On these issues see also Veselovskii, *Istoriia zemstva . . . ,* I, Chaps. 28-40.

305

though, this force had scarcely begun to coalesce. To be sure, gifted teachers would occasionally emerge as if by spontaneous generation from the peasantry,[51] but a far more common occurrence was for *zemstvos* to allocate funds to local schools and have them returned for lack of teachers.[52] And schools were not the only area in which *zemstvos* experienced this frustration. Petersburg legislators of the fifties and early sixties, in their eagerness to renounce what they referred to as "the bureaucratic principle," had completely neglected to make any provisions to train the requisite *zemstvo* specialists and technicians.[53] To make up for this oversight was thus a prime policy objective for *zemstvos* during the succeeding half century. The fact that the preparation of skilled cadres of professionals for the performance of local services became at least as great a concern of the *zemstvos* as of the central administration helps in part to explain the gulf that eventually opened between the "Third Element" and the state.

In large measure the obstinacy of personnel problems may be traced to another age-old stumbling block, the lack of funds. According to the *zemstvo* statutes the chief source of revenue was to be a tax on agricultural and forest land; in practice this levy yielded 75 percent of the *zemstvos'* total income in the 1860s. The remaining revenue derived about equally from taxes on other immovable property, from trade and industry duties, and from a number of minor levies on capital gains, turnpike traffic, etc. Together these fell far short of the needs in nearly every province.[54]

[51] "Pervoe desiatiletie . . . ," No. 7 (July 1875), 135.

[52] Ia. V. Abramov, *Chto sdelalo zemstvo i chto ono delaet? (Obzor deiatelnosti Russkogo zemstva)*, St. Petersburg, 1889, pp. 85ff.

[53] By contrast, Dmitrii Miliutin's military reforms fully anticipated this need. See Forrestt A. Miller, *Dmitrii Miliutin and the Reform Era in Russia*, Nashville, 1968, Chap. 4.

[54] Data from Veselovskii, *Istoriia zemstva . . . ,* I, 38ff. See also Anatole Leroy-Beaulieu, *The Empire of the Tsars*, Z. A. Ragozin, trans., 3 vols., London and New York, 1893, II, 176.

A special commission on the revenue issue in Smolensk spoke for local agencies throughout the empire when it declared that "our whole problem is caused above all by the absence of resources in the general public and in the peasant communes."[55] To remedy this, the Russian *zemstvos* anticipated the actions of provincial agencies in low-income nations everywhere and undertook an exhaustive search for new taxable resources. Boris Chicherin, the former apologist of central administrative control and now a delegate in the Tambov provincial *zemstvo*, speculated on the possibility of taxing the crown lands. Elsewhere levies on cottage manufacturies were considered, as well as taxes on farm produce.

Given the agrarian and antiurban majority of the early *zemstvos*, by far the most logical sources of additional revenue were levies on industry and trade. The 1864 legislation had empowered the *zemstvos* to take measures to promote commerce and manufacturers and had given them permission to tax the products as well. By the mid-1860s taxes on land had become so burdensome that gentry and peasant delegates willingly joined ranks to oppose further increases in land taxes.[56] Accordingly, wherever possible the *zemstvos* imposed substantial duties on gross receipts from trade and industry, particularly in the industrial western provinces.

Such a move put the Ministries of Finances and Internal Affairs on guard. The emancipation of the gentry's labor force in 1861 had temporarily retarded manufacturing as many industrial serfs fled the cities to claim land in their villages. Total investment in industry languished and the state began to consider seriously its future role in that

---

[55] Chicherin, . . . *Zemstvo i Moskovskaia Duma*, pp. 32-33.

[56] It must be acknowledged that the gentry's position on this matter included a generous measure of altruism. See, for example, the refusal of the Tver *zemstvo* to tax domestic cheese production because it would cause excessive hardship to the peasantry. "Pervoe desiatiletie . . . ," No. 7 (July 1875), 123.

sphere.[57] This occurred at a moment when governmental coffers were already reduced. So strained were the state's finances by 1866 that Minister of Finances Reutern proposed that all export of currency be banned, that foreign expenditures by the navy be curtailed, and that the servicing of internal loans to cover state debts be suspended so as to enable the economy to regain its footing.[58] Only two months after this rigorous belt-tightening, reports reached Petersburg on what the governors considered to be excessive taxation on provincial trade and industry.[59] Reutern and Valuev responded within days. Rather than simply establish temporary or even permanent ceilings, the two ministers forbade the *zemstvos* to tax anything except the immovable properties of manufacturing and commercial establishments.[60] Their law placed all raw materials and finished goods beyond the reach of *zemstvo* taxation. And in the same move, the state set maximum *zemstvo* imposts on wine and spirits, traditionally a rich source of revenue in Russia.[61]

These measures of November 21, 1866, tested the tolerance of the fledgling *zemstvos*. From Tambov, Petersburg, and other local assemblies came indignant charges against the ministries, to be followed by longer treatises enshrining the November laws as the first in a series of infamous measures by which the government hobbled provincial initiative.[62] Many critics pointed out that Reutern and Valuev had created a situation extraordinarily favorable to the

[57] Liashchenko, *History of the National Economy of Russia to the 1917 Revolution,* New York, 1949, pp. 477-78.

[58] TsGAOR, f. 678, op. 1, d. 620, p. 2. An extract from this memorandum was published by Zaionchkovskii in the notes to Valuev, *Dnevnik,* II, pp. 472-73.

[59] Tatishchev, *Imperator Aleksandr II . . . ,* II, 9.

[60] *PSZ,* XVI, otd. 2, No. 43874.

[61] *Istoricheskaia zapiska . . . ,* p. 345.

[62] See *Vest,* No. 7 (1867); Koshelev, *Golos iz zemstva,* pp. 11-14; and Golovachev, *Desiat let reform,* pp. 184-216; for the state's position see Count S. Iu. Witte, *Samoderzhavie i zemstvo . . . ,* St. Petersburg, 1907, p. 73ff.

merchant or industrialist: landowners commonly found themselves paying 100 rubles in taxes whereas traders of comparable wealth might have to pay as little as 30 rubles.[63] To a man, opponents of the trade and industries law vilified it as a frontal assault on the foundations of the economic system of local self-administration.

This charge was entirely appropriate so far as it went. But those who leveled it tended to underestimate drastically the meaning of Russia's broader economic evolution at the time. When the possibility of transferring the political, economic, and administrative center of gravity from Petersburg to the provinces was first discussed in the 1850s a profound and long-neglected truth had been forcibly brought to the attention of the public: for all the apparent centralization of the administration, the day-to-day life of Russia was lived on a local basis. We have seen how this awareness inspired scores of works devoted to provincial history, ethnography, and local economic conditions. This interest in provincialism was well grounded in economic reality, for a national market of exchange existed for only a limited number of commodities. Poor communications and transport hindered economic integration. At the end of the Crimean War the largest nation in Europe had well under 1,000 miles of rail lines to supplement a road system that was inadequate in any weather and nonexistent in autumn and spring; steam navigation on the major waterways was yet to be developed to its full potential due to the high cost of imported equipment. The limited development of manufacturing further discouraged the full development of a national market. It has been estimated that in 1861 there were fewer than 3,000 concerns worthy of being called factories, and these were concentrated in a few centers.

Under these circumstances it was not unrealistic to underscore the importance of local life at the expense of the national unit. Those who spoke of the coming of a different

[63] Golovachev, *Desiat let reform*, p. 197.

order of things did so as much by speculation as by concrete prognostication. One of the first Russians to detect the
source of future changes in the present was the economist
Ivan Vernadskii.[64] In the autumn of 1864 he entered the debate over provincial banks with a paper which he read at
the gentry assembly in Moscow and subsequently defended
before the Imperial Free Economic Society in Petersburg.
Vernadskii asked whether a single national banking system
or a series of provincial banks should exist, and he emphati-
cally opted for the former:

> . . . provincialism is yielding place to centralization. This
> is not taking place in the administrative and political
> sphere alone but in the economic and industrial sense as
> well; the improvement of means of communication, and
> [the introduction of] steam and electricity are smashing
> the narrow framework of local life and broadening the
> horizon of trade and commerce . . . by this means the
> most remote ties and controls are becoming possible.[65]

The autocracy officially encouraged this development,
warmly endorsing railroad entrepreneuers who promised
to build "an unbroken railroad line through twenty-six
provinces to link together the three capitals, our main in-
land waterways, the centers of our grain surpluses and two
ports on the Black Sea and the Baltic that are open almost
all year."[66] Such ambitious undertakings assumed the existence of nationwide control over the circulation of currency
and a body—public or private—competent to negotiate development loans from abroad. These demands necessitated
the formation of a State Bank in Petersburg; by the end of
the 1860s this governmental institution was so well devel-

[64] For a biased but competent general study of Vernadskii see N.
A. Tsagalov, *Ocherki Russkoi ekonomicheskoi mysli perioda padeniia
krepostnogo prava*, Moscow, 1956, pp. 365-428.
[65] I. V. Vernadskii, "O zemskikh bankakh," *Trudy Imperatorskogo
Volnogo Ekonomicheskogo Obshchestva*, 1864, vi, No. 4, p. 248.
[66] A. N. Kulomzin, ed., *Nasha zheleznodorozhnaia politika*, 2 vols.,
St. Petersburg, 1902, i, 38.

oped that it had established forty-three provincial branches, all of them strictly subordinated to the capital.[67] These innovations stood at the center of much official thinking after 1864. As they grew in importance they tended to reduce the *zemstvos* to being merely one factor in a complex web of policy considerations. The persistent inclination of officialdom to mount guard over its own sphere of activity to the exclusion of others further contributed to this demotion of the *zemstvos* to a lower level of priority. Their eyes set on broader economic issues and fearful lest the *zemstvos* appropriate any resources that the state might use to promote modernizing, Reutern and his colleagues in the Ministry of Finances acted logically, albeit harshly, in arresting the *zemstvos'* right to tax trade and industry.[68]

Zemstvo activists were slow to adjust to this government-imposed budgetary restriction. Once their initial indignation had cooled, however, they set to work to make the best of the situation. Most *zemstvos* established commissions to survey and reassess local properties in the hope that accurate apportionment of taxes would yield additional revenue.[69] So successful was this program that it alarmed local administrators who in several provinces challenged the new apportionments and even the *zemstvos'* right to carry them out.[70] At the same time, directorates of both district and provincial *zemstvos* redoubled their efforts to ensure that every ruble assessed was actually collected and deposited in their treasury. The failure of income to match the projected yields on taxes, along with the diminishing vol-

---

[67] *Ministerstvo finansov* . . . , I, 437-38; "Denezhnoe obrashchenie i Gosudarstvennyi Bank," *Istoriia Rossii v XIX veke*, VI, 80-87; Leroy-Beaulieu, *Un Homme d'état Russe* . . . , p. 29.

[68] Notwithstanding this prohibition, the *zemstvos* continued to derive income from taxing the overhead facilities of traders and manufacturers and from issuing various documents. See Veselovskii, *Istoriia zemstva* . . . , I, 38ff.

[69] See Chicherin, . . . *Zemstvo i Moskovskaia Duma*, pp. 34-35.

[70] Veselovskii, *Istoriia zemstva* . . . , III, 108-10.

ume of back-payments on tax deficits, constituted incontrovertible proof that this was not presently being done. Somewhere a weak link threatened the *zemstvo* tax system.

The culprits were those agents of the local executive police charged with responsibility for collecting all taxes in Russia. That the police should have continued to execute this vital public office even after the reform of 1864 seems glaringly at odds with the notion of local public autonomy and of functional specialization. Yet, as a practical matter the police agents, through the district *ispravniki* and their subordinates, had more contact with village life than did representatives of any other agency. Recognizing the difficulty and expense of establishing a *zemstvo* structure parallel to the executive police on this level, the legislators had simply left tax collection in police hands. The results were predictably bad. Police had to answer simultaneously to the central government for the collection of national taxes and to the *zemstvos* for the collection of local duties.[71] But whereas the ministries enjoyed a direct hierarchical control over police agents, the *zemstvos* had little control of any sort, with the understandable result that the *ispravniki* devoted most of their energies to the national levies at the *zemstvos'* expense. Spokesmen for self-government fulminated against this situation.[72] Individual *zemstvos* pondered means of rectifying it. Some petitioned for *zemstvos* to be allowed to collect their own levies. Others, less ambitious but more cunning, offered to pay the police a "fee" for successfully fulfilling their tax-collecting responsibilities. This Gogolian ploy proved quite successful until 1871 when the Senate forbade it categorically and backed its prohibition with a warning to those *zemstvos* wishing to express their "thanks" to the police to do so in nonmonetary ways.[73]

These strictures left the *zemstvos* fully subjugated to the

---

[71] N. N. "Zapiska odnogo iz prezhnikh gubernatorov," *Russkaia Starina*, xxx (January 1881), 139.

[72] Golovachev, *Desiat let reform* . . . , p. 199.

[73] A. Kuznetsov, *Sistematicheskii svod ukazov senata*, i, 339.

caprice of the executive police. When the police failed them they had recourse only to administrative sanctions. In a formal sense the executive police were to have been subject to juridical control,[74] but in practice the *zemstvo* directorate found it more expedient to bypass the courts and to complain directly to the governors. This they did with a vengeance, berating the local administrative heads with the shortcomings of the police and with the frequent and open derision shown by police agents toward *zemstvo* officials for their powerlessness.[75] But only rarely did such diatribes lead to the exercise of effective control; for all practical purposes the *zemstvos* remained at the mercy of their tax collectors.

By the end of the sixties more than a few *zemstvo* activists felt their condition to be helpless. The limitations imposed on their powers of taxation and their utter dependence upon the police for the collection of levies signified to these men that the *zemstvos* as constituted could never be true organs of public self-administration and provincial autonomy.[76] Many lost interest in *zemstvo* affairs. Mackenzie Wallace noticed the lack of internal debate and conflict at assembly meetings in the early 1870s and ascribed it to boredom;[77] the French political scientist, Anatole Leroy-Beaulieu, detected a similar absence of conflict between *zemstvos* and local administrators some years later and speculated that it was due to the impotence of the former.[78] As if acknowledging this as a fact, scores of *zemstvo* representatives followed their old habits formed in the days of the gentry assemblies and simply stayed away from meetings. In the years before 1870 the attendance at important annual meetings of provincial *zemstvos* ranged between 47 percent and 81 percent and was only slightly higher at the

---

[74] *MSVUK, otdel politseiskii*, Chap. 1, otd. 3, *Proekt obshchego uchrezhdeniia politsii*, p. 463.

[75] Veselovskii, *Istoriia zemstva . . .* , III, 113-14.

[76] Golovachev, *Desiat let reform . . .* , p. 199.

[77] Wallace, *Russia*, p. 215.

[78] Leroy-Beaulieu, *The Empire of the Tsars*, II, 173.

district level.[79] Poor attendance furthered *zemstvo* inefficiency and justified administrative incursions into their
work.[80] The State Council registered concern over this malaise as early as the winter of 1866-1867, and its Department
of Laws went so far as to propose that all representatives
failing to attend assembly meetings be replaced by state
appointees. Only the fact that the *zemstvo* quorum had already been set at a third of the members prevented the
State Council from acting upon this captious measure.[81]

A cynical onlooker might have taken sardonic pleasure
in seeing the autocracy planning measures to compel provincial delegates to attend the meetings of organs that Nikolai Miliutin had once promoted in terms of their utility as
"safety valves" for public agitation. But does this signify
that the *zemstvos* proved a failure during their period of
initiation? The case for such a conclusion is not convincing.
To be sure, there did take place a general decline in the
pioneering spirit of provincialism and public initiative that
was everywhere evident during the decade after the Sevastopol disaster. But such zeal, it may be argued, is always
more associated with the planning than with the institu-
tionalization of new departures. What was needed by the
late 1860s was not revolutionary euphoria so much as the
readiness to devote long hours to building up new infra-
structures. The majority of legislators in the early sixties
never intended this complex and demanding task to be the
work of the district or provincial assemblies; the function of
these bodies was rather to meet at infrequent intervals to
approve programs generally initiated by the directorates
and to check on the execution of these programs by the directorates' administrative "Third Element." What took
place during the years after 1864 was the predictable trans-

[79] Veselovskii, *Istoriia zemstva* . . . , III, 143.
[80] N. N., "Zapiska . . . gubernatorov," p. 141.
[81] TsGIA-SSSR, f. 1160, op. 1 (1866), p. 140. Valuev, *Dnevnik*, II, 177.

ference of the center of gravity in *zemstvo* life from the political to the administrative level, from the assemblies to the staffs of the directorate. This evolution, the fate of political movements everywhere, had a peculiarly Russian tinge as well, for during centuries of autocratic rule the bulk of public affairs had always slipped from the *dumas* and *zemskii sobors* back into administrative hands. This time, however, the administrators were on the *zemstvos'* own staffs. At the same time, the circumstances which had made provincial and antibureaucratic sentiment so strong while the *zemstvos* were being planned had changed considerably after 1864. The new institutions had to adjust to the now less aggressive localist mood, and the adjustment seemed to many to signify the end of self-government as it had been preached earlier. But, as we have noted, the main thrust behind the campaigns for self-government had been the pressing need to provide the underinstitutionalized provinces with the agencies and services essential to civil life. The *zemstvos* could not yet provide these due to the excruciating problems of personnel and finance, but they nonetheless laid the groundwork in many areas on which they could build over the succeeding decades.

CONTINUITY IN THE REFORMED ADMINISTRATION

It is impossible to appreciate fully the conditions of the new public agencies without at the same time considering the provincial administrations whose deficiencies so contributed to the *zemstvo* movement in the first place. Means of removing these shortcomings had been the specific concern of the Committee on Reducing Correspondence, of the reformist governors, of officials in the Ministry of Internal Affairs, of General Vasilchikov in Kiev, and of the Commission on Provincial and District Institutions. These individuals and groups proposed programs which tended to move in two complementary directions: first, they served to enhance the governors' powers and right of initiative by placing local functionaries of all ministries under his control and by enabling him to work more independently in respect to the central ministries. Second, their purpose was to revamp the entire police system by transferring most "economic" functions from the executive police to the *zemstvos* and by strengthening the remaining security police. It is important to point out that neither of these reforms—gubernatorial or police—had been instituted prior to the promulgation of the *zemstvo* statutes. The central offices of several southern and western provinces had been successfully reorganized along the lines proposed by Vasilchikov in Kiev, but it was June 1865 before this decentralizing scheme was applied throughout the empire.[82] Similarly, the broad principles of police reform had been confirmed by the tsar and applied as early as 1862 but only as "Temporary Regulations" which in 1864 had yet to receive their final definition. The resultant condition was anything but auspicious either for local administrators or for the *zemstvos*. During the very period when the new elective agencies were most in need of responsive local administrators, they instead found gubernatorial and police officials in an uncertain state of transition; and just as local officials were supposed to be devoting their full energies to their localities, their jobs were redefined and they were left groping desperately for a satisfactory relationship to their superiors in the capital.

A technological revolution occurring simultaneously with this search in the 1860s drastically reduced the range of possible solutions. Telegraphy was in a sense a Russian invention; a decade prior to S.F.B. Morse's work in the United States a member of the Petersburg Academy of Science, P. L. Schilling (1786-1837), had demonstrated the practicability of electromagnetic communication.[83] Except for a few experiments in the military, Nicholas' administra-

---

[82] *PSZ*, vi, No. 42180.

[83] See William L. Blackwell, *The Beginnings of Russian Industrialization*, Princeton, 1968, pp. 398-400.

tion failed to capitalize on this discovery, even though the telegraph would have facilitated the administrative concentration which his officials were trying vainly to achieve. Not until the late 1850s was the telegraph used in the Russian civil administration and even then only to a limited extent. Nikolai Muraviev-Amurskii, Governor-General of Eastern Siberia, was among the first to advocate its widespread use (after the collapse of his federative schemes).[84] Partly due to his urgings, the tsar thereafter allocated generous funds to telegraphy development. By the mid-1860s lines linked most provinces to the capital, a ready tool for powerful ministers and a crutch for insecure governors.

In the second half of the 1860s most provincial governors seemed delighted to resort to this aid even though the telegraph threatened, as a French visitor later remarked, to turn them into "secretaries shorn of all discretionary power, incapable of a decision [and] scared of the shadow of responsibility."[85] The reasons for which they so willingly abandoned their earlier demands for greater initiative and independence constitute the final chapter in the movement for decentralization within the state bureaucracy.

The prereformed administration had been structured on military lines and operated through quasi-military power relationships. The job of those at the top—or the center—was to formulate policy and the task of those below was to execute it. The slightest alteration of this simple formula was considered insubordination and cause for punishment. Though the aim of the decentralizers had been to adjust this blueprint to allow policy to be initiated at all levels and for two-way communications to be carried out, it was evident to all after 1864 that little if anything had changed. For instance, the Minister of Enlightenment happened once to be a guest at a provincial assembly where, in his opinion, incorrect procedures had been followed. Bypassing all nor-

---

[84] Letter to Grand Duke Konstantin Nikolaevich, October 1, 1858, cited in Ivan Barsukov, *Graf Nikolai Muraviev-Amurskii . . .* , I, 536.
[85] Leroy-Beaulieu, *The Empire of the Tsars*, II, 111-12.

mal channels, the minister acted on his own initiative to see that a reprimand was sent out from Petersburg within days.[86] On another occasion a respected provincial governor found himself in the capital on a brief holiday. Arriving at the country house of his ministerial superior for what he thought would be a social visit, he instead was handed orders to leave on an hour's notice to investigate a problem in remote Archangel.[87] Both situations reveal the extent to which the old military form of ministerial rule persisted after it had been officially denounced.

Such continuity was even more common as reformist governors passed out of office and were replaced either by nonentities or by men whose sole qualification was their impeccable military background. Even Valuev, who had never hesitated to propose military men for civil offices, scorned some of the post-1864 appointees as men "who know neither the region nor the administration."[88] Once set in motion, however, the return to the old policy of appointment proceeded apace: of the ten governors who supported a pitiable plea for help submitted to the tsar in 1869, not one had held a gubernatorial post prior to emancipation.[89] In addition, not one of the reformist governors who had responded to Lanskoi's great rescripts of 1856 and 1858 remained in office in 1870. A new generation had emerged which did not share the old concerns for administrative decentralization.

The continuity of earlier administrative practices and the demise of the reformist governors do not alone account for the changed attitude of provincial governors after 1864. Equally important was their highly unstable relationship with the new *zemstvo* organs. Russia's greatest historian of the *zemstvos* has taken pains to belittle the importance of the tensions which in fact existed between the state and so-

[86] P. D. Stremoukhov, "Iz vospominanii o grafe P. A. Valueve," *Russkaia Starina*, cxvi, April 1903, p. 284.
[87] *Ibid.*, p. 286.   [88] Valuev, *Dnevnik*, i, 33.
[89] MSVUK, iii, otd. 6, pp. 265ff.

cietal organs.[90] Yet such friction existed from the outset, and governors, plagued by the vague sense that they were slipping into the status of "very subordinate officials,"[91] struck out at real and imagined shortcomings of the elective bodies. In Simbirsk the governor accused the *zemstvo* of mismanaging the hospital, the Viatka governor accused his *zemstvo* of losing funds, and the Iaroslavl governor criticized the *zemstvo* for leading the welfare agencies to the verge of collapse.[92] Some of these splenetic attacks were patently false,[93] while others may be dismissed out of hand in light of the miserable *status ante quem*. Yet the widespread sense of rivalry which they reveal was serious indeed: the insistence of the governor of Tambov province that he be allowed to propose legislation to his *zemstvo*[94] was symptomatic of the mood that set in after the legislators failed to coordinate separate aspects of provincial reform that were planned simultaneously. Because of this failure of coordination the prospects of local administrators and *zemstvos* sitting together on the planned local super-agencies dwindled. In fact, not one Provincial Administrative Council was actually established.

Conflicts between governors and *zemstvos* followed a similar pattern everywhere: first the governor would lodge a protest with the elective body against its actions; then *zemstvo* leaders would complain over the governor's head to the ministries or Senate in Petersburg; finally the governor would attempt to defend himself before the same body. Rarely, if ever, were genuine conflicts between the public and the administration settled locally due to the absence of machinery in the provinces adequate for adjudicating such disputes. Nor could they readily be settled through force. Indeed, considering Russia's tradition of gubernatorial

---

90 See Veselovskii, *Istoriia zemstva* . . . , III, 104ff.
91 Wallace, *Russia*, p. 199.
92 *MSVUK, otdel politseiskii*, III, otd. 6, pp. 224ff.
93 *Ibid.*, pp. 249-52.   94 *Ibid.*, pp. 269ff.

stewardship, it is surprising that the governors had so few means at their disposal for compelling the cooperation of the *zemstvos* short of vetoing their legislation or refusing to confirm the appointment of elected officials.

The types of complaints lodged by governors against the *zemstvos* reveal the core of their concern. Most common were attacks on the local bodies for "exceeding their powers," which meant in practice anything from attempting to interrogate a vice-governor to initiating communications with the *zemstvo* of a neighboring province.[95] Summarizing his views on the local *zemstvos* in 1867, the Governor of Pskov declared that they needed "still more precise definition of the limits of their power and their duties must be brought in balance with their rights."[96] Almost as frequent were criticisms of the *zemstvos'* tax apportionments. Significantly, both criticisms touch on areas in which the governors and ministers had heretofore enjoyed unchallenged authority. This was precisely the root of the governors' dilemma: if the *zemstvos* had grounds for complaining of having been ceded competence but no power, the governors could argue with equal justice of having been left with ample power but only a limited sphere of competence. Accordingly, as the *zemstvos* worked to acquire the executive power essential to carry out their mandate, the governors campaigned overtly and covertly to be allowed to exercise their ample power in areas which the reforms had placed off limits to them. This is the dominant *motif* underlying many incidents of provincial life in the succeeding decades.

The chief reason that the governors could easily exercise power and the *zemstvos* could not is that the governors controlled the local executive police. But gubernatorial power had its own limits and these were particularly evident with respect to these same police. These agents of the state had been the object of considerable reformist energy earlier; in

[95] Veselovskii, *Istoriia zemstva* . . . , iii, 112.
[96] N. N., "Zapiska . . . gubernatorov," p. 159.

addition to removing *zemstvo* functions from their purview and asking for pay raises for police officers, the Commission on Provincial and District Institutions had hoped to increase efficiency by merging offices at the district and town levels and having the main agents in the districts, the *ispravniki*, appointed by the government rather than selected by the local gentry.[97] These efforts, entirely commendable in themselves, were all but inconsequential in the face of the problems that gave rise to them.

The difficulties of converting the old executive police into a modern corps of state servants are demonstrated in the attempts to increase their salaries. Once this was accepted as a worthy objective in 1859 the ministries set about finding the requisite funds. Since the Ministry of Finances remained in a virtual state of shock over its deficit, Reutern in 1862 suggested that fully three-fifths of the necessary 3 million rubles be borne by the *zemstvos*,[98] or, as would be the case in fact, by the local peasantry. Only a prudent reluctance to bleed the countryside further kept this from being enacted; and in 1866 the Commission on Taxes and Duties was still puzzling over ways of achieving the much-needed pay increases.[99] In the long run only modest gains were achieved and the police in many provinces began using their monopoly over the issuance of internal passports as an unofficial tax to make up for the government's failure to compensate them.[100]

As hopes for a real salary hike faded, attention turned to the related question of personnel. In the late 1860s police work fell, as it had earlier, to men deemed unfit for military service and to those with no prospects of achieving a posi-

[97] *MSVUK, otdel politseiskii,* I, otd. 3, pp. 24-26, 29ff. See also Robert J. Abbott, "Police Reform . . . ," Chap. II.
[98] *MSVUK, otdel politseiskii,* I, otd. 3, p. 115 (September 26, 1862).
[99] *Materialy o sborakh dlia usileniia soderzhaniia politsii,* May 1, 1865; *ibid.,* pp. 505-22; *Zhurnal II otdela komissii . . . dlia peresmotra sistemy podatei i sborov,* January 1866, *ibid.,* pp. 553ff.
[100] Leroy-Beaulieu reports that this yielded 3 to 4 million rubles annually, *The Empire of the Tsars,* II, 125.

tion of respect locally through other channels. Absolutely no tests had to be sustained beyond surviving a four-month trial period[101] and, even if it was hoped that police would have some schooling, as late as 1881 the capital's security police included many illiterates.[102] The few measures taken before 1870 to improve this situation were quite inadequate. Some officials suggested that the term of service be lengthened so as to enable men to remain on duty longer[103] while a plan to have the "tens" and "hundreds" (*desiatki* and *sotski*) appointed rather than elected received the endorsement of several governors.[104] Not one governor or central official, however, proposed that training programs be formalized and none of the various editions of the *Nakaz* on police work so much as mentioned the underlying problem of pay. Hence all the many suggestions fell short of establishing a truly professional executive force for the provincial and central administrations.

The grossly inadequate police staffs only exacerbated relations between the executive police and state and public agencies. On a modest level, the reformed police depended on the *zemstvos* for their horses and travel facilities, even when they were doing the government's business, just as they depended in their tax collection work on the goodwill of the communal elders.[105] Such inconveniences were symptomatic of the general failure of the reforms to spell out police duties with precision, particularly with respect to the *zemstvos*. In all the many legislative documents on the police ground out through 1865 there is not one specific discussion of the *zemstvo* institutions. Indeed, the first consideration of this critical issue came in a secondary document of 1866, *A Project on the Order and Forms of Procedure in*

---

[101] I. Tarasov, *Politsiia* . . . , pp. 62ff.

[102] Leroy-Beaulieu, *The Empire of the Tsars*, ii, 119.

[103] *MSVUK, otdel politseiskii*, 1, otd. 3, *O nekotorykh merakh k ulucheniiu uezdnoi politsii*, pp. 480ff.

[104] *MSVUK, otdel politseiskii*, 1, otd. 5, *Svod otzyvov o noudobstvakh sushchestvuiushchei sistemy politseiskogo upravleniia*, pp. 58ff.

[105] *Ibid.*

the Police.[106] Here, as *zemstvos* were opening across Russia, the government revealed for the first time that the earlier declarations on the segregation of *zemstvo* and police functions would not be honored fully and that a multiplicity of parallel agencies and responsibilities would exist at the provincial and district levels. Thus, both the *zemstvos* and the police would have medical staffs but "even in those districts and provinces where other civil doctors [i.e. *zemstvo* doctors] exist, the bulk of duties regarding all aspects of medical work lies principally with the [police]."[107] The same conditions were perpetuated in other spheres of *zemstvo* activity as well[108] and long after 1864 the executive police retained the multiple role of tax collector, sanitary engineer, architect, agent of the ministries, druggist, and inspector of roads, buildings, industry, and public welfare organizations. Lest anyone miss the point, the document goes on to specify seven areas in which the executive police could exercise the power of inspection and control over the *zemstvo* institutions. Not only were the police empowered to intervene in cases where the *zemstvos* exceeded their statutory powers but also in those cases where the "adequacy" of *zemstvo* measures was deemed "insufficient."[109] Insufficient to whom? Who could decide? According to all the relevant documents, the power to judge these matters was vested not in the courts but in the governor and the police.

It is surprising that the Commission on Provincial and District Institutions should have proposed such careless measures, for that same body advanced a detailed program for the relations between police and the new courts. By sanctioning parallel organs and granting to the police areas of control over the *zemstvo*, the Commission on Provincial

---

[106] MSVUK, *otdel politseiskii*, otd. 3, *Proekt instruktsii o poriadke i formakh deloproizvodstva v politsii*, pp. 389ff.

[107] *Ibid.*, p. 414.

[108] Tarasov, *Politsiia* . . . , pp. 72ff.

[109] *Ibid.*, pp. 421ff.

323

and District Institutions seemingly issued an open invitation to conflict. In Kherson, Vladimir, Kostroma, and elsewhere serious disputes developed between the executive police and the *zemstvos*.[110] Even if such conflicts were resolved the danger of further hostility remained so long as police power lacked sharp definition. This condition understandably frustrated the police themselves, who frequently refrained from acting against the *zemstvo* without first consulting the governor, a time-consuming procedure during which the *zemstvo* legislation stood in abeyance. The *zemstvos* reciprocated with undisguised contempt for the executive police, whom they accused of being better able to deal with horses than human beings and of treating *zemstvo* members as cattle.[111]

By 1870 Russians concerned with provincial affairs had to acknowledge that many of the worst features of the old system had survived to plague the new *zemstvos*. Once more provincial capitals buzzed with gossip of the venality of local agencies of government.[112] Once more governors struggled with an inundation of paperwork which is always the first product of poor administration.[113] As if signaling the completion of a cycle of reform, the governor of Orel used his report for 1869 to declare to the Minister of Internal Affairs that he believed relations between ministerial and police agencies and all other interests in the provinces to be on "a completely false road." Few could take exception to this. This condition, however, cannot be laid to some antireformist conspiracy in the higher bureaucracy, nor to the spread of "reaction" in the years after the reforms were promulgated, though both such tendencies were undeniably present. Far more important was the earlier fail-

---

[110] Veselovskii, *Istoriia zemstva* . . . , III, 111ff.

[111] "Pervoe desiatiletie . . . ," No. 8 (1878), 368-69ff; and Veselovskii, *Istoriia zemstva* . . . , III, 113-14.

[112] Leroy-Beaulieu wrote later on the police as if they had never been reformed. *The Empire of the Tsars*, II, p. 95.

[113] *Svod otzyvov* . . . , p. 79.

ure of the reformers to reckon fully with the attitudes and habits of the bureaucracy which they sought to reform. Rarely in the history of the Russian state had the introduction of a new institution been accompanied by the elimination of an older one; ordinarily the old agency continued to exist, either moving into a new sphere of activity or gradually claiming back its former functions. The basic principles of public self-government approved by Alexander II in 1859 specified that the centralized police agents would lose their role in local "economic" affairs entirely. This goal, so consistent with the ideal of local public initiative as practiced in the western European states, proved incompatible with Russian reality. The reinstallation of the executive police in many, but not all, of their former responsibilities represents the triumph of traditional administrative habits over the reformers' designs.

THE BRIDLING OF LOCAL INITIATIVE

The history of the postreform Russian province has been written largely by outspoken partisans of the *zemstvos* and supporters of any manifestation of centrifugal energy in the administration. Such predilections caused these writers to minimize the importance of constraints imposed on local authorities by the practical circumstances in which they existed, by their own heritage, and by the reforms themselves; instead they have blamed the reduction in localist fervor solely on efforts by the central government to bridle provincial initiatives. In sketching the development of the *zemstvos* and local administrations after 1864 we have underscored the neglected internal factors. Yet at the same time due recognition must be given to the antireformist machinations in Petersburg which have so frequently been cited as evidence that the reform era had ended.

No single event initiated the turn against the autonomy of local institutions. The centralizing currents which first made themselves felt during the debate on emancipation

325

and were then broadened during the years from 1861 to 1863 gained added momentum after 1864. Domestic radicalism and threats from abroad gradually convinced top administrators and the tsar of the need to preserve Russia's internal security by a return to the old practice of applying stringent measures from the center. The 1866 liberation of the millions of serfs owned by the state served to justify this policy in the same way that talk of emancipating the gentry's serfs had aided Muraviev's centralizing proposals in 1858.

This change was virtually a *fait accompli* when, on the afternoon of April 4, 1866, an attempt was made to assassinate Alexander as he strolled on the Summer Garden quay. Heartfelt expressions of gratitude at the "miraculous escape" poured into the Winter Palace by letter and telegram. *Zemstvos* across Russia shared in the general rejoicing, but deep fears alloyed their thankfulness. Few could share the optimism of the pro-*zemstvo* *Petersburg News* whose editors declared themselves convinced "that the crime of April 4 would not call forth a reaction."[114] After all, had not that old foe of local autonomy, Mikhail Muraviev, been called from retirement to head the commission to investigate the crime? And did not his investigation disclose that the would-be assassin, Dmitrii Karakazov, belonged to that class of small gentry with claims to education whose presence in the *zemstvos* so angered members of the court?[115] In its first days the feared reaction took the form of a sweeping cabinet change. The Ministry of Public Enlightenment was responsible for the university where the assassin was enrolled as a part-time student; at once the portfolio was taken from the then head of that ministry and handed over to the sinister Dmitrii Tolstoi. The Governor-General of Petersburg had allowed a dangerous criminal to go undiscovered in the capital; this official found his job

[114] *Sankt-Peterburgskie Vedomosti*, No. 122 (1866).

[115] Kn. V. P. Meshcherskii, *Moi vospominaniia*, 2 vols., St. Petersburg, 1898, II, 70.

eliminated and its functions allocated to a hard-fisted military man whose only prior distinction was having enforced order in the explosive Polish capital. Most important, the Chief of Gendarmes and Director of the Third Section was replaced with a terrifyingly able man known even to his intimates as "power loving" and "cunning"—General Count Peter Andreevich Shuvalov.[116] Shuvalov immediately established himself as the most powerful man in Russia excepting the tsar, and directed the full force of his authority toward tightening up the administration and restricting the freedom of all potentially dangerous groups including the *zemstvos.*

The tsar played at best a modest role in bringing about these ministerial changes which so strengthened the autocratic principle of rule. The removal of the Governor-General of Petersburg was initiated not by Alexander, who would have yielded to the tears of the incumbent, but by the newly appointed Count Shuvalov.[117] The institution of a new security official for the capital answerable only to the throne was also not Alexander's idea but the work of the administrative head of Poland, Count Fedor Berg, and of General Fedor Trepov; the general made the extra powers a condition of his assuming the new position.[118] And Prince Vasilii Dolgorukov, the Chief of Gendarmes, resigned on his own initiative within an hour after the attempted assassination. The tsar, taken completely aback by this unselfish gesture, at first tried to dissuade him; when he found Dolgorukov unrelenting, Alexander asked him whom he might turn to as a successor, to which Dolgorukov responded with Shuvalov's name.[119] Such incidents reveal with stark clarity the extent to which in crisis situations Russia's top bureaucrats needed the broad principle of autocracy[120] even if in daily practice they did not need the autocrat himself. This truth helps to explain the anxiety which all local

---

[116] *Ibid.*, pp. 62ff.
[117] *Ibid.*, pp. 33-36.
[118] *Ibid.*, p. 36.
[119] *Ibid.*, pp. 32-33.
[120] Valuev, *Dnevnik*, ii, 82.

initiatives, administrative or public, aroused in Petersburg during every crisis from the Crimean War to 1917.

The campaign waged against local initiatives by these new ministers and their allies could be carried out more easily because so few remained in the central administration to oppose them. In November 1866, Nikolai Miliutin suffered a near fatal stroke which removed him from service. Prince Vladimir Cherkasskii had resigned from the service after a nasty fight with the police administration, and both Iakov Soloviev and Viktor Artsimovich were by now far removed from power; when Baron Modest Korf retired from the Legal Section his opponents in the State Council carefully groomed a successor sympathetic to their side.[121] Even with these changes the new faces were slightly outnumbered by the old reform group in the Committee of Ministers, a situation which Shuvalov remedied by appointing Muraviev and other ministers *emeriti* to special seats on that body.[122] Through these changes the new forces gained a safe majority in the principal legislative bodies, leaving reformers such as Dmitrii Miliutin reduced literally to tears of frustration.[123]

The rise of Shuvalov's star was greeted with general fear that he would live up to the poet Tiutchev's estimation of him as "a second Arakcheev," with all the calculating sternness of Alexander I's adviser. Such fear was well warranted, for Shuvalov's cool and utterly confident manner enabled him to turn back to the traditional model of centralization as if he had himself discovered that technique of administration. His first measures were directed against the lawlessness which, widely noticed at the time,[124] was assumed to have been the soil from which the assassination attempt sprang.[125] The outspoken "radical" journals, *The Contempo-*

121 TsGIA-SSSR, f. 1291 (1863), op. 5, II, d. 65, pp. 216-23.
122 S. I. Seredonin, *Istoricheskii obzor* . . . , III, 135-38.
123 Valuev, *Dnevnik*, II, 228.
124 A. V. Nikitenko, *Dnevnik*, II, 393.
125 "O Razvitii idei kommunisticheskikh v Zapadnoi Evrope i

rary and *The Free Word* (*Svobodnoe Slovo*), were suppressed; measures were instituted against "nihilist women who wear no crinolines and round hats, blue glasses and short hair."[126] More concretely, approval was given for substantial increases in expenditures for security police, an old proposal of Muraviev's for a combined security and executive police command at the district level was revived,[127] as was Valuev's nearly forgotten proposal for small *vyt* units to serve as the lowest level of a highly concentrated security and administrative system.[128]

All of these various manifestations of the heightened preoccupation with security eventually focused on the governorship. Only a year earlier, the Vasilchikov program had been applied to all provinces of the empire. Now, in 1866 the new ministers noticed that this scheme, while rationalizing and deconcentrating administrative procedures, did nothing directly to enhance the powers of the central ministries. Yet, as Shuvalov observed in a memorandum to the tsar, "the correct structuring of administration in the provinces constitutes the chief means of preserving order and public tranquility."[129] He therefore resolved to strengthen the governors as much as possible, not as the earlier reformers had proposed, but by making them the local instruments of the autocratic will. At the same time that he made the subordinate governors directly dependent on directives from the capital, Shuvalov vastly enhanced their sphere of control. In a kind of inversion of the earlier deconcentration programs he empowered each governor, after consultation with Petersburg, to make surprise inspections of the local agencies of all ministries for the purpose of bringing

proiavlenii ikh poslednee vremia v Rossii . . . ," TsGIA-SSSR, f. 1149, op. vii, g., d. 31, partially quoted by Zaionchkovskii: Valuev, *Dnevnik*, ii, 481-82.

[126] TsGIA-SSSR, f. 1263 (1866), d. 3220, pp. 312ff.
[127] Valuev, *Dnevnik*, ii, 169.
[128] *MSVUK, otdel politseiskii*, i, otd. 3, pp. 186ff.
[129] Seredonin, iii, 130.

to light evidence of persons acting "against governmental order and security."[130] The governor could then require any public employee to appear before him for "questioning" and on the basis of this administrative trial, fire him. Shuvalov also applied this dark system of administrative justice against members of the judiciary, private persons, and heads of private societies, *artels*, corporations, and even the *zemstvos*.

Because it indirectly enhanced the power of the Ministry of Internal Affairs this program received Valuev's measured support. Since it all but guaranteed tranquility on the crown lands, it received the backing of Minister of State Domains Zelenyi. The ministries of justice and finances had solid grounds for opposing it, however; the former because it vastly expanded the sphere in which old forms of administrative justice prevailed and even placed the new judicial officers under it, and the latter because it would destroy the ability of the ministry to answer for the state budget.[131] Minister of War Miliutin also opposed the program on the grounds that the Vasilchikov reforms had already granted the governors all the power they required.[132] Notwithstanding these objections, Shuvalov and his supporters split the potential opposition in the Committee of Ministers and carried the day. Alexander II signed the new law on July 22, 1866; this convinced even the most optimistic that the spirit of the reform era had been drastically qualified.

By the autumn of 1866 rumors of a forthcoming *coup* against the *zemstvos* were daily gaining in plausibility as Shuvalov's administrative measures and the new law on taxing industry and commerce were instituted.[133] The Karakazov affair had electrified the political atmosphere in Petersburg and in the provincial centers; ministerial leaders and *zemstvos* each waited tensely for the other to over-

---

[130] *Ibid.*, pp. 130-38.   [131] *Ibid.*
[132] GBL, f. 169 (D. A. Miliutin archive), No. 15, d. 3, p. 206, partially cited by Zaionchkovskii: Valuev, *Dnevnik*, II, 469.
[133] Valuev, *Dnevnik*, II, 172.

step its bounds, knowing full well that such an occasion would subject the powers of each to hard and precise measurement for the first time. That occasion arose less than a year after Karakazov's assassination attempt and it occurred in Petersburg itself, in the same hall where a decade earlier the gentry assembly and Ministry of Internal Affairs had opened the first discussions on self-administration. Scarcely had the Petersburg *zemstvo* been called to order at its inaugural session in 1865 than a number of members proposed changes in the statutes to guarantee freedom from administrative interference, to assure them more funds, and to allow representatives of all *zemstvos* to form a national body.[134] The tsar and his advisers anxiously watched these actions but took no punitive measures. When the same spirit appeared during the next annual meetings, however, the post-Karakazov mood engendered a much tougher response from the government. This time the Petersburg *zemstvo's* directorate refused to comply with the ruling on commerce and industry on the grounds that the new law was promulgated after the *zemstvo* had drawn up its tax assessments for 1867. When the governor of the province interceded, the *zemstvo* at once drew into battle formation. Knowing full well that Valuev had sponsored the trade and industry bill and was otherwise hostile to the leadership of Petersburg province because of its outspoken support of Baron Korf's views, the local leaders decided after much debate to appeal directly to the Senate. Not only did the *zemstvo* appeal the governor's ruling on their tax assessments but it also forwarded to the Senate a personal attack on Valuev for failing to respond to twelve of their last twenty-six petitions. Valuev, of course, denounced the Petersburg assembly as a body of revolutionaries[135] while

[134] *Vest*, No. 27 (1865); Valuev, *Dnevnik*, II, 87, 90ff.; Veselovskii, *Istoriia zemstva . . .* , III, 100; S. G. Svatikov, *Obshchestvennoe dvizhenie . . .* , pp. 61-64.

[135] On this incident see Kornilov, *Obshchestvennoe dvizhenie . . .* , pp. 183-84; Valuev, *Dnevnik*, II, 184-85.

prominent *zemstvo* members in turn resigned from boards on which they had served with the minister. At length, over the objection of the Minister of Justice and Baron Korf, Shuvalov liquidated the Petersburg *zemstvo* on January 14, 1867, and exiled its president, a former official of the censorship, for four years to distant Orenburg. Other members of the directorate were either sent abroad or forced into retirement.

Judgments on these measures were as severe as were the punishments themselves. Valuev, who would have preferred to suspend rather than close the *zemstvo*, admitted that Shuvalov had outmaneuvered him;[136] the perceptive Nikitenko condemned the closure as a "fatal measure";[137] and the prominent *Moscow News* heaped scorn on government and *zemstvo* alike.[138] Long after the Petersburg assembly was permitted to reopen six months later it was acknowledged generally that public self-rule had suffered a complete rout in a battle that its partisans had courted intentionally.

This confrontation left Shuvalov more convinced than ever that the chief front on which to defend royal authority was not against Poles and nihilists but against the pretenses of the *zemstvos*. Even before the Petersburg confrontation he had drawn up a memorandum "On Introducing into the *Zemstvo* Assemblies a New Governmental Element. . ."[139] The crudity of this proposal rendered it unworkable and it was quickly dropped. Then, in June 1867, Alexander II approved a more subtle version of the same idea which Valuev had worked out for the Combined Departments of Law and Economy and for the State Council. The new law forced no government appointees on the *zemstvos* but instead held the presidents of assemblies and directorates to

---

[136] Valuev, *Dnevnik*, II, 182.   [137] Nikitenko, *Dnevnik*, III, 69.
[138] S. Nevedenskii, *Katkov . . .* , p. 440.
[139] Valuev, *Dnevnik*, II, 142. This proposal bears some resemblance to the right granted earlier to governors to appoint "governmental representatives" to the provincial committees on emancipation; cf. Soloviev, "Zapiski . . . ," May 1881, p. 29.

full account for the legality of any measure passed under their chairmanship. Specifically, presidents were expected henceforth to open and close all meetings, approve the agenda, cut debate on unscheduled topics, maintain order, and close the meeting in the event of any actions violating the general interests of the state. In other words, Valuev's "compromise" introduced Shuvalov's "governmental element" into the *zemstvos* by all but impressing their presidents into the police force. This law was applied at once to all clubs, societies, and organizations as well as to *zemstvos*, and placed vast realms of civic life under administrative rather than civil law.[140] In a similar vein, Valuev ordered his governors to report immediately and in detail to Petersburg on all *zemstvo* meetings, even while they were in progress.

On the same day that the law drawing assembly presidents into the police was signed, the tsar gave his assent to the first of several measures that stripped the *zemstvos* of the right and ability to communicate with one another. A major oversight of the legislators earlier had been to ignore the entire question of *zemstvo* publishing and the related issue of censorship of their public statements. These issues came innocently to the surface during 1865 and 1866: the *zemstvo* of Kharkov proudly sent word of its new tax system to neighboring provinces; the *zemstvo* of Petersburg hired a stenographer to record its meetings; the *zemstvos* of Tambov and Kazan published their proceedings without consulting the local governor; the *zemstvo* of Kherson established a newspaper of its own; the *zemstvos* of Kostroma, Samara, and Novgorod sought to establish their own publishing houses.[141] A communication network developed rapidly. So fast did it grow, in fact, that it threatened

---

[140] TsGIA-SSSR, f. 1149, op. vii, d. 75 (1867); Tarasov, *Politsiia* . . . , pp. 76ff.; Valuev implies that the original idea was Panin's which is scarcely likely since Panin defended the rights of the new court system as against administrative procedures, *Dnevnik*, ii, 189.

[141] Veselovskii, *Istoriia zemstva* . . . , iii, 65, 112, 126ff.

to swamp the government's struggling *Provincial News* sheets and to rival even the official organs of the ministries.

Provincial administrators sounded the first alarm. By 1866 several governors had complained to Petersburg of local resistance to their efforts to censure *zemstvo* publications. As Dmitrii Tolstoi took the reins of the Ministry of Public Enlightenment and Shuvalov tightened his grip on the security system, such conspicuous assertions of independence seemed marked for suppression. This occurred with a law of June 13, 1867, which categorically forbade publication of all *zemstvo* documents—newspapers, reports, proceedings, technical papers, etc.—unless they carried the governor's imprimatur.[142] Once more a chorus of criticism from all quarters, including prominent censors, met the government announcement.[143] The censorship successfully clamped down on criticism of itself, however, and the attack collapsed.

No sooner did public indignation on the publication law subside than further restrictions were imposed on the ability of *zemstvos* to communicate with one another. Interprovincial projects and relations of all sorts were forbidden. Next, the *zemstvos'* franking privileges were revoked. In Russia, the right to send mail free of charge was extended as a matter of course to corporations and charitable agencies as well as to local or public administrative organs. The statutes establishing the *zemstvos* had assumed this point and Valuev had confirmed it by administrative fiat as late as July 1865. Then, in an abrupt reversal of policy this privilege was withdrawn in 1867. The juridical dimensions of this decision were extraordinarily grave. On the one hand it denied the *zemstvos* any hope of being considered government agencies, a change that the tsar upheld in an 1869

---

[142] This ruling had been anticipated by Valuev's 1865 ban on the use of the provincial *vedomosti* for *zemstvo* news. *Sbornik rasporiazhenii po delam pechati s 1863 do 1-oe sentiabria 1865 goda*, St. Petersburg, 1865, pp. 29, 47-48.

[143] Nikitenko, *Dnevnik*, iii, 94; Koshelev, *Golos iz zemstva*, p. 19; Veselovskii, *Istoriia zemstva . . .* , iii, 128ff.

pronouncement issued jointly with the Committee of Ministers. "Zemstvo institutions," the pronouncement declared, "are not governmental powers either by their composition or their fundamental principles [of organization]."[144] At the same time, it went on to imply that they did not even enjoy the rights of private corporations.

The restrictions imposed on the *zemstvos* and the obligatory duties placed on provincial governors in the wake of the crises endured by the imperial autocracy after 1866 challenged the understanding of contemporaries. Most went no further than to blame the whole unfortunate turn of events on the Karakazov affair. A few men closer to the events traced the turn in policy to the turnover of personnel in the central administration, thus stressing the administrative rather than purely autocratic character of decision making in imperial Russia. Such were the conclusions of Vladimir Cherkasskii when he complained to Soloviev of "reckless and immoderate" leadership in the ministries.[145] What neither of these insightful statesmen could see, of course, was that the state for which they so indefatigably labored was chronically subject to change from external shocks.

Few if any of the counterreforms instituted after 1866 under pressure of civil disorder, radical political movements, and attempted assassinations can be considered as absolutely new departures. The dogged attempts by Valuev in 1862 and 1863 to come to grips with the Polish crisis and draw from it lessons to apply to Russia's provincial reforms foreshadowed much of what Shuvalov drove through after 1866. In both situations ministerial leaders concluded on the basis of meager evidence that public self-rule and local administrative initiative constituted threats to the autocracy. In both cases the governors were called upon to be the provincial mouthpieces for ministries and defenders of the

---

[144] Witte, *Samoderzhavie . . .* , pp. 87ff.
[145] GBL, f. 327 (Cherkasskii archive) III, 3rd. khr. 7, p. 29 (Cherkasskii to Soloviev, March 1, 1867).

autocracy; and in both cases, too, the leaders in Petersburg wavered between drawing elective agencies fully within the administrative orbit and pushing them completely outside it where they could be dealt with harshly as private organizations and, if necessary, stripped of their powers. Nor was this to be the last instance of such administrative reaction to crisis. When Alexander II was murdered by an assassin's bomb in 1881 the old commission on provincial reform was revived once more; its chairman announced that he would seek "to subordinate all actions taken locally to the law and to . . . the decisions of the central organs of government."[146] Such a statement, identical in spirit to Valuev's position in 1862-1863 and the position of Shuvalov and Valuev in 1866-1867, suggests strongly that these instances of "reaction" are not merely the consequence of "reckless and immoderate" leadership but rather the persistence of a deep-rooted pattern of response to crisis. Never fully confident that they actually ruled the sprawling nation, leaders tended to meet most crises by reclaiming prerogatives and powers from whatever bodies, groups, or individuals had succeeded in obtaining them during the earlier period of calm. Only in cases of extraordinary gravity, such as the fall of Sevastopol or the defeat by Japan in 1905, was the state forced to acknowledge that it had temporarily lost the capacity to impose control. In the mid-1860s the general pattern prevailed as Shuvalov and his colleagues reverted to the old ideal of centralized control.

THE PROVINCIALIST IDEOLOGY IN DECLINE

The expressed purpose of these many assaults on public self-government and administrative decentralization was to remove any lingering possibility of local agencies taking corporate actions inconsistent with national policy. In contrast to their fear of corporate actions, the administrators

[146] Korf, *Administrativnaia iustitsiia* . . . , I, 362.

involved seemed relatively unconcerned with preventing the purely ideological statements that earlier had been so much a part of the provincial movement. This apparent neglect was not as imprudent as it may at first appear, however, for by the late 1860s the anticentralist fervor of the post-Crimean years had cooled considerably. To be sure, a number of publicists followed Alexander Koshelev in pamphleteering in behalf of the *zemstvos*, but the old pugnaciousness was gone.[147] This is not to say that the censors let down their guard, for their continued watchfulness affected even such a self-confident pro-*zemstvo* organ as the *St. Petersburg News*. But this factor should not be exaggerated, for an inspection of the archives of *The Voice* (*Golos*), a moderately pro-*zemstvo* paper, reveals that very few "provincial" essays of the old type were written but not published.[148] A factor of greater import than censorship in cooling ideological ardor was the mere existence of the *zemstvos*. Numerous writers followed Alexander Vasilchikov, Boris Chicherin, and Alexander Golovachev into *zemstvo* work, plunging into practical activity that allowed little time for the sort of polemics which would come down to us today in published form. Yet even this does not suffice to account for the change of temper between 1864 and 1870. The fact is that when the future of the reformist legislation was placed in jeopardy in the period after 1864 there were fewer voices raised in its defense than had been mustered over fine points of debate a half decade before.

In the particular case of several men whose "provincial" writings we have already considered, their silence must be attributed to special conditions. Nikolai Ogarev, who had campaigned for provincial reform in *The Bell*, fell on hard times and was already living on handouts that were to sustain him to the end of his life. After 1864 the federalist his-

---

[147] Koshelev, *Golos iz zemstva*; Koshelev, *Zapiski* . . . , Chap. 4. See also material collected in V. Iu. Skalan, *Po zemskim voprosam*, St. Petersburg, 1882.

[148] PD, *Golos* archive.

torian Afanasii Shchapov turned to the theory of geographical determinism devised by Buckle in England and wrote several works in that vein while in exile in Siberia.[149] The colorful émigré Prince Peter Dolgorukov was lost to provincial causes during several years of journalistic failures and fruitless lawsuits and eventually died in Paris in 1868.[150] Several other veterans of early reformism were still actively writing but no longer in the old vein. This was the case with Prince Cherkasskii who had opened the discussion on provincial self-rule with his review of Tocqueville in 1857. Though he participated actively in urban reforms, Cherkasskii's voice was not heard on provincial questions after 1864. Katkov's influence was if anything greater than it had been in the 1850s, but he now devoted most of his energy to defending the interests of the nation-state rather than its constituent corporative groupings. Similarly, the historians Nikolai Kostomarov and Konstantin Bestuzhev-Riumin had long since established their professional eminence, but by the late 1860s had completely outgrown their earlier interest in the provinces.

Many thinkers who earlier tackled the problem of local rule had passed from the scene or experienced a basic change of heart. But what of the younger generation? During the 1860s a fresh coterie of talented young scholars appeared in the legal and historical faculties of Petersburg and Moscow universities. The names of Alexander Lokhvitskii, Alexander Gradovskii, Vladimir Sergeevich, and Ivan Andreevskii stand out among this group. These specialists in the history of Russian juridical institutions all began their careers as Chicherin had before them, with studies of provincial organs of government.[151] In respect to subject mat-

---

[149] Kuzmin, A. P. Shchapov v Irkutske, pp. iv-v.

[150] Lemke, "Kn. P. V. Dolgorukov . . . emigrant . . . ," pp. 180-91.

[151] See A. Lokhvitskii, Guberniia, ee zemskie i pravitelstvennye uchrezhdeniia, St. Petersburg, 1864; A. D. Gradovskii, Istoriia mestnogo upravleniia, St. Petersburg, 1869; A. D. Gradovskii, Istoricheskii ocherk uchrezhdeniia general-gubernatorstva v Rossii, St. Petersburg,

ter and the questions they asked these men stood well within the framework of the great debates of the late 1850s, but in their relation to the world of contemporary politics and in the conclusions to which their studies led them they clearly represent a different tendency. Only Andreevskii, in his book comparing the modern governorship with earlier forms of state representation in the provinces, followed the strongly antibureaucratic line so familiar after the fall of Sevastopol; and when the volume appeared the government released heretofore classified documents to refute it.[152] Gradovskii and Sergeevich showed a certain practical respect for the local public's involvement in government and for administrative deconcentration but they concerned themselves principally with the growth of state authority. With a fascination that is not to be detected even in the histories of Soloviev or Chicherin this new group of scholars followed the course of the state's development and penetration into diverse societal relationships. They all accepted this process as necessary and desirable and accused historians of the federalist school of bringing a romantic bias into their scholarly research. In a word, these younger thinkers were far too enamored of national states, "the highest creation of the human spirit" as Lokhvitskii called them,[153] to criticize out of hand the system that was so rapidly evolving around them.

At few times in modern history has the character of European governments undergone more profound changes. Whereas liberal reformers in 1848 had placed implicit trust in the proper ordering of institutions, in the 1860s all signs

---

1869; V. I. Sergeevich, *Veche i kniaz. Russkoe gosudarstvennoe ustroistvo i upravlenie vo vremia kniazei riurikovichei*, Moscow, 1867.

[152] Ivan Andreevskii, *O namestnikakh, voevodakh i gubernatorakh*, St. Petersburg, 1864; Count Bludov released the records of the Committee of December 6, 1826 to refute Andreevskii; these were utilized by Nikolai Kalachov, *Razbor sochineniia g. Andreevskogo "O namestnikakh, voevodakh i gubernatororakh,"* St. Petersburg, 1867.

[153] Lokhvitskii, *Guberniia . . .* , p. xxvi.

indicated that the decisive factor in the lives of nations was raw power. The victory of the Union forces in America pointed to this conclusion, as did the successful imposition of a Franco-Piedmontese administration throughout Italy. Above all, the efficacy of brute force was demonstrated by the man who coined the phrase "blood and iron," Prince Otto von Bismarck. Under his sole direction Prussia brought all the royal houses of Germany to their knees in 1866 and united the nation for the first time under a single modern government.

The lesson of these political pyrotechnics was not lost on Russia. One evening at dinner in the Summer Palace at Tsarskoe Selo the empress, who was of German birth, commented to Valuev that any nation could be pleased to have a Bismarck, which Valuev understood to imply that Russia needed its own Bismarck but had none.[154] Though the Russian minister insisted that such a man was not wanted in Petersburg, the very success of Bismarck's policies demanded attention. This he received in ample measure from Russian journals, in which the general topic of Germany quickly displaced both England and France.[155] Bismarck's Germany, in other words, provided Russians with a new model of state development.

Not all Russian opinion on the unification of Germany "from above" was favorable. One Russian federalist commented sourly that "if the fracturing of Germany into numerous district states does not advance the broad development of political life, then even less would it be promoted by the establishment of a single military and bureaucratic monarchy on the pattern of Napoleonic France or the Prussia of Bismarck."[156] Especially strong in their criticism of Bismarckian centralism were the two *zemstvo* mouthpieces,

---

[154] Valuev, *Dnevnik*, II, 71. Nikitenko believed similarly that Russia needed a second Peter I. *Dnevnik*, II, 521.

[155] Data from Mezhov, *Russkaia . . . bibliografiia*, 1864-1866.

[156] *Vestnik Evropy*, II (1866), 106-07; see also Nikitenko, *Dnevnik*, III, 178, 180.

the *St. Petersburg News* and *The Voice*, which unleashed on united Germany all the criticism that they were forbidden to express about Russia itself.[157] But German unification was of paramount importance in forcing even those Russians who opposed it to consider their empire once more as a single unit impelled by ideals transcending local interest. The new German model of state development was even more attractive because of changes in French political thought. Though the issue of decentralization was still under debate in France and was the subject of decrees in 1861, 1866, and 1871, the old leaders of Tocqueville's generation were dead and their successors had changed their demands.[158] After 1863 Napoleon's interest in the entire provincial issue slackened,[159] which gave Russians still less cause for following the internal debate in France. When France attempted to thwart Russia over the Polish insurrection, their indifference changed to hostility which in turn gave way to *hauteur* when the Second Empire collapsed under German attack in 1870.

At the height of the post-Karakazov panic Minister of Internal Affairs Valuev observed in his diary that "The organism of the state either develops or decays; there is no middle course."[160] This learned rationalization of a course of events over which Valuev himself had been able to exert little control is characteristic of statements made in the late 1860s in Russia. It embodies the new concern for the state as a monolithic national body welded firmly together so as to maintain its position in a world of similar and competing nation-states. Nikolai Danilevskii raised this call for unity

[157] *Sankt-Peterburgskie Vedomosti*, No. 203 (1865); *Golos*, No. 16 (1864). A competent review of Russian attitudes toward Germany at this time is A. I. Nachnochnitskaia, *Rossiia i voiny Prussii v 60-kh godakh XIX v. za obedinenie Germanii "sverkhu,"* Moscow, 1960.

[158] See Charles Samary, *Un projet d'une loi sur la décentralization*, 3rd edn., Paris, 1870.

[159] Avalov, *Detsentralizatsiia i samoupravlenie* . . . , p. 214. Letter of Napoleon to the president of the Conseil d'État, June 24, 1863.

[160] Valuev, *Dnevnik*, II, 143.

in the face of foreign enemies in his ponderous book, *Russia and Europe*, published in 1869.[161] Equally evocative versions of essentially the same vision were propounded by other members of that highly diverse, often inconsistent, and always volatile movement known as Pan-Slavism.[162]

For all their internecine differences, Pan-Slavists stood in essential agreement on the question of provincial reform and their statements on that subject present a common silhouette that is starkly different from the one presented by the reformist ideologues of the 1850s. First, unlike thinkers of the early reform period, the Pan-Slavists were intensely—almost obsessively—preoccupied with the relation of Russia to the outside world, particularly Germany. If Cherkasskii or other provincial reformers ventured occasionally to speak on such issues as the Balkans, they had always retreated quickly to domestic concerns.[163] Second, because of their fear of internal division in the face of foreign enemies, the Pan-Slavists were unalterably opposed to federalism, whether applied to the reform of Russia's provinces or to the entire Slavic world. The Pan-Slavist Ivan Aksakov was typical in accusing federalist historians and the entire provincialist movement of being an anachronism: "[In Europe] Naples and Piedmont are merging and Venice is being joined to Rome, but here people want to split the country into Poltava, Kursk, Voronezh and Kiev."[164] The same argument against federative organization was extended to

161 N. Ia. Danilevskii, *Rossiia i Evropa*, St. Petersburg, 1869; see Robert E. MacMasters, *Danilevsky, A Russian Totalitarian Philosopher*, Cambridge, 1967, Pt. 2.

162 A. N. Pypin, *Panslavizm v proshlom i nastaiashchem*, St. Petersburg, 1913; S. Sharapov, *Teoriia gosudarstva u slavianofilov*, St. Petersburg, 1898; Michael Boro Petrovich, *The Emergence of Russian Panslavism*, New York, 1956, Chaps. 3, 9; Hans Kohn, *Pan-Slavism; Its History and Ideology*, New York, 1960, Pt. 2.

163 V. A. Cherkasskii, "Dva slova po povodu vostochnogo voprosa," *Russkaia Beseda*, IV (1858), 65-92.

164 Aksakov's views on this issue are set forth in Barsukov, *Zhizn . . . Pogodina*, XVII, 124, 136-42.

large groups of Slavic peoples by the brilliant linguists A. F. Hilferding and V. I. Lamanskii. Hilferding constructed an oppressive hierarchy of Slavic languages and dialects with Great Russian at the top, while Lamanskii ridiculed the ideal of federal equality among peoples by observing that "until such a federation is established, the Slavs are living under the rule of the Germans and the Turks."[165] Like Valuev and Danilevskii, the Pan-Slavists took all localism and anything suggesting division within the Russian Empire to be a sign of weakness. They scorned the broader claims of the zemstvos as divisive and wanted Russians to seek their principal identity in small village communes and in a powerful national state.

One of the few movements of social thought in the late 1860s to maintain close links with the ideology of provincial reform was that dynamic if amorphous current known as Populism.[166] But the journalists, ethnographers, and students who can be numbered in this movement tended to look with skepticism on the zemstvos because of the preponderance of gentry in provincial assemblies, and rejected the existing provinces outright on account of their bureaucratic origin. Like the earlier thinkers and in contrast to Pan-Slavists, however, these people were on the whole little concerned with Russia's foreign relations and advocated a federative form of internal state organization. For their federalism they were no less indebted to west European thinkers than were the men of the fifties, but instead of turning to Regnault, Odilon-Barrot, or Tocqueville, they took *Du Principe Fédératif* . . . by the anarchist Proudhon as their main text. This work was a lively call to arms for revolutionary federalists against precisely the sort of reformist localism that the earlier Russian movement had actively

[165] Cited by Petrovich, *The Emergence* . . . , p. 157.

[166] The argument for continuity between early post-Crimean social thought and Populism, particularly on the issue of federalism, is supported by Ogarev's clandestine papers published in *Literaturnoe Nasledstvo*, Moscow, 1953, i, 494ff.

promoted.[167] Even when the institutional forms coincided, those of the Populists were intended to serve new social ends that were held to be more important than the particular structural means of achieving them.

The last attempt in the Reform Era to present a reasoned case for public self-administration was made in 1865 by a now forgotten legal scholar and publicist, Vladimir Leshkov. Since the 1830s Leshkov had lectured on police law at Moscow University and been a participant in the intellectual circle led by Mikhail Pogodin.[168] In a lecture in 1840 Leshkov could still speak of the province as merely "a part of the state"[169] but immediately after the Crimean War he threw himself wholeheartedly into the movement for provincial reform. His debut in this field was a response to the dissertation of his former student, Boris Chicherin and was entitled *The Social Customs of Ancient Russia*.[170] In this Slavophile tract he investigated the territorial basis of the ancient princedoms, a subject which led naturally to his next work, "The Division of Russia into Provinces According to the Ukazes of Peter the Great and Catherine II."[171] Here Leshkov accused Peter and Catherine of acting "mechanically and arithmetically" in their provincial legislation and pleaded with the present government to reverse old errors by establishing a decentralized administration. These works borrowed heavily from the leading ideologists of provincial reform and in no way advanced the study. After such an undistinguished beginning, Leshkov's next work, "Towards a Theory of the Public and Its *Zemstvo* Institutions According to the Act of January 1, 1864," came as

---

[167] P. J. Proudhon, *Du Principe Fédératif et de la nécessité de reconstituer le Parti de la Revolution*, Paris, 1863.

[168] GBL, f. 231 (Pogodin archive), II, karton 18, ed. khr. 89, pp. 18-89, Pogodin-Leshkov correspondence.

[169] GBL, M. 4890, 1, p. 58. Notes of unknown student on Leshkov's lectures.

[170] V. Leshkov, *Obshchestvennyi byt drevnei Rossii*, St. Petersburg, 1856.

[171] V. Leshhov, "Razdelenie Rossii na gubernii po ukazam Petra Velikogo i Ekateriny II," *Russkii Vestnik*, No. 22 (1859).

a complete surprise. Writing scarcely a year after the promulgation of the *zemstvo* reform, Leshkov cut boldly to the heart of the juridical problems underlying all public self-administration and proposed solutions that foreshadow even much Soviet thought on the problem today.

Administrative decentralization, he argued, offered little hope for long-term success because whatever authority was delegated to local officials could be withdrawn whenever circumstances demanded it. Public self-government would necessarily suffer from the same defect, he continued, so long as the statutes governing it remained a branch of the state law. Leshkov therefore dismissed in a stroke the entire mainstream of Russian jurisprudence which attempted futilely to derive a coherent basis for provincial self-rule from the narrow state law tradition. On the other hand the system of private law promised little more, for private rights would always remain subordinate to the general needs of the public. Leshkov therefore proposed that a new sphere of law be created, one that would be independent of both state law and private law: "The rights of public institutions, taken in the sense of the rights of the *zemstvos*, [should] henceforth constitute a special and independent system of laws distinct both from the civil or private law and from state law. This is the essence of *zemstvo* or *societal* law."[172] The germ for this new corpus of law he found in the *zemstvo* statutes. If it could be nurtured and developed, the "public" would become a force complementary to but independent of the state.

In retrospect, the very boldness of this proposal has a pathetic quality, for the first restrictive measures against the *zemstvos* lay less than a year in the future. More pathetic still, Leshkov's daring theoretical resolution of a

[172] V. Leshkov, "Opyt teorii zemstva i ego zemskikh uchrezhdenii, po Polozheniiu 1864, g., Ianv., 1," *Den*, No. 42 (1865), 999, essentially the same arguments were repeated in his later "O prave samostoiatelnosti, kak osnovoi samoupravleniia," *Iuridicheskii Vestnik*, No. 1 (1872).

fundamental problem of provincial and public life was rejected by his colleagues. As if to demonstrate how disillusioned Russian jurists had become with the dream of provincial self-government, six months after this landmark of Russian legal history was published its author was blackballed by his colleagues from further teaching at Moscow University. Only the timely intervention of the Minister of Public Enlightenment saved Leshkov from utter ruin.[173]

What, then, was left of the old ideology of provincial reform? Administrative decentralization had been roundly attacked by Alexander Lokhvitskii,[174] who demonstrated in a few powerful paragraphs that it provided no security against revolution, that it could impede progress, and that it might hinder intellectual endeavor. Ivan Vernadskii had undermined the economic justification for the policy by claiming that in an industrialized state greater centralization would be imperative. Provincial self-government had failed to hold the attention of its three best apologists among the historians, Kostomarov, Shchapov, and Bestuzhev-Riumin. Ethnographic study of the Russian countryside continued and even expanded after the 1860s, but its practitioners either ceased to be immediately involved with politics or, as was more frequent, rejected the artificial province as the unit of study.[175] Finally, juridical research on the province was either submerged in the study of the national state as a whole or it trailed off into a morass of ever more arcane issues defined not by Russian conditions but by the irrelevant attempts of German scholars such as Rudolph Gneist to deal with the Bismarckian state. A contemporary summed up the situation in these words: "Among the diverse issues with which Russian writers have been deeply concerned in recent years, special attention has

[173] GBL, f. 87 (Gerie archive), papka 87, No. 20, B. Chicherin, *Zapiska o prichinakh otstavki shesti professorov v M. universitete,*" 1868. In protest against Leshov's reinstatement six professors including Chicherin resigned.
[174] Lokhvitskii, *Guberniia . . . ,* p. xv.
[175] Pypin, *Istoriia russkoi etnografii,* III.

been accorded to the renowned question of *centralization,*
the representative of which appears to be France. . . . The
victory has evidently gone to the adherents of centralization, and this question, settled at last, has been sent to the
archives."[176] This sweeping pronouncement of 1866 surely
overstated the case, but few would have contested its general validity.

[176] M. I. Zarudnyi, *Obshchestvennyi byt Anglii; Ocherki zemstva,
goroda, suda,* St. Petersburg, 1865, p. 88.

VI | Conclusion

By way of conclusion, let us draw back from the mass of data which survives to our time—the debris from which the great debate on provincial government in nineteenth-century Russia must be reconstructed—and briefly review the general observations to which this evidence has led us. We can present them in the form of a tentative hypothesis on reform of local institutions at other periods of recent Russian history. It is appropriate to begin with an obvious point and yet one that is easily overlooked in the pursuit of more arcane truths: the Great Reforms, so far as they affected provincial administrative and public agencies, were first of all a response to the conditions of Russian provincial life over the preceding generation. Attempts to anticipate the problems of the future played at best a secondary role in the planning and legislative process. Hence to study these reforms outside of the context of the laws, habits, and customs which were the common inheritance of all the reformers—even those from the cities—would be unthinkable. Ideology and the dynamics of the reform process itself could guide the legislation to a degree, but not to the extent that the process could lose touch with the conditions that were the legacy of the era of Nicholas I.

348

Most contemporary observers, including men whose views diverged on other issues, agreed tacitly or explicitly that the chief deficiency of the prereform province was that it was underinstitutionalized and undergoverned, notwithstanding the conspicuous growth of bureaucracy in the countryside. Before 1855 this view was expressed in attacks on the bureaucratic mentality, praise for the primitive rural commune, complaints by the gentry about their own and the government's agencies, and a general awareness that the real needs of the provinces were ill-served by the existing way of doing things. It took the Crimean War and the near bankruptcy of the state to crystallize this malaise into tradition-breaking thought on institutions, and it took the example of the well-developed localist ideologies of western Europe to translate that thought into programs for reform in Russia. Together these factors stimulated widespread sympathy for new policies that were at odds with Russia's centralist past, and at the same time appeared consonant with the seemingly inevitable course of development of national institutions in other countries. Throughout the early reform era the dominant current of reformist thought on the provinces, both in educated society and in the government, favored either decentralized administration, local self-rule, or both.

The concurrent debate on the emancipation of the serfs immensely stimulated the general exchange of ideas on this issue, but at the same time hindered the implementation of a program for local reform by raising fears over national security that could be satisfied only by keeping the planning for emancipation and other reforms within the central administration in St. Petersburg. Yet this by no means rid the local reform issue of "politics." Indeed, the procedure by which the reforms of local government were drafted was an eminently "political" one with bureaucratic factions and defined interest groups making their influence felt at every stage of the legislative process.

During the preparation of this reform legislation a chief

source of pressure for change lay within the upper civil service. This highly diverse body was at times split vertically, with the ministries of Internal Affairs, Finances, and State Domains competing vigorously for control of general policy making and for the largest possible share of scarce resources. At other times the bureaucratic infrastructure was cleaved horizontally, with groups of governors presenting demands to their ministerial superiors as if they, as governors, constituted a special interest group. Of course, such behavior only reproduced in microcosm the conflicts that raged in the society as a whole.[1] In defending their interests against those of the larger system of which they were themselves a part, the governors resembled closely the other chief action group of the period, the reformist provincial gentry. Together, gentry and governors introduced greater elements of diversity and complexity into the decision-making process than had existed in the memory of any Russian then alive. With the politically active segment of Russia's elite divided along both vertical and horizontal lines, it is impossible to delineate sharply the borders of each new political style. Suffice it to say that during the planning of the reforms the tsarist system exhibited many of the characteristics of bureaucratic and interest-group politics and relatively few of the traits of the autocracy it claimed to be.

From this skein of contradictory pressures emerged reforms which, for all their shortcomings, rendered possible the birth and development of many new institutions serving public ends in the provinces, the involvement of a significantly enlarged number of people in public life, and the limited but real growth of rationalization and specialization in the state administration. The reforms also sharpened and gave ideological focus to an old tension between two rival patterns of institutional growth. The one called for local organizations endowed with broad autonomy. It would turn over as many functions as possible to such inde-

[1] Joseph LaPalombara, *Bureaucracy and Political Development*, Princeton, 1963, p. 15.

pendent bodies, which would then develop local life with little or no outside interference. The other pattern looked upon all local organizations and officials as simply agents for the execution of programs planned centrally. Whatever powers local officials or bodies might exercise would necessarily be delegated to them from above and subject to revocation if local officials or institutions failed to communicate general goals and policies to their constituents. Lenin referred approvingly to organs constituted in this way as "transmission belts."

Debate over these two alternative patterns of state building was at the center of the provincial reforms of the 1860s, just as it played an important part in French political thought in the mid-nineteenth century and continues to influence public controversy in many developing nations today. By the end of the reform period an apparent victory had been won by those advocating administrative concentration and public participation on the "transmission belt" pattern. Gradually emerging economic forces, the continuity of long-established administrative habits, heightened pressures on the state from without and within, and a renewed confidence that traditional policies could control the situation combined to render decentralization and self-government as preached in the late 1850s and early 1860s unrealizable models. To be sure, the *zemstvo* organs still existed and were rapidly expanding their activities in many provinces. But such expansion occurred only because national leaders were confident that they were by then closer to being "transmission belts" than to being the fully autonomous bodies originally conceived by provincialists in the 1850s. That the *zemstvos* continued in any sense to be independent instrumentalities must be attributed more to the belief of national leaders that such groups provided a convenient means of moderating and regulating the flow of demands to and from the central bureaucracy than to any lingering inclination on their part toward the autonomous pattern of development. A generation and a half before the

351

creation of a national *zemstvo* with the *Duma* in 1906, the probable sphere of its autonomy was severely proscribed.

Yet the story does not end here, for, like a fire in an old mine shaft that continues to smolder and occasionally rises to the surface, the defeated provincial program of the era of the Great Reforms continued to make its presence felt in Russian life. Examination of these issues in the terminology of the late 1850s remained a part of Russian legal training until the October Revolution, becoming the common heritage of everyone from Paul Miliukov to Lenin. Throughout the late nineteenth and early twentieth centuries articulate and occasionally influential writers and activists continued to call for deconcentration of the bureaucratic apparatus, the ceding of state functions to self-regulating provincial bodies, and even federalism.[2] During the First World War the *zemstvos* assumed control of an unprecedented range of projects,[3] and in 1917 the Social Revolutionaries put "self-government," "antibureaucratism," and "federalism" on their party's banner.[4] Shortly thereafter the Bolsheviks went so far as to restructure the state on nominally federalist lines. The debate over the powers of local officials and over the relation of "societal" organs to the state administration continued to be waged under Soviet rule, becoming particularly intense during the decade following the Twentieth Party Congress of 1956.[5]

Russian liberals of the 1905 to 1917 generation and numerous west European and American writers and jour-

[2] See, for example, M. P. Dragomanov, who advocated all three programs. Iashchenko, *Teoriia federalizma*, pp. 757-59.

[3] Tikhon J. Polner, and others, *Russian Local Government during the War and the Union of Zemstvos*, New Haven, 1930.

[4] F. A. Danilov, *Gosudarstvennaia vlast i mestnoe, gorodskoe i zemskoe, samoupravlenie*, Petrograd, 1917.

[5] See Akademiia nauk SSSR, Institut gosydarstva i prava, *Mestnye sovety na sovremennom etape*, Moscow, 1965; P. S. Cheremnykh, *Sochetanie gosudarstvennykh i obshchestvennykh nachal v upravlenii obshchestvom*, Moscow, 1965; A. Aimbetov, M. Baimakhanov, M. Imashev, *Problemy sovershenstvovaniia organizatsii i deiatelnosti mestnykh sovetov*, Alma-Ata, 1967.

nalists have found in this recurrent theme evidence of a persistent striving for "freedom"—in tsarist Russia and the Soviet Union. It is not my intention to deny this thesis or the beliefs underlying it, but it is worth pointing out a broad similarity among all of the periods in which the programs that I have called "provincialist," but which might also be called "societal" or simply "antibureaucratic," flourished. The post-Crimean years, the period immediately before and after the Revolution of 1905, the First World War years, the first phase of Soviet rule, and the post-Stalinist decade were all periods during which the Russian state endured some particular physical or financial stress or in which its leaders were themselves experiencing doubt and uncertainty as to its principles of organization. At such times, one may hypothesize, the efficacy of the centralist and administration-centered tradition of organization is cast in doubt, and the possibility of refounding the structure on opposing principles is raised. These public-centered alternatives are naturally the more appealing when the state itself is deficient in the managerial resources or funds that local administrators or public bodies promise to tap. If these conditions exist, the state itself may lead in the institution of "provincial" or "societal" programs.

Those accustomed to view the world philosophically or through the lens of ideological categories may see these measures as laudable acts of political morality, comparable in import to Russia's medieval liberation from the Tartar yoke. Meanwhile, their more realistic (or perhaps more distrustful) contemporaries view them as temporary steps backward along the ever-forward course of state-sponsored institutional development—as provisional measures to be rescinded when the government apparatus is once more capable of resuming its traditional leadership role or when it is forced to do so by threatening circumstances. Such general hypotheses cannot, of course, be verified by reference to any single period, and a more comprehensive evaluation of them would take us beyond the scope of this book. None-

353

theless, it may be said that the latter view most adequately describes the Reform Era's experience with "decentralization" and "self-government." Given the still underdeveloped state of provincial society, the attitudes and habits of most officials, and especially the experience of national leaders with internal disorder, it would have seemed most unlikely by 1870 that the Russian state would ever be restructured on a more deconcentrated basis or on any basis in which the local public would be directly responsible for the execution of functions deemed of primary importance to the government.

Selected Bibliography

I. ARCHIVAL SOURCES

Tsentralnyi Gosudarstvennyi Istoricheskii Arkhiv SSSR
(TsGIA-SSSR)

fund	91	Imperial Free Economic Society.
fund	572	Commission on Taxes and Duties, Ministry of Finances.
fund	573	Department of Taxes, Ministry of Finances.
fund	651	Vasilchikov archive.
fund	772	Chief Directorate of Censorship.
fund	775	Central Directorate of the Censorship.
fund	869	Miliutin archive.
fund	908	P. A. Valuev archive.
fund	1149	State Council, Department of Laws.
fund	1159	State Council, *Memoriia* of the General Assembly and of Departments.
fund	1160	State Council, Journals of Departments.
fund	1162	The Imperial State Chancellery.
fund	1180	Main Committee on Peasant Affairs.
fund	1181	Main Committee on Rural Conditions.
fund	1250	Papers of the President and Members of the State Council.

fund 1261   Second Section of His Imperial Chancellery.
fund 1275   Council of Ministers.
fund 1281   Council of the Ministry of Internal Affairs.
fund 1282   Chancellery of the Minister of Internal Affairs.
fund 1284   Department of General Affairs.
fund 1286   Department of Executive Police of the Ministry of Internal Affairs.
fund 1287   Economic Department of the Ministry of Internal Affairs.
fund 1291   *Zemskii* Section of the Ministry of Internal Affairs.
fund 1313   Committee on Equalizing Local Duties, Ministry of Internal Affairs.
fund 1316   Commission on Provincial and District Institutions, Ministry of Internal Affairs.
fund 1341   First Department of the Senate.
fund 1386   Revision of Vitebsk Province by Senator M. P. Shcherbin.
fund 1387   Revision of Penza Province by Senator S. V. Safonov.
fund 1389   Revision of Kaluga Province by Senator A. Kh. Karger.
fund 1405   Ministry of Justice.

Tsentralnyi Gosudarstvennyi Arkhiv Oktiabrskoi Revoliutsii (TsGAOR)

fund 109   First Secret Archive of the Third Section of His Imperial Chancellery.
fund 647   Grand Duchess Elena Pavlovna archive.
fund 678   Alexander II archive.
fund 722   Marble Palace archive.

Gosudarstvennaia Publichnaia Biblioteka im. Saltykova-Shchedrina (GPB)

fund 379   F. P. Kornilov archive.
fund 380   M. A. Korf archive.

fund 738 V. V. Stasov archive.
fund 781 I. I. Tolstoi archive.
fund 827 N. P. Sobko archive.
fund 833 V. A. Tsie archive.
Otdel Rukopisei Gosudarstvennoi Biblioteki im. Lenina v
Moskve (GBL)
    fund 69 Herzen and Ogarev archive.
    fund 87 Gerie archive.
    fund 169 Miliutin archive.
    fund 231 Pogodin archive.
    fund 265 Samarin archive.
    fund 327 Cherkasskii archive.
    fund 334 Chicherin archive.
Tsentralnii Gosudarstvennyi Istoricheskii Arkhiv Lenin-
gradskoi Oblasti (TsGIALO)
    Gentry Assembly of Petersburg
    Province.
Arkhiv Instituta Literatury; Pushkinskii Dom (PD)
    fund 3 Samarin archive.
    Golos archive.
Sterling Memorial Library, Yale University:
Miliutin collection.
Columbia University Russian Archive:
P. P. Semenov-Tian-Shanskii archive.

II. NEWSPAPERS AND JOURNALS

Aksioner
Biblioteka dlia Chteniia
Birzhovye Vedomosti
Den
Ekaterinoslavskie
  Gubernskie Vedomosti
Ekonomist
Golos
Kharkovskie Gubernskie
  Vedomosti

Kaluzhskie Gubernskie
  Vedomosti
Kievskii Telegraf
Kolokol
Moskovskie Vedomosti
Nashe Vremia
Odesskii Vestnik
Osnova
Otechestvennye Zapiski
Pravdivyi-La Véridique

Russkaia Beseda
Russkii Invalid
Russkii Listok
Russkii Vestnik
Sankt-Peterburgskie
   Vedomosti
Severnaia Pchela
Severnaia Pochta
Sovremennaia Letopis
Sovremennik
Sovremennoe Slovo

Svobodnoe Slovo
Trudy Imperatorskogo
   Volnogo Ekonomicheskogo
   Obshchestva
Vest
Vek
Zhurnal Ministerstva
   Iustitsii
Zhurnal Ministerstva
   Vnutrennykh Del

III. RUSSIAN PUBLISHED DOCUMENTS, MATERIALS, AND SPECIALIZED BIBLIOGRAPHIES

Avinov, N. N., *Opyt programy sistematicheskogo chteniia po voprosam zemskogo samoupravleniia*, Moscow, 1905.

Baraba, A. Z., and others, eds., *Otmena krepostnogo prava na Ukraine: sbornik dokumentov i materialov*, Kiev, 1961.

Barsukov, N. P., *Zhizn i trudy M. P. Pogodina*, 22 vols., St. Petersburg, 1888-1906.

Gavrilov, D. P., *Materialy i svedeniia o sushchestvuiushchem poriadke i sposobakh otpravleniia naturalnykh zemskikh povinnostei v tsentralnykh guberniiakh imperii* (Ministry of Finances), St. Petersburg, 1860.

Istoricheskaia zapiska o khode rabot po sostavleniiu i primeneniiu polozheniia o zemskikh uchrezhdeniiakh, St. Petersburg, n.d.

Kashkarov, M., *Istoricheskii obzor zakonodatelnykh rabot po obshchemu ustroistvu zemskikh povinnostei*, St. Petersburg, 1894.

Kaufman, I. I., *Statistika russkikh bankov*, St. Petersburg, 1912.

Kopoliuk, P., Marakhov, G., and others, eds., *Obshchestvenno-politicheskoe dvizhenie na Ukraine v 1856-1862 gg.*, 2 vols., Kiev, 1963.

Materialy dlia istorii uprazdneniia krepostnogo sostoianiia pomeshchichikh krestian v Rossii v tsarstvovanii imp. Aleksandra II-go, 3 vols., Berlin, 1860-1862.

Materialy po zemskomu obshchestvennomu ustroistvu. Polozhenie o zemskikh uchrezhdeniiakh, 2 vols., St. Petersburg, 1885-1886.

Materialy redaksionnykh komissii dlia sostavleniia polozheniia o krestianakh, vykhodiashchikh iz krepostnoi zavisimosti, St. Petersburg, 1859-1860.

Materialy sobrannye dlia vysochaishei uchrezhdennoi komissii o preobrazovanii gubernskikh i uezdnykh uchrezhdenii, Pt. 1, *Materialy istoricheskie i zakonodatelnye*, St. Petersburg, 1870.

Mezhov, V. I., *Zemskii i krestianskii voprosy. bibliograficheskii ukazatel knig i statei no pervomu voprosu s samogo nachala vvedeniia v deistvie zemskikh uchrezhdenii i ranee, po vtoromu-s 1865 g. vplot do 1875 g.*, St. Petersburg, 1875.

Morozov, P. O., ed., *Istoricheskie materialy iz arkhivov ministerstva gosudarstvennykh imushchestv*, St. Petersburg, 1891.

O glavnykh nachalakh preobrazovaniia zemskikh povinnostei, St. Petersburg, 1863.

Obzor tsarstvovaniia gosudarstva Imperatora Aleksandra II i ego reformy 1855-1871, St. Petersburg, 1871.

Olkhin, S. A., *Svod suzhdenii i postanovlenii zemskikh sobranii o zemskikh povinnostiakh*, St. Petersburg, 1868.

Poiasnitelnaia zapiska o rabotakh po soglasheniiu otsenkov gosudarstvennykh imushchestv mezhdu guberniiami, St. Petersburg, 1863.

Polovtsov, A. A., ed., *Zhurnaly komiteta, uchrezhdennyi 6 dekabria 1826*, 2 vols., St. Petersburg, 1891-1894.

Predtechenskii, A. V., ed., *Krestianskoe dvizhenie v Rossii v 1825-1849 gg*, Moscow, 1961.

Prilozhenie k trudam redaksionnykh komissii po krestianskomu delu. Otzyvy chlenov gubernskikh komitetov, 2 vols., St. Petersburg, 1860.

359

Proekt uchrezhdeniia Volynskogo gubernskogo upravleniia, n.p., 1861.

Proekt uchrezhdeniia Podolskogo gubernskogo upravleniia, Kamenetsk—Podolsk, 1861.

Proekt uchrezhdeniia Kievskogo gubernskogo upravleniia, Kiev, 1860.

Rumovskii, I. P., *Istoriko-statisticheskie svedeniia o podushnykh podatakh,* St. Petersburg, 1862.

Sbornik materialov po istorii Tverskogo gubernskogo zemstva, 1866-1886, 4 vols., Tver, 1887.

Sbornik postanovlenii Vladimirskogo zemskogo sobraniia 1865-1895 gg., 4 vols., Vladimir, 1896.

Sbornik pravitelstvennykh rasporiazhenii po ustroistvu byt krestian, vyshedshikh iz krepostnoi zavisimosti. 3 vols., St. Petersburg, 1861-1862.

Skrebitskii, A. I., ed., *Krestianskoe delo v tsarstvovanii Imperatora Aleksandra II-ogo. Materialy dlia istorii osvobozhdeniia krestian,* 4 vols., Bonn, 1862-1868.

Trudy komissii vysochaishei uchrezhdennoi dlia peresmotra sistemy podatei i sborov, 6 vols., St. Petersburg, 1861-1866.

Trudy komissii o 'gubernskikh i uezdnykh uchrezhdeniiakh, 6 vols., St. Petersburg, 1860-1863.

Trudy komissii vysochaishei uchrezhdennoi dlia ustroistva zemskikh bankov, 4 vols., St. Petersburg, 1861.

Trutchenko, B. E., ed., *Materialy ob ustroistve upravleniia zemskimi povinnostiani,* St. Petersburg, 1861.

Zhurnaly sekretnogo i glavnogo komitetov po krestianskomu delu, 1857-1861, 2 vols., Petrograd, 1915.

IV. CONTEMPORARY NON-RUSSIAN STUDIES AND THEORETICAL WORKS

Béchard, F., *Essai sur la centralisation administrative,* 2 vols., Paris, 1836-1837.

360

Constant de Rebecque, Henri Benjamin, *Cours de politique constitutionelle*, 3rd edn., Brussels, 1837.

Courcelle-Seneuil, Jean Gustave, *Traité théorique et pratique des opérations de banque*, Paris, 1857.

Custine, Astolphe Louis Léonor, Marquis de, *Journey for Our Time*, Kohler, Phyllis Penn, ed. and trans., New York, 1951.

Dupont-White, Charles, *La Centralisation*, Paris, 1861.

Eötvös, Joseph Baron, *Der Einfluss der herrschenden Ideen des XIX Jahrhunderts auf den Staat*, 2 vols., Vienna, 1851-1854.

Fauchet, Léon, *Études sur l'Angleterre*, 2 vols., Paris, 1845.

Gneist, Dr. Rudolph von, *Die Geschichte des Self-Government in England, oder die innere Entwicklung des Parliamentsverfassung bis zum Ende des achtzehnten Jahrhunderts*, Berlin, 1863.

Hauser, P., *De la décentralisation*, Paris, 1832.

Haxthausen, Baron August von, *Studien über die innern Zustände, das Volksleben, und insbesondere die ländlichen Einrichtungen Russlands*, 3 vols., Hannover and Berlin, 1847-1852.

———, ed., *Das constitutionelle Princep, seine geschichtliche Entwicklung und seine Wechselwirkungen mit den politischen und socialen Verhältnissen der Staaten und Volker*, Leipzig, 1864.

———, "Ob otmenenii i vykupe pomeshchichikh gospodskikh prav v Prussii," *Russkii Vestnik*, XII (1857).

Leroy-Beaulieu, Anatole, *The Empire of the Tsars*, Ragozin, Z. A., trans., 3 vols., London and New York, 1893.

Mill, John Stuart, *Considerations on Representative Government*, London, 1861.

———, *The Letters of John Stuart Mill*, Elliot, H.S.R., ed., 2 vols., London, 1910.

Montalembert, Charles Comte de, *De l'avenir politique de l'Angleterre*, 3rd edn., Paris, 1856.

Odilon-Barrot, Camille, *De la centralisation et de ses effets*, Paris, 1861.

Proudhon, P. J., *Du Principe fédératif et de la nécessité de reconstituer le parti de la Revolution*, Paris, 1863.

Regnault, Elias, *La Province; ce qu'elle est, ce qu'elle doit être*, Paris, 1861.

————, *La Question Européenne improprement appelée Polonaise Réponse aux objections présentées par M. M. Pogodine . . . Solowiew, etc. contre le Polonisme*, Paris, 1863.

Samary, Charles, *Un projet d'une loi sur la décentralisation*, 3rd edn., Paris, 1870.

Simon, Jules, *De la démocratie et de la décentralisation en France*, Paris, 1849.

Smith, J. Toulman, *Local Self-Government and Centralization: The Characteristics of Each; and Its Practical Tendencies, as Effecting Social, Moral and Political Welfare and Progress*, London, 1851.

Tocqueville, Alexis de, *De la démocratie en Amérique*, 2 vols., Paris, 1835.

————, *Demokratiia v Amerike*, 4 vols., Kiev, 1861.

————, *Oeuvres complètes*, 9 vols., Paris, 1864-1866.

————, *The Old Regime and the French Revolution*, Stuart Gilbert, trans., New York, 1955.

Wallace, D. Mackenzie, *Russia*, New York, 1887.

V. BOOKS AND MAJOR ARTICLES BY NINETEENTH-CENTURY CONTEMPORARIES

Aksakov, I. S., *Dnevnik*, St. Petersburg, 1910.

————, *Sochineniia I. S. Aksakova*, 7 vols., Moscow, 1886-1887.

Andreevskii, Ivan, *O namestnikakh, voevodakh i gubernatorakh*, St. Petersburg, 1864.

Anon., "Pervoe desiatiletie zemstva," *Otechestvennye Zapiski*, ccxxi (1875).

Antonov, A. A., "Chetvert veka nazad: vospominaniia stepnogo pomeshchika," *Sankt-Peterburgskii Istoricheskii Vestnik*, xxx (1887).

Artsimovich, V. A. (subj.), *Viktor Antonovich Artsimovich —vospominaniia—kharakteristika*, St. Petersburg, 1904, p. 155.

Bakunin, M. A., *Narodnoe delo: Romanov, Pugachev ili Pestel?*, London, 1862.

Bestuzhev-Riumin, K. N., "Istoricheskoe i politicheskoe doktrinerstvo v ego prakticheskom polozhenii," *Otechestvennye Zapiski*, cxxxix (1861).

———, (unsigned), "O neobkhodimosti novogo metoda v naukakh gosudarstvennykh," *Moskovskoe Obozrenie*, No. 2 (1859).

———, *Vospominaniia K. N. Bestuzhev-Riumina (do 1860 g)*, St. Petersburg, 1900.

Bezobrazov, N. A., *Predlozhenie dvorianstvu*, Berlin, 1862.

Bezobrazov, V. P. "Iz dnevnika," *Byloe*, September 1907.

———, *Gosudarstvo i obshchestvo*, St. Petersburg, 1882.

———, *Ob ustroistve zemskikh bankov v Rossii*, St. Petersburg, 1882.

———, *Otchet o deistviiakh komissii vysochaishei uchrezhdennoi dlia ustroistva zemskikh bankov*, St. Petersburg, 1861.

———, *Pozemelnyi kredit i ego sovremennaia organizatsiia v Evrope*, St. Petersburg, 1860.

———, *Zemskie uchrezhdeniia i samoupravlenia*, Moscow, 1874.

"Biurokraticheskaia voina 1839-ogo g.," *Russkaia Starina*, xxxii, 1881.

Bodianskii, O. M., "Vyderzhki iz dnevnika," *Sbornik obshchestva liubitelei russkoi slovesnosti*, Moscow, 1891.

Chernyshevskii, N. G., *Polnoe sobranie sochinenii*, 16 vols., Moscow, 1939-1953.

Chicherin, B. N., *Neskolko sovremennykh voprosov*, Moscow, 1862.

———, *Oblastnye uchrezhdeniia Rossii v XVII-m veke*, Moscow, 1856.

———, *Ocherki Anglii i Frantsii*, Moscow, 1858.

———, *O narodnom predstavitelstve*, 2nd edn., Moscow, 1899.

Chicherin, B. N., *Vospominaniia Borisa Nikolaevicha Chicherina: zemstvo i Moskovskaia duma*, Moscow, 1934.

——, *Zapiski proshlogo (vospominaniia i pisma)* Bakhrushin, S. V., Tsiavlovskii, M. A., eds., Moscow, 1929.

Danevskii, P., *Ob istochnikakh mestnykh zakonov nekotorykh gubernii i oblastei Rossii*, St. Petersburg, 1857.

Dolgorukov, P. V., *Des Réformes en Russie*, Paris, 1862.

——, *Kn. M. V. Muraviev*, London, 1864.

——, *O peremene obraza pravleniia v Rossii*, Leipzig, 1862.

——, *Peterburgskie ocherki; pamflety emigranta, 1860-1870*, Bakhrushin, S. V., and Shchegelov, P. A., eds., Moscow, 1934.

——, *Russkii administrator noveishei shkoly*, Berlin, 1868.

Eshevskii, S. V., *Sochineniia*, 3 vols., Moscow, 1870.

Golovachev, A. A., *Desiat let reform, 1861-1871 gg.*, St. Petersburg, 1872.

——, *Mysli, vozbuzhdennye pri chteniia proekta Polozheniia o zemskikh kreditnykh obshchestvakh*, St. Petersburg, 1860.

Golovine, Ivan, *Russia under the Autocrat, Nicholas the First*, 2 vols., London, 1845.

Gradovskii, A. D., *Istoricheskii ocherk uchrezhdeniia general-gubernatorstva v Rossii*, St. Petersburg, 1869.

——, *Sobranie sochinenii*, 9 vols., St. Petersburg, 1898-1908.

Herzen, A. I., *Sobranie sochinenii*, 30 vols., Moscow, 1954-1966.

——, *Gertsen i Ogarev*, in *Literaturnoe Nasledstvo*, vols. 61, 62, 63, Moscow, 1953-1956.

I. D. (pseud.), *Neskolko slov po vroprosu o zemskikh bankakh*, Kiev, 1860.

Kalachov, Nikolai, *Rezbor sochineniia g. Andveevskogo "O namestnikakh, voevodakh i gubernatorakh,"* St. Petersburg, 1867.

Kavelin, K. D., *Sobranie sochinenii K. D. Kavelina*, 4 vols., St. Petersburg, 1904.

——, and Turgenev, I. S., *Pisma K. D. Kavelina i I. S. Turgeneva k A. I. Gertsenu*, Geneva, 1892.

Konstantin Nikolaevich, Grand Duke, "Iz dnevnika V. K. Konstantina Nikolaevicha," *Krasnyi Arkhiv*, x, 1925.

Korf, Baron M. A., *Zhizn Grafa Speranskogo*, St. Petersburg, 1861.

Koshelev, A. I., *Golos iz zemstva*, Moscow, 1869.

——, *Kakoi iskhod dlia Rossii ot nyneishei ee polozheniia?*, Leipzig, 1862.

——, *Konstitutsiia, samoderzhavie i zemskaia duma*, Leipzig, 1862.

——, *Zapiski Aleksandra Ivanovicha Kosheleva, 1812-1883 gody*, Berlin, 1884.

Kostomarov, N. I., "Avtobiografiia Nikolaia Ivanovicha Kostomarova," *Russkaia Mysl*, 1885, Bks. 5, 6.

——, *Istoricheskie monografii Nikolaia Ivanovicha Kostomarova*, 3rd edn., 16 vols., St. Petersburg, 1886.

——, "K bratiam ukraintsam," *Byloe*, February 1906.

——, *Katalog biblioteki N. I. Kostomarova*, Kiev, 1903.

——, "Pisma N. I. Kostomarova k K. M. Sementovskomu," *Russkii Bibliofil—Le Bibliophile Russe*, Petrograd, 1916, III.

——, *Ukrainskii separatizm. Neizvestnye zapreshchennye stranitsy*, Iu. G. Oksman, ed., Odessa, 1921.

Kropotkin, P., *Memoirs of a Revolutionist*, Boston, 1899.

Lamanskii, I. E., "Iz zapisok I. E. Lamanskogo," *Russkaia Starina*, CLXI, January 1915.

Lebedev, K. N., "Iz zapisok senatora K. N. Lebedeva," *Russkii Arkhiv*, No. 1 XLIX, 1911.

Leshkov, V., *Obshchestvennyi byt drevnei Rossii*, St. Petersburg, 1856.

——, "O prave samostoiatelnosti, kak osnovoi samoupravleniia," *Iuridicheskii Vestnik*, No. 1 (1872).

——, "Opyt teorii zemstva i ego zemskikh uchrezhdenii po polozheniiu 1864 g., ianv. 1," *Den*, No. 42 (1865).

——, "Razdelenie Rossii na gubernii po ukazam Petra Velikogo i Ekateriny II," *Russkii Vestnik*, No. 22 (1859).

Levshin, A. I., "Dostopamiatnye minuty v moei zhizni, Zapiska Alekseia Irakleevicha Levshina," *Russkii Arkhiv*, xxiii, No. 8, 1885.

Lokhvitskii, A. V., *Obzor sovremennykh konstitutsii*, 2 vols., St. Petersburg, 1862.

——, *Guberniia; ee zemskie i pravitelstvennye uchrezhdeniia*, St. Petersburg, 1864.

Meshcherskii, V. P., *Moi vospominaniia*, 2 vols., St. Petersburg, 1898.

Mikshevich, Iu., *Neskolko slov o novoi osnove doveriia*, Kazan, 1862.

Miliutina, Mariia A., "Iz zapisok Marii Agleevny Miliutinoi," *Russkaia Starina*, xcvii, January 1899.

N. N., "Zapiska odnogo iz prezhnikh gubernatorov," *Russkaia Starina*, xxx, January 1881.

Nikitenko, A. V., *Dnevnik A. V. Nikitenko*, 3 vols., Moscow and Leningrad, 1955.

Obolenskii, D. A., "Moi vospominaniia o Velikoi Kniagine Elene Pavlovne," *Russkaia Starina*, cxxxvii, cxxxviii, March, April, May, 1909.

Obolenskii, E. P., *Souvenirs d'un Exilé en Sibérie*, Leipzig, 1862.

Odoevskii, V. F., "Dnevnik V. F. Odoevskogo, 1859-1860," Kosmin, B., Briskman, M., Aronson, M., eds., *Literaturnoe Nasledstvo*, 1935, Nos. 22-24.

Ogarev, N. P., *Essai sur la Situation Russe; Lettres à un Anglais*, London, 1862.

——, *Izbrannye sotsialno-politicheskie proizvedeniia*, 2 vols., Leningrad, 1957.

Pavlov, Platon, *Tysiachiletie Rossii*, St. Petersburg, 1863.

Polezhaev, P., "O gubernskom nadzore," *Zhurnal Ministerstva Iustitsii*, No. 5, 1859.

Pravdin, Kassian, *Pia desideria. O preobrazovaniiakh v grazhdanskom upravlenii*, St. Petersburg, 1858.

Saltykov, M. E., "M. E. Saltykov-Shchedrin: pisma, 1845-1889," *Trudy Pushkinskogo Doma pri Rossiiskoi Akademii Nauk*, Leningrad, 1925.

——, *Polnoe sobranie sochinenii M. E. Saltykova,* Arseniev, K. K., ed., 12 vols., St. Petersburg, 1905-1906.

Samarin, Iu. F., *Sochineniia Iu. F. Samarina,* 10 vols., Moscow, 1877-1911.

Schedo-Ferroti, D. K. (pseud. for Baron Firks), *Études sur l'avenir de la Russie,* 2 vols., Berlin, 1857-1858.

Semenov-Tian-Shanskii, P. P., *Epokha osvobozhdeniia krestian v Rossii 1857-1861, v vospominaniiakh P. P. Semeneva-Tian-Shanskogo,* 4 vols., St. Petersburg, 1911-1916.

Sergeevich, V. I., *Veche i kniaz. Russkoe gosudarstvennoe ustroistvo i upravenie vo vremia kniazei riurikovichei,* Moscow, 1867.

Serno-Solovevich, N. A., *N. A. Serno-Solovevich; publitsistika i pisma,* Volodarskii, I. V., Kaikova, G. A., eds., 2 vols., Moscow, 1963.

Shchapov, A. P., *A. P. Shchapov v Irkutske (neizdannye materialy),* Kuzmin, V. K., ed., Irkutsk, 1938.

——, *Neizdannye sochineniia,* Chernyshev, E. I., ed., Kazan, 1926.

——, "Pismo k Aleksandru II," *Krasnyi Arkhiv,* vi, 1926.

——, *Sochineniia A. P. Shchapova,* Luchinskii, G. A., ed., 3 vols., St. Petersburg, 1906-1908.

—— (unsigned), "reglamantatsiia i biurokratiia," *Sbornik statei nedozvolennykh tsenzuroi 1862 g.,* St. Petersburg, 1862.

Shill, I. N., *Predpolozhenie ob uchrezhdenii Russkogo gosudarstvennogo ili zemskogo banka,* St. Petersburg, 1861.

Sollogub, Count Vladimir, "Chinovnik," *Russkii Vestnik,* i, No. 3 (1856).

Soloviev, Ia. A., *Nastoiashchee i budushchee Smolenskoi gubernii,* Moscow, 1857.

——, "Pamiatniki i predaniia Vladimirskoi gubernii," *Otechestvennye Zapiski,* cxii, 1857.

——, *Selsko-khoziastvennaia statistika Smolenskoi gubernii,* Moscow, 1855.

Soloviev, Ia. A., "Zapiski senatora Iakova Aleksandrovicha Solovieva; krestianskoe delo v tsarstvovanii Aleksandra II," *Russkaia Starina*, XXVII-XLVII, 1880-1885.

Soloviev, S. M., *Istoricheskie otnosheniia mezhdu Russkimi kniaziami Riurikogo doma*, Moscow, 1847.

————, "Istoricheskie pisma," *Russkii Vestnik*, No. 4 (1858).

Speranski, M. M., "Zamechaniia o gubernskikh uchrezhdeniiakh," *Arkhiv istoricheskikh i prakticheskikh svedenii otnosiashchikhsia do Rossii*, St. Petersburg, 1859, Bk. 4.

Stremoukhov, P. D., "Iz vospominanii o grafe P. A. Valueve," *Russkaia Starina*, CXVI, April 1903.

Tatarinov, V., *Preobrazovanie gosudarstvennoi otchetnosti*, St. Petersburg, 1861.

Tegoborskii, L. de, *Études sur les forces productives de la Russie*, 4 vols., Paris, 1852-1855.

Terner, F. G., *Svedeniia o pozemelnom naloge v inostrannykh gosudarstvakh*, St. Petersburg, 1863.

Tiurin, A., *Obshchestvennaia zhizn i zemskie otnosheniia v drevnei Rusi*, St. Petersburg, 1850.

Tolstoi, D. N., "Zapiski grafa Dmitriia Nikolaevicha Tolstogo," *Russkii Arkhiv*, XXIII, No. 2, 1885.

Trubetskaia, O., *Materialy dlia biografii kn. V. A. Cherkasskogo; kn. Vladimir Aleksandrovich Cherkasskii, ego stati, ego rechi, i vospominaniia o nem*, 2 vols., Moscow, 1901-1904.

Turgenev, Nikolai (Tourgueneff, Nicolas) *La Russie et les Russes*, 3 vols., Paris, 1847.

————, *Vsgliad na dela Rossii. Russkii zagranichnyi sbornik*, Pt. 5, Leipzig, 1862.

Unkovskii, Aleksei, "Zapiska," *Russkaia Mysl*, No. 7, 1906.

Valuev, P. A., *Dnevnik*, Zaionchkovskii, P. A., ed., 2 vols., Moscow, 1961.

————, "Dnevnik za 1847-1860 gg.," *Russkaia Starina*, LXX, LXXI, April–August, 1891.

————, "Duma Russkaia (1855)," *Russkaia Starina*, LXIX, March 1891.

————, "O vnutrennom sostoianii Rossii," Garmiza, V. V., ed., *Istoricheskii Arkhiv*, No. 1, 1958.

Vasilchikov, A. I., *O samoupravlenii*, 3rd edn., 2 vols., St. Petersburg, 1869-1870.

Vernadskii, I. V., "O zemskikh bankakh," *Trudy Imperatorskogo Volnogo Ekonomicheskogo Okshchestva*, vi, No. 4, 1864.

Zarudny, M. I., *Obshchestvennyi byt Anglii; ocherki zemstva, goroda, suda*, St. Petersburg, 1865.

VI. BOOKS AND ARTICLES

Abbott, Robert J., "Police Reform in Russia, 1858-1878," Ph.D. diss., Princeton University, 1970.

Abramov, Ia. V., *Chto sdelalo zemstvo i chto ono delaet? (Obzor deiatelnosti Russkogo zemstva)*. St. Petersburg, 1889.

Artsimovich, V. A. (subj.), *Victor Antonovich Artsimovich, vospominaniia—kharakteristika*, St. Petersburg, 1904.

Anuchin, E., *Istoricheskii obzor razvitiia administrativnykh-politseiskikh uchrezhdenii v Rossii s uchrezhdeniia o guberniiakh 1775 g. do poslednego vremeni* (Ministry of Internal Affairs), St. Petersburg, 1872.

Andreevskii, I., *Leksii po istorii politseiskogo prava i zemskikh uchrezhdenii v Rossii*, Moscow, 1883.

Aristov, N. Ia., *Afanasii Prokofevich Schapov*, St. Petersburg, 1883.

Avalov, Z., *Detsentralizatsiia i samoupravlenie vo Frantsii*, St. Petersburg, 1905.

Avinov, N., "Graf M. A. Korf i zemskaia reforma 1864 g.," *Russkaia Mysl*, No. 2, 1904.

B.P.Z., "Biurokratiia i samoupravlenie. Ocherki iz istorii zemskikh uchrezhdenii," *Iuridicheskii Vestnik*, No. 10, 1882.

Backor, Joseph, "M. N. Katkov, Introduction to His Life and His Russian National Policy Program," Ph.D. diss., Indiana University, 1966.

Barsukov, Ivan, *Graf Nikolai Muraviev-Amurskii (materialy dlia biografii)*, 2 vols., Moscow, 1891.

Bermanskii, K. L., "Konstitutsionnye proekty tsarstvovaniia Aleksandra II-ogo," *Vestnik Prava*, No. 9 (1905).

Blinov, Ivan, *Gubernatory; istoriko-iuridicheskii ocherk*, St. Petersburg, 1904.

Blum, Jerome, *Noble Landowners and Agriculture in Austria, 1815-1848: A Study in the Origins of the Peasant Emancipation of 1848*, Johns Hopkins University Studies in History and Political Science, LXV, No. 2, Baltimore, 1948.

——, *Lord and Peasant in Russia from the Ninth to the Nineteenth Century*, Princeton, 1961.

Borovoi, S. Ia., *Kredit i banki Rossii (seredina XVIII v.-1861 g.)*, Moscow, 1958.

Chebaevskii, F., "Nizhegorodskii gubernskii dvorianskii komitet 1858 g.," *Voprosy Istorii*, No. 6, 1947.

Chernopatov, V. I., "Dvorianskoe soslovie Tulskoi gubernii," *Zapiski Moskovskogo Arkheologicheskogo Instituta*, Vol. 6, Moscow, 1910.

Curtiss, John Shelton, *The Russian Army under Nicholas I, 1825-1855*, Durham, N. C., 1965.

Czap, P., "P. A. Valuev's Proposal for a Vyt' Administration, 1864," *Slavonic and East European Review*, XLV, No. 105 (1967).

Driesen, Baron N. V., "M. E. Saltykov v Riazane," *Istoricheskii Vestnik*, XXI, February 1900.

Druzhinin, N. M., "Moskovskoe dvorianstvo i reforma 1861 g.," *Izvestiia Akademii Nauk SSSR, Seria istorii i filosofii*, 1948, No. 1.

——, "Zhurnal zemlevladeltsev, 1858-1860," *Trudy instituta RANION*, Moscow, No. 1, 1926, pp. 463-518.

Druzhinskaia, E. A., "*Russkaia Beseda*; istoriia zhurnala kak otrazhenie 'krizisa verkhov,'" diss., Moskovskii Oblastnoi Pedagagicheskii-Institut, Moscow, 1952.

Dzhanshiev, G. A., *A. M. Unkovskii i osvobozhdenie krestian*, Moscow, 1894.

————, *Iz epokhi velikikh reform*, 5th edn., Moscow, 1894.

————, *Epokha velikikh reform, istoricheskie spravki*, 7th edn., Moscow, 1898.

Emmons, Terence, *The Russian Landed Gentry and the Peasant Emancipation of 1861*, Cambridge, 1968.

Evgenev-Maksimov, V., *Sovremennik pri Chernyshevskom i Dobroliubove*, Leningrad, 1936.

Garmiza, V. V., "Iz istorii razrabotki zakona o vvedenii zemstva v Rossii," *Vestnik Moskovskogo Universiteta*, No. 1, 1958.

————, *Podgotovka zemskoi reformy 1864 goda*, Moscow, 1957.

Gershenkron, A., "Agrarian Policies and Industrialization: Russia, 1861-1917," *The Cambridge Economic History*, VI, Pt. II, Cambridge, 1965.

Gershenzon, M. O., ed., *Epokha Nikolaia I*, Moscow, 1910.

Gindin, I., *Gosudarstvennyi bank; ekonomicheskaia politika tsarskogo pravitelstva, 1861-1892*, Moscow, 1960.

Gronskii, P. P., "Teoriia samoupravleniia v russkoi nauke," in *Iubileinyi zemskii sbornik*, Frenkel, Z. G., and Veselovskii, B. B., eds., St. Petersburg, 1914.

Grot, I. K., "M. A. Korf, biograficheskii ocherk," *Russkaia Starina*, x, 1876.

Grothusen, Klaus Detlev, *Die historische Rechtsschule Russlands*, in *Osteuropastudien der Hochschulen des Landes Hessen*, Series I, Giessen, 1962.

Hammer, Darrel Patrick, "Two Russian Liberals: The Political Thought of B. N. Chicherin and K. D. Kavelin," Ph.D. diss., Columbia University, 1962.

Iakovlev, N. V., *M. E. Saltykov-Shchedrin v Tveri, 1860-1862*, Kalinin, 1961.

Ioanniian, A. G., *Vopros natsionalnosti v publitsistike Mikhaila Nalbandriana, 1829-1866*, Erevan, 1955.

Iordanskii, N. I., *Konstitutsionnoe dvizhenie 60-kh godov*, St. Petersburg, 1906.

Ivaniukov, I. I., *Padenie krepostnogo prava v Rossii*, St. Petersburg, 1882.

Ivanovskii, V. V., *Istoricheskie osnovy zemskogo upravleniia v Rossii*, St. Petersburg, 1892.

Jones, Robert Edward, "The Russian Gentry and the Provincial Reform of 1778," Ph.D. diss., Cornell University, 1968.

Kataev, I. M., *Do-reformennaia biurokratiia po zapiskam, memuaram i literature*, St. Petersburg, 1914.

Katz, Martin, *Michael N. Katkov—A Political Biography*, The Hague, 1966.

Kirshman, V. V. "Pechat Peterburga i Moskv-1856-1874, gg. o zemskoi reforme 1864 goda," diss., Pedagogicheskii Institut im. Lenina, Moscow, 1949.

Kizevetter, A., *Istoricheskie ocherki*, Moscow, 1912.

——, *Istoricheskie otliki*, Moscow, 1914.

Korf, Baron S. A., *Dvorianstvo i ego soslovnoe upravlenie za stoletie 1762-1855 godov*, St. Petersburg, 1906.

——, *Administrativnaia iustitsiia v Rossii*, 2 vols., St. Petersburg, 1910.

Kornilov, A., *Zemskoe i gorodskoe samoupravlenie v tsarstve Polshi v 1861-1863 gg.*, Petrograd, 1915.

——, "Gubernskie komitety 1858-1859," *Velikaia Reforma*, Moscow, IV, 1911.

——, "Gubernskie komitety po krestianskomu delu," *Russkoe Bogatstvo*, 1904, Nos. 1-5.

Kornilov, A., *Obshchestvennoe dvizhenie pri Aleksandre II, 1855-1881; istoricheskie ocherki*, Moscow, 1909.

Kotliarevskii, Nestor, *Kanun osvokozhdeniia, 1855-1861. Iz zhizni idei i nastroenii v radikalnykh krugakh togo vremeni*, Petrograd, 1916.

Kovanko, P., *Reforma 19 fevralia 1861 g. i ego posledstviia s finansovoi tochki zreniia*, Kiev, 1914.

Kozmin, V. P., "Artelnyi zhurnal Vek (1862g.)," *Iz istorii revoliutsionnoi mysli v Rossii*, Moscow, 1961.

Kulomzin, A. N. and Reuter, B. G., *M. Kh. Reutern*, St. Petersburg, 1910.

Lemke, M., "Kn. P. V. Dolgorukov v Rossii/emigrant, 1859-1868 gg.," *Byloe*, February and March 1907.

————, *Nikolai Mikhailovich Iadrinstsev*, St. Petersburg, 1904.

————, *Ocherki osvoboditelnogo dvizheniia 60kg godov*, St. Petersburg, 1908.

Leroy-Beaulieu, Anatole, *Un Homme d'état Russe (Nicholas Milutine)*, Paris, 1884.

Leslie, R. F., *Reform and Insurrection in Russian Poland, 1856-1865*, London, 1963.

Liashchenko, P. I., *Poslednyi sekretnyi komitet po krestianskomu delu, 3 ianvaria, 1857-16 fevralia, 1858, po materialam arkhiva gos-a soveta*, St. Petersburg, 1911.

Lincoln, William Bruce, "Nikokai Alexandrovich Miliutin and Problems of State Reform in Nicholaevan Russia," Ph.D. diss., University of Chicago, 1966.

Linkov, L., *Revoliutsionnaia borba A. N. Gertsena i N. P. Ogareva i tainoe obshchestvo "Zemlia i Volia" 1860-kh godov*, Moscow, 1964.

Mazour, Anatole G., *Modern Russian Historiography*, Princeton, 1958.

Meshcheriakov, N., "Nachala literaturnoi deiatelnosti Shchedrina," *Polnoe Sobranie Sochinenii M. E. Saltykova-Shchedrina*, Moscow, I, 1941.

Miller, Forrestt A., *Dmitrii Miliutin and the Reform Era in Russia*, Nashville, 1968.

Ministerstvo finansov, 1802-1902, 2 vols., St. Petersburg, 1902.

Ministerstvo vnutrennykh del; istoricheskii ocherk, 3 vols., St. Petersburg, 1902.

Molok, A. I., "Istoriia Frantsii v trudakh N. G. Chernyschevskogo," *Trudy iubileinei nauchnoi sessii Leningradskogo gosudarstvennogo universiteta*, Leningrad, 1948.

Mosse, W. E., *The Rise and Fall of the Crimean System, 1855-1871, The Story of a Peace Settlement*, London, 1963.

Nachnochnitskaia, A. I., *Rossiia i voiny Prussii v 60 kh godakh XIX v. za obedinenie Germanii "sverkhu,"* Moscow, 1960.

Nechkina, M. V., "N. P. Ogarev v gody revoliutsionnoi situatsii," *Izvestiia Akademii Nauk SSSR, seriia istorii i filosofii,* Moscow, IV, No. 2, 1947.

————, ed., *Revoliutsionnaia situatsiia v Rossii 1859-1861 gg.,* 4 vols., Moscow, 1960-1965.

Nevedenskii, S. Katkov i ego vremia, St. Petersburg, 1888.

Nifontov, A. S., *Rossiia v 1848 godu,* Moscow, 1952.

Nolde, B. E., *Peterburgskaia missiia Bismarka, 1859-1862,* Prague, 1925.

Orlov, V. S., *Otmena krepostnogo prava v Smolenskoi gubernii,* Smolensk, 1947.

Ozerov, I. Kh., *Osnovy finansovoi nauki,* 2 vols., Moscow, 1905.

Pazhitnikov, K., *Gorodskoe i zemskoe samoupravlenie,* St. Petersburg, 1913.

Pintner, Walter McKenzie, *Russian Economic Policy under Nicholas I,* Ithaca, New York, 1967.

————, "Inflation During the Crimean War," *American Slavic and East European Review,* XVIII (February 1959).

————, "The Social Characteristics of the Early Nineteenth-Century Russian Bureaucracy," *Slavic Review,* XXIX, No. 3 (September 1970).

Pokrovskii, M. N., ed., *Russkaia istoricheskaia literatura v klassovom osveshchenii,* 2 vols., Moscow, 1927.

Povalishin, A., *Riazanskie pomeshchiki i ikh krepostnye,* Riazan, 1903.

Proklamatsii 60-kh godov, Moscow and Leningrad, 1926.

Pypin, A. N., *Istoriia russkoi etnografii,* 4 vols., St. Petersburg, 1890-1891.

Raeff, Marc, *Michael Speransky: Statesman of Imperial Russia,* The Hague, 1957.

————, "The Russian Autocracy and Its Officials," *Harvard Slavic Studies,* IV, 1957.

————, "Russia after the Emancipation: Views of a Gentleman Farmer," *American Slavic and East European Review,* XXIX (June 1951).

————, "L'État et gouvernement et la tradition politique en

Russie impériale avant 1861," *Revue d'histoire moderne et contemporaine*, xv (October-December), 1962.

Rashin, A. G., *Naselenie Rossii za 100 let (1811-1913); statistikicheskie ocherki*, Moscow, 1956.

Rein, T., *Iogan Vilgelm Snelman, Istoriko-biograficheskii ocherk* (trans. from Swedish), 2 vols., St. Petersburg, 1903.

Reingart, A. K., *Istoriia nachalnoi shkoly v Orlovskii gubernii; ocherk deiatelnosta mestnykh zemstv, 1866-1895*, Orel, 1896.

Repszuk, Helma, "Nicholas Mordvinov (1754-1845)," Ph.D. diss., Columbia University, 1962.

Rieber, Alfred J., *The Politics of Autocracy: Letters of Alexander II to Prince A. I. Bariatinskii, 1857-1864*, Paris and The Hague, 1966.

Romanovich-Slavatinskii, A., *Dvorianstvo v Rossii ot nachala xviii veka do otmeny krepostnogo prava*, 2nd edn., Kiev, 1912.

Rosenberg, H., *Die Weltwirtschaftskrisis von 1857-1859*, Stuttgart and Berlin, 1934.

Rosental, V. N., "Obshchestvenno-politicheskaia programma russkogo liberalizma v seredine 50-kh godov XIX v.," *Istoricheskie Zapiski Akademii Nauk SSSR*, Moscow, No. 70, 1961.

Rubenstein, N. L., *Russkaia istoriografiia*, Moscow, 1941.

Saveliev, A. A., "Neskolko slov o byvshem Nizhegorodskom gubernatore A. N. Muravieve," *Russkaia Starina*, xciv, xcv, June-July 1898.

Shcherbina, F., *Voronezhskoe zemstvo za 1865-1889 gg.: Istoricheskii-statisticheskii obzor*, Voronezh, 1891.

Semenov, N. P., *Osvobozhdenie krestian v tsarstvovanii imperatora Aleksandra II-ogo. Khronika deiatelnosti komissii po krestianskomu delu*. 3 vols., St. Petersburg, 1889-1892.

Semenov-Tian-Shanskii, P. P., *Istoriia poluvekovoi deiatelnosti Imperatorskogo russkogo geograficheskogo obshchestva, 1845-1895*, 3 vols., St. Petersburg, 1896.

Semevskii, V. I., "N. I. Kostomarov, 1817-1885," *Russkaia Starina*, XLIX, January 1886.

———, *Politicheskie i obshchestvennye idei Dekabristov*, St. Petersburg, 1909.

Seredonin, S. M., *Istoricheskii obzor deiatelnosti komiteta ministrovy*, 3 vols., St. Petersburg, 1902.

Sharapov, S., *Teoriia gosudarstva u slavianofilov*, St. Petersburg, 1898.

Shefer, A., *Organy "samoupravleniia" v tsarskoi Rossii*, Kuibyshev, 1939.

Shompulev, V. A., "Provintsialnye tipy 40-kh godov," *Russkaia Starina*, XCV, August 1898.

Skalan, V. Iu., *Po zemskim voprosam*, St. Petersburg, 1882.

Sladkevich, N. G., "K voprosu o polemike N. G. Chernyshevskogo so slavianofilskoi publitsistikoi," *Voprosy Istorii*, No. 6, 1948.

———, *Ocherki istorii obshchestvennoi mysli v Rossii v konste 50-kh godov-nachale 60-kh godov XIV-ogo veka*, Leningrad, 1962.

Smirnov, V., "Zemskaia reforma 1864 g. i ee posleduiushchie izmeneniia," *Russkaia Starina*, CLXVII, July 1916.

Svatikov, S. G., *Obshchestvennoe dvizhenie v Rossii, 1700-1895*, Rostov-on-Don, 1905.

Tarasov, I., *Politsiia v epokhe reform*, Moscow, 1885.

Tatishchev, S. S., *Imperator Aleksandr II. Ego zhizn i tsarstvovanie*, 2 vols., St. Petersburg, 1911.

Torke, Hans-Joachim, *Das russische Beamtentum in der esten Halfte des 19. Jahrhunderts. Forschungen zur osteuropaischen Geschichte*, XIII, Berlin, 1967.

Tsagolov, N. A., *Ocherki russkoi ekonomicheskoi mysli perioda padeniia krepostnogo prava*, Moscow, 1956.

Tseitlin, S. Ia., "Zemskaia Reforma," in *Istoriia Rossii v XIX veke*, 9 vols., St. Petersburg, 1906, III.

Varadinov, N. V., *Istoriia ministerstva vnutrennykh del. 3 vols.*, St. Petersburg, 1858-1863.

Velikaia reforma: Russkoe obshchestvo i krestianskii vopros v proshlom i nastoiashchem, 6 vols., Moscow, 1911.

Venturi, Franco, *Roots of Revolution*, New York, 1964.

Vernadsky, Georges, *La charte constitutionelle de l'empire russe en l'an 1820*, Paris, 1933.

Veselovskii, B. B., "Detsentralizatsiia upravleniia i zadachi zemstva," *Iubileinyi zemskii sbornik*, Frenckel, Z. G., Veselovskii, B. B., eds., St. Petersburg, 1914.

———, *Istoriia zemstva za sorok let*, 3 vols., St. Petersburg, 1911.

Vucinich, Alexander, "The State and the Local Community," in *The Transformation of Russian Society*, Black, C. E., ed., Cambridge, 1960.

Wachendorf, Josef, *Regionalismus, Raskol und Volk als Hauptprobleme der Russischen Geschichte bei A. P. Ščapov*, Cologne, 1964.

Witte, Count S. Iu., *Samoderzhavie i zemstvo; konfidentsialnaia zapiska ministra finansov stats-sekretaria S. Iu. Witte (1899)*, St. Petersburg, 1907.

Zaionchkovskii, P. A., *Otmena krepostnogo prava v Rossii*, 1st edn., Moscow, 1954.

———, *Voennye reformy 1860-1870 gg. v Rossii*, Moscow, 1952.

Zelenyi, P., "Khersonskoe dvorianstvo i Khersonskai guberniia v 1862-om godu," *Severnyi Vestnik*, VIII (August 1889).

Zimina, V. G., "Krestianskaia reforma 1861 g. vo Vladimirskoi gubernii," diss., Moscow University, 1956.

VII. MODERN THEORETICAL BOOKS AND ARTICLES

Akademiia Nauk, Institut Gosudarstva i Prava, *Mestnye sovety na sovremennom etape*, Moscow, 1965.

Binckley, Robert C., *Realism and Nationalism, 1852-1871*, New York, 1935.

Bird, Richard M., Oldman, Oliver, eds., *Readings in Taxation in Developing Countries*, Baltimore, 1964.

Cheremnykh, P. S., ed., *Sochetanie gosudarstvennykh i obshchestrennykh nachal v upravienii obshchestvom,* Moscow, 1965.

Crozier, Michel, *The Bureaucratic Phenomenon,* Chicago, 1967.

Danilov, F. A., *Gosudarstvennaia vlast o mestnoe, gorodskoe i zemskoe. samoupravlenie,* Moscow, 1917.

Eisenman, Charles, *Centralisation et décentralisation: Esquise d'une théorie générale,* Paris, 1943.

Heffter, Heinrich, *Die Deutsche Selbstverwaltung im 19. Jahrhundert,* Stuttgart, 1950.

Hintze, Hedwig, *Staatseinheit und Föderalismus in alten Frankreich und in der Revolution,* Berlin and Leipzig, 1928.

Huntington, Samuel, "Political Development and Decay," *World Politics* (April 1965).

Iashchenko, A., *Teoriia federalizma,* Iuriev, 1912.

LaPalombara, Joseph, ed., *Bureaucracy and Political Development,* Princeton, 1963.

Livingston, William S., *Federalism and Constitutional Change,* Oxford, 1956.

MacMahon, Arthur W., ed., *Federalism, Mature and Emergent,* New York, 1955.

Maddick, Henry, *Democracy, Decentralization and Development,* London, 1963.

Merton, Robert K., ed., *Reader in Bureaucracy,* New York, 1952.

Moore, Barrington, *Political Power and Social Theory,* Cambridge, 1958.

Riggs, Fred, *Administration in Developing Countries: The Theory of Prismatic Society,* Boston, 1964.

Simon, Herbert A., *Administrative Behavior,* New York, 1957.

Tannenbaum, Arnold S., *Control in Organizations,* New York, 1968.

Index